THE NECESSITY OF MUSIC

Variations on a German Theme

In *The Necessity of Music*, Celia Applegate explores the many ways that Germans thought about and made music from the eighteenth to twentieth centuries. Rather than focus on familiar stories of composers and their work Applegate illuminates the myriad ways in which music is integral to German society. Music reflected the polycentric nature of social and political life, even while it provided many opportunities to experience what was common among Germans. Musical activities also allowed them, whether professional musicians, dedicated amateurs, or simply listeners, to participate in European culture. Applegate's original and fascinating analysis of Mendelssohn, Schumann, Brahms, Wagner, and military music enables the reader to understand music through the experiences of listeners, performers, and institutions. *The Necessity of Music* demonstrates that playing, experiencing, and interpreting music was a powerful factor that shaped German collective life.

(German and European Studies)

CELIA APPLEGATE is William R. Kenan Jr. Chair in History at Vanderbilt University.

CELIA APPLEGATE

The Necessity of Music

Variations on a German Theme

UNIVERSITY OF TORONTO PRESS
Toronto Buffalo London

Toronto Buffalo London
www.utppublishing.com

ISBN 978-1-4875-0068-9 (cloth)
ISBN 978-1-4875-2048-9 (paper)

(German and European Studies)

Library and Archives Canada Cataloguing in Publication

Applegate, Celia, author
The necessity of music : variations on a German theme / Celia Stewart Applegate.

(German and European studies ; 26)

Includes bibliographical references and index.
ISBN 978-1-4875-0068-9 (hardback) ISBN 978-1-4875-2048-9 (paperback)

1. Music – Social aspects – Germany. 2. Music – Germany – History and criticism. I. Title. II. Series: German and European studies ; 26

ML3917.G3A648 2017 780.943 C2016-907308-4

University of Toronto Press acknowledges the financial assistance to its publishing program of the Canada Council for the Arts and the Ontario Arts Council, an agency of the Government of Ontario.

Canada Council for the Arts
Conseil des Arts du Canada

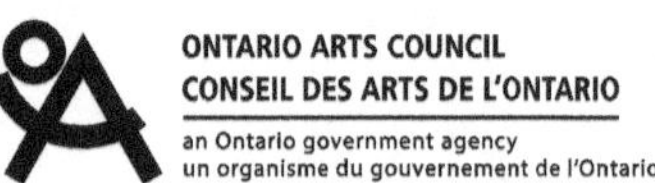

Funded by the Government of Canada
Financé par le gouvernement du Canada
Canada

To Cea and Henry,
with gratitude, admiration, and love

Contents

Part III: Public and Private

Illustrations

Acknowledgments

This volume of essays reflects the work of many years and the conversation and community of many colleagues and friends. From Rochester to Nashville, from Helsinki to Padua, in Berlin and Kalamazoo, at Princeton and Cornell, in Quebec, South Carolina, Louisiana, and many other places in between, abroad, and at home, I have been very lucky in my audiences and my hosts. Most of these chapters emerged from lectures or from papers at conferences or from essays for journals and books, and so I am very grateful to the presses that have allowed me to republish this body of writing in its own volume.

For giving me the opportunity to prepare the papers or essays that make up these chapters, I would like to thank David Blackbourn, Geoff Eley, Jane Fulcher, Peter Hohendahl, Michael Kater, Roe-Min Kok, Ingeborg Majer-O'Sickey, Sven Oliver Müller, Jürgen Osterhammel, Neil Christian Pages, Martin Rempe, Jan Palmowski, James Retallack, Mary Rhiel, Albrecht Riethmüller, Daniel T. Rodgers, Jonathan Sperber, Laura Tunbridge, Anne Schreffler, Nicholas Vaszonyi; and to thank *19th Century Music*, Boydell & Brewer, Continuum Press, *History and Memory*, Indiana University Press, *Journal of Modern European History*, C.H. Beck Verlag, Laaber Verlag, Oxford University Press, Princeton University Press, Rodophi Verlag, and the University of California Press.

I am also very grateful to the following individuals and institutions that have granted me permission to use images from their collections: AKG Images; BosseVerlag; Mike Brubaker; the Buffalo and Erie County Historical Society; the Deutsches Historisches Museum, Berlin; the Germanisches Nationalmuseum, Nuremberg; the Arthur M. Sackler Gallery of the Smithsonian Institution; the San Francisco History Center at the San Francisco Public Library; and the Museum in der Widumspfiste Fügen (Tyrol).

Finally, at the University of Toronto Press, I am deeply grateful to Richard Ratzlaff for his enthusiastic support for this project, to Catherine Frost for her deft and thorough editing of the manuscript, and to Frances Mundy for seeing it through to completion. Heartfelt thanks to Cassandra Painter for her superb work on the index at a busy time of year.

Wisdom and friendship have lightened the way, starting most especially with Pamela Potter's generosity in welcoming me into the mysteries of musicology; continuing education from Melina Esse, Ralph Locke, and Holly Watkins; and Joy Calico's welcoming friendship at Vanderbilt. Special thanks also to Stewart Weaver, Joanna Scott, James Longenbach, Suzanne Marchand, Nira Wickramasinghe, Lynn Binstock, Daniel Borus, Robert Westbrook, Harold Wechsler, Helmut Smith, and Meike Werner. I dedicate Chapter 4 to the memory of my dear friend Lynn Gordon, who would have been amused to find Buffalo, New York, lurking in these pages.

In acknowledgment of debts of another order, I thank David Blackbourn, who also suggested the possibility of the title by introducing me to Ernst Fischer's *The Necessity of Art.* My mother, Joan Applegate, always provides her knowledge, good sense, and loving support as I navigate this musical terrain; chapter 11 on Wagner's Women is dedicated to her and my late grandmother Virginia Strait.

I dedicate this volume to my children, Celia Magdalena Weaver and Robert Henry Weaver, present at the creation of anything I have done since they were born, always on my mind, and in my heart.

THE NECESSITY OF MUSIC

Variations on a German Theme

Introduction

Music is necessary, and people have found it so for millennia. "Let me not live without music," sang the chorus in Euripides' *Heracles*. For the ancient Greeks, music helped to constitute social life itself, weaving together the disparate activities of work and play, public and private, peace and war.[1] The Graecophilic Germans thought along the same lines. "He who does not love music does not deserve the name of man," wrote Goethe in 1822 to the French composer Ignace Pleyel, "he who loves it is still just half a man, but he who devotes himself to it is a whole man."[2] In 1947, a century and a quarter of music-making in Germany later, we find another Frenchman (Jean Arnaud, a French musical control officer in occupied Germany) rebuking the Germans for believing themselves to be "the only really musical people," the only people to "penetrate the mystical-musical depths." He suggested that the Germans could be returned to humanity and civilization only if they could be "brought to think that music is no longer a German monopoly."[3] He never suggested, however, that they should make it any less a part of their lives; indeed, he thought music properly understood was a key to the recovery of their humanity. The notion that music is necessary, that music in any number of forms must be part of our lives, continues to mark what Germans say about themselves and what others say about Germans. In her obituary of Kurt Masur, Margalit Fox wrote that the former conductor of the Leipzig Gewandhaus Orchestra, "brought to the podium the ardent conviction that music-making was a moral act that could heal the world."[4] The essays gathered in this collection fill in some of the history of performing and thinking about music in Germany between these disparate moments – moments when the necessity to play, to understand, to promote, and to experience music informed what Germans did in their own country and beyond it.

These essays represent my own wanderings over the past several decades through the great storehouse of European musical achievement to which countless people, famous and obscure, have contributed over the centuries. I came to musical investigations as a historian of modern Germany who had some limited musical training. I wondered why so few of my fellow German historians, many of whom I knew to be passionate about music, "classical" and otherwise, wrote about it in their scholarship. I knew, of course, that an entire discipline had devoted itself to the study of musical works and their authors, and I knew something of how that discipline went about its work. I was also aware of musicology's ongoing work of renovation and redefinition of its disciplinary norms. Musicologists were expanding the canon, interrogating distinctions between popular and art music, investigating the histories of performance and reception, and questioning the ideological origins of the methodologies of musical analysis itself. There seemed no reason why I could not venture into this vibrant, increasingly ecumenical field of musical studies and ask questions native to the discipline of history in which I had been trained. The enormous range of ways in which people have made and made use of music over the centuries represented a rich source of knowledge about how people lived, the beliefs they held, and the means they devised to express themselves, both in public and in private. Historians could look to musical life as a way to understand more fully the other aspects of the past we had long studied – social classes and gender roles, parliaments and protest movements, wars and revolutions, religions and ideas, and identities of all kinds. When I started my music-historical studies in the early 1990s, there seemed no end to the possibilities, and it seems that way to me still.

Over the past twenty years, a number of other historians have come to the same conclusion. As I recently wrote elsewhere, a kind of Schengen zone of scholarship now exists among historians and musicologists, "where people cross disciplinary borders without hindrance yet remain conscious of differences in language, custom, knowledge, and ways of going about their work."[5] For musicologists, growing doubts about the adequacy of formal analysis as the primary means of understanding music led them out from that dense centre of musical works in search of context. Historians for their part rarely adopt the signature methodology of musicology, that of the close analysis of a musical score. Instead, we have worked mainly on reconstructing the endless flow between text and context, between the music and the world in which it sounds, without saying much about the text itself. We have been drawn more to performance than to composition, more to the social and political analysis of performers and composers than to the formal analysis of their music-making. The opus takes on different meanings under such redirection of our attention and is in any case a concept that music scholars have questioned and historicized.[6] Our subject is musical culture, a capacious term that includes social and political contexts as well as musical institutions, philosophies, and what we might call music's everyday life. Music regarded in this way becomes, in other words, a species of cultural history.[7]

To name it as such does not necessarily answer the question of how one goes about one's work. Those who practise cultural history have at their disposal an enormous range of options in terms of both subject matter and method. Cultural historians seem to stand, deciding which way to turn, in the middle of some spacious piazza from which many streets and alleys go forth. Shall one take the path on which popular and elite musical cultures meet and mingle? Shall it be the Actor-Network-Theory path, where material and semiotic objects link together and come apart? Shall it be the path of Roger Chartier, where forms of appropriation take place, or of Michel Foucault, where discourses abound and yet one has hardly any control over what to think and do? Shall it be the Bakhtinian play of authority and carnival or Pierre Bourdieu's fields of action, the doxa that define them and our capital endowments, cultural and otherwise? Or simply Geertzian thick description? And in the end what do we do with the sounds themselves, so quick to disappear, so fleeting in their effects? If we take the musical context as our subject, then we run the risk of letting context overwhelm the music, to such an extent that the important concepts in our trade, causality and consequence chief among them, can force music into the role of a mere reflection of the real action happening elsewhere in time and space.

My own approach has been eclectic, with an emphasis on social and political contexts – a bit of Bourdieu and Bakhtin, a chaser of Chartier, and a gram or so of Geertz, here less the practitioner of thick description than the advocate of a "social history of the imagination," in which the arts feature as the means by which a particular culture's "way of experiencing" its collective life comes "out into the world of objects where men can look at it."[8] More so than other historical subfields, cultural history practises descriptive analysis and interpretation rather than determination of causes and consequences, and music poses particular problems of evanescence and subjectivity.[9] Nevertheless, music-making does constitute action in the world, and as such we have work to do as historians explaining the circumstances under which people make music and the effects these actions have upon themselves and the larger communities in which they live.

The new cultural history of music divides roughly into two research agendas. In the first, making music is simply one part of what people do in society, and from that observation we can focus on circumstances and institutions that enable the composition, performance, and consumption of music and then ask how this music-making interacted with other social forms, with politics and state formations. Topics such as the role of the musician in totalitarian regimes or the introduction of the violin into Meiji Japan or the use of hymns in maintaining minority religious communities fall within such broad parameters of research. The second agenda approaches music as intellectual history, both through well-established topics such as aesthetic theory and through more recent and elusive ones such as the history of subjectivity. In the latter case, music becomes an object of study because it has been the means by which people experience, express, and develop their interior lives and, in the boldest formulation, free themselves from imagined or real constraints upon their sense of self. The historian John Toews has argued, similarly to Geertz's position quoted above, that music is a "privileged site ... for imagining and enacting the organization of individuals into historical subjects ... and for the integration of individuals into collectivities through processes of subjective identification." Musical performance and experience, he suggests, "helped European individuals organize and perform their self-activity and self-consciousness in relation to the past, to other individuals within the networks of communal relations, and to the transcendent."[10]

Summing up, then: the new cultural history of music has developed a number of different ways to articulate the social and individual effectiveness of musical activity as part of the effort to explain in the broadest possible way what music means. Music organizes society. It creates and reinforces bonds among people. Its circulation in and between individuals and communities forms networks that have the capacity to reinforce, subvert, or transcend existing social, cultural, and political boundaries. Music has enormous powers of expression, whether with words set to it or wordless, and this capacity to articulate and dramatize a mood or a program, to make imagination or ideology audible, is a form of action in the world, created and performed by humans but also doing its work a degree removed from its creators in an individual space of sensuous experience. Music also constitutes a record of the past, providing an infinitely renewable form of access to the sensuous experiences of our ancestors and the great reservoir of their creative energies, living on into the present. The prominence of what musicologists have taken to calling in self-mocking language "the works of dead composers" on concert programs since the nineteenth century epitomizes this phenomenon but by no means exhausts it. This prominence has to some extent distracted scholars from undertaking a more social and cultural history of the concert repertoire (not just the concert itself) – in contrast to the histories of influence and the gradual evolution of genres and styles that have been the central task of musicology.

All these forms of effective social action allow a surprisingly wide field for the historian who wishes to write music into history. My own efforts to exploit the riches of the musical past have focused on Germany and its composed art music. At the outset, I posed two questions – "what is German music?" and "how German is it?"[11] Since my first essays on German musical culture I have also been concerned with the problems of when music became German and the Germans became the people of music and why, seemingly, music has carried such cultural weight in the collective life of people who identify themselves as German. The essays in this volume amount to variations on these themes, in the musical sense of development and transposition, elaboration and transformation. Simple questions sometimes have simple answers, but in this case the weight we should give to the term "German" in musical matters is not self-evident. A reasonable person might well regard the designation as irrelevant to the pleasure or the quality of the music so indicated, at most a mere convenience to indicate in a general way the provenance of the composer or the site of the music-making. The important distinctions would be generic (e.g., opera, symphony), functional (e.g., dance music, march music), stylistic, chronological, or any number of ways to organize lists of music. Geographical attributions would seem otiose. Nevertheless, musicologists, eager to cast off the burden of the Germano-centric concert repertoire (e.g., Bach, Mozart, Beethoven, and Brahms), have over the past decades brought the hermeneutics of suspicion to bear on the significance of "German" in musical texts of the past, and in the process they have made the designation a matter for discussion and debate. They have forced into the open the chauvinistic foundations and practices of musicology, enumerated the many aspects of musical and musicological participation in the Third Reich, and traced the uneven and inadequate reckoning with a tainted legacy in the post-war period. Most fundamentally, they have called into question the notion of German musical superiority. This notion is the product of two centuries of textual reception of the music of German composers in the form of music histories, criticism, journalism, concert notes, analytical techniques, and cultural policies. The truth of it remains, of course, a matter of opinion. It is a myth of sorts, complete with claims that German composers gave us privileged access to transcendent experience. In the words of musicologist Albrecht Riethmüller, Germany's special musical genius was an illusion – an "*Einbildung*, with its multiple meanings of imagination, imprint, fantasy, and concept, that stems from a feeling, is based on a belief, and belongs to the realm of opinions and convictions."[12]

The origins and the trajectory of this particular illusion are of considerable historical interest and form the major theme of a collection of articles that musicologist Pamela Potter and I published in 2002.[13] A decade or so later maverick musicologist Peter van der Merwe provided a deliberately breezy account of this "illusion" in his engaging, sometimes exasperating book *Roots of the Classical: The Popular Origins of Western Music.* "In the early 18th century," he wrote, "Germany had been generally regarded as a *Land ohne Musik* – or rather a *Paese senza musica.*" But by the late eighteenth century, he continues, echoing the French musical control officer Jean Arnaud, they had "managed to acquire a reputation as a musical people," then eventually as *"the* musical people," and finally, "music itself – or at any rate 'good' music – was widely thought to be a peculiarly Teutonic thing." "It was natural," he concluded in deadpan fashion, "that this should go to the Germans' heads."[14] Still, the need to dethrone Germano-centric musicology has lost much of its urgency since the publication of Richard Taruskin's six-volume *Oxford History of Western Music,* a sustained rejection of such, with generous helpings of social and cultural history included.

But even if we cannot take the idea of musical superiority as seriously as people once did, we can identify and assess the cultural activity by which Germans, paraphrasing van der Merwe, acquired and maintained their musical reputation, without pathologizing the process as a one-way path to the Nazi regime. In the chapters that follow, the idea of a special German endowment for music forms just one thread within a multicoloured skein of music-making in German-speaking Europe. These essays seek to provide glimpses of a complex history of the cultivation of a particular form of artistic expression. They do not, taken together, provide a narrative development by which German music and musicians rose to greatness, developed hubris, suffered downfall, then rebuilt in a chastened manner. There are other non-heroic, non-teleological ways to think about Germans and their music and other themes to consider that are less about accusing Germans of loving their music too much and more about trying to understand what, if anything made German musical culture distinctive. In the last decades of the eighteenth century developments in the practice and organization of music in central Europe intersected powerfully with the emergence of a self-conscious nationalist movement, and over the next century organized musical life and the musical performances it made possible helped to strengthen various forms of national organization. But this convergence was not a unitary phenomenon. Musical life continued to reflect the polycentric nature of German social and political life, even while it provided many opportunities to experience what was common among Germans. Moreover, musical activities encouraged Germans, whether professional musicians, dedicated amateurs, or simply listeners, to participate in European culture more generally, increasingly a culture of nations and peoples rather than courts and dynasties.

These essays also share a focus on composed and mainly art music, as opposed to folk or popular music, improvised or commercial music. Art music did not exist in some kind of sacred precinct, breathing only the rarefied air of the concert hall or opera house and complicit in processes of canonization that, allegedly, reproduced social hierarchies with near pitch-perfect accuracy. Nor is the study of art music itself an act of disdain towards popular culture in all its manifestations. On the contrary, I offer these essays as a means of submitting the "canon," a recent construct without clear edges, and "high culture" in general to the same kind of treatment that has honoured popular culture, that is, treating art music as an integral part of cultural and social life, subject to life's turmoil and not in itself intrinsically classist, racist, or sexist. I would rather not use either term. The term "high culture" is deceptive, because it conflates seriousness with high social status, complexity with luxury, and art with snobbery. Likewise the term "popular culture" can be meretricious, attractive at first blush but lacking integrity. It is difficult to define, and wailing spirits haunt it – the spirits that have animated the long search, begun in the eighteenth century, for authenticity on the one hand and the vast machinery of commercialization on the other. If popular culture is an "elusive quarry," as Peter Burke put it, then high culture is an easy target – easy to dismiss and marginalize by pretending that it is a taste acquired by only a few, and therefore the loser in the great and never-ending cultural popularity contest.[15] Looked at as cultural practice, the boundaries among the variegated forms of musical practice are easily and productively crossed in every era. Hybridity and multiplicity are the nature of cultural production, just as they are of identities, national and otherwise.

The chapters in this volume are organized into three sections: places, people, public and private. People listen to music in actual physical locations, and the sounds of music also carry with them – through knowledge of their authors and through the sounds themselves – intimations and associations of place. The first group of chapters explores why the places where music happens can be as important to its meaning as its historical origins or the instruments that play it and the people who perform and hear it. The place that is foremost is, of course, Germany, but each explores Germany's significance as a place of music-making from a different perspective. The first chapter juxtaposes the cultural and political nature of German nationalism in the first decades of the nineteenth century to the struggles of musicians to make a living. This was a time when the vagaries of the marketplace increasingly replaced court and church employment. With Carl Friedrich Zelter as the exemplary figure, we find Germans emphasizing the German identity of their music and its necessity for the moral improvement of German society as a means to secure a place for serious music in this changing sociopolitical environment. The second chapter focuses on classical musicians and their audiences as place-makers, endowing meaning on the spaces where they perform. It pushes back against the assertion of sound-studies pioneer R. Murray Schafer that the art music of the nineteenth century took place in a vacuum, abstracted from the "soundscape" of real life. The third chapter, on musical itinerancy, further explores the extent to which musicians were always on the move, crossing borders, creating networks, reinforcing and reinventing national identities as they travelled – in short, a necessary ingredient in the making of new cultural identities. The fourth chapter interprets the musical offerings at the great world's fairs of the late nineteenth and earlier twentieth centuries as paradigms of both nationalism and internationalism, each dependent on the other for its appeal to the large audiences who heard them. These events were paeans to the peaceful coexistence of nations, thanks to the beneficent workings of technology, commerce, and capitalism, and as a result, they were also occasions when music's essential variety could be celebrated all at once and in one (albeit large and slightly chaotic) place. World's fairs provided juxtapositions of popular and highbrow repertoires, amateur and professional musicians, and military and civilian ensembles, in the forms of serious, light, and comic entertainment. By building artificial places (in the form of the fairgrounds) the fairs aspired to a world in miniature, and in their circumscribed space music played a necessary, even crucial, role, binding all the parts together through sonic experience.

The chapters that make up the second part of this volume continue to explore the nature of music's national identities, but here in the context of how particular musicians of the nineteenth century embodied and understood them. Place, travel, the profession of music, its reception, and its history are woven into accounts of how four prominent figures in nineteenth-century German musical life helped to shape musical experience and make the case for just how necessary music was for the development of nation and society. While biographical in focus, these essays do not offer biographical sketches of famous musicians. The fifth chapter uses Mendelssohn's extensive visits to England to illuminate how the musical world became over the course of the nineteenth century a world of nations rather than of courts, religious institutions, or the road itself. Mendelssohn was an internationalist rather than a cosmopolitan, and his work on the road as well as back home in Germany helped to clarify – for Germans and the rest of the world – the practice and the meaning of German music. The music critic, theorist, commentator, and composer A.B. Marx, the focus of the sixth chapter, provides the critical commentary on the musical world in which Mendelssohn had flourished. Marx had been an older, somewhat detached member of Mendelssohn's youthful circle in the Berlin of the 1820s. He and Mendelssohn remained close in the decades after Mendelssohn left Berlin to pursue his career, and Mendelssohn remained an exemplar to Marx of the kind of musical life he hoped to see develop further in Europe – serious, demanding, and nationally centred yet open to the world. By the end of his life (he died in 1866), his internationalist sympathies had become even more pronounced. But he remained consistent in his attention to Germany, seeking to recover the music of the past, invigorate the music of the present, and lay the foundations of music in the future by helping the public become more musically literate.

Robert Schumann, the subject of the seventh chapter, appears in his position as a music journalist, claiming a necessary role for music in the public life of Germany. His *Neue Zeitschrift für Musik* asserted a musical voice into what he saw as an activist public sphere, where attention to the urgent needs of the present might help to "stimulate artists into effectiveness." In the most general sense his journalism sketched out a musical map of Germany made up of places where important musical developments were unfolding, not places where commercialism, fashion, and triviality reigned. Before 1848 it seemed possible that like-minded musicians could change musical Germany into a network of such excellence. After the failure of the liberal nationalists to effect significant change during the German revolutions of 1848–9 Schumann wrote more gloomily of the scattering of "true people of art" (*wahre Kunstmenschen*). Others, once sympathetic to his liberal musical vision, turned his notion of a Germany divided between true artists and "false prophets" (Theodore Uhlig's term for Meyerbeer) towards a more integral, less liberal nationalism.

Meanwhile, Brahms, the young eagle from Hamburg who in 1853 had landed unannounced on Schumann's doorstep in Düsseldorf, himself came from one of the musical centres where *wahre Kunstmenschen* dwelt – the free city of Hamburg. The eighth chapter explores the nineteenth-century evolution of the *bürgerlich* (civic, middle-class) institutions of choral societies and symphony orchestras that sustained art music in many German cities. Brahms's own relationship with Hamburg was a conflicted one – insofar as he felt settled anywhere, it was in his sparsely furnished Vienna apartment. To outsiders, then and now, it seemed a judgment on Hamburg, an allegedly unmusical city of philistine merchants, that it had not appointed Brahms to any position of musical leadership in the city. But Hamburg's musical scene of touring artists coming and going and thriving local institutions was more typical than otherwise. The degree to which the repertoire of symphony and chorus settled on the "great German masters," with space at the margins for new masters or non-German ones, is striking but not surprising. It reflected the process of consolidation and consensus about the substance of German identity and music's contribution to it. This was a process that had begun early in the century and was carried forward by hundreds of musicians, music lovers, and associations at the local level. Brahms was a beneficiary of this process – but as composer, pianist, and conductor, not as city music director or impresario. The work of organizing and maintaining musical institutions was of a different order, yet Germany's reputation as the land of music would not have existed without it.

The third and final set of chapters brings into focus some of the many ways in which music became necessary in the lives of Germans. The ninth chapter provides a general account of German musical culture over the course of the long nineteenth century, with particular attention to what, if anything, changed after the foundation of the German Empire in 1871. Take, for instance, the case of Vienna. The Bismarckian solution to the German problem of political multiplicity had, of course, extruded

Austria from the new nation of Germany. But the political dualism of Vienna and Berlin made no sense from the perspective of a music lover. In the Holy Roman Empire, even with its scores of residential and free cities each maintaining more or less significant ensembles of musicians and performance schedules, Vienna had reigned supreme among them. The reasons for its musical centrality – seat of the Habsburg rulers, presence of wealthy aristocratic palaces, crossroads of Catholic Europe – lost much of their strictly musical significance over the course of the nineteenth century, and other German cities became, again for a variety of reasons, important musical centres. Nevertheless, it still remained unthinkable that German musical culture could thrive, remaining vibrant, innovative, and influential throughout the world, without the Austrian capital as part of it – as it has always been. The problem of Vienna, if problem it were, is indicative of the degree to which political unification changed very little in how Germans went about their musical business. This chapter is thus a study of continuities across the long nineteenth century, stretching from the French Revolution to the outbreak of war in 1914, with musical life developing and changing more often because of economic or stylistic developments than because of political ones.

Subsequent chapters focus on particular aspects of the public and the private cultivation of music. The tenth chapter draws our attention to military brass bands over the course of the long nineteenth century. This immensely popular form of musical ensemble could be seen and heard in every town and city by the end of the century, throughout Europe and the Americas. For contemporaries military bands were a feature of everyday life, encountered in parks, parades, and the grander public occasions that ritualized state and local authority. With a few exceptions musicologists have paid them little attention, and historians, even military ones, even less. Yet they were ubiquitous in German life. Because their performances expanded to include brass band versions of the entire musical repertoire, from high to low, from Beethoven to popular song, the phenomenon of military brass bands forces us to consider – especially in the German case – whether they were agents of a pervasive militarization of society on the eve of the Great War. For the Weimar satirist Kurt Tucholsky military music was the synecdoche for the militarism of the pre-war German Empire: “Let it finally be silenced, oh Republic, this military music, this military music!”[16] Still, the interaction of civilian and military musicians, repertoires, and venues suggests that military brass bands became as necessary for civilian musical experience as civilian musical contributions were for military routines and ceremonies.

The eleventh chapter provides reflections on the scattered reception of Richard Wagner's works. The women who are its subject lived in Germany, England, and the United States from the 1860s to the 1930s. None was an important figure in Wagner's life or in the public world of music-making in Europe or America. Several of them were "ordinary" women; others were women of enormous accomplishment; and their levels of musical knowledge varied. They have in common that they attended his operas or played transcriptions on the piano or collected long-playing recordings of them, and then they left traces – in writings and in other people's memories – of what they thought of him and his music. The chapter is an effort, then, to explore the private experiences engendered by a public figure and his works. The response of listeners and the role of music in people's lives is one of the most elusive quarries of musical history, buried in letters and diaries, if written down at all, and made all the more difficult to pin down by the evanescent nature of a musical performance and the emotions it stimulates. Wagner's own enormous public presence – his fame and his notoriety – made the search for responses to his music from people who were neither critics nor performers somewhat easier. What these women set down in the way of responses to Wagner's music suggests experiences of emotional intensity that left their traces even after the music stopped.

A less individualized approach to music's role in German life is investigated in successive chapters on aspects of music in the twentieth century, the first focused on private life and the second on the musical background noise to a very public display. Chapter 12 discusses how making music in the home, or *Hausmusik* – four hands at one piano, a string quartet, a singer and an accompanist, a small vocal ensemble, solo players of every sort – had historical roots in Germany as far back as the era of Reformation. Advocates of Hausmusik in the Third Reich understood themselves as rescuing a practice fallen into decadence and decay. In order to put these claims into perspective, the chapter explores the heyday of Hausmusik in the nineteenth century, its expansion in the Weimar era, and the characteristic National Socialist effort to control, reconfigure, and take credit for an activity that had been and remained part of the texture of everyday music-making, especially in middle- and upper-class households. Chapter 13, on filmmaker's Leni Riefenstahl's use of music, continues to focus on the Weimar and National Socialist periods in German history. A nimbus of Wagnerianism surrounds the music Riefenstahl used as part of the soundtrack to her two major films at the behest of the Nazi regime – *Triumph of the Will* and *Olympia.* Yet neither film score was particularly beholden to Wagnerian motifs or styles, except in a sense so general as to be meaningless. Familiar sounds – military marches prominent among them – characterized the musical background in these films, making the new and still unfamiliar rituals of the Nazi regime seem to emerge seamlessly out of the past. By considering Riefenstahl's relationship to music and the scores of composer Herbert Windt, this chapter makes a case for the continuities of musical life, in some respects an area of Nazi cultural politics in which carrying on as before was the order of the day. Disruptions such as the exclusion of Jewish musicians and works by Jewish composers were papered over and music's power to intensify feelings of belonging together, across time and space, was fully exploited.

The final chapter in this volume explores the compromised nature of the cultural citizenship that music has offered to Germans over the course of the nineteenth and twentieth centuries. Since 1945 Germans searching for things that persist in the face of catastrophe and disintegration have sought out what seemed to be the enduring experience of music, whether in symphonies, operas, folk songs, or yes, military marches. No matter how entwined music has been in the workings of the discredited and failed German states of the past, it remains for better or for worse an arena of social activity in which people express and consolidate new collective understandings. As David Blackbourn recently wrote, "Germans have a special relationship to their own past because of a broken, discontinuous history."[17] Yet for many Germans – and music lovers outside central Europe – the history of music has been continuous, unbroken, persisting through the rise and fall, expansion and contraction of states, seemingly impervious to state boundaries.

The resilience of musical culture in itself does not constitute a moral lesson. It does, however, allow for, and even encourage, meditations on the past and present because of the mutability, variety, and contemporaneity of any musical act. The unending and sometimes tedious debates about Wagner and how to stage his operas are essentially hopeful gestures at confronting the past, understanding it, and making it present, unforgotten. The necessity of music, then, has little to do with repertoire, performer or composer, aesthetic theory, social claim, or political performance. It is, and has always been, necessary because it lives and thereby gives life to us.

PART 1

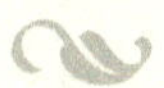

Places

Chapter One

How German Is It?

Sometime early in the nineteenth century, or perhaps the late eighteenth, students of the science of music discovered the national idea, adopted it, lived and wrote within it, and often, but not always, made it central to their assessments of what music was excellent and what not and where music had come from and where it was going.[1] Time went by, regimes came and went in Europe, wars swept across it, scholarship matured, and the national idea lost much of its influence. Indeed, throughout much of the post–Second World War era, the national idea had little purchase on the musico-scholarly imagination, except insofar as the tradition of judgment that still shaped the outlook of musical scholarship was, in often subterranean ways, the legacy of the nation-obsessed nineteenth century. But in the last few decades musicologists have again embraced the national idea, this time as a tool both of disciplinary self-scrutiny and of critical historical analysis. References to the nationalist allegiances of schools of music theory and musicology abound; efforts to link the history of reception to the history of various nationalisms seem likely to proliferate; and investigations of the contributions of musicians to the promotion of nationalist agendas are no longer deemed an inappropriate use of musicological training.

The quantity of recent scholarship on music and nationhood warrants a few observations about the emerging methodology of such work in light of what historians, sociologists, and anthropologists have contributed to the study of nationalism over the past several decades. The pitfalls in the study of nationalism are many and the path through them is difficult to negotiate. The meanings of the key terms in the debate – nation and nationalism – are by no means self-evident, particularly when one descends to the ground of specific historical experience. Those who use them are chronically at risk of reifying something that is protean, controversial, and hence by nature unstable. Yet if one bears in mind the essential instability of the phenomenon in question, the study of music in the context of nations and nationalism is a rewarding way to understand music's place in the societies that made it. Since the major thrust of musicology's interest in nations and nationalism has been to demystify the western canon in general and to shake off German influences, whether musical or musicological, in particular, what follows concerns the German case.[2] A brief survey of how American musicology since the 1930s has understood the significance of nations in musical composition will provide a general context, within which we may examine a specific moment in the emergence of the idea and institutions of serious music in the German-speaking lands.

Musicology's German Problem

American musicology from the 1930s until the recent past has adhered to a straightforward assessment of what nations and nationalism signify in the history of musical development. For the most part the answer has been that they constitute a category of negligible importance. The most striking characteristic of musicology's relation to nationalism has been inattention, possibly deliberate renunciation. Even in periods when the question of music's national valence took on great intensity elsewhere (as in Germany throughout the interwar period), surveyors of music history in the United States managed – politely ignoring the polemics of a Europe gone mad – to say very little about it. And in the post-war decades the tendency to devote little analytical attention to the role of the nation in the history of music only became more marked. If one cautiously takes textbooks of music history as a rough measure of the state of the field, then one finds in an author such as Donald Jay Grout a distinct retreat even from the clichéd national characterizations of Paul Henry Lang or Howard McKinney and W.R. Anderson, who, alongside their explicit belief in the universalist character of all truly great music, were given to pronouncements about the "German spirit," the "dainty and pointed manner" of French musicians, or the "sensuously beautiful" melodies of the Italians.[3]

When musicologists did talk about the national character of certain music, their remarks were confined to general references to geographical locations or to the musical compositions in a self-consciously "national" style characteristic of countries on the German periphery in the second half of the nineteenth century. Particularly this second practice – that of confining the term *national music* to the music of non-Germans and, even more strictly speaking, to non-Germans attempting to overcome German influences – had the effect of loosening German music from its national moorings, until even the term *German music* sounded slightly absurd. This practice has in a more sophisticated form continued in the musicological survey literature. Robert Pascall writes reasonably that "national boundaries offer a rationale for the writing of national history in music," but within that category of "national music" he discusses primarily non-German music.[4] Something that starts out as a straightforward proposition – national boundaries exist, and a history of music within those boundaries makes sense or at least as much sense as they do – quickly becomes complicated precisely when one tries to explain why, and since when, the music of so nationally minded a group as the Germans nevertheless does not seem, in the ears of the listening world, to sound "national."

Levels of awareness and acknowledgment of this phenomenon have varied. For an earlier generation, the universality of German music was an unproblematic fact of European musical development. McKinney and Anderson wrote that the Germans were "somehow able to express ideals which we can definitely recognize as German in a manner that emphasizes their universal content rather than their nationalistic manner of speech."[5] Lang dissolved the paradox with a similar reliance on the distinction between form and content; national forms are good only if they can be absorbed into world art as a new tone or colour, which in turn happens only when they represent something universal that does not belong "only to the nation that produced it."[6] Others relied on the clarities of reception. "The great aim of all nationalistic art," observed Donald Ferguson, "seems to be to attain to international recognition. How much that is purely national must be sacrificed in such a process is a question too complex to be debated here" – or indeed, anywhere.[7]

Post-war writers were even less explicit about the nationality of music by Germans, while the influence in the United States of German musicological scholarship, cleansed of the embarrassment of its more nationalistic overtones, increased.[8] One sophisticated formulation of the problem of what to do with nationalism in music may be found in *The New Oxford History of Music* series, which directly addresses the question of the national in music only once. This comes in Robert Pascall's treatment of nineteenth-century programmatism, of which self-consciously national music was a subcategory, to be treated in tandem with musical exoticism as one element of musical coloration. Satisfactory though this formulation ultimately proved to be, in Pascall's version there was no explicit reference to the music of German-speaking composers; so what might be called the German problem, the problem of whether one can or indeed ought to place music by Germans in a national context, remained unresolved.[9]

Perhaps the national problem in music was simply an artefact of the awkwardness of writing general surveys, a process that necessarily involves even the most circumspect author in unsustainable generalizations and inelegant aggregations. The bulk of musicological work could then concentrate on individual composers, works, genres, and even eras, thus avoiding a heretofore unproductive confrontation with the contingencies of place and nationality. Unfortunately, the national problem in music, particularly as it does or does not apply to German music, is like pulling a weed only to find that its roots are intertwined with everything you wish to keep in your garden. The first sign of trouble for musicological research was that, try as one might to limit it, the national in music is not just a question of "distinctive creative styles," as Pascall puts it.[10] Even his flexible and defensible definition of them, in which the putative nation itself has dropped out – a "generalized conceptual construct based on groupings of individual composers and their personal styles" – inexorably leads away from style to its perception and perhaps even construction in the minds of … whom? Composers? Listeners? Musicologists? And so from style, the features of which might be catalogued and compared, one moves quickly to the far less manageable, in fact, nearly open-ended, set of empirical data posed by musical contexts and musical valuations. It is precisely at this point of opening out onto society, politics, and culture, that musicology confronts the inadequacy of its own artificially limited definitions of the words *nation* and *nationalism*, definitions that have long shut out such complicated problems as what is the German nation and what has been the cultural force of German nationalism over the centuries.

To be sure, a confrontation is under way. That, for instance, German nationalism of an unspecified variety has had a hand in shaping the underlying assumptions of the musicological enterprise as a whole has become a truism of the musico-critical debates of the past several decades. From Joseph Kerman's encompassing calling into question, "How We Got into Analysis, and How to Get Out," we learned that much of the responsibility for the first part of the problem, the long reign of analytical musicology, lay with the dominant influence of German scholarship of the nineteenth century. *Musikwissenschaft* taught the superiority or (what was the same thing) the universality of German music, particularly of the nineteenth century. Universality in turn immunized this music against extramusical criticism, indeed against anything other than respectful and elegantly scientific demonstrations of its internal musical coherence. The intellectual basis of such scholarship was not scientific, however, but in Kerman's formulation was ideological; moreover, the ideology in question was "Viennese or Pan-German in origin, and certainly profoundly guided by nationalistic passions."[11] And with so much else to be done in setting new and German-free agendas for musicology, it is little wonder that there would be no time for filling in the picture on those nationalistic passions, explaining where they came from and why they settled on music to press their Pan-German programs. We would all agree that Wagner had a lot to do with it, but does that really allow us to "take for granted" J.N. Forkel's "German nationalism," as Hans Lenneberg urged us to do in his 1988 reflections on musical biography?[12] Or to accept without further explanation James Hepokoski's assurance that a "connotation-saturated repertory" of nineteenth-century German music "had been pivotal in establishing a German national identity in the nineteenth and twentieth centuries"?[13] Or to understand as too obvious to require demonstration the apparent fact that, as William Weber stated, "the German nationalist movement" drew "heavily on musical culture for its ideological equipment"?[14]

These examples have in common a desire to harness to some other interpretive enterprise the additional force of the nationalist explanation without filling in the historical detail that would make such an explanation plausible. In each case the author moves on to other matters – the usefulness of criticism, Bach's changing reputation, Carl Dahlhaus's project, Vienna's concert life – but before doing so seeks to establish German nationalism and the German nation as a significant circumstance of European musical development. In each case German nationalism or national identity, or indeed nationhood, looms as an undifferentiated whole, lurching its monolithic way through the nineteenth century into the disastrous twentieth and contaminating musical culture along with everything else. Such historical shorthand has its uses but also its misuses. Turning to a more detailed look at two recent articles – Sanna Pederson's "A.B. Marx, Berlin Concert Life, and German National Identity," and Stephen Rumph's "A Kingdom Not of This World: The Political Context of E.T.A. Hoffmann's Beethoven Criticism" – one finds both *Nutzen und Nachteile* are in full evidence.[15]

These articles represent to an admirable degree one of the new directions that musicology has taken, which is towards a more concerted engagement with the problem of musical contexts and hence with the other academic disciplines, chiefly historical and literary studies, that have examined them. Both claim an array of New Historicist literary critics as inspiration and practise a kind of historical-materialist criticism. Both look to the early nineteenth century for the origins of the present crisis in musicological hermeneutics (particularly in regard to German music). Both seek to give more centrality to the early practitioners of musical criticism. Most important, both wish to demystify the "idea of absolute music" and with it the hegemony of symphonic music composed by German speakers, especially Beethoven, and both seek to effect this demystification by revealing the workings of worldly interests, above all nationalist ones, in constructing such musical ideologies in the first place. If it can be shown that the shapers of musical taste and judgment endorsed some incipient version of Germany's drive to world power, then perhaps the legitimacy of their judgments of musical value is thrown into question – and by extension ours also.[16]

Were nineteenth-century music critics like A.B. Marx and E.T.A. Hoffman German nationalists, and did their musical criticism reflect nationalist agendas? Pederson and Rumph think that the answer to both questions is yes. For Pederson, A.B. Marx was one of the chief architects of a "new, exclusionary ideology directed at other nations"; and Hoffmann, in Rumph's view, was "disposed" to a "deep loyalty to the Prussian government" and wrote in an "unmistakably patriotic," if not "fiery nationalist," mode. "There can be no doubt," writes Rumph, that Hoffmann "came under the influence of the reform movement and the political ideology of the Romantics," thereby developing "anti-Napoleonic, nationalist sympathies."[17] Such dispositions had consequences. Marx, according to Pederson, championed the symphony "as a national treasure" and established a "strong connection" between "nation building and concert going."[18] He consolidated a canon, constructed an "other," promoted an elitist high culture, built a nationalist constituency, and laid the groundwork for our own nostalgia for this glorious past. Hoffmann's accomplishment, in Rumph's account, was just as sweeping and just as unfortunate in its long-term consequences. In the "laboratory" of his Beethoven criticism Hoffmann developed a "political model" of musical culture, characterized by "totalizing structures" and ruled over by a "musical monarch" (the "autonomous genius" composing "in fine disregard for the public"), who in turn is "reverently interpreted by an elite class of conductors, performers, and critics" whose real-life originals were the Prussian civil servants.[19] "Vested political interest," whether in Hoffmann's "nationalist," "Germanic" civil servant reformism or in Marx's "exclusionary" nationalism, thus constructed an aesthetic doctrine, that of absolute music, and a musical institution, that of the symphony concert, which together would shape musical culture for the next hundred or more years.[20]

The thesis is intriguing because it is counter-intuitive. It proposes a reversal of meaning: while absolute music and the concerts that performed it would appear on the surface to attest to a new musical autonomy and to unprecedented freedom from social, political, and indeed linguistic limitations on musical possibilities, these arguments imply that to believe in this kind of aesthetic autonomy, to admit music into a realm beyond the reach of language, is paradoxically to be in thrall to the original politics present at its birth. In Pederson's formulation, playing Karl Marx to Dahlhaus's Hegel, it is not that the "idea of absolute music ... became the esthetic paradigm of German musical culture," but rather that "the idea of a German musical culture ... became the paradigm of absolute music." As a result, even now we lament the decline of the symphonic repertoire with a degree of alarm that fails to take account of the nationalist origins of symphonic canonization.[21] Likewise Rumph believes that if we can only sense behind Hoffmann's aesthetic doctrine the "sordid violence of the all-too-real kingdoms of this world," we will open our ears to political representations in the music as well.[22]

Nevertheless, both authors exaggerate the significance of nationalism in Prussian Berlin and in these critics' imaginary, largely because they simplify the politics of the time. In the case of Hoffmann, Rumph is able to make a case for the "vested political interests" at work in his criticism only by positing a powerful cultural and political salience to German nationalism, both in its effects on Prussian politics and statecraft and in its thematic centrality to contemporary literary culture. Writing about the Napoleonic era in central Europe, historians are now more likely to emphasize the extent to which German nationalism in the early nineteenth century was a diffuse and divergent group of phenomena, with only tentative links to the princely states. There was no centrally organized national movement at work during the reform era and so-called wars of liberation; the tentative state modernization accomplished after 1807 in Prussia did not involve "nationalist reforms"; and the reformers themselves were not united in a desire to address "deficits in the national spirit."[23] Moreover, the vast majority of the soldiers who fought

Napoleon's armies were motivated not by *völkisch*-nationalist fervour but, as James Sheehan put it, by the usual "military motivators," "diffuse loyalty to state and sovereign, the habits of discipline, and the fear of punishment."[24] Hence, while it is true that Hoffmann was a dutiful civil servant in the Prussian state on the one hand and a self-conscious cultural German on the other, this combination does not add up to an aesthetician of vested political interests, certainly not of the proto-Bismarckian stance that Rumph detects. Hoffmann's political and cultural loyalties, like those of many of his contemporaries, often worked at cross-purposes and were marked by misconceptions and false hopes. His case illustrates the difficulty of saying what was and was not "nationalistic" in this period, one in which the national "coding" of such cultural artefacts as the music of Haydn, Mozart, and Beethoven was far from fixed or obvious, when the passage from folk to national stereotypes was under way but unstable and in flux, and when German culture and Germanness were inventing themselves, consciously and not.[25] There was nothing official about German nationality in 1810 or 1815 or 1830.

Certainly writers like Hoffmann were central to the process by which a discourse of the nation emerged and ramified, entering into more spheres of social life, and it is useful to speak metaphorically, as Rumph does, of a "cultural war" with France. But such metaphors have a way of literalizing themselves, to the extent that to the national imaginings of writers like Hoffman and A.B. Marx one begins to impute intentions that probably were not there. To put it otherwise, not all nationalisms are state-seeking, not all forms of nation-building are state-building or state-centred, and sometimes a symphony is just a symphony.

For instance, Pederson regards Marx as being so focused on the superiority of German music (and German character), particularly as exemplified in the symphonies of Beethoven, that he strangled a lively musical culture in Berlin, forcing on concertgoers and performers alike a "narrow repertory" of works "embodying German national identity." There are several problems with this portrait. First, it probably overstates the effectiveness of Marx as a shaper of public opinion in ways that he might have found gratifying. Instead of reckoning him a failure as a journalist who could neither recruit nor keep good writers and who never established a firm audience for his editorializing, Pederson seems to take Marx at his word when he writes that he has brought "the public of Berlin out from the poverty and shallowness of earlier concert life to the more noble path."[26] Moreover, Berlin's problems as a musical city had little to do with a nationalistic repertoire: Mendelssohn left the city not because of too many Marx-inspired Beethoven concerts but because he was fed up with the calcified Prussian establishment (to simplify a complicated situation). Marx did indeed, as Pederson argues, urge "the German people" to "listen to the symphonies of Haydn, Mozart, and Beethoven not only for the music itself but also for themselves as a nation."[27] But he also urged them to listen to Italian and French operas, in order to place German music in its proper European context. He seems to have believed that listeners in Berlin would come to understand the greatness of native musical composition only if they were broadly educated in the European musical idiom – the kind of call for greater learning and the hopeful attitude towards questions of nationality that were so characteristic of the German Enlightenment.[28] Certainly Marx distrusted Rossini and "Italianate" music, and he saw the Germans as more capable of deeper and higher aesthetic experiences than were other nationalities. Neither of these attitudes meant that he was an exclusivist in his sensibilities or intent on nation-building. Like Hegel himself, whose philosophy and historical method he admired, A.B. Marx must be read within a different and more flexible interpretation of early-nineteenth-century nationalism.[29]

The Crisis of the Music Profession and German Nationalism

To be sure, many scholars exaggerate the nature and strength of nationalism in early nineteenth-century Germany, perhaps reflecting their knowledge of Germany's future. But there are more general problems here with how we conceptualize nationalism as well. The root cause of overstatements regarding nationalism is a tendency to regard it, first, as a coherent ideological doctrine, like Marxist socialism, to which one becomes convert and adherent, and, second, as a doctrine that describes some political reality or is at least affiliated with some kind of politics of interest, whether those interests be the legal-statist ones of the Prussian bureaucracy or the liberal-representative ones of various dissident groups seeking political power. Such a tendency necessarily gives the reader of an allegedly nationalist text the task of finding the interest it expresses behind what is then construed as the "nationalist rhetoric." This is not a very interesting task for musicology to set itself. It forces musicology back on yesterday's models of German national development: the tendentious and deterministic Luther-to-Bismarck-to-Hitler models. Must we now insert E.T.A. Hoffmann and A.B. Marx into that trajectory simply for the sake of proving that music is indeed a part of intellectual and political history?[30] Among other shortcomings, such models have an inevitable tendency to anachronism and musical melodrama: like the Hollywood soundtracks that render the most banal conversation pretentious, knowledge of how it turned out can distort understanding of how it once was.

Nationalism can become powerfully attached to political agendas of various stripes, but for the early nineteenth century it makes better sense of the evidence to look at nationalism as an emergent cognitive model for a number of educated Europeans, a way of ordering experience, of looking at the world and making sense of one's place and identity in it – in Bourdieu's terms, a mode of "vision and division" of the world.[31] An understanding of "nation-talk" that emphasizes the instability and varieties of its relationship to the fields of social interaction would allow us to reconstruct more accurately the context in which nineteenth-century Europeans increasingly regarded certain music as "serious." Understanding talk of the nation as a cognitive disposition also opens the way to more pluralistic descriptions of the connections between the sphere of musical activity and those of politics, the marketplace, state administration, family and private life, religion, and literary and intellectual culture. The task of explaining why a number of educated Germans became so serious about music in the early nineteenth century and what, if anything, their new orientation had to do with their nationality will occupy the remainder of this chapter.

The emergence of a new aesthetic of music in the first part of the nineteenth century suggests the existence of a problem in the musical sphere to which the thesis of musical autonomy posed a solution, and indeed the polemical tone of musico-critical debates of the period itself implies a sense of crisis among contemporary musicians and their various audiences. But identifying the nature of the crisis and its relationship to nationalism is no straightforward matter. For Dahlhaus the problem was aesthetic-philosophical, a crisis of intellectual justification. The idea of absolute music presented a new, though not unprecedented, solution to music's status as art, and so he analysed the idea in terms of intellectual genealogies and affinities, in the tradition of a hermeneutic *Geistesgeschichte.*[32] While acknowledging the importance of a cultural Germany as the frame for this discussion and occasionally as a factor in the paired antimonies that carried through its development, Dahlhaus was otherwise uninterested in the national/nationalist issue. Bernd Sponheuer too regarded the distinctions between high art music and low entertainment music as the outcome of a sophisticated battle of ideas, a philosophical problem (Kant's dismissal of music) with a philosophical solution (music dichotomized, then differentially valorized).[33] In contrast, Rumph and Pederson have redefined music's problem in political and loosely economic terms, with the idea of absolute music serving to gather audiences and promote nationalist agendas and programs of political quietism.[34]

But there is an additional and simpler explanation for the early-nineteenth-century shift in musical paradigms, one that engages the social and political world but does not require us to regard either musicians or their audiences as committed German nationalists – a characterization that involves anachronism, simplification, and inaccuracy. The idea that music was a serious art form was a solution to problems not in Prussian political development or German national development but in the music profession itself. The transposition of aesthetic arguments from the literary to the musical sphere, which Hoffmann accomplished and A.B. Marx further developed, formed the cognitive counterpart to the slow and difficult birth of an autonomous musical field. To say this is to say little more than that thinking about music underwent a process of crisis and redirection in the early nineteenth century, which was dependent on the crisis and redirection in the ways by which people made their living from music. Nation-ness, specifically Germanness, enters into this story, as it does into so many, as a strengthening and linking agent, an explanatory framework that connected the problems and possibilities of musical life to social life as a whole and to larger problems of cultural meaning. Its presence in debates over musical meaning thus signifies not the hidden presence of political agendas but a more general upheaval in social life and, connected to it, the perceived importance of music in regard to basic social attributes of community and identity.

The crisis in the musical professions in the German-speaking lands arose from fundamental transformations in the larger social formations that had sustained musical production up through the eighteenth century – that is, princely states, churches, and home town guilds. Each entered into the period of French hegemony in various stages of decline and internally generated reform efforts; each emerged from the period of French hegemony profoundly altered. In each case, the process of confronting change in the form of French armies and administration diminished the capacity of society to support a sphere of musical activity. The case of the aristocracy is most often cited, the decline of aristocratic patronage serving as one of those truisms, like a rising middle class, without which one seems unable to think historically. Its significance has probably been exaggerated: from Arno Mayer's 1981 reminder about the "persistence of the old regime," especially in cultural matters, to Tia

DeNora's account of the Viennese aristocracy's constructive efforts on behalf of Beethoven's genius, a number of scholars have insisted that we leave the titled classes in play at least until 1914, if not later.[35]

Despite such qualifications, it remains true that the possibilities for musicians to live off the landed gentry were in decline by the start of the nineteenth century. If one focuses less on lords and more on the princely rulers of Germany's thousand fatherlands, whose many *Kapellen* were more important to music than titled music lovers as such, then one must acknowledge the precipitous decline in numbers of courts. From 1803, when the Holy Roman Empire began the complex process of its own reorganization, to 1806, when it shut itself down, the number of sovereign entities roughly under its purview diminished from several hundreds to about forty. This decrease and the generalized state of financial distress that followed in the wake of French invasion resulted in the disbanding of musical ensembles and the dislocation of musicians.[36] Moreover, native German musicians and instrumentalists were hurt proportionally more than the Italian and French stars at the top of much court musical life in Germany.[37]

The reorganization of lines of authority and the state of financial hardship affected musicians in towns as well, where the social configuration of musical life was more complicated than in the German courts. Town and church musicians occupied a baffling array of positions, true in their multiplicity to the variety of local constitutions but unique in the range of statuses they held. A baker was a baker no matter the home town one considered, but a musician could be beggar-wanderer or citizen, servant or *Bürger*, lay or cleric, and Catholic or Protestant, thus cutting across all the distinctions that operated in early modern Germany.[38] Local aristocrats and ecclesiastical sovereigns financed some musical positions, town councils and churches some others, and so on. In addition, the localization of much of the response to French hegemony makes it difficult to generalize about the effect of these upheavals on town musicians. It seems clear that the number of available cantorships had declined drastically by the first decade of the nineteenth century, reflecting not only social and political upheavals but a fifty-year decline in the importance of music within Protestant worship. Those that survived often involved few and sometimes no musical duties.[39] Music-making in the Catholic churches of Germany was enjoying a revival by the end of the eighteenth century along with Catholic intellectual life in general. The Reich reorganization of 1803–6 reversed that hopeful trend, however, coming down with its most devastating force on the many ecclesiastical principalities, which suffered wholesale loss of land and revenue to middle-sized secular states. Finally, in the eighteenth century there is some evidence that town musicians increasingly sought the security of guild structures to clarify their status within the home towns, but the more powerful trends of state centralization and bureaucratic consolidation worked against that solution, making it something akin to rats running onto a sinking ship.[40] Even in the German territories that remained part of what W.H. Riehl called the "individualized country" of classic guild-based constitutions only the most powerful guilds retained the full control over membership and standards of production that was the sign of guild health, and musicians' organizations, Wagner's fairy tale to the contrary notwithstanding, had never been among the central home town guilds.

At the same time, the musical sphere was developing new means of support and new structures of social organization and performance; indeed, so dominant did these new developments in society become in a short time that one tends to forget that, just like modern industry itself, they arose in a context of ruin and insecurity, even if they themselves were rarely the chief cause of the old world's decline. The list of modern musical institutions is a familiar one. Its centrepiece was the public or semi-public concert, singly or in series, the commercial structure of which implied a commodification of music, its capacity to transform sound into money.[41] The commodification of music through growth of the public concert was slow to develop, but music publishing was a powerful motor, servicing a growing market of domestic performance and contributing to the freeing of musicians from patronal or guild relationships, even while forcing them to submit to the discipline of supply and demand. As in industrialization itself, all aspects of the musical marketplace – subscription concerts, amateur duet-playing, and so on – reinforced and encouraged one another, becoming eventually a self-sustaining set of products and desires. Finally, confirming the social significance of these trends, the characteristic organizational form of musical life became the voluntary association, which had precursors early in the eighteenth century and proliferated from the turn of the nineteenth century on, particularly in German-speaking lands. Musical associations, whether groups that performed music for their members, groups that performed music for others, or groups that mainly organized musical performances, had characteristics in common with all voluntary associations of the period. Men and some women, amateurs in spirit if not always in actuality, organized as free individuals on the principles of self-constitution, self-cultivation, and self-rule.

This familiar story is nevertheless worth retelling to draw attention to the social implications of these changes. Their overall impact for musicians themselves was a simplification and clarification in their social status, at least potentially, if not right away and for all. Thanks to Max Weber, we are used to thinking about the process of modernization as one of increasing specialization of functions within an ever-thickening web of institutional structures, but modern complexity is of a different, more coordinated nature than premodern complexity. For musicians the premodern world of home town and court had consisted of unlike and incomparable relationships, each governed by its own rules and presenting its own possibilities or lack of them. The category of musician as a predictable set of professional experiences and expectations hardly existed in the sociopolitical world of central Europe before 1790. But the economic, social, and political transformations that changed this state clarified the situation, establishing commonalities among divergent types of musical performers and placing the musician among the movers and doers. These were the free professionals known not by what they had or were in a particular community but by what they did, by their ambition, aggressiveness, skills – in short, their achievement.[42] Performers in the independent orchestras, which embodied the increasingly public nature of concertizing, had to sustain a certain level of musicianship to flourish; this performance requirement was, of course, even more stringent in the case of solo players, the famous virtuosi, whose careers of constant moving and striving represented not an exceptional but an intensified case of the new musical career, open above all to talent. Some musicians also moved into the commercial realm of publishing and selling music; as Klaus Hortschansky has pointed out, much of the early business in music was "in the hands of the musicians themselves," in roles ranging from publishers and sellers to agents, composers of transcriptions, and copyists.[43]

"Out into the world with you!" wrote Carl Maria von Weber in 1809 as the opening line of his never-finished novel, *Tonkünstlers Leben*, "for the world is the artist's true sphere. What good does it do you to live with a petty clique and to earn the gracious applause of a patron ... Out! A man's spirit must find itself in the spirits of his fellow creatures."[44] Weber's exhortation has the boldness of a Nietzschean transvaluation of values. What had previously marked the musician as a man without honour – his mobility his restlessness, his association with peddlers, beggars, and Jews – now was proclaimed as the mark of true nobility, indeed of membership in Fichte's *Geistesaristokratie*.[45] A series of social-historical transformations lay behind this shift in valuation, by which professional mobility became virtue rather than vice. Under the influence especially of the French Revolution in its European impact, mobility increasingly meant survival – being able to take advantage of opportunities whenever they arose and to change when change was all there was. The new man of music, on the move and on the make, was also gradually removing himself from his old circles of acquaintance and experience and coming into contact with the other movers and doers – state officials, merchants, free professionals, clergy, and intellectuals. That many of the "fellow creatures" worked for the state or depended on the noble families who hired them as tutors did not prevent them from developing a distinctly non-servile and non-statist collective identity: again, in Mack Walker's words, they conceived of themselves collectively "as individuals, free of social restraints and prejudices, outside the static dull complexities of Germany's predominant home town and country life."[46]

The institution that more than any other accounted for this collective identity, providing a common experience of "mixing and changing," was the university. Long before the celebrated period of early nineteenth-century reform, the most advanced German universities (Göttingen, Halle, and a few others) represented that rarest of institutions in German-speaking lands, a place where people could "transcend the limits of provincialism and gain an introduction to cosmopolitan thought patterns and life-styles."[47] Successive waves of reform resulted finally in a peculiarly German synthesis of utilitarian training for the free professions and state service, on the one hand, and a neo-humanistic education of individual cultivation and self-development (*Bildung*) on the other.[48] Binding together these unlike, even mutually cancelling, goals into a single educational institution were the accomplishments and the ambition of a small elite – the bureaucratic intelligentsia, made up partly of modernizing segments of the old aristocracy and partly of the well-to-do bourgeoisie – who administered the German states. This elite had in common the possibility of leisure, which is not the same as a fully idle life, expensive secondary schooling, and a commitment to both aristocratic refinement and bourgeois hard work and self-improvement.[49]

To be sure, enrolling in a university was not what Carl Maria von Weber had in mind when he urged his musician to seek wider horizons, but mixing with people and impressing people who *had* been to university was an essential part of successful participation in "the world," particularly when the old world began to fall apart. Mixing with the commercial bourgeoisie was not, from that perspective, a sufficient survival strategy, for the commercial bourgeoisie held little power in central Europe (except in the so-called free cities) and had no control over the course of events, whereas the university-educated elite stratum, with their hands increasingly on the levers of state, to some limited extent did. The commercial bourgeoisie also lacked a sustained tradition of financial support for arts and learning and by the end of the eighteenth century were rarely sending their sons on to university training. Its members operated largely within the marketplace, and while, as noted above, new musical institutions like the concert did begin to commercialize music, the musical marketplace was not fully viable – it offered constant insecurity and meagre returns on effort. The musician who relied on the sale of his talents risked financial ruin, a fact that Klaus Hortschansky sees as having produced a "latent crisis in the musician's life," a lurking fear that music was doomed to become, in the words of one contemporary, a "breadless art."[50]

Marketplaces have never been a wholly effective means of ensuring the existence of artistic endeavour in the west, but have operated best in conjunction with state and private patronage. So although it would be a mistake to attribute too much conscious understanding of their situation to individual musicians making more or less independent decisions about their careers, nevertheless what Bourdieu has called the "objective divisions of the social world" inevitably impose themselves on social actors, enabling us to identify certain "genetic" links between social structures and the cognitive schemata by which people organize their lives.[51] Everything – their own mobility and lack of clear status as a group, their association with traditions of Latinate and theological learning, their acquaintance with the German courts if not with the state bureaucrats per se, their familiarity with the activities of leisured people, the limited salability of their product – suggested to forward-looking musicians the desirability of association, of some as yet unrealized sort, with the bureaucratic intelligentsia and, by extension, with the state.

Yet the obstacles to building such relationships were considerable: as Sponheuer in particular has shown, some of the most influential thinkers among the educated elite had a low opinion of music's capacity to express serious thought. Nor did music yet have a sufficiently articulated history, which might have demonstrated its place among the arts cultivated by the ancients and hence worthy of modern attention.[52] Winning the respect of the educated elites thus required that a new case be made for music, in order to demonstrate both the suitability of music as part of the philosophical project of neo-humanism and the competence of musicians to embody and carry forward that project. As long as music remained the decoration of a moribund court culture or the accompaniment of equally moribund liturgical and provincial ceremonials, its practitioners had little hope of moving fully and successfully "out into the world." As both Dahlhaus and Sponheuer have shown, music-loving philosophers struggled for and won in this period a place for music in the modern philosophical and aesthetic debate, but securing intellectual prestige would not have mattered so much to musicians themselves had not access to funding and support, whether state or private, depended on such distinction. Institutionally, a Kantian underestimation of music's significance meant the absence of musical scholarship from the most modernizing universities; this in itself both reflected and, as the stakes became higher after 1806, threatened to perpetuate the state's indifference to music as art and all that such indifference implied.[53]

Thus, the paradigm shift, by which literary models of artistic autonomy and transcendence began to shape a new musical hermeneutics as well, can be seen as a new set of mental schemata made necessary by a significant reordering of forms of social integration and employment of musicians. Musical autonomy at the cognitive level of a new collective representation of musical meaning referred back to the need, the desire, and the struggle for professional autonomy of the practising musician. From the same perspective the persistent concern that runs through musical writings of the time that the whole musical endeavour will be dragged down into triviality and mere entertainment represented not only ambivalence about the marketplace and sensitivity to a literate culture's doubts about musical seriousness, but an unavoidable status anxiety – a pervasive doubt about the musician's ability to find an honourable and tenable place in the social order. It is thus understandable that by the end of the eighteenth century calls to improve the standing of practising musicians increasingly took the form of exhortations to further education: a 1787 pamphleteer lamented the condition of professional musicians who worked as mere "machines," "with their hands and not with their heads." This author went on to argue that "public institutions such as the secondary schools and the *Gymnasien* could do much to refine the study of music ... The choice of a way of life, the poor methods of studying music, the lack of intellectual development – these are the factors which produce such a small number of really musical instrumentalists." In the same vein J.F.K. Arnold, in his 1806 advice on the "art of developing an orchestra," urged not only "industry and constant practice" but "aesthetic education" through "a library of books on music," first anecdotal and biographical, then moving on to truly serious "readings on the critique of pure artistic taste."[54]

This advice brings us finally to the question of national culture, because those for whom debates over musical meaning and the improvement of musicians were carried on – the university-going, state-serving, journal-writing, association-joining mostly men of the educated stratum – were at the same time the makers and shapers of Germanness. The final piece of this puzzle, then, is to answer the question initially posed: how German was it, this turn to absolute music, this new configuration of ideas about the seriousness of music?[55] That these developments took place in the German states and were conducted in the German language is no sure guarantee that the nationalizing impulse was either central to or even present in these changes. For some outsiders musicality and national character seemed to be intertwined. Charles Burney observed that "a musical spirit" was "universally diffused through the empire," and though Germans for the most part lacked a "national music," they had a distinctive musical style, which was characterized by "*patience* and *profundity*," along with "*prolixity* and *pedantry*."[56] In any case, Germans who actually thought of themselves as such did not think of their wholeness in musical but in linguistic and literary terms. By the second half of the eighteenth century and through the journals and associations that constituted their "Germany" these people had achieved a certain "unity of taste and judgment which transcended territorial boundaries."[57] This unity had its first classical centre in the grand culturalizing project that was Goethe's and Schiller's Weimar, a place with links to practically every endeavour of the literate elite and with aspirations to create a native culture for Germans. But by native culture they meant above all a national literature with a common style and a shared national spirit in sympathy with past and present.[58] It was, in other words, a notably non-musical unity and native-ness; nor did the experiences that had led some German-speaking people to feel bonds of commonality include to any significant degree listening to, performing, or even talking about music – even though they lived in an era of remarkable music-making and probably heard a great deal of music themselves, without thereby connecting it to their conception of the German nation.[59]

Music's non-linguistic character is part of the explanation for this cultural dissociation, for it posed a challenge to meaningful inclusion in a common (nationalizing) culture, particularly one based on language and later concerned, as a matter of philosophical and scholarly inquiry, with the capacity of language to shape human groups. But one must also look to the incompleteness of the nationalizing impulse itself, which in Friedrich Meinecke's phrase consisted of a "slowly sharpening vision," turned both inward on the self and outward on the world. Germanness represented, from such a perspective, "a great extension of the individual personality and its sphere of life," and the cultural nation, "a jointly experienced cultural heritage," arose out of "an era of individualistic strivings" – "the nation drank the blood of free personalities, as it were, to attain personality itself." Meinecke's entire formulation, problematic though its celebratory tone ultimately proved, emphasized the gradualness of the nationalizing perception and its deep affinities with the neohumanistic, universalistic projects of self-discovery. Becoming "national" was an infinitely expansive Enlightenment project of education, a search for knowledge about self and environment. Indeed, men like Wilhelm von Humboldt believed, with reason, that the more society itself became educated, the more national it would become as well: a "finer cultivation of language, philosophy, and art" would in turn lead to more "national differentiation," which itself would then call for higher efforts at understanding and hence more education. "Whoever occupies himself with philosophy and art belongs to his fatherland more intimately than others," wrote Humboldt to Goethe from Paris, for "philosophy and art are more in need of one's own language, which emotion and reflection have formed and which forms them again in turn."[60]

Given such an understanding of Germanness as an attribute of educated, widely travelled, and cultivated men and an aspect of heightened self-knowing, music had much to gain by aligning itself with the national habitus; asserting the national-cultural significance of certain music and musicians was tantamount to claiming inclusion in educated society, a kind of shortcut to relevance and respect. By the same token, evidence of increasing national inflections in writings about music after 1800 is a strong indication, not that musicians and music lovers had become nationalists, but that they were working towards fuller integration into the circles of the educated elite. If some music could indeed be seen as an integral part of the cultural past, present, and future, then serious people, musically gifted or not, must undertake to acquire a better understanding of it.

This is what J.N. Forkel suggested in the oft-quoted introduction to his 1802 biography of J.S. Bach, probably the first fully realized statement of the existence of a specifically German music. One does not need to assert the existence of some "tide of nationalism" to make sense of his remarks: Bach's works were "an invaluable national patrimony, with which no other nation has anything to be compared," and the "preservation of the memory of this great man … is an object in which not merely the interest of the art but the honor of the nation itself is deeply involved."[61] Forkel, as befit the author of the first general history of music in the German language, placed Bach at the centre of an educational project that he explicitly compared to that of training in Greek and Roman classics at gymnasium and university. Bach himself, in Forkel's comparison, was the musical counterpart to the Greek and Roman authors; he was "the first classic that ever was, or perhaps ever will be," at least in terms of the higher musical education of a cultivated person. This ingenious transposition of classical status from the ancient world to the near contemporary one and from the semi-exotic Mediterranean to a provincial German *Heimat* was, to be sure, anticipated by the English in their celebrations of a Handel centennial in 1784. Still, in the context of German society Forkel's homemade classicism not only exploited the German intelligentsia's susceptibility to invocations of Greco-Roman culture but also managed at the same time to finesse the troublesome problem of music's shaky status in the neo-humanist world view.[62] Finally, it hinted, very gently and perhaps not even consciously, at the superiority of Germany's musical monuments over any other of the young cultural nation's products. After all, only seven years earlier Goethe had been driven to a public defence of German prose for being not yet capable of classic grandeur but certainly full of promise: true classics asserted Goethe, could not be conjured out of thin air but rather must be developed out of the efforts, good and bad, of one's predecessors and contemporaries.[63] Music, it seems, was already there, or so Forkel wishfully claimed. However, it would take more grounding in the institutions of social and intellectual life to make this status real. I turn now, by way of conclusion, to that process of institutional reform.

Carl Friedrich Zelter: Musical Reform, the Prussian State, and the German Nation

I have until now dealt at a general level with the interdependence of social and cognitive levels of reality in the emergence of the distinctively German idea of serious music; but social changes, like ideational ones, appear to us most forcefully in their embodied form, in people's lives. Carl Friedrich Zelter (1758–1832), whose life extended across the full range of these changes in musical status and meaning, grasped their import more fully and struggled with mastery of them more successfully than his relatively obscure reputation might suggest. His significance as a figure in European musical development indeed does not lie in his compositional efforts, vast though they were, nor in his specifically musical judgments which, although sound, lacked prescience and flair.[64] And as long as the history of musical reception has focused on specific (and usually enduringly famous) composers or on the influence of such composers on other famous composers, there was indeed no reason to think of Zelter as a man of much importance.[65] But he is centrally important to the history of music in society, not just because he put together a couple of organizations and mentored a generation of new musicians, but because his institutional reconfigurations of musical life in Prussia gave a self-regulating and systematic form to the labile musical relationships of his times. Zelter should be seen as the great stabilizer in the transition of musical life from premodern to modern forms and dispositions. Dahlhaus provides us with a characteristically insightful summary: Zelter's new institutions, he wrote, "constituted a nearly complete system, a system through which the participation of music in the *Bildungsidee* of the classical-romantic era was institutionalized."[66] Including among his institutions the impact of his own highly visible life, I shall conclude with a brief account of Zelter's story, as it illuminates that of the ideas and institutions of serious music at the start of the nineteenth century.

His own pursuit of a musical career, as he recalled it, initially followed the *stürmisch* trope of young Werther's flight from practicality to unrestrained sensibility and from health into febrility and illness. From our perspective it illustrates the extent to which a life in music increasingly drew someone into conflict with the static certainties of the German home town. Zelter's father was a successful mason in and around Berlin and owned his own lucrative brickyard on the outskirts of Potsdam. His second son, like his first, was trained from childhood to join the trade, a natural path made all the more irresistible by the early death of young Zelter's elder brother.[67] Music entered his life during breaks from construction work: he wrote of listening to orchestra rehearsals at Sans Souci while his father repaired palace buildings or chatting with military musicians while working on the new cadet academy in Berlin. In 1775, at age seventeen, he nearly died of smallpox and during his convalescence took up the violin to promote his return to "bodily health." The health regimen quickly turned into an unhealthy passion – a new form of illness, it seems, to which his father strenuously objected, saying that "one cannot eat bread" from music.[68]

The next twelve years involved a series of after-hours efforts to obtain musical instruction, while chiefly pursuing training in the science and practice of building houses. The latter process culminated in Zelter's achievement of master mason status in 1783. The former included experiences across the range of musical activities, from hanging out with the "rough" but "talented" city musicians of Berlin, to playing briefly in the Döbbelin'schen Theater orchestra, to composing a cantata on the dedication of a new church organ. All these episodes skirted the edges of a respectable *bürgerlich* lifestyle, so Zelter pursued them half-furtively. In particular, his association with Lorenz Georg, the Berliner *Stadtmusikus*, had him serenading women and blowing trumpets from city towers, both legitimate parts of the job, to be sure, but at the same time indications that this was no job for an honourable guildsman, let alone something more elevated: according to Ledebur, the city-musician period was bad for Zelter's morals (*Sitten*), and Georg himself, recognizing this fact, eventually sent him away.[69] Even the church cantata, which seems stodgy enough to suit any parent, partook a bit too much of the new public world of concertizing and publicity. Zelter's father read about the performance of his son's composition in one of the Berlin dailies and was not so much angry as confused – who was *this* Zelter? The home town citizen was known by who he was: his *Eigentum* did not refer to the property he owned; it referred to the qualities, the worthiness, that inhered to him and his place – earned, certainly, not by striving and pushing, but rather by steady effort and proper behaviour. In contrast, young Zelter had thrown himself before the public as an unknown quantity and let the public make their own judgment on his worth. A new, modern world opens up for us in those judgments; to be a musician at the end of the eighteenth century increasingly meant that one had to join it.

After the death of his father in 1787 Zelter moved more and more in these circles of movers and doers, like the *Kenner und Liebhaber* (experts and lovers – both voluntary statuses) of C.F. Rellstab's public concerts with which Zelter was involved in 1788.[70] One of the most characteristic acts of his new-found identity as a member of the modernizing set was to join C.F. Fasch's summer singing circle, an embryonic voluntary association that had its first fully public performance in 1791, at the Marienkirche in Berlin, and therefore dates its founding to that year. From Zelter's point of view participation in the Singakademie, as it was called after 1793, meant a definitive entrée into good society as well as a statement of intent about his own career change. The social status of the organization is most evident from its female members, all of whom carried the spousal monikers of the bureaucratic elite: Medizinal-Räthin, Legations-Räthin, Hof-Räthin, Stadt-Räthin, Geheime Registratur-Räthin.[71] Music had its own peculiar way of forwarding new social statuses, within strict limits, and so a man, if he were a *Berufsmusiker*, was not only welcome but excused from dues (a gentle status reminder, in its own way). Good tenors are hard to find; moreover, Zelter had long been a pupil of Fasch, time permitting, since they first met at Potsdam as servants – one a musician, the other a mason – in the court of Frederick the Great. Berlin and the Singakademie together show us how a musician lacking the university experience went about "mixing and changing." The group was the making of Zelter, and he of it: after Fasch's death in 1800 he led it (with a stable membership hovering around 150, all the best people of the city) through war, occupation, more war, and restoration, until his own death in 1832. He not only made the directorship of an amateur singing group into a professional musical post of a highly respectable sort – something unlikely to occur in 1791 – but he gradually made concrete the social and political linkages implicit in its membership, to the *gebildete* elite, on the one hand, and to the state, on the other.[72]

One year before Fasch's death, Zelter had had the unexpected honour of a letter from the man who was already regarded as the living expression of German cultural achievement, a figure whose authority and achievement were unique in the German-speaking lands, Johann Wolfgang von Goethe. Goethe's interest in Zelter sprang initially from his pleasure in the musical settings Zelter had composed in 1796 to a few of his poems. Ambitious publishers routinely sent Goethe the latest batch of song settings of his poems, in the hopes of publishable expressions of approval; Zelter's, sent by the Berlin publisher Unger, was one of the few that Goethe genuinely liked. In any case Goethe's interest in pursuing an actual acquaintance seemed to derive less from Zelter's music than from the piquancy, sure to appeal to a collector like Goethe, of his dual career as mason and musician.[73] Goethe wrote directly to Zelter only after his interest had been aroused a second time by August Wilhelm Schlegel, whose letter about Zelter to Goethe in 1798 compared Zelter's house building to Orpheus's ability to raise structures with his music. Besides giving him classical credentials of a sort, Schlegel's letter cast Zelter in the role he would play effectively and even authentically throughout his correspondence with Goethe, that of a plain-spoken man, with integrity and practical sense, but also with the tender sensibilities and aesthetic interests of an artist. As Goethe wrote of Zelter to Charlotte von Stein in 1805, "One begins to have faith in human beings again when one sees such a man, who lives so vigorously and honestly, in contrast to the many who are blown back and forth like the roar of the wind ... If excellence in ordinary things should ever be lost, then he will restore it to us."[74]

The Weimar connection, as it played itself out over the following thirty-three years, would be of inestimable value not just to Zelter himself but to the prestige of the institutions that were closely associated with Zelter's, and hence Goethe's, name. Scholars who have looked at their friendship have mostly bypassed this aspect, wondering instead at what Goethe saw in the man (the implication being that if what he wanted was a musical correspondent there were many more promising candidates around, Beethoven, for instance, or E.T.A. Hoffmann) or waxing sentimental about the affection between two such exemplary and yet dissimilar German men.[75] But the relationship always had about it the air of a public exchange and a *Bildungserfahrung* for both. Nor was their increasing intimacy, which reached the *duzen* stage in the wake of the suicide of Zelter's stepson, at all in contradiction with their mutual understanding of the symbolic significance of the correspondence. Zelter was Goethe's connection to Berlin, where he rarely visited yet with which he wished to stay current, and to music, which in a similar way he felt he did not understand well but was beginning to think he should.[76] And Goethe was, to paraphrase Heine, Zelter's entrée card into European culture, in the wide, cosmopolitan, nationalizing sense that characterized the "classical centre" at Weimar.

His approval may also have emboldened Zelter, one year after his first long visit to Weimar, to write directly to the Prussian state seeking some kind of official recognition for his musical activities and in particular for the Singakademie. In 1803 Hardenberg – at that point, among other things, a trustee of the Prussian Academy of Arts and already part of the reform-minded clique among the Prussian bureaucracy – had sent out a call to members for suggestions on how to enable the academy to "have a sure and measurable impact on the spirit of the age and the productivity of this epoch," as well as to "awaken the artistic energies of the country." Zelter, through his growing connections to the Berlin elite, obtained a copy of the memorandum and sent Hardenberg a response – a reasonably bold move for the son of a mason.[77] His suggestions to Hardenberg were also bold in their simplicity: include music, he urged, make the promotion of good musical instruction and performance among the people a basic goal of the Academy of Arts, improve music in churches and schools and you will improve people altogether.

The memorandum reflected his views, developed in the course of his transitional musical career, on the problems that musical life faced in German lands, specifically Prussia. His diagnosis was shaped by his own varied experience of court, guild, and urban life: it reflected the moral and spiritual concerns of the German Enlightenment and shared its inclination to look to the state, not for solutions, but for its support and implementation. Zelter believed (not wrongly, in fact) that musical instruction and musical cultivation had fallen to a low level among the town and city population as a whole; that church music, particularly church singing, was in the midst of a full-blown crisis of existence; and that the population would benefit morally from a renewal of church and urban musical sociability. Although Zelter declined to lay specific blame for what he saw as the superficiality, frivolity, and dilettantism of much of contemporary musical life, he strongly implied that the princely rulers of the German states had too long neglected "serious" music in favour of the narrow and morally suspect cultivation of court opera. Although the Europe-wide debate over opera and its meanings would quickly connect to emerging national movements, Zelter himself excluded opera altogether from the category of serious music, preferring to focus his energies on forwarding non-operatic traditions in German-speaking lands. Above all, he was concerned that musical life of the future not be confined to an operatic high culture and worthless imitations of it at lower social levels.

Zelter's eight-page proposal, which Goethe and Schiller later read and amended before Zelter resubmitted the document to the Prussian king in 1804, should be seen – along with such more famous writings as Wackenroder's outpourings of a music-loving friar or E.T.A. Hoffmann's review of Beethoven's Fifth Symphony or J.N. Forkel's biography of J.S. Bach – as one of the key documents in the transformation of music from a courtly decoration to an essential part of the cultivated person's education. Unlike the writings of those others, however, it made its appeal to the educated elite through the vehicle of state recognition – in other words, through a bid for recognition by the shapers of "taste and judgment" actually in a position to take practical steps. The 1803 memorandum was the first of a long and not always fruitful correspondence between Zelter and officials of the Prussian cultural establishment. It initiated a twenty-year process of continual pestering, prodding, cajoling, and pleading on the part of Zelter to include music on the state's agenda of moral and cultural renewal.

Over time Zelter's efforts paid off. He won approval to rehearse his singing society in the building of the Academy of Arts and eventually persuaded the state to contribute prime land, near the Zeughaus on Unter den Linden, on which to erect a prominent new building for the group. He himself was made first an honorary member of the Royal Prussian Academy of Arts, then the first professor of music at Humboldt's University of Berlin.[78] Alongside these marks of inclusion in the state-sponsored project of cultural renewal, Zelter sought and received the participation of the Berlin elite in music-making itself. Besides his continual and successful efforts on behalf of the Singakademie, he founded a small singing group for patriotic German men, a *Liedertafel*, which became the model for countless other such groups in Germany. In pursuit of his goal to raise standards of education among practising musicians, he also founded a school for instrumentalists, a school for the training of school singing instructors, and a state-sponsored institute for church music, of which he was the first director.

All this activity helped to raise the profile of non-operatic music as a public art, the cultivation of which was necessary to the well-being of the community as a whole. Piece by piece, his institutions took over functions in musical life – training, regulation of quality and quantity of musicians, professional placement – that the decline of guild, town, and court musical life had left in neglect. They did this, moreover, by establishing direct relationships with state authorities and the favoured cultural institutions of the state, from academy to university. Although Zelter himself was sceptical of abstract discourse about the public and its capacities, his institutional achievements coincided in time and in essential ideological orientation with the better-known developments in musical journalism, publishing, and performing, each of which in its own way forwarded the development of a musical public sphere. Informing all these developments was the new aesthetic of musical seriousness, which asserted *some* music's capacity to work positively on the moral sensibilities of its performers and listeners – "a salutary influence on morality," in Zelter's straightforward formulation.[79] For Zelter this ethical aesthetic, the practical realization of which was the performance of what he liked to call "eine tüchtige Musik," represented the possibility of regrounding collective life in the age of revolution on the solid foundation of the traditions and achievements of his craft, now working in a new partnership with the reformist state.[80]

That Zelter's reformist activity on behalf of music in Prussia should have had any affinities with nationalism in any of its forms is not, however, immediately obvious. To be sure, Zelter did sprinkle his memoranda with references to his "patriotic heart" and his "duty" to his "fatherland," but none of these terms implies anything more than loyalty to the Prussian king. A perfectly responsible rendering of his life's work might mention them only in passing, as marginal notes to his real accomplishments, which were, on the one hand, the composition of hundreds of quite pleasant Lieder and, on the other hand, tireless but dull organizational activity within the musical circles of Berlin. Yet I think such a portrait would be incomplete, in its own way as misleading as the stridently nationalist portrait of Zelter that emerges from Georg Schünemann's work, in which Zelter, like Stein, Hardenberg, and all the rest, prepared the ground for a destined unification of Germany under Prussia.[81] For Zelter the nation, conceived of as a cultural and ethical commonality among German-speaking people, existed as the ideal community in which music ultimately was heard and performed. If Berlin was his *Heimat* and Prussia his fatherland, then Germany the nation was his culture in which and for which his music resounded. No more than Goethe, Humboldt, or Fichte did Zelter imagine this community as a political entity. It was, instead, the context for all cultural and ethical work, the community on which this work would presumably have an influence and that would, in turn, shape the spirit and character of the individuals who were part of it. Music, like all the arts, had a "communal purpose" (*gemeinschaftliche Zweck*), and that was *Bildung*, which, as Zelter defined it, was the "activity of inner or spiritual forces, to the end that man realizes his complete existence and becomes nobler."[82] Bildung was the property of men who lived as part of a nation, that is to say, as part of a cultural and ethical community. Thus, art, nation, and Bildung stood together and intertwined, as the markers of a distinctive elite with aspirations to represent something greater than themselves.

Concern for the preservation and promotion of this nation pervaded Zelter's memoranda to the Prussian state, going beyond a mere rhetorical frame for practical proposals. In his first memorandum Zelter's argument about the nation followed immediately on his dramatic characterization of music as the one missing piece in the state's promotion of art. No other art, he declared, had had such an influence on the "formation [*Ausbildung*] of the German nation" in the preceding seventy years as had music; no other art had by its excellence so distinguished the Germans among the other nations of Europe as had music. Finally and most tellingly, Zelter claimed that no other art lay so close to the essence of being German: its deterioration, he asserted, "threatened the German nation in its most essential characteristics of constancy and seriousness" (*Treue und Ernsthaftigkeit*).[83] To preserve the "old German seriousness" (*alte deutsche Ernst*), something Zelter saw as tantamount to maintaining the German nation, it was necessary to keep alive the institutions that had fostered seriousness, serious people, serious craftsmen, and serious art. For music, this meant reinventing an organizational structure for church music. The old institutions had fallen apart. Without renewed ones there would be no new "Bach, Fasch, Graun, Quantz, and Benda" (Zelter's tradition of greatness and seriousness), and their music, with all its life-improving capacity, would be lost to Germans forever.

Zelter's decision to mobilize this conception of the nation and of its vulnerability on behalf of musical activity was an important key – perhaps *the* key – to the acceptance of his reformist ideas among members of high Prussian bureaucracy, among whom such ideas were widely disseminated and widely accepted, at least in their apolitical form. Zelter's claims about the role of music in raising the religious and moral sensibilities of "the nation," of exerting "an important influence on the spirit of the nation," appeared repeatedly in the paper trail of ministerial correspondence surrounding the inclusion of music in the Prussian Academy of Arts. Wilhelm Humboldt himself echoed Zelter's language in a memorandum of 1809 that Schünemann has characterized as the "founding document of the musical section of the Academy." Music's influence "on the character and the formation [*Bildung*] of the nation" had been too long neglected by public authority, argued Humboldt, in an unmistakable echo of Zelter's language. A few days later the king answered, graciously allowing the formation of a special musical section, in recognition, again echoing Zelter, of the "unmistakable influence of public music on national development."[84]

Humboldt's advocacy of the state's patronage of "serious" music had been decisive; in 1809 his influence over cultural affairs in Prussia was at its height.[85] But his conversion to the cause of serious music is also significant, given his own marked indifference to all things musical. Here was no musical enthusiast putting forward acceptable public arguments to clothe his own aesthetic preferences, but rather someone apparently persuaded into a new view of music by way of his recognition of its relevance to the cultural nation he so valued. Humboldt represented precisely those members of the educated elite who had long regarded music as lacking in ideal or intellectual content – regarded it, in short, as the entertainment of the uneducated, whether they be lords, peasants, or townsmen. If Humboldt could embrace a new aesthetic of musical seriousness, then there was hope yet for musical progress. His memorandum in effect enshrined in official educational policy in Prussia a conception of serious music that would influence German music-making for decades to come. According to this conception, the more serious a piece of music was, the more demands it placed on the technical, intellectual, and emotional resources of an individual; the more fully it expressed the capacities of a free human being; the more German it was as well and, the more German, the more universal. For to be German was to learn freely from other cultures, to (in Humboldt's words) "lack … a circumscribed nature," or (in Schiller's) to "keep company with the spirit of all worlds."[86]

Humboldt, moreover, picked up on Zelter's oft-repeated claims to a privileged insight into the mind of the "common man," the marker of whose participation in the cultural nation (so said Zelter) was not philosophical depth or poetic sensibility, but rather "Prussian probity and constancy, the sum of which is piety" (*Preußische Redlichtkeit und alter Treue … deren Summe Frömmigkeit ist*). In Humboldt's rendering, music constituted the key to reaching this "common man" and integrating him into the great educational project that was the German nation. Because music was essentially a language of feeling, its "strength and completeness" could be apprehended by all human beings without special knowledge; music was, therefore, "a natural bond between the lower and higher classes of the nation." As in a religious service, in fact in conjunction with one, musical performance allowed "all members of the nation to unite purely as human beings and without the accidental distinctions of society."[87] The implications of Humboldt's arguments to the king were clear: give people this experience of equality in the context of culture and religion, and they will not seek it in political life. Nationalism liberates and enlarges the human soul; it need not at the same time destroy the framework of an ordered society. Here, through music, the collective uplift of nation could reinvigorate Prussia without opening it up to the mob.

Thus, serious music, as Zelter understood it, cultivated it, and promoted it to the educated elite of his country, was German indeed. It served as a key definer of national character, which was in Zelter's time emerging out of a combination of folk and elite traditions into that "unity of taste and judgment" which is the marker of a cultural nation. His work attempted to lay the foundation (an appropriate metaphor for the master mason, and one that he himself used often to describe his activities) for the permanent contributions of music to German national character and social cohesion. In his perception of the problems music faced and the likely sources for their solution, Zelter was a man of his time, ready to pursue reform and progress in concert with the state and its servants, ready to identify the nation and the national soul with the moral improvement of the people. That his national conceptions were essentially innocent of exclusionary and imperialistic coloration is to say no more than that he reflected the state of German culture at the time. His originality lay in his perception that music could and should be at the centre of national culture, not for its folksiness or its entertainment value or its aristocratic tones, but for its seriousness. The first dramatic demonstration of the influence of his work came with the enthusiastic participation of Berlin's educated elite in Felix Mendelssohn's revival of Bach's *St Matthew Passion* in 1829, two decades after music's admission into the Prussian Academy of Arts. After attending the performance Johann Wilhelm Loebell wrote that this was music that was "strong above all ... and serious."[88] Mendelssohn's triumph was unthinkable without the preceding decades of musical preparation, much of it sponsored by Zelter, among Prussia's now more musically inclined *Bildungsbürgertum.* The task for the historian of this period is not just to identify the presence of such national contexts and motivations, but to keep them in their proper place, as one part of an increasingly rich and complicated musical scene, in which German musicians and non-musicians alike were gradually learning how to live in a national culture.

Chapter Two

Music in Place

Over recent decades historians of Germany have done much to complicate and otherwise confound the sweeping effect of narrative, its ability both to soar above the details of life at ground level and to gather this detail into manageable if inevitably distorted general statements.[1] With its attention to micro-history and the history of everyday life the new cultural history provided theoretical justification for setting aside concerns about narrative coherence and attending instead to side-stories, counter-stories, submerged stories, and forgotten stories, all the things that make particularity seem more important than generalization and incommensurability more compelling than aggregation.[2] But if we revert to an older way of thinking about culture, not in broad anthropological ways but more as the ladies of the opera society or Matthew Arnold thought about culture ("the best that has been thought and said in the world"), then we will notice that the study of arts and art culture has remained aloof from the process of dismantling and complicating the stories we tell.[3] Relatively few works by German historians, working in the discipline of history itself, have much to say about the vast store of cultural treasures that have accumulated over the centuries. As a result, a number of conventional assumptions about the forward march of artistic innovation and the like remain in place, awkward companions to what are by now significantly reconstructed narratives of political, social, and economic development. This chapter aims to renovate the study of so-called high culture or, more accurately, art culture through examples from the history of music, understood here as a cultural activity shaped in significant and intriguing ways by the places in which it sounded.

Place as a "Hidden Dimension" of Musical Culture

Both place and space have been oddly neglected in the study of music and musical culture. David Blackbourn has observed that "space is too often a hidden dimension" in our efforts to understand the past, and this holds just as true for the history of music as for other aspects of the past.[4] To be sure, one can find many histories of music in this or that country or in city or court, but place in these works is passive in its relationship to the music-making, leaving one curious about how our understanding of music in nineteenth-century society would change if we consistently attended to the *where* of it – where people heard it; what kind of places these were; what cultural, political, and social connotations they carried; and so on. We have often been content to restrict our consideration of the where of music culture to descriptions of concert halls and opera houses, the survival of which into our own times has somehow worked to obscure the particular positions they occupied in earlier times and places. Once one looks for the ways that music and place interacted in the nineteenth century, each giving meaning to the other, the more one finds these interactions, some hidden in unexplored corners of musical life, many others hidden in plain sight.

The geographer Robert Sack has called us "place-makers," always in the process of transforming the physical reality we encounter into meaningful space.[5] Our capacity to make sound and to listen to sound is a crucial aspect of this conversion. The appropriation or claiming of space is a matter of sound, something that is quite obvious in, say, the household, where sounds such as refrigerators turning on and off, door hinges squeaking, people talking, and stereos playing make this space familiar and known to us. It may be a conceptual leap to move from that space to an orchestral concert or a band playing in an outdoor pavilion, yet we ought to make that leap and ask both how those sounds affected people's experience and interpretation of these places and, contrariwise, how these places shaped the sounds heard in them. Both perspectives on music in place might teach us something about how these human communities worked. Walter Benjamin famously observed that "even the most perfect reproduction of a work of art is lacking in one element: its presence in time and space, its unique existence at the *place* where it happens to be."[6] When he wrote that, of course, he was interested in art in the age of "mechanical reproduction" and was not thinking about music. What, one then wonders, might a history of musical aura before the age of mechanical reproduction include?

The interest of musicians and musicologists in music and place has tended to cluster at either end of the chronological spectrum of serious music in the western tradition: medieval and Renaissance music on the one hand and twentieth-century experimentalism on the other. As is well recognized, in the Middle Ages a close relationship that was more than just acoustic developed between music and the Gothic cathedral; both were expressions of the medieval concept of cosmic order. Medieval philosophers thought of the universe in terms of Pythagorean ratios, called musical consonances, and in recognition of this theory churches like St Denis, of seminal importance to medieval architecture, were proportioned according to these same consonances. Thus, the church stood as a microcosm of the universe, and the liturgical chant sounded in it was the reverberation of the spirit animating this order. Here, then, was aura in its most obvious form, a kind of human magic the loss of which Benjamin associated with modernity.

Fast forward around 800 years, from the twelfth to the twentieth century, and one finds many efforts among twentieth-century composers to recreate the close, organic relationship between music, man, and place often associated with the origins of music itself. Much of this twentieth-century work was intended as a direct rebuke to the music of the nineteenth century, allegedly cut off from any meaningful relationship to the world around it. It took as its polemical starting point the notion that nineteenth-century music lacked connectedness, lacked context, and lacked *place.* In the words of R. Murray Schafer, a contemporary Canadian composer who coined the term "soundscape" and with it launched the now vibrant field of sound studies, "in the western tradition music is an abstract entertainment for the pleasure of the ears alone ... In order to achieve this purity it was necessary to separate music from the soundscape. The soundscape is a plenum. The music room is a vacuum."[7] The suggestion that art music has existed in a kind of vacuum, starting, as Schafer implies, with the construction of the first concert hall, is evident in a volume of cultural studies explicitly concerned with music's relationship to place and space. This is a collection of essays on global and indigenous popular music called *Soundtracks: Popular Music, Identity, and Place.* "*Popular* music is spatial," write the volume's editors, Australian musicologists John Connell and Chris Gibson; it is "linked to particular geographical sites, bound up in everyday perceptions of place, and a part of movements of people, products, and cultures across space."[8] But they have nothing to say about art music, as though exempting it from the earthbound fate and worldly relevance of popular music and musicians, as though the harmony of the spheres still sounded in the concert halls of Europe.

Bayreuth: The Making of a Musical Place

To be sure, nineteenth-century music critics and theorists must bear some of the blame for this distorted view of musical life in the nineteenth century. So eager were many theorists, especially Germans, to raise the prestige of instrumental music in a social world dominated by opera that they developed an ideology of "absolute music," or music freed from earthbound meaning and purpose. Such was the success of their efforts that the musical public, first in Germany and England and soon across Europe, began to form a reliable, paying audience for concert and chamber music performances, to an extent unprecedented in the previous century. Yet the idea of absolute music was more a conceit than a description of actual musical practice in the nineteenth century. When twentieth-century musical writers take it as a description, they inadvertently contribute to our neglect of the context of music so designated. Speaking very generally, then, much of the great quantity of art music composed between 1700 and 1900, together with the musical practices that realized it, needs to be better placed. Art music was spatial, too: the music room was not a vacuum. To paraphrase Connell and Gibson, it is and was linked to particular geographical sites, it is and was bound up in everyday perceptions of place, and it is and was a part of the movements of people, products, and cultures across space.[9]

A few years ago, Terry Eagleton posed the question: "What is it that connects culture as a way of life and culture as artistic creation?"[10] For musical culture the easiest way to illustrate how we might approach this question is briefly to consider Wagner's Bayreuth. The sounds of the music at this particular geographical site so obviously included the reverberations of a broader cultural space that one has no excuse for regarding it as a vacuum. But Bayreuth also points beyond its singularity in two directions: first, to art music's complicated relationship to German provincialism, and second, to its equally intricate intertwining of nationalist and internationalist tendencies in European cultural life. Wagner shaped the so-called Bayreuth experience in opposition to both these aspects of his native musical culture, the provincial and the international, with ambiguous success.

The Bayreuth story is a familiar one, since properly told it reflects every step of Wagner's troubled passage through the nineteenth century –

and few individuals' steps have been more closely followed than his.[11] Nevertheless, it is worth reviewing in order to emphasize Wagner's acute and unusual awareness of the role of places in the shaping of musical meaning and experience. Whether or not we consider this attention to place visionary, Bayreuth was the product of his sustained engagement with place, the culmination of his efforts to re-engineer the settings in which people experienced the musical arts. His choice of Bayreuth was, first of all, a reaction against the capital cities where he had suffered (Paris, Dresden, Munich, etc.) and against everything they represented in cultural and political life. His writings on the failings of metropolises as sites for music date before the 1848 revolutions, and his views did not change even after he gave up revolution for Schopenhauer.[12] In brief, the trouble with music in cities was that people arrived at the theatre after stressful days spent in pursuit of profit, too distracted really to listen, too weary to be anything but amused or asleep. Concerts were designed for the short attention span; people spent the intervals drinking and further dissipating their mental energy in mindless chit-chat. Such distraction was disastrous and prevented people from achieving the kind of transformation through music that he always believed to be its highest purpose.

As his thinking developed about the kind of place that would be most effective for the artistic experience he believed people desperately needed, he proposed a number of outré ideas, each of which attests to his sense of the impossibility of finding appropriate space in society as it existed. For instance, having completed the libretto for *Siegfrieds Tod* (ultimately *Götterdämmerung*) in 1850, he told a friend he wanted it to be performed once only, in a temporary structure in the fields outside Zurich, which would then be burned to the ground in the finale of the opera. He also imagined it being performed in a temporary structure along the banks of the Rhine, or on a floating theatre on Lake Lucerne, and in any case (in a letter to Liszt) in a "beautiful quiet place far from the smoke and disgusting industrial smell of our urban civilization."[13] The preface to the published edition of the Ring libretto, which came out in 1863, proposed the building of a temporary, wooden theatre in a small town. Then, finally, after a lengthy episode of scandal and extravagance in Munich between 1865 and 1869 (when his erstwhile revolutionary friend Gottfried Semper drew up elaborate plans for a custom-built Wagnerian opera house in Munich, only to be dumped and bilked and forced to resort to lawyers), the town of Bayreuth finally emerged in 1871 as a possible site for the theatre of the future – "my instinct's greatest

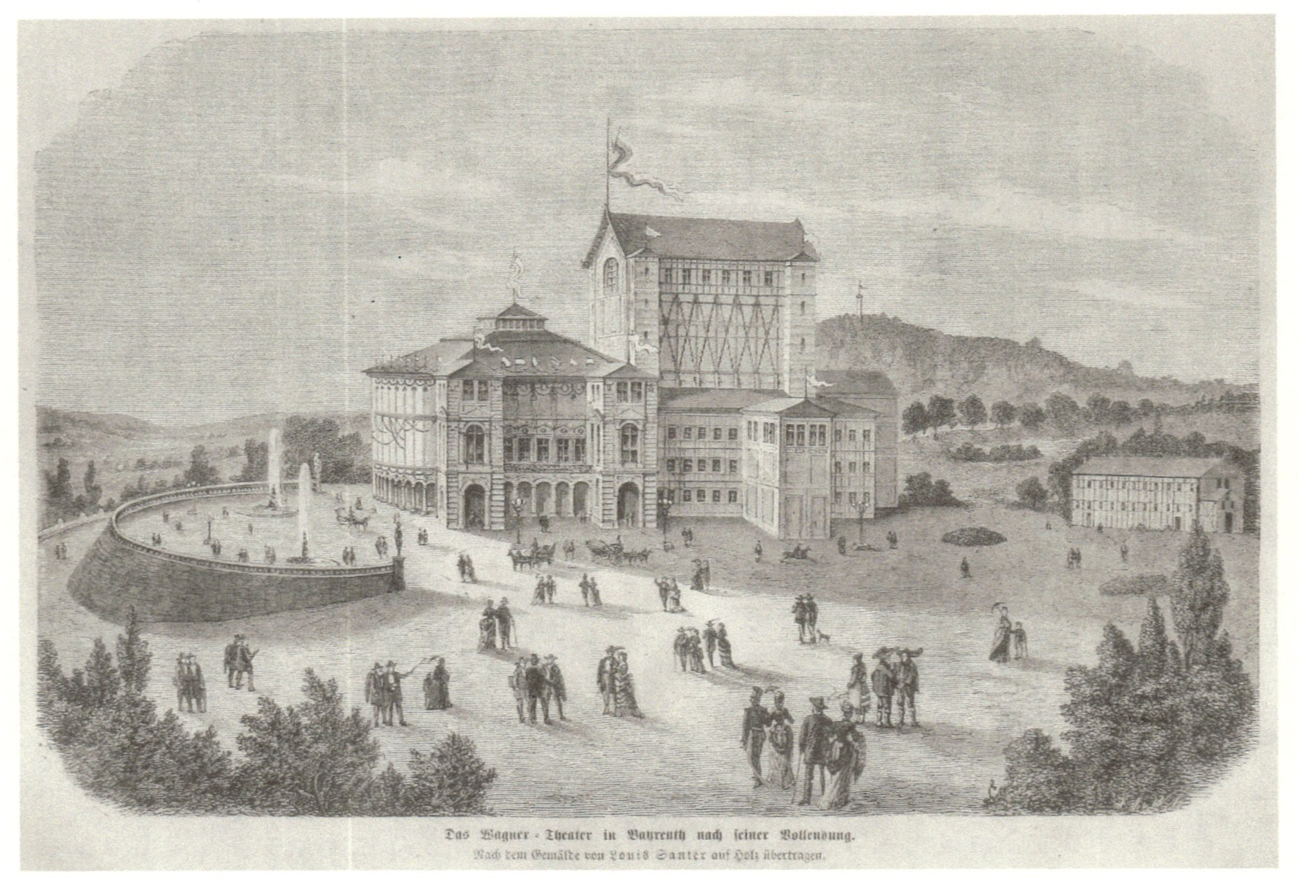

2.1 Wagner's Festspielhaus in Bayreuth on the Green Hill. Contemporary lithograph in *Die Gartenlaube* (Leipzig), 1873. Wikimedia Commons.

success," he told Nietzsche.[14] The cornerstone was laid in 1872; the theatre opened in 1876.

Wagner, of course, intended to create at Bayreuth something that Germany lacked, that is, one central place to which all Germans could come to experience one common thing – *his* art, which he understood as the culmination and embodiment of all previous German art, musical and otherwise. Much about the place-ness of Bayreuth and how he appropriated it reveals this conception. He considered it to be geographically in the heart of Germany, not in a borderland, yet isolated enough to be a place without distractions – in that sense, like the fields outside Zurich. In the town itself he settled on a spot not in its centre but off to the side and up on a hill, hence also in that sense close yet separate. And while other buildings of that era dedicated to art were distinguished in the midst of their busy cities by means of decorative gestures evocative of cathedrals and palaces, Wagner deliberately eschewed architectural references to the sacred or the splendid in favour of functionality. Bayreuth thus emerged as distinct in every way (architecture, ambiance, environs) from its exact contemporary, the Paris Opéra of Jean-Louis-Charles Garnier, opened in 1875. It had more in common with a spa than an urban temple of art. Even the means of getting there (a long train journey) and the daily rhythm of a visit (walks, leisurely meals, and episodes of mentally demanding, physically uncomfortable healing) evoked the atmospherics of the magic mountain more than the metropolis. The only thing the *Festspielhaus* did share with the Paris Opéra was an implicit aspiration to singularity and centralization in national culture – one place, *über alles*.

But in that, Bayreuth failed. It easily became the centre of a cultic Wagnerianism, which was certainly consequential for German culture as a whole. But it did not become the vital centre from which national cultural life emanated, nor did it become the touchstone for authentic Germanness, even though a belief that it embodied both bound together Wagner and his followers. National cultures are not so easily manipulated, and German musical culture in particular resisted both centralization and nationalization in ways that Wagner and the Wagnerians either misunderstood or refused to acknowledge. When he designed the Bayreuth experience, Wagner was not in the grip just of anti-urbanism, but also of anti-provincialism, and thus he fell, seemingly unconsciously, into the old trap of wanting Germany to be more like France. He tried to create in Bayreuth an artificial centre for a nation that had no centre, to take the provinciality out of the place. Instead, he created a kind of limbo, a musical Neverland, well suited to the demands of the music with all its mythological abstraction but ill-suited to the everyday interaction between people and art.

It is not surprising to find that one of Wagner's most impassioned opponents in this effort was that tireless defender of German particularism, the conservative folklorist and cultural historian Wilhelm Heinrich Riehl. Riehl was a Bavarian citizen and a resident of Munich. He also described himself as "the longest-standing opponent of Wagner" set against him "since the esteemed Royal Saxon Court *Capellmeister* stood behind the barricades in Dresden." Generally not shy about publicizing his disapproval, Riehl nevertheless stayed silent on the subject of Wagner until 1873, when the latter's appeals to the German people, German honour, and German genius to help save the faltering Bayreuth project were making daily headlines, especially in Munich. Although he deplored Wagner's display of base ingratitude to a royal patron in 1848, Riehl's objections went more to the kind of musical culture he saw Wagner foisting onto a susceptible German public. For Riehl Germany was "a land and a people at once homogeneous and unified and also polymorphic and disparate," and the challenge of his times was to preserve the diversity while achieving unity. He thought that Wagner's Bayreuth experiment, and his claim to leadership of German musical life altogether, were too singular, too grand in their claims, and as a result far too dismissive of the cultural diversity of German life. "As a friend of freedom and fairness," he declared, "I could never become a follower of Wagner, even if I held his art in the highest esteem. The kingdom of art is republican, aristocratic-republican, if you will; it does not tolerate the dictatorship of one individual, and Wagner is an art-dictator, as none before him."[15]

Bayreuth was, in his eyes, a circus, and just as he rejected any notion that one composer could encompass or inherit or represent all of German music, so too did he dismiss the possibility that one place could be the site of its deliverance. For him the essence of German musical life resided not just in theatres (though he was an opera-lover and theatregoer), but in thousands of churches, concert rooms, public halls, and above all – his most constant theme – in the German home. German musical life was, in other words, a geographically dispersed phenomenon and as such a perfect mirror of German life. The "artistic greatness" of the German nation – or any nation, he argued – never rested in a single great individual "but rather in the combination of all, and the more diverse its parts, the richer and more powerful the whole."[16]

Music-Making in the Nation of Provincials

Riehl thus draws our attention from particular geographical sites or particular individuals to the second of Connell and Gibson's concerns: how music was bound up in everyday perceptions and experiences of place. To turn to this is necessarily to consider the more geographically diffuse phenomena that are often encompassed in vague phrases like "the role of music in German life." Riehl and Wagner were in agreement on one point at least, as were any number of travellers to Germany in the nineteenth century, in thinking that one of the most noticeable aspects of German life was the ubiquity of organized music making in every corner of the land, much of it taking place below the notice of the more widely read music periodicals. The German always remains a provincial, wrote Wagner in 1840 with both affection and exasperation, and we know Riehl agreed with him in this belief. To illustrate the point, both conjured up similar images of an intimate group of musicians: in Wagner's telling, "a father and his three sons, at a small round table in their home; two play the violin, a third the viola, the father the cello," playing a quartet composed by one of them; in Riehl's, a group around a piano, one playing, others singing, another playing the violin.[17]

But the two observers drew different conclusions about what the phenomenon meant. For Wagner, such scenes were symptomatic of a serious problem – the lack of a single, national public for German musicians. Already in 1840, in his essay "De la Musique Allemande," published in the *Gazette Musicale* in Paris, Wagner sought to distinguish the German musician from the French one (a virtuoso, a creature of society life) and the Italian one (a singer, a lover). The German musician was purely a musician, "capable of writing music merely for himself and friends, uncaring if it will ever be executed for a public – the desire to shine by his creations but rarely seizes him and he has no idea how to make it happen." The reason for this state of affairs lay in the "political barriers" that "obstruct him from publicity": "his fatherland is cut up into a number of kingdoms, electoral principalities, duchies, and free towns." The musician cannot shine in a small town, because it has no public; if he seeks a public nevertheless, he will move to the residential city of the duke, but there he will find so many good musicians competing for so little work that he will give up or grow old and die searching for that elusive German-wide fame. All that is left for the talented German musician is to "choose a trade to earn a living and give oneself to music with all the greater zest in one's leisure hours; to refresh oneself, to grow nobler by it, but not to shine." Moreover, take this musician out of his home, out of his small town concert hall or his regional music festival, put him "before a full-dress audience in a crowded salon,'" and he falls apart. He sounds mediocre, his native musicianship is ruined, denatured, his talent is for naught. "A great national work of music," wrote Wagner, would never come about until "this mournful chapter in the history of German music" was brought to a close.[18]

Riehl, as is hardly surprising, was far more worried about the disappearance of this provincial musician than his failure to win acclaim in the salons of Europe. As far as he was concerned, the best, most essential German music and musicians were "*einfach, frisch, sinnig und innig*" (simple, fresh, thoughtful, and sensitive), not the first adjectives that come to mind in describing Wagner or his music. Riehl showed particular concern for the fate of the amateur musician, who, he felt, had been increasingly ill served by German composers since the era of Mozart and Haydn. Their genius, he thought, had welcomed the participation of the amateur, but Beethoven, the hero of German music, had composed works increasingly difficult for the amateur to play or even to understand, thus driving a wedge through the middle of musical social life. His late compositions were "a musical necessity and in technical terms a great leap forward," but for the "education of society" they brought about a "painful regression."[19]

By the 1870s, and even more so in the decades after Bayreuth, Riehl saw himself surrounded by soulless music-making in artificial places, while music in the home, of the "good old German masters," seemed discouraged and overwhelmed. Still, Riehl's polemical mission, to combat a public infatuation with all things Wagnerian – and "Slavic," a close relation – tended to make him oblivious to the actual state of provincial music-making. There is little to suggest that provincial and domestic music-making were atrophying, or that Bayreuth or Wagner had much effect on the shape and conduct of such activities. Instead, one finds a dramatic expansion in the music publishing business, the bread and butter of which was music for home and amateur performance.[20] Music publishing involved making available both the work of famous composers, in particular those such as Mozart, Haydn, Schubert, and Beethoven, who essentially enjoyed no copyright protection – indeed, there was something of a "classics boom" after 1867 and the introduction of offset lithography. But publishers also became active recruiters of people who could churn out, in industrial fashion, works that were easy to learn, entertaining, and graced by a modest amount of virtuosic display – *faux*

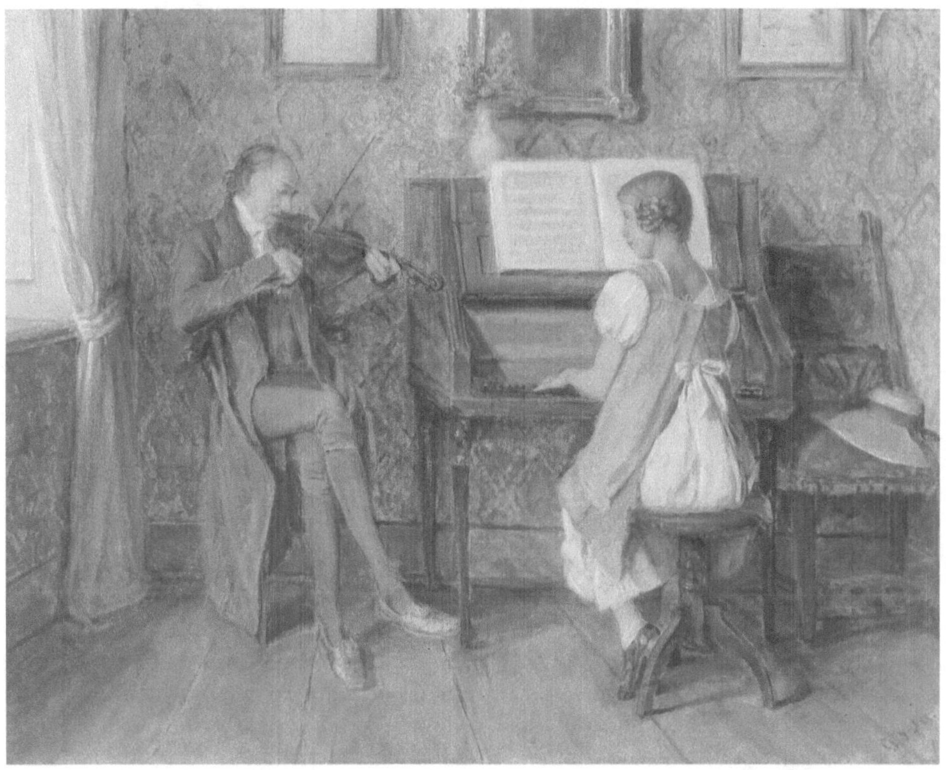

2.2 *Hausmusik.* Painting by Gustav Igler (1842–1908), popular nineteenth-century Austrian genre painter. Wikimedia Commons.

fireworks, as it were. They were usually little more than some right-hand trilling and scales, along with the occasional glissando or crossing-over the left hand, which was, for its part, consigned to infinitely repeatable accompaniments of chordal boom-chuck-chuck or simple arpeggiation. Arrangements of operatic favourites, sentimental songs, and instructional pieces rounded out the home repertory. The explosive increase in the amount of printed music available reached a high point around 1910, gradually receding thereafter in response to the advent of sound recording and broadcasting, and German firms such as Schott, Simrock, and Breitkopf & Härtel were the dominant players in this commercial market, both in Germany and abroad. The period of the Second Empire thus coincided with the peak of music publishing, and the market for its products consisted of players and consumers of music in every city and small town of Germany.

There was a similar rise in numbers of people participating in amateur music associations, regional music festivals (which bore no relation to Bayreuth), and city orchestras and theatres. After the Second World War a great outpouring of local history volumes recounted the musical history of one's town or region – from the accounts of gymnasia choruses to exhaustive lists of every local musical organization. No other European nation has a similar body of writing about its musical life, nor does the United States, even though amateur musical groups established themselves very prominently across the British Isles and the United States. But in Germany the phenomenon became linked to national identity, even national mission, in a way it did not in other countries. And although we can certainly regard the commemorative and antiquarian writing as a post-war search for continuity, it also speaks to a longer-standing pride in local and regional music-making. It documents the phenomenon to which music publishing records point, that below the level of high-profile music centres such as Vienna and Berlin art music was cultivated and practised in a steady, everyday kind of way, along with a hard-to-classify mixture of other, simpler music. The city of Ludwigshafen, for instance, had twenty or so amateur choral groups, such as the Singverein Ludwigshafen, whose director, the grammar school teacher Jakob Gutwein, kept them on a steady diet of "folk songs and the easier art songs." He rehearsed them to "stand up to the most exacting criticism" and, like Riehl, showed a particular partiality for Mozart and Schubert.[21]

Moreover, in the nineteenth century no other country produced the kind of serious compositional attention to this level of music-making as did the Germans. The music historian Carl Dahlhaus (a lover of paradox) has gone so far as to call most of Schumann's oeuvre "provincialism of the highest order" and "*Hausmusik* for cognoscenti."[22] The same could be said for much of Brahms's work; he wrote quantities of music for amateur choir or private performance at the parlour piano, including waltzes, Hungarian dances, and simple religious motets. Even his great symphonies were written in expectation of an audience of people who would have enjoyed his other music in the home. Art was for him part of the social fabric, not removed from it, and the fabric was German, provincial, and dispersed across place. Even Wagner wrote a song cycle, the *Wesendonck Lieder*, intended mainly for private singing and indeed was little performed in recital halls, then or now.

Although the full social and cultural contexts of this music-making remain somewhat obscured in histories of music, overshadowed as they are by the forward march of great composers and their works, the density and distribution of such music-making across German-speaking Europe contributed to the vitality of local and regional cultures. In the course of the nineteenth century, music-making became one of the most public expressions of local pride and solidarity, every town boasting of its musical offerings, however meagre, and regions and cities competing with each other in the choral festivals that became a common part of the musical landscape from the 1820s on. Through the planning and carrying-out of such activities both amateur and professional musicians forged networks among localities and regions, reinforced by the presence of music in schools and homes. Music, to put it another way, formed an important experiential bridge between these places of everyday life, crossing over from public to private and back again without much ado. Moreover, as already noted, the evidence of local musical life suggests considerable diffusion of art music or serious music, in various adapted forms, across a fairly broad spectrum of social classes and local milieus. Even industrial cities had factory-based brass bands, wind ensembles, and singing groups, which inherited both the town-musician repertoire and adaptations of the concert hall and opera house repertoire.[23] A great deal of Wagner, for instance, proved especially adaptable to the brass band. Finally, military bands and orchestras were ubiquitous in Germany and well integrated into local life, often providing musical backup for the more numerous choral groups (good instrumentalists being a bit rarer than singers, as is still the case).[24]

Finally, a significant portion of the serious or classical music of nineteenth-century Germany was, of course, sacred music or church music, which, starting in the 1820s, began to be performed in places other than churches to a significant degree, sometimes in concert halls, often in regional music festivals. One of the major types of amateur musical associations in the nineteenth century, the choral society, whose prototype was the Berlin Singakademie, dedicated itself largely to the cultivation of sacred music. Much of the repertoire of such groups came from the "museum'" of the musical past, from Palestrina to Schütz to Bach, Handel, and Mozart. The event that, more than any other, signalled their arrival on the German cultural landscape was the 1829 Berlin revival of the Bach's *St Matthew Passion* in a secular hall and under the auspices of the Berlin Singakademie. By the 1840s major regional choral festivals, usually featuring oratorios performances, were an annual event across

Germany, and by the 1870s most cities and towns included at least one performance of *Messiah* or *St Matthew Passion*, or preferably both, as part of the Easter season. Contemporary composers wrote for this growing market of choral societies. Brahms, for instance, composed a series of *Marienlieder* for his Hamburg women's choir, a wholly secular organization that nevertheless held its rare performances in a church.[25] The characteristic feature of all these groups, their intermixture of the sacred and the secular, expressed itself most clearly in the miscellaneous character of the spaces in which they practised and performed, from back rooms of music stores to choir rooms of churches. The very unpredictability of their placement in urban culture reflected a significant, long-term redefinition of space within German communities and across the complicated confessional geography of Germany itself.

Our consideration of confessionalism in nineteenth-century Germany needs to draw music into the conversation. It was a fundamental aspect of religious expression in Germany and provides strong, if complicated, evidence for Lucien Hölscher's ideas about the transformation of religious practices and piety in the nineteenth century. Hölscher has argued that the late eighteenth century saw the virtual disappearance of a powerful integration of church and society, the visible sign of which had been "regular and communally enforced participation in all the religious festivals and services." This process of *Entkirchlichung*, or de-churching, created a more metaphorical religious community and a "modern piety," just as widespread but less church centred. The nineteenth century, in other words, saw belief made individual and religious experience made private.[26] It was marked not by the decline of religious belief but by the free-floating of piety outside traditional sacred spaces. If the visible demonstrations of this modern piety were Bible-reading in the home or charitable good works in the community, its audible demonstration was heard in the strains of the local choral society at its weekly rehearsal in some town hall or upper room in a local restaurant.

Musicians as Travellers

Between music in the parks and music in restaurants, music in the parlour and music in the concert hall, music in schools and music in factories, the German who disliked the sound of it would have found few places in which to escape it completely. But beyond music's connection to particular places and infusion into everyday life, Connell and Gibson mention a third aspect of the geography of music – its participation in the movements of people, products, and cultures across space. This was, arguably, the dominant feature of art music from the eighteenth century on, or so at least the circulation of musicians across borders and the cross-currents of compositional styles and genres would seem to demonstrate. No clearer evidence for the cosmopolitanism of court culture in central Europe can be found than the diverse origins of court musicians and the common repertoires of court performance. Musicians did not cease to travel in the nineteenth century, even as court culture became less prominent, but with the increasing importance of nation-states and national markers of identity the significance of travel changed along with the affect, the conduct, and the meaning of the travelling musician. In the first place the motive force behind musicians' travel became the tremendous expansion of the market for concert performers. Moreover, the enormous commercial potential of the middle-class concert public lay at least as much in the provincial centres as in capital cities, owing to their permanent but often limited musical institutions. For the performers who made their living from this demand a measure of independence, of control over their careers, was its happy consequence, but independence came at the price of a kind of social marginality, the marker of which was their itinerancy, their lack of settled place. It came also at the price of a kind of ambiguous, or hybrid, identity. To be a well-known figure was to have crossed the boundaries of the national markers of identity that were becoming so overt in the public life and consciousness of people in the nineteenth century. Fame meant hybridity, with very few exceptions. Unless one died young, as did Franz Schubert, or started late in life, as did Anton Bruckner, a successful musical career demanded that the performer or the composer cross borders.

One can grasp how varied were the ambiguities of identity yet how ceaseless was the movement inherent in the musical career by considering briefly the very different careers of Franz Liszt and Johannes Brahms – an antipathetic pair in musical terms, yet sharing at least the restlessness of musical internationalism. Born on the Esterhazy estates near Raiding (in a German-speaking part of Hungary), Liszt was the descendant of Danube Swabian Germans through his father's family, and his mother was Viennese. He never learned Hungarian, initially spoke German, and became fluent in French as a teenager. As a boy of prodigious musical talent, he attracted the attention of several Hungarian noblemen who financed his studies in Vienna. He and his family then moved to Paris, where his career as pianist and composer took off – tours of Europe that reached from Russia to the Ottoman Empire to England, turbulent affairs, and extraordinary, unprecedented fame. In 1842 he accepted a position as *Kapellmeister in ausserordentlichem Dienst* (Kapellmeister in extraordinary service) in Weimar, where to everyone's surprise he settled, effectively making the small town a centre for avant-garde music (what came to be called, significantly, the New German School). But he eventually tired of life in provincial Weimar, was frustrated by lack of support from his noble patrons, and moved to Rome, where he hoped to reform church music. He began to spend more time in Hungary, continued to travel a great deal in Europe, made another major tour to Great Britain, and in 1886 died and was buried in, of all places, Bayreuth.

Brahms, on the other hand, spent his entire life lamenting his state of exile from his native Hamburg, from which he departed at age twenty on a fledging concert tour with the Hungarian violinist Eduard Remenyi to make his way in the world. He kept coming back to Hamburg over the course of his life, and he wrote constantly in his letters about his homesickness: "I yearn for Hamburg perpetually and I pass my favourite, albeit melancholy, hours sitting alone in the evening and reminiscing"; "In a somewhat old-fashioned manner I am suffering from homesickness"; "Here I sit, somewhat homesick for Hamburg."[27] In 1853, in what he framed as the greatest setback in his life, the Hamburg Philharmonic passed him over as conductor, which unleashed a storm of anguish. In a letter to Clara Schumann he wrote, "How seldom do people like us find a fixed abode, and how I would have liked to find it in my native city. Here [in Vienna] I will always feel that I am a stranger and can find no peace." Clara responded, laconically, "to which artist was it ever given to be able to establish hearth and home in his native city?"[28] Brahms came to see himself as condemned to vagabondage. Although he ostensibly had a permanent home in Vienna, his apartment was spartan, lacking the usual gewgaws and excessive furnishings so characteristic of the nineteenth-century home. It spoke of transience, lack of rootedness, displacement, and exile. He is said always to have had his suitcase packed, and indeed his basic schedule, repeated year after year throughout his adult life, was to travel for performances and visits in the autumn and to spend the winter months in Vienna, the spring travelling again, and the summer in some resort village in the Austrian or Swiss Alps or in Lichtenfeld outside Baden-Baden. In those places, he would register with the local authorities as "itinerant musician," a typical Brahmsian joke, all irony and self-mockery. Certainly, Brahms moved in a much more confined geographical space than Liszt (Italy and the Netherlands are the only non-German-speaking countries he ever visited), but as a famous composer and sometime performer he was a border crosser and hybrid persona nevertheless. His career mapped out a kind of amalgamation, even reconciliation, between Austria and the Germany of 1871, and his music was received, feted, and performed far outside the confines of German-speaking Europe.

One could find versions of these journeys throughout the ranks of professional musicians, yet the meaning of this moving about and consequent confusion of identity remains obscure. The case of Liszt's reception is the only one for which we have a careful study, by the musicologist Dana Gooley, who shows how the virtuoso "was constantly and insistently mobilizing, destabilizing, and reconstituting borders." Liszt was especially adept at exploiting whichever aspect of himself was appropriate for wherever he happened to be. Gooley describes this process as a mutual one between Liszt and his audiences, who sought to "naturalize" him, closing off "the gap between his uprooted, cosmopolitan identity and the national or regional spirit of the local community."[29] In 1844, midway through his amazing career, a French music critic accused Liszt of being a chameleon: "Posterity will be ... baffled at the location of Franz Liszt's real country. Everywhere the great pianist appears he receives homage as a compatriot, as a local glory ... He goes to Russia? Franz Liszt is a Muscovite of pure blood; he has slaves and has knout distributed to them. He goes to Berlin? He becomes a merciless Prussian, he intones arch-teutonic and anti-gaulish couplets. Is he at Marseilles? There's Provençal in his soul and he fraternizes with the bouillabaisse ... He molds himself to every zone and takes the mold of all patriotisms."[30] Throughout his life, no one was ever sure of what he was, but nor did they ever find the question of his identity unimportant or uninteresting.

Looked at from the perspective of their consumers, that is, the audiences that sustained their careers through ticket sales and music purchases, the nationality of musicians mattered, their place of origin mattered, in short, their place-ness mattered. At the same time, the virtuosity of Liszt's place-shifting might also be somewhat misleading, because people did not expect, as the Parisian critic sarcastically put it, that every visiting musician be "a local glory," though certainly that could be a selling point. Rather, the musicians who travelled from city to city and country to country had a larger-than-life, symbolic function in the places where they performed, embodying not just art but national identity. They taught people the meaning of difference. One aspect of this has long been recognized as a feature of "exoticism" in music. Audiences responded with great approval to musical gestures that evoked

Spanishness or Hungarianness or gypsy-ness or Turkishness.[31] But this kind of artificial exoticism existed within a larger societal experience of music that tied it firmly to places on the map, even as it allowed it free passage, as it were, across borders. As Wagner inimitably put it in 1840, "People have begun to demolish the barriers which are destined perhaps eternally to sever the nations themselves, yet should never separate their arts."[32]

The case of Liszt is thus once again helpful in the effort to understand how the incessant movement of art and artists across national borders nevertheless contributed to the process of nation-building. Gooley tells us that, starting in 1840, Liszt put his mind to becoming German. He did so not with a single dramatic gesture, as in the infamous Budapest sabre incident of 1840, but "by force of accumulation, by giving a little bit for the nation in each of the locales he visited."[33] And what was true for Liszt was also true, with variations, for other travelling musicians, whether they were elaborately manipulating nationality, as in the case of Liszt, or embodying it in less deliberate ways. One must remember that concerts featuring soloists from outside the community were not everyday happenings outside major cities – they took place perhaps three to four times a year and were therefore much remarked upon and remembered. Further, as we know, most Germans travelled only within the narrow compass of their region; the kind of travel that Brahms undertook annually, from Vienna to Munich to Karlsruhe to Leipzig to Düsseldorf to Berlin, criss-crossing the length and breadth of the country – was very unusual.[34]

Given such a context we might speculate that the effect of the circulation of musicians was an intensified version of the effect of national newspapers or literature, insofar as these travellers provided a kind of enactment of the reality of the nation as they moved from one city to the next, linking them all in a common musical culture. In addition, they had a larger-than-life function, bringing a certain distinction to the places they visited (or perhaps leaving it behind), helping to sustain a locality's pride in its musical sophistication, that is, its participation in the larger worlds to which it belonged. The most transitory of the arts, even if the most German, music disappeared into the imagination when the last note of the concert ceased to sound, yet in community after community we can find evidence of the impulse to recapture the moment and somehow make it permanent, as part of daily life. This evidence consists not only of piano transcriptions of the symphony just heard or easy keyboard versions of the virtuoso piece well beyond the capacity of most

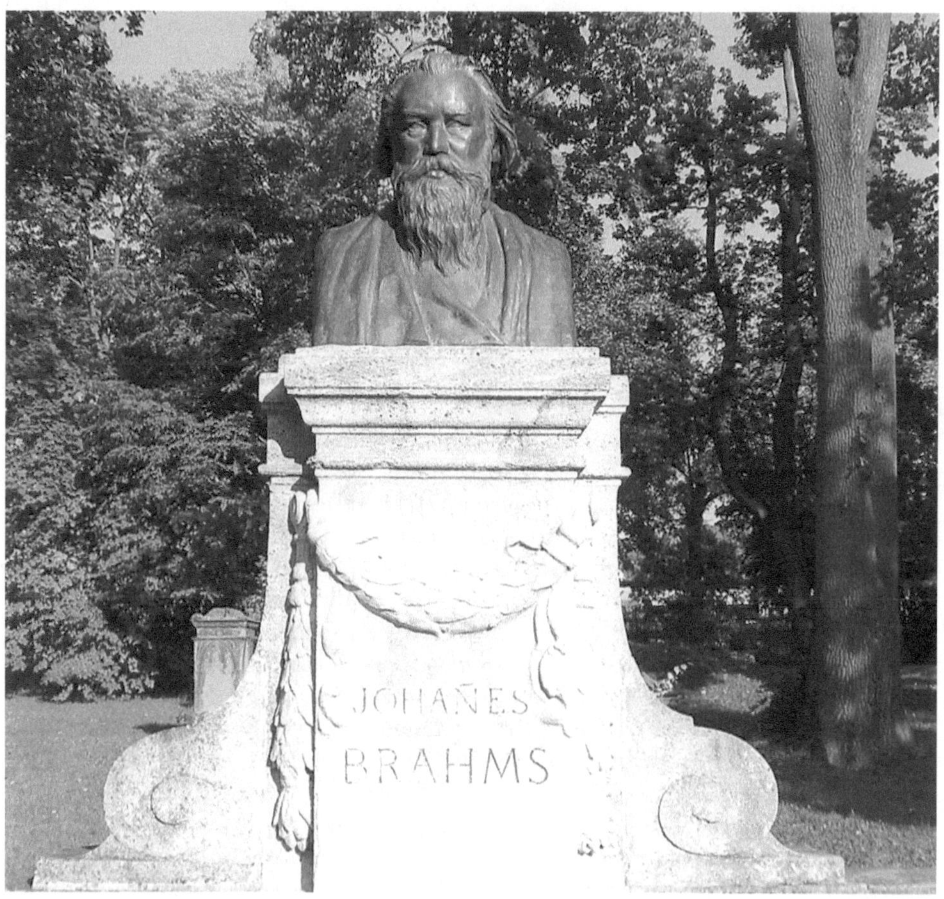

2.3 The first Brahms monument after his death, erected in 1898 in Meiningen. Sculptor Adolf Hildebrand. Wikimedia Commons.

amateurs. By the latter half of the nineteenth century it consists also of a lively trade in photographic images of composers. Brahms's correspondence has a number of references to his opinions (mainly unfavourable) of the commercial photographs for which he had just sat. Music stores sold such pictures along with the music or in conjunction with ticket sales for an upcoming performance. Bronze, marble, or plaster busts of famous composers and performers also were created, a product of the commercialization and diffusion of classical music in the nineteenth century that lingers into the twenty-first in the form of student recital favours and middle-brow aestheticism.[35] An extensive material culture of musical life – print reproductions of Hans Sachs at his cobbler's bench, postcards of Brahms's birthplace in Hamburg, ashtrays formed out of the head of Beethoven – came to clutter the bourgeois parlour, along with the piano, of course. And on a more imposing scale was the monument building. Even the mere visit of a famous musician could be memorialized by at least a plaque, and performance spaces, grand and humble, would bear the names and images of the men who had passed through and whose music would, presumably, still sound in that place.

Of course, not all travelling musicians were German, but even the non-German ones, especially when in Germany, spread the gospel of German music, of Germanness in music, of German superiority in all things musical. Whether Hungarian or Russian or Norwegian or English, the core of what they played was German, with some other works thrown in for the usual exoticist reasons of colour and contrast. In the course of the nineteenth century performing in Germany had indeed become something like a pilgrimage for non-German musicians, a phenomenon demonstrable in the biographies, memoirs, and letters of these famous men and women but the impact of which on German audiences needs further study. Anton Rubinstein, whose career as an international pianist spanned the latter half of the nineteenth century (from his first European tour as an adult in 1854 to his death in 1894), was born and raised in Russia, but received much of his musical training in Berlin and Vienna. In his marathon concerts, their length both a wonder and a torment for his audiences, he often performed entirely German works. Back in Russia he became an important, sometimes controversial, leader in musical life, calling for what amounted to the Germanization of Russian musical training and composition and more or less explicitly granting universal status to German music alone.[36] In Germany his passionate and reckless style of playing surrounded him, almost immediately, with the legendary aura of Beethoven. People regarded him as the reincarnation of, possibly even the illegitimate son of, and certainly the musical heir to this figure already well established as the hero of German music. People who had known Beethoven well, like the pianist Ignaz Moscheles, helped to sustain such middle-class fantasies. "Rubinstein's features and short, irrepressible hair remind me of Beethoven," said Moscheles, and Liszt referred to him as "Van II."[37]

Conclusion

It has long been recognized that the nineteenth century saw the canonization of a symphonic and instrumental repertoire dominated by the works of Germans, but the mechanisms of this canon's formation are less well studied than its deleterious effects on those composers and performers on the periphery of this great centre. Studying the way these increasingly canonical works circulated, the meanings that audiences attached to the performances and the performers in particular places, and the everyday practices of art music appreciation provides us with the possibility of looking at canon formation as a process that involved not just critics, patrons, and other taste-makers but also a mutual interaction of audience and performer. Robert Schumann wrote of Beethoven in the 1830s that Germans should "take a hundred century-old oak trees, and write his name with them in giant letters. Or carve his likeness in colossal proportions, like Saint Borromaeus on Lake Maggiore, that he may gaze above the mountains, as he did when living; and when the Rhine ships pass, and foreigners ask the name of that giant form, every child may answer – it is Beethoven, and they will think it is the name of a German emperor."[38] Perhaps it is unfortunate for Germans that the civic activists of the Rhine Valley took on their Germania project instead; but with or without a Mount Rushmore of great composers, music was inscribed on the landscape of German-speaking Europe, not literally but in musical practices that have outlasted a good many nineteenth-century monuments. Our own expectations of the sound of serious music and its meaning derive from what developed in concert halls, opera houses, and music rooms in the course of the nineteenth century. In their evolution as sites of music-making, and in the musical practices they made possible, we may also glimpse many of the tensions that marked European society in the nineteenth century and gain some sense of how people understood the distinctions between public and private, between sacred and secular, between confessions and classes, and between local, national, and international identities. Seen this way, the music room was indeed a plenum, not a vacuum – a space entirely filled with matter and meaning.

Chapter Three

Musical Itinerancy in a World of Nations

In November 1862 Johannes Brahms wrote an anguished letter to Clara Schumann about being passed over as conductor of the Hamburg Philharmonic – "where may I and can I [go now]," he wrote, "[I am] set loose to fly about all alone in empty space."[1] Two decades later, in 1884, he composed five songs (Opus 94), the fifth of which was a bleak setting of a poem by Friedrich Halm: "No house, no homeland, no wife and no child; thus I am whirled like a straw in storm and wind." That summer he identified himself, when registering with the police for his (usual) summer sojourn in the Austrian mountain village of Mürzzuschlag, as "itinerant musician."[2] At age fifty he saw himself as a refugee, a man without place, a vagabond with only his music to recommend him. For Brahms's biographers these documents allow speculation about his psychology. For the cultural historian their appeal lies in his illumination, deliberate at times, of the relationship of the musician to society. His description of himself to the settled folk of Mürzzuschlag as itinerant musician was, of course, ironic, but the irony derived from the contrast between this portly professional man and a folkloric figure of dubious musical skills and doubtful morals. It invites us to explore the historical reality of both musicians, the legendary scapegrace evoked by Brahms and the professional musician Brahms himself embodied, along with the lines of development that stretch in both directions from them.

Itinerancy was, and continues to be, one of the persistent features of the musical life. Evidence for the existence of musical travellers of one kind or another date back to as far as evidence for music-making can be confirmed. In every time and place for which a history can be written, one can find musicians on the move. In the modern period of travel and exploration, European musicians travelled to all places that Europeans lived and colonized.[3] Brahms's term "itinerant musician" encompasses a great range of musical people – professionals and amateurs, early moderns and moderns, stars and worker bees, men and women, composers, performers, writers about music, and those who travelled simply to listen to music. And if we further stretch the term itinerancy to include the travels not only of musicians but also of their music, then one comes quickly to the conclusion that movement represents the defining characteristic of the art form itself, at least in western culture.

This chapter expands upon chapter 2, providing further scenes from the long history of musical itinerancy and travel, mainly in the places of German-speaking Europe, in order to illuminate the means by which Germans shaped and expressed their collective identity. Itinerant musicians and music-making formed the German nation, not in the sense of determining its borders or shaping its politics but in the sense of making it a lived experience. That musical travel of any sort, whether constant or occasional, should have anything to teach us about nationhood is not, however, immediately apparent. All cultures are "travelling cultures," wrote James Clifford in his essays on how "culture makes itself at home in motion," but the claim is much easier to substantiate in postcolonial, globalizing cultural development than in the age of nationalism.[4] National cultures seem on the face of it to be the opposite of travelling ones, located in bounded spaces and rooted, at least in the minds of their creators and adherents, in the soil itself. Music, for its part, is different from some of the more obvious markers of nation-making, like monuments, museums, and memorials, paintings, poems, and parks. Its participation in nation-making cannot be described through metaphors of construction, because the work music does exists in the moment of its performance and, like Renan's daily plebiscite, relies on repetition and continual recreation. Even after the advent of the age of mechanical reproduction, music still involves continual production and reproduction to exist in the world.

Yet this momentary quality of music, its "dying fall," its immediacy, and its accompanying demand to be made again and again, is precisely what has made it so powerful an agent in the making of national cultures and, by the same token, made travel and circulation so fundamental to its social effectiveness. The movements of musicians must be a central element in any history of music in national cultures. Nationalizing societies, just as much as our contemporary globalizing ones, took shape in part through displacement, and "tangled cultural experiences" as well as "impure, unruly processes of collective invention" formed their collective life.[5] Travelling musicians of all kinds dramatize the generalized place-ness of the nation by moving around the national space and representing the nation outside its borders. Musical practices thus formed a transnational space, predicated on the existence and recognition of national cultures. The phrase "the musical world," which came into circulation in the latter decades of the eighteenth century, was a world not of courts, religious communities, and the road itself but of musical nations.[6]

What did the travel of musicians achieve? First, travel transmitted knowledge, practical and theoretical, among people in many places, and that transmission of musical knowledge brought about the development of new musical styles, instruments, and institutions. Music has so often been called a universal language that the sentence practically writes itself. For their part, ethnomusicologists have shown that it is not so, and a new cultural history of music has tried to bring their insights to bear on western music. Yet it still remains the case that the social processes of musical transfer and exchange, how they were both limited and promoted by the existence of national and nationalizing states, remain less well understood than the musical evidence that such processes were at work. Bach's French Suites were so called because they followed the sequence of dance forms common to seventeenth-century instrumental suites by French composers; Mozart's Piano Sonata No. 11 (*alla Turca*) represented his homage to Turkish Janissary bands then fashionable in the capitals of Europe; and Bizet made *Carmen* sound both Spanish and gypsyish without ever meeting a gypsy or travelling to Spain ("that would only confuse me").[7] These examples manifest successive "cultural waves" across the ethnic and national boundaries of Europe and beyond, the movement of which we have only begun to map.[8]

Second, these cultural waves themselves were signs of how musical travel helped to form multilayered senses of belonging to communities beyond the local one in which the traveller performed. Europe was one such community, though its borders were vague. Musical travel and travelling music also reinforced pan-European confessional identities, even while some music – Bach's for instance – was capable of crossing confessional boundaries. By the nineteenth century national communities, even and perhaps especially before they were nation-states, were the most important of the supra-local identities that musical travel helped to form. To call such communities "imagined" is to diminish the importance of musical practices in making them real, practices in part formed and sustained by the incessant travel of musicians. Musical interchange, within and among nations, may have been all the more rapid and pervasive because of the non-linguistic nature of music – that "fatal diversity of human language," on which Benedict Anderson put so much conceptual weight. But it still required, or perhaps better, created feelings of mutual understanding among those who undertook such acts of cultural transfer. In 1988 Akira Iriye asked, "Who can deny that thinkers, artists, and musicians ... have contributed decisively to the making of contemporary history?" His main interest lay in the "alternative community of nations and peoples" that could emerge from their activities, but cultural interchanges are relevant to the history of national communities as well.[9] Such exchanges illuminate the strange nature of national boundaries, not singular but marked by varying degrees of permeability. Not everything changes when one crosses a political or cultural national border, and musical differences among nations or national groups, whether we are talking about musical practices or the music itself, can be extraordinarily difficult to identify objectively.[10] The history of how well music functioned as a boundary among nations or how persuasively its practitioners represented their nations could help to clarify what nations were, and remain.

What, then, was the meaning of musical itinerancy and travel for those who travelled and those who listened to or performed with the travellers? If we wish productively to revise the conceptual behemoths of modernization, nationalization, and imperialism, we need to disaggregate them and see how people experienced the changes of past centuries in their everyday lives. Musical life provides a wide field for such investigations precisely because it is pervasive, various, dispersed, and unstable. From concert hall and opera house to parlour piano and town choral society, music-making helped to condition people's adjustment to rapid, relentless alterations in their social worlds. It may not be the most sensitive barometer of change, nor should we seek only the sounds of upheaval and transformation. But to account for the reasons that musicians have travelled or to draw out the views that people have held about musical travellers is to illuminate constitutive experiences of the national community. In a period that stretches from the end of one Thirty Years' War in the mid-seventeenth century to the end of another in the mid-twentieth century, the ties that bound such a German community together broke and re-formed dozens of times, but it came to seem to its members that the music would always be there.

On the Road: Early Modern Musicians and Their Worlds

In 2009 the *New York Times* ran a human interest story about Gerry Niewood and Coleman Mellett, two men killed in the crash of Continental Flight 3407, under the headline "For Two Jazzmen, Work Meant Life on the Road." For both, "flying in a cramped turboprop plane to play a show in Buffalo in February was not an unfamiliar routine," yet both, according to the article, also had a "middle-class existence": as a friend said of Mellett, he "loved his wife, he loved his home, he loved the town where they lived" in his "ranch-style house."[11] Centuries of suspicion echo faintly in these bland remarks. As long as people have written about musicians as a group, they have been accusing them of immorality or trying to defend their honour. To explore the long history of perceptions of itinerant musicians is to illuminate processes of Christianization, urbanization, and the uneven development of law and sovereignty across disparate territorial arrangements (among other things). Terminology alone presents a daunting problem, and much of the acrimony over the centuries is centred on titles and their consequences.[12] The baroque writer and musician Johann Beer dramatized this conflict in his picaresque novel *German Winter Nights* (1681) by staging a brawl between courtiers and musicians over whether the latter would be called *Stadtpfeifer* or *Spielmänner*.[13]

For centuries this had been a distinction that made a difference. The *Spielmann* (and similar names) was someone who had neither regular employment – in a court or a town or a church or some combination of all those – nor fixed abode and who thus wandered around picking up work when he could. He belonged to the category of "un-honourable people" (*unehrliche Leute*), along with executioners, sheep shearers, gravediggers, linen weavers, and unmarried daughters.[14] Many of these positions required that people live semi-permanently on the road, and as a result only with difficulty can we separate their movement from their work in explaining their lack of honour. Because of their violation of the mimetic taboo, their association with the libidinous, ecstatic, and unruly powers of music, *and* their lack of settled place, travelling musicians lacked honour and, with that lack, rights to be a witness or juror or to win damages as plaintiff in a trial, to hold civic office, to own land, or to be a member of a guild.[15]

Not surprisingly, for townsmen the last exclusion became the nub of the matter. One might regard the travelling musicians as those left over after long-term processes of institutional growth had regularized the ways in which people composed, performed, and heard music in Europe, but that would be to diminish the dynamic force they represented in the development of musical styles and institutions. In the history of the musical profession the employment of musicians by towns was the last kind of employment to emerge, after centuries in which the mainstay of musical life had been the church, supported and increasingly rivalled by royal and noble establishments that required larger and more ambitious musical programming. But as towns too sought to formalize their soundscape – bells calling people to church, trumpets announcing the arrival of people and goods at the city gates, pipers and drums accompanying civic ceremonials – musicians were able to settle down in towns and train their children in the profession.[16] They were still johnny-come-latelies in the money and moral economies of early modern towns and cities. The earliest existence of musicians' guilds dates probably to the fourteenth century, and town records of localities all across Europe are filled, from then until the near total disappearance of musicians' guilds in the early nineteenth century, with evidence of endless bickering over who did and did not belong to a guild, or deserve to belong to one, or perform services that should be restricted to one. In 1593 Bartoldt Snider and Peter Gerken, a pair of travelling musicians perhaps similar in their partnership to Niewood and Mellett, were ejected from the city of Bremen for playing at a wedding without authorization, that is to say, without membership in the local musicians' guild. They unsuccessfully defended themselves by claiming that they had been playing without harassment in many places – "Saxonland, Braunswig, Westphalia, Hamburg, Lünenborg, Magdeburg, the state of Lyppe Schomburg, and many other honorable cities."[17]

But in fact pursuit of the guild strategy by musicians who had managed to find positions as town trumpeters never entirely worked. Henry Raynor has written that "there was never a period in their history when the town musicians were not engaged in a bitter struggle to preserve their monopoly" and, one might add, to maintain their place among existing and higher-ranking guilds in the towns and cities.[18] Even before the loosening of guild cohesion in the eighteenth century, other guilds regularly challenged their presence among them, a circumstance that in 1653 led to an unusual supra-local effort on the part of German musicians to obtain imperial approval for uniform standards within communities. The Saxon Town Musician Articles, which the emperor himself confirmed, consisted of twenty-five specifications of musicians' guild privileges, ranging from a monopoly over local performances to moral instruction of journeymen.[19] And although scores of musicians signed onto them, the articles represented not a step towards gradual unification of musical employment across central Europe but only an attempt to strengthen the position of musicians in a handful of localities. Moreover, the guilding of musicians did not work, because even guilds could not ensure that the salary of a town trumpeter would support a family, thus guaranteeing that all musicians, whether in guilds or not, would compete for occasional work at weddings and wakes. The search for supplementary work also meant that travel always beckoned – travel especially to courts, of which Germany had, of course, many.

The limited effectiveness of musicians' guilds raises the question of whether one ought indeed to regard travelling musicians merely as throwbacks in a modernizing musical world.[20] But such a perspective would obscure the extent to which even musicians with regular employment in court, church, and town continued to travel throughout those long stretches of time in which most Europeans were settling down and staying put. One can distinguish between different types of travel, between the true vagabond and the purposeful traveller, but in both cases, travelling musicians did the cultural work that created and sustained the European musical world. The story of the development and spread of styles and genres – monophony, polyphony, functional harmony, plainchant, organum, motet, madrigal, opera, concerto grosso – is one of explorations and elaborations of patterns in sound, which depended on the creation of a system of musical notation that could record exact pitch and time and thus provide the possibility of building on the explorations and elaborations that had come before. Musical notation was portable, and thus the very development of musical style in the western tradition resulted from travel among monasteries, courts, and towns, and by musicians, whether monks or minstrels, saints or scoundrels, and all those in between. Conditions of service accounted for most travel, like that of all musicians in court employment, and, when the papacy itself went on the road in the fourteenth century, it had rippling effects on patterns of training and recruiting musicians.

Musicologists have never ignored the existence of travel and of cultural transfers and networks. The spread of "northern polyphony" and the contributions of the Franco-Flemish school to the development of the motet, for instance, are staples of music history, as are the multiple interactions between German and Italian musicians that defined the transition from Renaissance to baroque music. Nevertheless, the significance of musical travel to the crossing of social, not just geographical, boundaries and to the formation of national, not just musical, identities has necessarily remained out of focus in the picture musicologists have drawn. As to the first, the constant infusion of influences from popular music into church and court music relied in part on the movement of musicians without honour who travelled the roads of Europe in the company of beggars and thieves. So did developments in instruments and their technique: Georg Philipp Telemann greatly admired the Polish and Moravian fiddlers he heard during his own extensive travels, and the violinist Franz Benda wrote in his autobiography that he learned techniques from a Jewish tavern fiddler in Prague.[21] As to the second, the gradual stabilization of notions of what constituted German, French, or Italian musical styles came about through increasing familiarity with the work of musicians coming from these places and speaking these languages. And over the course of the late seventeenth and eighteenth centuries the question of just where exactly musicians belonged in the increasingly dynamic social and political structures of European countries came more sharply into focus, generating not just anxiety and ambition among musicians but also considerable reflection in print about what role music and musicians played in European life.

After all, it was not so easy then – or now – to distinguish between the reputable and the disreputable travellers, between the Italian composing French music or the Bohemian composing Italian music or the German turned Englishman composing German music now dubbed quintessentially English. All such distinctions were especially difficult to discern in places disrupted by warfare, expansionist states, and changing economic opportunities (often for the worse). Yet discerning such differences became, at the same time, all the more important, especially since the quickening circulation of new knowledge about the world had the effect of making it all the more important to possess a stable and legible identity. People needed to read and to be read, especially if those people were travellers. In the last decades of the seventeenth century a growing number of musicians in German-speaking Europe took up the pen to write prose about music and musicians, establishing a literary pendant to music-making itself. Through novels and treatises they made musicians legible to German literary culture, in James Sheehan's words, "a culture of readers and writers for whom print had become the essential means of communication and printed matter the primary source and subject of cultural activity."[22] Its social core consisted of a mélange of the merchants, patriciates, and pastors of the burgher order alongside the new bureaucratic elites that served the prince, and, from the late seventeenth century on such people created a self-supporting, sustained, and secular reading public. Numbers of books and new periodicals rose dramatically, each feeding off the other. This was also the only truly national culture in the German-speaking lands, constituting a social network of shared concerns that crossed geographical, social, and political barriers dividing one locality from another and the privileged aristocracy from all. It expressed the nationality of Germany, and in its products, whether they were comic accounts of imaginary travels or learned treatises on ecclesiastical law, nationality was a quality that grew ever more distinct in the contemplation and description of it.

The literary products of musician-writers, less scrutinized today than their musical compositions, shed considerable light on the question of how musicians fit into an emergent national culture in Germany; these writings show us how people infused the national into the German pursuit of the musical. And in much of the fictional writing in the decades before and after 1700 the travelling musician was always present, often a stock figure whose calling made him (or occasionally her) useful for narrative twists and turns, but sometimes the central figure of the whole tale. The mother of all these works was the sprawling picaresque novel *The Adventures of Simplicius Simplicissimus the Vagabond* by Hans Jacob von Grimmelshausen, published in 1669 and celebrated for its depiction of the horrors of the Thirty Years' War. In one of its episodes Simplicissimus poses as a musician in order to seduce a countess, and in one of the "Simplician" sequels to the original novel, *Der seltsame Springinsfeld* (The Odd Spring-into-Action), the main character is a musician of an exceedingly marginal sort, a one-legged mercenary turned beggar-fiddler, whose mother was Greek noblewoman turned itinerant singer and whose father was a Turkish tightrope walker. By the 1670s, thanks to the popularity of Grimmelshausen's writings, the pace of literary production began to pick up. In Johann Beer's fifteen or so novels, Daniel Speer's five, Wolfgang Caspar Printz's three, and Johann Kuhnau's three, all written between 1677 and 1704, not only are musicians usually the principal characters in the novels but all the writers were principally musicians.[23] Between the musical experiences of the authors themselves and those of the characters they created, one encounters the range of musical travel, from penny-ante scoundrels to itinerant but honest entertainers to *Kapellmeisters*, cantors, city trumpeters, and a whole host of boys orphaned at a young age, whose musical training takes place on the road of life. The sites of education and performance consist of inns and castles, monasteries and bedrooms, cities and villages, places as exotic as Babylon and as provincial as Ulm.

Given the satirical tone of these works and the incoherence of their narratives, they might seem merely to confirm the poetic theory of Christian Weise (1642–1708), who held that literature had the power to dispel melancholy and depression (as did, of course, music).[24] But Weise also tried to bring an element of instructive social commentary into the so-called political novels he pioneered. Precursors of the more celebrated *Bildungsroman* and *Künstlerroman* a century later, these works adopted satire for the purpose of plain speaking. These were anti-court, anti-French, à la mode works that expressed the need to find a literary language that could defend "*alte teutsche Redlichkeit und Aufrichtigkeit*" (old German integrity and honesty).[25] The "political" in this context – and one finds it often in the titles of books, for instance, Weise's *Politische Näscher* (Political Climber) or Beer's *Politische Bratenwender* (Political Sausage Roaster) – means something like prudent or worldly; hence, the political met the picaresque in the journey, through which characters learn about the world and their place in it. And the world was, as these books showed, a dangerous and terrible place for a young German on his own.

Literary historians have found in these works a kind of proto-realism, with dashes of magic thrown in, and preposterous though these characters and plot lines can be, nevertheless even the strangest of them remains powerfully grounded in the circumstances of the late seventeenth century. One does not have to believe that everything Simplicissimus experienced actually happened to Grimmelshausen, the one-time boy soldier and musketeer, in order to see in the novel a remarkable working-through of the trauma of the Thirty Years' War – sinners in the hands of an indifferent God.[26] Likewise, in the musician novels, two closely related aspects of the musical world come to the fore repeatedly: the problem of the musician's social identity and that of his national identity. Both problems are reflected in the lives of the authors themselves, and both are worked out through the theme of travel. In Johann Beer's *Der simplicianische Welt-Kucker oder abentheuerliche Jan Rebhu* (The Simplician World-Observer or the Adventurous Jan Rebhu), the title character, an orphan of course, becomes a soprano at a court dominated by Italian musicians, is taught by a castrato, barely escapes becoming one himself, and then wanders in and out of more or less dangerous love affairs, getting into all kinds of trouble, including shipwrecks, near executions, and battles with Turks. In Daniel Speer's *Haspel-Hanss*, the main character, this time a deformed orphan, half learns the musical trade and proceeds to practise it badly in university towns all across Germany. In Speer's *Dacianische Simplicissimus*, the main character, this time a religiously persecuted orphan, takes to the road, learns to play the drum and the trumpet, then serves as a military musician in the wars against the Turks, travelling through Galicia, Bohemia, Hungary, and Austria before moving on to Constantinople and the Middle East in the book's sequel, *Türckische Vagrant.*

Beyond the book-selling exoticism of their adventures, the marginality of these characters serves a common admonitory purpose. All suffer from deficient musical training, and none is able to find a settled place in his native land. Buffeted by fate, exploited and abandoned by nobles and courtiers, they embody the displacements and sufferings of a Germany victimized by its more powerful neighbours and its selfish or incompetent rulers. Their travelling, as much symptom as cause of their vulnerability, can produce no worldly experience that would make up for what it takes away; a life of adventure is no substitute for a craft well learned. Moreover, the problems they face, as Beer made explicit in the polemical pamphlets he wrote shortly after the Jan Rebhu series, were not moral ones arising from their musical profession. In 1696 a school rector and scholar named Gottfried Vockerodt had published an anti-musical fulmination in which he suggested that music led people into lives of dissipation and evil deeds (being a classicist, his prime example was young Nero and his violin). Beer retorted that harmony was the very foundation of the universe (a familiar argument); the creation of harmony through music made this art the finest and most humanly important of all arts (an unfamiliar one); and the occasional rackety behaviour associated with some musicians and music-lovers could not be changed by the banning of music.[27] It could be resolved, however, by thorough education in the musical craft, which would foster a deep understanding of the rules of harmony and composition. That in turn required that German musicians resist the siren call of foreign names and foreign ways, learn their trade, and practise it well.[28] It required, in short, not that musicians cease to travel but that they cease to wander aimlessly.[29]

A declared enemy of musical scholasticism and someone who himself had led a rackety life before and during his successful career as concertmaster and singer for Duke August of Saxony-Weissenfels, Beer did not always see eye to eye with his fellow musician-authors. He attacked in print, among others, Wolfgang Caspar Printz, like him a successful and widely travelled court musician but a man less tolerant of disruptive behaviour.[30] In writing style and professional experience, Beer also had little in common with fellow novelist Johann Kuhnau, Johann Sebastian Bach's immediate predecessor in the respectable position of cantor of the Thomaskirche in Leipzig. But viewed from our perspective, removed from the disputatious atmosphere of this emergent German public sphere, they shared a basic understanding of the importance of the role of the musician in German life. This was an understanding that went beyond a defence of the craft and honour of the guild musician against his roguish Doppelgänger and beyond the *Untertan*'s ineffectual complaining about his noble employer – though, to be sure, the novels can be seen as expressive of pervasive anxiety about the insecurities of court employment and the possibility of a settled life in troubled times.[31] The kinds of social tensions these novels depict, and the kinds of resolutions they propose, go further and assert a new order, which their authors were simultaneously working to achieve in their musical activities. At the purely musical level this period saw the full articulation of a system of functional harmony, by which, in the striking characterization of Joseph Kerman, "chords seem to be going where we expect them to, harmonies no longer seem to wander, detour, hesitate, or evaporate."[32] At a more broadly cultural level these activities – composing, performing, organizing, writing, travelling – ultimately shaped a new transnational musical world, in which German musicians, *as* Germans and in both German-speaking lands and abroad, strove for recognition outside the older structures of guild and court and thereby helped to make Germany audible, legible, and real.

Music and Nationalizing Culture in the Eighteenth Century

The baroque musician-novelists of the late seventeenth century first posed the problem of who is the musician in the world, a theme that plays out in a rich set of variations over the course of the eighteenth century. To call eighteenth-century Germany a nationalizing culture is to acknowledge that many, indeed most, aspects of social, political, and cultural life were *not* nationalizing in this period and that signs of German consciousness must be seen within the complexity of milieus from which this nationalizing project emerged. Consider, for instance, the extent to which J.S. Bach, musical colossus that he was, straddled the interlocking spheres of worship, political display, learning, and sociability, each of which was marked by, to widely varying degrees, a consciousness of German national identity. In the period in which he worked, from January 1703 to his death in July 1750, he earned money, in descending order of importance to his income, from municipal authorities, noblemen, and the anonymous paying public, and he held gradually more prestigious posts as minor court musician, organist, music director, concertmaster,

Kapellmeister, and finally (a lateral move to a different kind of prestige) cantor. The geographical spread of places where he held these positions is small, as scholars often point out, and the furthest extent of his own travels was to Lübeck in the north.

During this period the most active and well-funded centres of musical life lay in the princely courts and residential cities, in which a distinctive courtly "institutionalization of music," following the French model and employing mainly Italian musicians, served to domesticate the nobility – through rituals, etiquettes, and entertainments, which Italian opera, with its elaborate plots and theatrical realizations, dominated.[33] This cultural milieu was cosmopolitan and its makers notoriously indifferent to anything like native cultural development. Princely preference for Italian or French musical culture reflected not disdain for native German musical work as such but the function of art in connecting princes and nobility to their social and political counterparts across all of Europe. Italian-dominated musical establishments thus asserted an aristocratic identity over a national or local one. Moreover, even if they did not set the dominant musical style or fill the most prestigious courtly positions, many German musicians travelled to Italy to study music and subsequently found employment in the courts as well as opportunities for modest social advancement within their ensembles. Bach worked this system as much as he was able, serving for extended periods of time in the ducal court at Weimar and the princely court of Anhalt-Cöthen, but his reputation was not made in the service of princes.

As for town musicians of the eighteenth century, the only independent and vibrant urban centres were the trading cities of Hamburg, Bremen, Frankfurt, and Leipzig. All managed to sustain astonishingly rich musical cultures well into the era when independent urban culture elsewhere declined in the face of the rising domination of princely states and their cities. Leipzig, although not an imperial free city, managed after 1648 to reclaim its position as the most important trade centre of central Europe by 1710.[34] Its renewed prosperity allowed it to spend some money on its cultural institutions, which thus enjoyed independence from princely intervention. The powerful city council of Leipzig, in concert with church authorities, controlled the Thomasschule and city churches. The university was a proudly self-governing corporation, with extensive (though not complete) control over its musical activities. This plethora of alternately competing and cooperative authorities characterized many a smaller German community, ensuring equilibrium, if not excellence or innovation. In Bach's frequent clashes with authorities he usually deployed arguments about his rightful corporate privileges, never his needs as an artist. His career illustrated the profound differences between the local and courtly musical milieu. Bach, like many practising musicians by the start of the eighteenth century, moved back and forth between these two, submitting at times to the contentious discipline of corporate town institutions and at other times to the humiliating servitude and insecure tenure of the court musician and struggling throughout to extract the best from both worlds.[35]

It is hard, nevertheless, to avoid the conclusion that court music provided more scope for creativity and individual achievement than did the "static dull complexities" and the "monotony and melancholy" of German town life.[36] Duke Johann Ernst of Weimar, for all that he is remembered as the patron who consigned Bach to a month in the local jail, made it possible for Bach to immerse himself in a great body of Italian instrumental music (Vivaldi, Corelli, et al.), in part by bringing back thousands of scores of the latest works from his own travels. To say that Bach, who himself had never been able to travel to Italy or anywhere outside Germany, absorbed this material, worked on it, and synthesized it into works at once Italianate and wholly his own is an understatement. The circumstances that made possible the full expression of his musical potential thus included, prominently, networks of travel and cultural exchange linking European court cultures and rippling out from them into town and church milieux.

Finally, Bach's career reveals glimpses of the literary culture, to the growing significance of which the musician-novels and musical polemics attested. The first printed reference to Bach – Johann Mattheson's (1681–1764) remark in 1717 that he had "seen things by the famous organist of Weimar, Mr Joh. Sebastian Bach ... that are certainly such as must make one esteem the man highly" – was a direct indication of this third culture's existence. So too was his request to Bach in 1720 for biographical information for a planned dictionary of musicians (Bach never provided any). Likewise, when the mayor of Leipzig pressed for Bach's appointment because he was eager to appoint a "famous man" to the cantorate in order to "bolster the attractiveness and reputation of the city," we sense the presence of a new set of cultural assumptions at work.[37] All these moments concern Bach's reputation – a simple enough concept, one would have thought, but in early eighteenth-century Germany it was anything but. The milieu of locality and home town, the one into which Bach was born and spent much of his life, understood reputation in terms of membership in the community, what Mack Walker once described as "a silhouette projected on community" that can be "rendered and reflected only by community."[38] Divorced from this community, individual artistic achievement made little sense. Reputation in court circles was, by contrast, a matter of virtuosity and display, the purpose of which was to cast not one's own shadow upon the world at large but rather that of the prince one served. And those who had it tended not to be Germans, or if they were Germans, they had become cosmopolitans, known for their extensive travels and conversant in many languages.[39]

Mattheson was deploying a third notion of reputation when he referred to the "esteem" in which Bach ought to be held. This kind was earned through striving and merit. It marked one out for notice from a larger world than a single community, and most important, it was both the product of the musician's circulation and a literary artefact, written about and discussed among the educated inhabitants of independent and princely cities. For the most part historians have explored literary culture as a project that consisted of writing literature and developing the expressive capacities of the German language. As a result, the participation of musicians, including those writing about music, in the nationalizing project of literary culture is more obscure to us, even though the writings of musical novelists, scholars, and aesthetic philosophers, extracted from this context, have long drawn the attention of scholars in their respective disciplines. But musical matters were more central to the makers of this new nationalizing culture than we have acknowledged; and vice versa: the makers of this national culture contributed substantially to new developments in musical life in ways that may have been recognized, though not often in such terms.

Two major trends in musical life in the eighteenth century reflected the growth of nationalizing culture and the social groups defining it. The first was a trend towards a musical marketplace, separate from court institutions and free of guild restrictions, in which musicians could earn money – teaching and playing with growing numbers of amateurs; performing in the new phenomenon of public concerts; and participating as middlemen, copyists, publishers, sellers, and, of course, composers in the expanding commerce of music publishing. All these adjustments required movement, travel, and flexibility, not unprecedented for musicians but now in a changed context. Inevitably, some commentators experienced this difference as loss – not just of security but of something more like standards, the craft itself. Klaus Horschansky argues that by the latter half of the eighteenth century a "latent crisis" existed in the music profession; music was doomed to become, in the words of composer J.W. Hässler in 1787, a "breadless art," in which no distinctions could any longer be maintained "between beer fiddlers, town musicians, and true artists."[40] A few years earlier, composer Johann Friedrich Reichardt lamented that "from the prince's *Oberkapellmeister* to the beer fiddler who drags operettas into the peasant pub, everyone has become an artisan producing cheap copies for the going market price."[41] Established institutions of court music furthered the growth of this marketplace by opening court performances to a limited audience and supporting the development of national theatres.[42] Princely courts also stood behind the development of the social core of new audiences consisting of educated and culturally ambitious people who were often members of the bureaucratic elites. They consumed music in concerts, on their travels, in their own homes, commidifying music but at the same time establishing the beginnings of organized public interest in the arts.

The second trend, no less important in shaping the meaning of music and musical travel, was a slow accumulation of writings about music: critical, scholarly, imaginative, and concerned – far more than was the case in works of the baroque novelists such as Johann Beer and others – with the question of music's role in the humanistic project of enlightenment and social improvement. In Johann Kuhnau's cheerful *Der musikalische Quacksalber* (*The Musical Charlatan*), published in Dresden in 1700, the story begins in a prosperous, bustling market town, with substantial citizens and an educated cadre of town musicians engaged in musical and academic undertakings and considering themselves men of the world – all that is to say: the novel's setting is Leipzig.[43] But Kuhnau also invokes the broader milieu of literary culture with his greeting to the "amiable reader" and his references to antiquity, the "stage of our world," and the Leipzig Book Fair catalogue. Finally, he makes clear his purpose is not to attack "the upright virtuosic *musici* who adorn not only foreign countries but also our own" but to show "how great a gulf exists between art and ignorance," and "how much something splendid and delicate is to be preferred to that which is rustically wild and maladroit," and how much in the world is "good and moral."[44]

The assertion and defence of German identity is the undertow of the whole work, pulling the reader along through surface actions and distractions of his anti-hero, the musical charlatan. This "so-called Caraffa," a German from Swabia with a false name who "for approximately a year had carried the instruments of some famous musicians in Italy," returns to a town in Germany, sure that he will be able to fool people there as he could not in Italy. Caraffa considers that most Germans belong to "that silly company who think a composer or *musicus* who hasn't seen Italy is a foolish dunderhead" and who believe "that the air of Italy can impregnate people with the most perfect skills."[45] He also counts on being unknown – Kuhnau's depiction of the limits of local knowledge amounts to a running commentary on German fragmentation, as Caraffa travels through Germany's provincial backwaters. There are, then, three kinds of fools in this novel: the ordinary fools, country bumpkins who know nothing and have spent their lives gossiping around the parish pump; the pretentious, insecure fools who have a little learning and no sense; and the fool Caraffa, who thinks that all his fellow Germans are as ignorant of true learning, true art, and true music as is he.

We meet Kuhnau's heroes on the first page, the members of the Collegium Musicum. This characteristically German musical organization, of which Leipzig's was among the most famous, dated probably to the Reformation era and consisted of professional and amateur musicians, gathering for the pleasure of performing instrumental and vocal music. Under Kuhnau himself and his successors Georg Philipp Telemann and J.S. Bach, the Leipzig Collegium Musicum began to perform weekly in public, usually at the storied Zimmermann's Coffee House. Music historians regard it as one of several points of origin for the rise of the public concert and symphony orchestra; it represented a form of sociability through small-scale music-making that proliferated from the late eighteenth century onward.[46] Kuhnau's account describes it as "indeed a praiseworthy undertaking, partly because [its members] thereby continue to improve themselves in their splendid profession and partly because from their pleasant harmony they also should learn an even, harmonious agreement among their personalities which from time to time must prevail among such people."[47] Music makes society, and in this case the members of the group know how to act in concert. They quickly identify Caraffa as a fraud, through reports of a member who knows Swabia and so knows the "real" Caraffa (travellers' knowledge) and, more profoundly, through his inability to participate in their performance. The charlatan continually interrupts it by taking snuff, the marker of French affectation and equally as suspect as his Italian disguise.

Travel in this story represents, then, both a danger and a promise for Germans. On the one hand it clearly fosters trickery like Caraffa's; on the other it can enlighten and strengthen Germans in their craft, as we see in members of the collegia musica, not bumpkins or fools but Germans of broad experience and "*alte teutsche Redlichkeit und Aufrichtigkeit.*" Their judgment on Caraffa is unequivocal. "All those who are ashamed of their German names and commit a fraud by changing them deserve to have Germany be ashamed of *them* and expel them from its borders along with other frauds," says one musician; another adds, "because he prefers the Italian language, manners, and names to the Swabian and thus disdains his good fatherland, I can't recognize him as an honest fellow."[48]

Piquant though *The Musical Charlatan* may be, Kuhnau himself was not the most important figure in defining and defending music to the German reading public of the eighteenth century. That status belongs to Mattheson of Hamburg, organist, composer, and the true founder of the tradition of musical writing in central Europe.[49] He was born, lived, and was buried in Hamburg, and his life's work reflected the ethos of this trading hub of enduring importance and the site of the absorption of English influences in German Europe. Though he lived only briefly in England, Mattheson was a conduit of such influences, a tutor to the English ambassador's son, then a fully invested diplomat attached to his entourage. He retained this post for much of his life, and it brought him income, elevated social status, and marriage to an Englishwoman. Mattheson's physical travels were limited; his was the travelling of the mind, by which he ranged across Europe, including the fractured, musically scattered landscape of Germany. He extended the possibilities of music writing in several directions: a pedagogic one, by providing useful aids to fellow musicians, which in turn circulated widely even into the nineteenth century; a learned one, by writing treatises for the scholarly community; and a public, political one, by translating from English numerous political and economic tracts, and by writing quite a few himself, often commenting on the musical scene.[50] He was not, of course, the first to bring music into such discursive contexts, but his contributions were wide-ranging, substantial, and timely. They ensured that discussions of music in Germany for the next two-and-a-half centuries would implicate and debate nationality. Otto Dann has called Hamburg the "point of departure for modern patriotism in Germany" and, because of Mattheson, we can add for modern musical patriotism as well.[51]

In 1713 Mattheson published his first sustained work on music, *Das neu-eröffnete Orchestre* (The Newly Established Orchestra), a "universal and fundamental guide" for the "educated gentleman" to understand "fully the greatness and worth of noble music." The first musical compendium for non-musicians in Germany, it included information, in non-technical terms, about musical qualities and terminology, as well as rules and national schools (Italian, French, English, and German) of composition.

His book was at once useful and critical, universalizing and comparative, and he used it to point out the urgent need for musical composition to develop with changing times, something that would never happen in Germany without improving the deplorable educational and economic condition of German musicians.[52] In 1722 Mattheson's first venture in musical journalism, *Critica Musica*, became the first musical periodical in Europe, modelled explicitly on the scholarly periodicals and moral weeklies of literary culture, including that of England.[53] In 1728 he began a second periodical, called *Der musicalische Patriot* to signal its kinship with *Der Patriot*, a journal aimed at the "German-speaking community" of Hamburg and beyond. A number of further treatises on the principles of harmony and melody followed, liberally sprinkled with his views on the wretched state of musical Germany (operatic music, church music, instrumental music, courts, cantorates, universities). His crowning achievements came close on each other's heels, in 1739 and 1741. The first and most famous was his book *Der vollkommene Capellmeister*, containing "the fundamental information about all those matters that anyone who would preside over an ensemble with honor and competence must know, be able to do, and completely master."[54] The second was his *Grundlage einer Ehrenpforte* (Foundations for a Gateway of Honour), a biographical encyclopedia of the 148 "most excellent" musicians of his day (not including J.S. Bach, though that was possibly Bach's own fault). Both the latter in its essential nature and the former in its digressions constitute documents of a nationalizing culture. Both were widely read in their day and influential long after it; both attest to an understanding of music as a vital part of European life, in which Germany could, with considerable effort at reforming itself musically, be playing a more substantial role.

Might we then consider Mattheson a nation-builder and a nationalist? His was a nationalism grounded in the observation and emulation of other nations and in his efforts to experience and understand the rest of the world. Perhaps better than "nationalist" would be "patriot," as reflected in the title of his periodical, *Der musicalische Patriot*. In his day the word carried overlapping connotations, including devotion to one's native land (a place of indeterminate boundaries but essentially local and limited) and consciousness of membership in an indeterminate entity called *Deutschland*. It also evoked a discourse of "baroque language and cultural patriotism" and a search for the missing ground of national consciousness that dated back more than half a century.[55] "The unity of the citizenry," he wrote in a brief section of the *Vollkommene Capellmeister*, "the use of music for the common good [*gemeine Wesen*]" is the foundation of the "strongest empires," and what better way to achieve such unity than through the promotion of music. All great peoples, from the Greeks to "today's clever Chinese" to the French and the English, "have structured their social life with such felicity by musical means" as to bring "the entire political body into a proper and harmonious order."[56] Mattheson's choice of the term patriot also reflected his belief in a common good, as well as defensiveness about Italian music (especially opera) and other influences from outside the communities to which the patriot belonged. Reinhart Koselleck has described this defensiveness as a "concrete fear of the cultural infiltration of foreigners [*Überfremdung*] and political powerlessness."[57] Literate people knew that German culture existed, but lacked the confident assertion of a deeply rooted existence for it that Herder would deliver half a century later, German culture seemed to them a vulnerable, elusive thing, too dependent on the changing fortunes of princes and easily lost through the bumbling ignorance of the people.

Choral Societies and Nation-Building in the Nineteenth Century

Any consensus on what actually constituted German culture, compared with, for instance, the German manners and German names that Kuhnau's learned musicians so confidently recognized, proved difficult to articulate. Mattheson himself danced around the problem, saying a great deal about canons and fugues, Italian and French styles of declamation, and problems such as carpet-bagging Italian musicians (they "make all the money and then return home"). But neither he nor anyone else managed to describe in words what Johann Philipp Praetorius called the "ingenious character of the German nation" that music alone expressed.[58] Putting aside, then, the further development of musical writing along the meandering paths that led eventually to the Romantics, we need to consider people in the act of making music, in order to illuminate further aspects of the work both music and travel did in a world of nations.

Choral activity formed a large a part of nineteenth-century music-making in German-speaking Europe. It was simultaneously local, national, and transnational, and singing in choral groups and travelling to choral festivals probably did more to provide ways in which people understood and lived their nationality than did any number of canonizing composer biographies or concert and opera performances. Nevertheless, its rapid growth after 1815 and the large numbers of people it mobilized pose a nagging "why" question for which neither social nor aesthetic nor political explanations suffice. The first large-scale choral performances, immediate ancestors of the sort that became widespread in the nineteenth century, took place not in Germany but in England. They took shape in mid-century in the Lenten performances of Handel's oratorios and had an early apotheosis in 1784, in the enormous centenary commemoration of Handel in Westminster Abbey. Apart from the composer's birthplace, little was peculiarly German about these origins.

Still, the British developed in a short amount of time a "social and musical ritual" that, in the words of William Weber, "proved remarkably appealing and adaptable," and portable.[59] It brought together from a nationally extensive space large numbers of amateur and professional singers to perform revered older or serious newer works. In 1786 Johann Adam Hiller, the first director of Leipzig's Gewandhaus concerts, organized the first full performance of *Messiah* in German-speaking Europe, imitating the British. It took place in the Berlin Cathedral, with an orchestra and chorus numbering in the hundreds, and he followed it up with similarly large-scale performances in Leipzig in 1786 and 1787, then in Breslau in 1788 – taking it on the road to the leading musical centres of north-central Germany. The nineteenth century added a degree of institutionalization to the spread of choral festivals, with the proliferation of musical societies.[60] Number, size, and purposes of festivals expanded apace, crowding the civic calendars of the nineteenth century with celebrations of composers, monarchs, events, and inventions. The Great Exhibition of 1851 included round-the-clock oratorio performances of the Anglo-German line-up of Handel's *Messiah*, Mendelssohn's *Elijah*, and Haydn's *Creation*, and thereafter, in the characteristic dynamic of imitation and amplification, thousands of singers descended on every world's fair for friendly international competition.[61] In short, nineteenth-century singers leave the impression of having spent their time in a state of constant motion and tireless enthusiasm.[62]

What is not so obvious is whether all this travelling and singing meant the same thing. The Handel festivals in England, says Weber, were national celebrations that stabilized the relationship between state, state church, and society.[63] The situation was otherwise in German Europe, where state and society were too decentralized and scattered for any music festival to have Germany-wide consequences. Still, this was not for want of aspirations. Hiller, who moved to Leipzig in 1751, the year after J.S. Bach's death, had more in common with Mattheson, or indeed with Handel, than he did with Bach, and he hoped his work would improve musical life beyond that of any single locality. Bringing Handel back to the Germans thus formed one part of Hiller's varied career as composer, theorist, pedagogue, and impresario, in which he travelled often from place to place.[64] He organized concert series, established musical societies for amateurs, ran a school for singers, and founded a musical periodical. His treatises on singing instruction were revolutionary, and his collections of songs for children and household music-making reflected progressive ideas about music in the home and the enlightening sociability inherent to music-making as a whole.

All these activities echo far into the nineteenth century, marking them as a point of origin for a number of key transformations in the musical culture of Germany, Europe, and North America – festivals, big groups, careful training regimens, easily accessible collections of songs for home and amateur singing, and attention to national traits and traditions. Yet his impact dissipated in the era of the French Revolution, when Germans became aware of models of choral activity at once more inspiring and more disturbing. After 1790 the open-air festivals of revolutionary and Napoleonic Paris, which included massed choral singing and large military bands, recruited music to the cause of the new regimes. In German-speaking Central Europe these French models implicitly competed with the English Handelian ones for the soul of the German choral movement, winning at least a few initial victories for what in the German context was a destabilizing nationalism. The first large-scale festival in Germany, in 1810 in the small Thuringian town of Frankenhausen, was not overtly political, but its place and time sounded themes of a nationalizing consciousness that became louder over the next decades. Its organizer, an obscure local cantor and court musician named G.F. Bischoff, was so encouraged by a performance of Haydn's *Creation* in his native Frankenhausen that he convinced Louis Spohr, then conductor of the court orchestra in nearby Gotha, to direct a larger-scale festival in his home town.

Frankenhausen lies at the foot of the Kyffhäuser mountain, deep inside of which, according to German legend, Emperor Frederick Barbarossa slept in a hidden chamber, waiting to arise and come to Germany's rescue in his country's hour of greatest need – a fanciful notion with surprising resonance. The participants in the festival did not cry "Wach' auf!" to the emperor or to their fellow Germans, like the singing townspeople of Wagner's *Meistersinger of Nuremberg*, first staged some sixty years later. Still, hundreds of German musicians, both amateur and professional, did gather to perform Haydn's *Creation* and Beethoven's Fifth Symphony. Five years later, even more gathered again, this time to commemorate the victory over Napoleon two years earlier at the Battle of the Nations in Leipzig. They sang Gottfried Weber's *Te Deum* as well as Spohr's newly composed cantata, *Das befreite Deutschland* (Germany Liberated), and gave speeches consonant with the aggressive, even sacralized, nature of German nationalist discourse during the period of the Napoleonic wars. In 1818 the first of what became the most musically ambitious of the German festivals, the Lower Rhine Festival, took place in Elberfeld, with a large orchestra and chorus from the surrounding area.[65] The emperor, it seems, had awoken.

The development of German nationalism after the monarchical restorations of 1815 takes one through many political detours and disappointments, but a concern for the cultural achievements of the German nation never disappeared. Nationally minded people of this era did not make neat distinctions between the cultural content of nationhood and its political implications; to believe that Germany existed as a cultural reality was also to believe in the political ideal of self-government and unified statehood.[66] But people expressed their consciousness of their nationality in different ways, and when the opportunities for political activism diminished, especially after 1819, the promotion of cultural unity and national fulfilment through the consumption of culture became more important, and not simply as a cover for forbidden political gatherings. Events like the Lower Rhine Festivals exemplified such activism with their performances of oratorios and symphonies by composers whose German nationality the organizers and participants found deeply satisfying. The international significance of these compositions were to them truths they held to be self-evident, and hence the performance of such works asserted, in very public fashion, the existence of a German nation among nations. They were a cultural declaration of national independence.

We can also regard the Lower Rhine Festivals, and others like them, as the most public face of the many respectable singing societies that had developed in central Europe since the founding of Carl Friedrich Fasch's Berlin Singakademie in 1791, the first permanent amateur singing organization in German Europe and accidental heir to the Handel tradition in Germany begun by Hiller. Fasch's Singakademie had grown to more than 100 singers by 1800 and more than 200 by 1815. Under him and his successor, Carl Friedrich Zelter, it became known for its careful study of sacred choral music, much of it no longer regularly heard in either Catholic or Protestant churches. In January 1794 Fasch introduced J.S. Bach's double-chorus motet *Komm, Jesu, Komm* into rehearsals, setting the Singakademie off on a thirty-five-year journey to its celebrated revival of his *St Matthew Passion* in 1829 – an event, like the Lower Rhine Festivals, of profound national significance to performers and audiences alike.[67] Groups seeking a similar kind of musical experience soon began to appear all over German-speaking Europe. The Singakademie's first wave of imitators, starting with the Leipzig Singakademie (founded in 1800) included within a couple decades more than a dozen new choral societies from Stettin to Innsbruck.[68]

The German festival movement, with its large, mixed-sex choruses, did not challenge established authority, but its exponents did maintain a presence in the public eye. They adopted formal statutes, elected officials, held fundraisers, and made claims on public space that were anything but modest.[69] The desire to assert themselves publically was even more the case with a rowdier strand of the choral-festival movement, that of male choruses. Starting in 1809, when Carl Friedrich Zelter founded in Berlin a singing group, or *Liedertafel*, for men only, hundreds of similar organizations sprang up all across German-speaking Europe. By the 1830s these men's singing societies represented one of the most important outlets for the public participatory impulses of people whose political activism was virtually shut down. Frequent gatherings of singers in the years preceding the outbreak of revolution in 1848 were occasions for cautious speech-making and unrestrained singing, both making a case for a single German nation, as well as celebrating German nature and the German people.[70] Whether unveiling a monument (Gutenberg in 1840, Beethoven in Bonn in 1845), honouring a restored cathedral (two for the Cologne cathedral in 1842), or celebrating the patriotic fellowship of song, these events mobilized several thousand male singers and drew even larger audiences from the city and surrounding towns. None of the festivals or groups contributed directly to the outbreak of the revolution, and they more or less ceased as a form of public activism in the revolutionary years themselves, thus making this kind of massed singing different from its French predecessors. Nevertheless, the men's singing movement of the pre-1848 period established its credentials as the authentic voice of the German nation.

The general tendency of the nineteenth century, no matter the country or the activity, was to consolidate and institutionalize, and singing everywhere was no exception. After the revolutionary period had faded away, massed singing returned to central Europe, in greater numbers than before. In 1862 a German Singing Confederation (*Deutscher Sängerbund*) solidified the fluid ties among different localities, and soon an

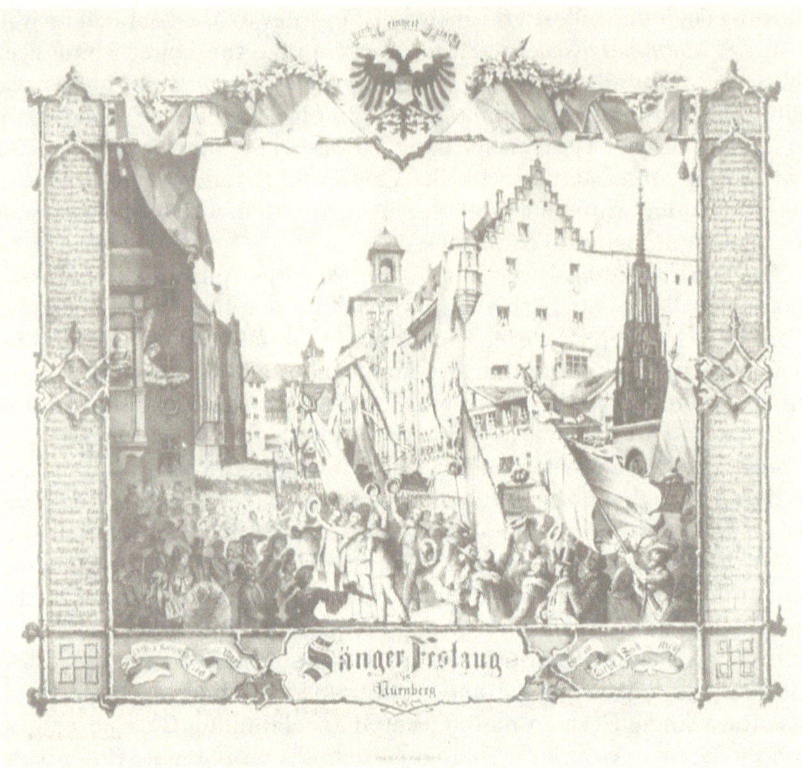

3.1 Postcard depicting the festival parade for the *Sängerfest* of 1861 in Nuremberg, an event with strong nationalist overtones to which more than 20,000 singers travelled, many by rail. Lithography, Rudolph and Julies Geißler, 1861. Germanisches Nationalmuseum, Nuremberg.

annual Confederation Festival became a regular, ever more staid event on the musical calendar of a soon-to-be-united German Empire. Yet the Liedertafel model, with its combination of small local groups and periodic large festivals, had not simply become establishment. It proved influential in showing eastern European nationalities a way to express their sense of belonging together and to give workers, students, and veterans a satisfying and relatively peaceful way to make noise. Workers' choruses, which began to form in large numbers in the 1860s, took the middle-class Liedertafel as both model and counter-model, adopting its earlier method of using singing as a way to pursue politics and consciousness-raising through non-political means. Especially after the new German Empire passed anti-socialist laws in the 1870s, massed singing became, once again, as much a way to evade authority as to celebrate it.[71] Regardless of the political valence of German men's singing groups, all in one way or another served the cause of nation-building. Germany and other modernizing nations became real to people because many thousands of them travelled around them, first by coach or horseback or on foot, later most often by train, meeting their fellow countrymen and singing together.[72]

Finally, all these choral groups, including those in other European nations and in the United States, showed a lively, even maniacal interest in competition. By the latter half of the nineteenth century neither a year nor an exposition went by without a choral competition taking place. For the exhibition organizers, this was a winning proposition, promising to bring "music-lovers in all parts of the country" to the event; for singers, this pursuit of war by other means brought the pleasure of travel and the thrill of defeating others. For all the differences between the development of choral singing and festivals in Germany, Great Britain, and the United States, if one simply closed one's eyes and listened, one would have been hearing the same thing, and that held true over a surprisingly long period of time. From Handel to Haydn to Mendelssohn and beyond, these societies converged on a repertoire that was the joint creation of German-English musical interaction, institutionally and compositionally. Probably the most notable difference between singing societies and choral festivals in England and in Germany was not the music but the absence of alcohol at the former and its overindulgence at the latter. In contrast to the teetotal temperance activists who filled the English choral societies, German festivals of local Liedertafeln had already by 1844 earned the reputation of being, in the words of the *Allgemeine Musikalische Zeitung*, "drinking bouts with shouting and tobacco smoke."[73]

The pleasures of participation in the public world were the hallmark of singing in big groups, but we should not allow the peremptory claims of publicity to blind us to more intimate forms of small-group singing that were just as important to nineteenth-century music lovers. Composers wrote for them; publishers catered to them; parents encouraged their older children to participate in them, likewise employers their employees, and eventually all levels of schooling, from the elementary to the university, included them. Small-group singing was often, though not always, a single-sex activity. The German Liedertafel in Zelter's original formulation consisted of a small number (fifteen or so) of like-minded men, who would gather "with German gaiety [*Fröhlichkeit*] and conviviality [*Gemütlichkeit*]" for a "frugal repast" and the singing of songs that the members themselves had written. Within a decade of its founding, it had become stodgy enough that a rival organization, of *younger* like-minded men, had formed in Berlin. And so it went, all across Germany and soon across the United States. The logic of the diffusion was the logic of sociability, that is, of finding people with whom one wanted to spend time. Some societies organized themselves around certain genres, such as madrigals or motets, and thus considered themselves chiefly motivated by the work of historical recovery. Others grew out of the isolation of immigrants in foreign lands or small-town people in big cities and so affirmed regional and local identities in unfamiliar places. The whole superstructure of festivals, competitions, and national dreams grew out of this basic experience of "keeping together in time" and also creating together in time. As William McNeill put it, this togetherness constituted and reconstituted social bonds on a daily basis – it did not simply reflect the fact that society already existed.[74]

Take the Berlin Singakademie, for another instance. At the start of the century in which it became the model for so many other choruses, Zelter described it as "a kind of artistic corps" in which "every serious-minded friend of art" would find "as much satisfaction through serious art as is possible." Its gatherings encompassed "attentiveness without visible exertion, beauty without privilege, multiplicity of all estates, ages, and trades, without affectation; delight in a fine art without weariness; the young and the old, the aristocrat and the burgher; the joy and the discipline; the father and the daughter, the mother with her son, and every possible mixing of the sexes and the estates."[75] The musicologist Erich Valentin once wrote that groups of people singing in homes "formed the foundation on which public music life first began to constitute itself, radiating from within society to more outward forms."[76] Zelter's description, in which his group is a family, and indeed a rapidly growing one, confirms the truth of this. Many choral societies in the nineteenth century, especially those that began almost casually, as did the Singakademie, had their roots not in church practices or public, state-centred ceremonials, but in the semi-private and private settings of domestic music-making.

As a result, the organizational structures of this quasi-formal, quasi-private singing varied enormously, from occasional gatherings in someone's music room or parlour to highly organized groups with regular rehearsal space, statutes, dues, membership lists, and annual reports. Women's choruses in German-speaking Europe sometimes traced their activity to the singing that went on in the spinning rooms of premodern households, and there were plenty of folklorists who were willing to play the game of "find the origins" as well.[77] Richard Wagner gave the theory his own peculiar blessing in the "Spin, Spin, Fair Maiden" chorus that opens Act II of *Der Fliegende Holländer*, and in the way of such things, versions of this popular scene in the opera circulated back into the women's chorus repertoire. Singing and spinning did go together naturally, as did song and work, edification, education, moral improvement, and conviviality, with or without alcoholic lubrication. If one follows the yearly activities, for instance, of the University of Munich men's chorus in the late nineteenth century, one finds a group that maintained in its yearbook a list of all former members, honorary members, auxiliary members, and "philistines" (i.e., community people who paid dues), thus constituting social bonds across time as well as in place. Rituals abounded in such groups. An annual party before Lent included elaborate shenanigans that usually involved cross-dressing (imagine a young Max Planck, future Nobel Prize winner, writing an operetta for this group, of which he was assistant director, about the unexpected arrival of a harem at the Vienna world's fair). An annual expedition took the group to some town in the surrounding countryside, where much wining, dining, and singing with the town men's chorus would take place, followed often by an early morning hike to the local promontory or castle ruin, where a patriotic song of some sort would ring forth, followed by more wining and dining and singing.[78] Nature itself was inscribed with social and national significance in such practices, and the combination of movement and music created vital bonds of belonging that could be mobilized in other settings and for other purposes as well. To invoke again the biological and the anthropological, singing was work done together. It enacted the struggle to come together and the satisfaction of achieving it. It was the synchronization of individual bodies (ears, minds, eyes, lungs, arms holding music, legs standing and sitting). Particularly when one realizes that behind every performance lay months and years of weekly rehearsals – the warm-ups, the repetitions, the tea breaks with sweet cakes, the talking and exchanging of opinions and experiences, the coming together and leaving only to return again the next week – then one comes to acknowledge that singing together was a central experience of the quotidian for hundreds of thousands of Europeans and Americans, made all the more memorable by the unconscious effects, so impossible to measure, of the music itself.

Conclusion

Ethnomusicologist John Blacking wrote:

> Music cannot change societies, as can changes in technology and political organization. It cannot make people act unless they are already socially and culturally disposed to act. It cannot instill brotherhood, as Tolstoy hoped, or any other state or social value. If it can do anything to people, the best that it can do is to confirm situations that already exist. It cannot in itself generate thoughts that may benefit or harm mankind, as some writers have suggested; but it can make people more aware of feelings that they have experienced, or partly experienced, by reinforcing, narrowing or expanding their consciousness in a variety of ways.[79]

When thinking about the Germans and their music (if indeed we should even consider it "their"), this is bracing good sense to counteract the more vulgar notions of music's implication in the crimes of the German people. Still, in his effort to get past the sentimentalizing, heroizing, and demonizing discourses about music that are among the many legacies to western culture from its musical past, Blacking may restrict too severely the historical contributions of musicians to society and underplay the centrality to collective life of the actions he does allow that music can perform. It is particularly easy to underestimate music's broader cultural importance if we regard it as something that can be neatly sorted into hierarchies of low, middle, and high; filed under genres of blues, Christian, classical, country, jazz, rap, and reggae; confined to certain times of the week or modes of leisure – in short, a kind of decorative motif carved onto the iron cages of our modern existence. The study of how musicians and music have moved around in the world can provide an escape from these interpretative cages. "Out into the world with you!" wrote Carl Maria von Weber in 1809, as the opening line of his unfinished novel,

A Musician's Life, "for the world is the artist's true sphere ... What good does it do you to live with a petty clique and to earn the gracious applause of a patron. Out! A man's spirit must find itself in the spirits of his fellow creatures."[80] German musicians followed his exhortation in ever greater numbers in the centuries that followed, out of ambition, curiosity, idealism, restlessness, and every kind of necessity including, of course, exile and flight. One result was the German nation itself.

Chapter Four

Music at the Fairs

Just in time for the opening of the 1915 Panama Pacific International Exposition (Pan-Pacific) the American Telephone and Telegraph Company managed to complete the first transcontinental telephone line from New York to San Francisco.[1] AT&T President Theodore Vail undertook this enormous task mainly for the chance to display his company's technological derring-do, and the publicity department touted the achievement as the means by which people all across America would be able to hear the Pacific Ocean roar. A nice idea, perhaps, but in truth there was far too much other noise at the Pan-Pacific for anything so sonically unemphatic as the surf splashing against the sea walls of Fort Mason to be heard amid the cacophony that was the soundscape of the fair. An article in the *San Francisco Examiner* in April 1915, discussing only the music at the fair, complained, "there is just too much of it." Three months into the Pan-Pacific the exhibitors in the Liberal Arts Palace had filed an urgent appeal to the music organizers asking them to please cancel or, at the very least, move the daily concerts of the Third Coast Artillery Band, which was drowning out three talking machine exhibits, as well as exhibits of Hawaiian, Japanese, wind and stringed instruments, an organ, and a "very extensive" piano exhibit, and a "continuous entertainer" mechanical instrument exhibit. "When a talking machine concern is playing [Anton Rubinstein's] Melody in F," according to the *Examiner*, "what avail has it against a forty piece brass band playing 'I'm on My Way to Dublin Bay'? When an organ is soulfully rendering Ave Maria what effect shall it have against a 16 inch brass band howitzer playing 'Tip Top Tipperary Mary'?"[2]

Together, these reports suggest the two conceptual issues in the study of musical culture that music at the great international fairs of the nineteenth and twentieth centuries raises for us. First is the issue of displacement and the kinds of transformations that came about when music moved. Movement of all sorts is, of course, intrinsic to the idea and practice of the world's fairs, as they evolved into a gigantic circuit of what *Punch* magazine already in 1851 called "the great derby race" of nations.[3] The organizers and participants in the fairs celebrated the movement of goods and peoples in this proudly modern, ever modernizing world. Transnational, transcontinental, transoceanic, trans-hemispheric – the fairs created something that historians of these phenomena have taken to calling a global village or, more abstractly, a global public space. But it was an odd kind of village space – artificial, temporary, monumental, and hypertrophied, utterly lacking in the everyday – rather, every day was a special day. "There is a peculiar atmosphere about all expositions which causes commonplaces to become uncommonly interesting," wrote American humorist and cartoonist Thomas Fleming in his account of going *Around the "Pan" with Uncle Hank.* "This is partly due to the holiday air pervading," said Fleming, "and to the fact that the visitor has come to be entranced and that he intends upon his return home, to dilate on the wonderful things seen."[4] Annegret Fauser has written of the musical effects of this displacement – the time out of time, place out of place, coming, seeing, hearing, and going home again – at the 1889 Universal Exposition in Paris.[5] This chapter will consider displacement in other directions, mainly from Europe to America.

Second is the theme of interactions. The Third Coastal Artillery Band's drowning out of mechanical Ave Marias was a kind of interaction, or certainly a juxtaposition, but the main concern of this chapter will be interactions across lines collectively understood to be national (French, American, German, and so on), interactions in and among status designations (our continuing reliance on those familiar distinctions among highbrow, lowbrow, middlebrow), and interactions among the means of musical production (orchestra, band, chorus, mechanical). The military band playing a popular tune and drowning out a mechanical device playing a classical one encapsulates the confusion that resulted from such interactions in the artificial, representative space of the world fair.

Musical sounds had been an integral part of expositions ever since the Sacred Harmonic Society of London had launched round-the-clock oratorio performances (in a regular rotation of Handel's *Messiah,* Mendelssohn's *Elijah,* and Haydn's *Creation*) to accompany the Great Exhibition of 1851.[6] In her "thick description of music making and listening," Fauser suggests that we look upon them as "a laboratory both of musical perception and of modes of musical usage," in her case of late nineteenth-century France.[7] The 1889 Exposition Universelle set a new standard for musical participation in a world's fair, but of course, worlds' fairs were always works in progress, more concerned with upping the ante and inventing the future than with following whatever traditions had been already established. The 1889 event had easily the most culturally diverse musical offerings so far, and all subsequent fairs imitated its method of insinuating music into every aspect of the fair – tableaux vivants, ceremonial events, technological displays, as well as actual staged performances. The 1901 Pan-American Exposition in Buffalo, New York, ostensibly a celebration of the electricity generated by nearby Niagara Falls, was smaller in scale, certainly, than the Parisian fairs (1889, 1900) and smaller even than the Chicago Columbian Exposition of 1892, but it still gave music a prominent role in its limited space filled with tightly packed amusements and edifying exhibitions. The Temple of Music, an elaborately decorated concoction, lit up with electric lights and located in the centre of the fairgrounds, held hundreds of concerts, including a daily one on the enormous organ built for the exposition by Emmons Howard & Son of Westfield, Massachusetts.[8] On 6 September 1901 organist William J. Gomph was playing a piece of transcribed orchestral music (either Schumann's "Träumerei" or Wagner's "To an Evening Star" from *Tannhäuser* – accounts differ) to President William McKinley when Leon Czolgosz, the home-grown American anarchist, walked up to the president and shot him.

The Louisiana Purchase Exposition of 1904 in St Louis, Missouri, had a single impresario to select and coordinate the musical offerings: George W. Stewart of Boston, a veteran band player (trombone), member of the Boston Symphony Orchestra, and a founder of the Boston Festival Orchestra, which toured the United States around the turn of the century. Under Stewart's guidance music at the Louisiana Purchase Exposition was considered to have been a great success, though again much of the attention went to an organ of Brobdingnagian dimensions, built by Murray M. Harris of Los Angeles and advertised as "the largest organ in the world," capable of "producing musical effects never before heard outside the Grand Orchestra."[9] It included 130 miles of electric wire, 13,000 magnets, and 250,000 pounds of pipes and chests, many of which had to be imported from Germany, and thirteen freight cars were needed to transport it from Los Angeles to St Louis. But after all the usual delays, cost overruns, inadequate seating, and ticket price inflation, the organ's sold-out recitals with international superstar

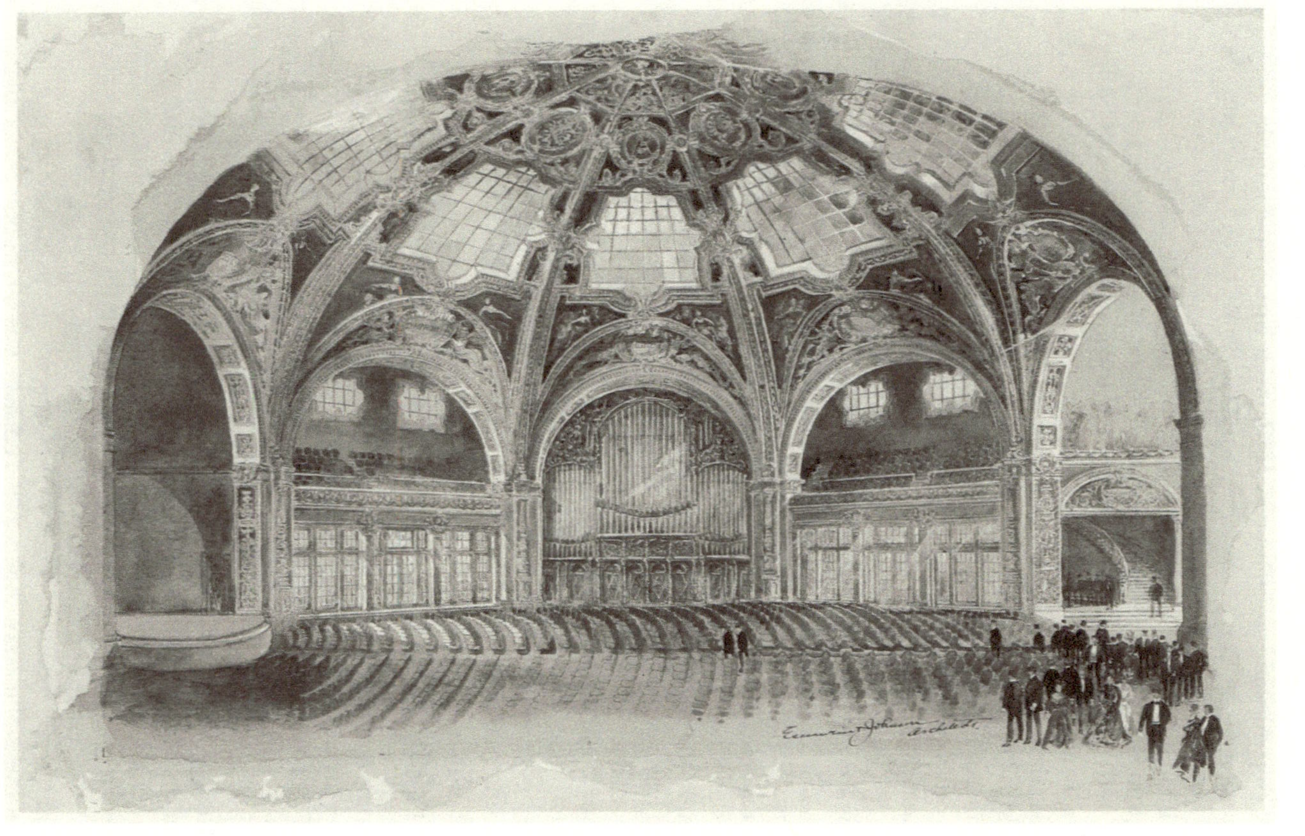

4.1 Interior of the Temple of Music, Pan-American Exposition in Buffalo, NY, 1901 (Eisenwein & Johnson). *The Rainbow City: Celebrating Art, Color, and Architecture at the Pan-American Exposition, Buffalo, 1901*. Buffalo and Erie County Historical Society.

organist Félix-Alexandre Guilmant at the console proved as compelling an attraction as the ferris wheel (first unveiled in Chicago a decade earlier). During one of Guilmant's concerts large chunks of the ceiling in the exposition's Festival Hall broke off and crashed to the floor, but such mishaps only added to the excitement of music at the fairs. In July 1901, for instance, the undaunted organist in the Temple of Music had rallied the crowd during a severe thunderstorm by playing on in the darkness: "during the long interval of waiting for a release from the grip of the elements all sorts of popular airs were played, and the immense but undismayed crowd joined in singing pretty much the whole round of old and new from the latest coon, or ragtime, to the finest sacred melodies."[10]

Planning for the Panama-Pacific International Exposition

Thus, by the time the San Franciscans began planning their own Pan-Pacific Exposition, scheduled to stand for eight months in 1915, the possibilities and pitfalls of music's participation in fairs were well known. The Pan-Pacific had better than the usual unconvincing array of high-minded justifications for a big trade fair. The planners began their work in expectation of the Panama Canal's completion, after a long and tragic history of construction. The canal formally opened in August 1914, almost two years ahead of schedule and well in advance of the exposition designed to celebrate this "meeting of two oceans." The organizers also began their planning among the ruins caused by the 1906 earthquake and fire, which had claimed more than 3,000 lives and caused $400 million in property losses. Rushed efforts to rebuild in time for the exposition resulted in construction weaknesses that still plague the city, but the main point had to be made to the world – San Francisco was rising from the ashes as an economic and a cultural powerhouse. In 1912 J.B. Levison of San Francisco, a successful businessman, frequent traveller to Europe, and enthusiastic amateur musician, became chair of the Music Committee for the fair. In his first official act, he appointed as music director the same George W. Stewart of Boston, who set sail for Europe on 2 June 1914 on the Hamburg-American steamer *Cincinnati* to recruit organizations and individuals of "reputation and importance" to bring lustre to the exposition. The stage was set for music to serve (in the words of a official 1915 description of the exposition) as "a means not only of entertainment but as a means of cultural development, and as an intellectual factor in the evolution of the race."[11] The stage was set, in other words, for Europe to do its usual work of bringing cultivation and edification to the Americans, even to their farthest shores.

Yet matters did not turn out that way, not in 1901 in Buffalo, not in 1904 in St Louis, and not again in 1915, despite the conventional gloss put on these events by contemporary commentators and official chroniclers. Stewart himself, a veteran of middlebrow musical organizations, was never so high-minded. To Levinson and the organizers, he stated his conception of the exposition's music: "instead of serious symphonic compositions to be rendered in a solemn temple, and of interest but to a limited cult, there should be great military bands playing in the open, and playing music that would appeal to all classes – not trash for that purpose, but good, popular compositions, and especially things that [are] new." Even the professional artist at the exposition, he thought, would not be "in a frame of mind to enjoy the more technical exemplifications of his art." As for the general public, it could "not be expected to."[12]

The scheme that emerged was indeed extensive, even elaborate, but not otherwise especially ambitious – though in the words of Frank Morton Todd, the fair's official chronicler, "no phase of the exposition was more popular, more satisfactory, more attractive to more people and better worth the imposing amount of money devoted to it than the music."[13] The organizers set up four bandstands around the exposition grounds, on which a constantly changing array of bands played for free, day and night: some were small-time bands from the Bay Area; some were big-time ones such as Sousa's Band and the *Garde Républicaine* of Paris; and some were unknown but symbolically potent ones, such as the Philippine Constabulary Band. On a stage in a restaurant visitors could hear two performances daily, mostly by the Exposition Orchestra, whose members had been recruited largely from the Bay Area and the expense of which was shared with the Union Pacific Company (more on that later). And a very large Festival Hall with a very large organ saw more than daily organ recitals – 368 recitals to be exact (1.3 organ recitals per day, on average, performed by more than 25 different organists, including the man billed as the "greatest living organist," the Englishman Edwin Lemare, who alone accounted for 100 of these performances). The Boston Symphony Orchestra (BSO), "the most famous of all orchestras," also had an extended engagement at the exposition in the spring of 1915, under the great Dr Karl Muck, and finally, Stewart also managed to bag an actual living European composer, though an elderly one: Camille Saint-Saëns, about to turn eighty.[14]

European Musicians Come to the Fair

The ceremonial arrival of Saint-Saëns at the exposition, on 21 June 1915, raises the question of how we are to interpret this phenomenon of musical displacement, that is, the appearance of scores of European musicians at these events explicitly designed to display American achievements. Besides the great Frenchman himself, many famous as well as journeyman players appeared, from the incessantly "organ-izing" Edwin Lemare of London to the Czech-German singer Emmy Destinn (advertised as among the "Half Dozen Greatest Sopranos ... idealized in all parts of Europe as well as in the Southern Hemisphere") to the violinist Fritz Kreisler, wounded veteran of the Austro-Hungarian infantry on the Eastern Front, to Karl Muck, late of Berlin and the Kaiser's favourite conductor, his orchestra saturated with a German repertoire and populated by German-born musicians.[15] If one were to expand the category of European musicians to include those trained in Europe, the list would include many more musicians and almost all the conductors. Further, if one were to look at the repertoire of the orchestral concerts – not just those of the BSO, the organ recitals, the band and choral concerts – and if one counted up the national origins of the works in their original forms, one would find an overwhelming amount of German music, followed in a distant second place by French and Italian music, with American and British music hardly in evidence at all.[16] In the concert series presented by the BSO the organizers offered two "French Programmes" and a "Wagner Programme"; as for the rest, which consisted of works by Beethoven, Brahms, Mendelssohn, Bach, Strauss, and Weber, a label was neither provided nor needed.

But what does this exercise of counting national heads actually tell us? To consider the most obvious explanation, it meant that Americans, in search of prestige, looked to find it in Europe. Contemporaries talked about the transatlantic exchange that way – prestige for payment – but the simplicity of the phrase belies the complexity of the exchange itself. By 1915, even by 1904, the time was long past when Louis Gottschalk could remark about a volunteer military band, "is it necessary for me to say that it was composed of Germans? (all musicians in the United States are Germans)."[17] As Frank Trommler and Jessica Gienow-Hecht, among others, have argued, the two decades before the decision of the United States to join the Allied effort against the Central Powers in 1917 were characterized by a considerable loosening of America's enthralment to German culture, German scholarship, and even German music and its

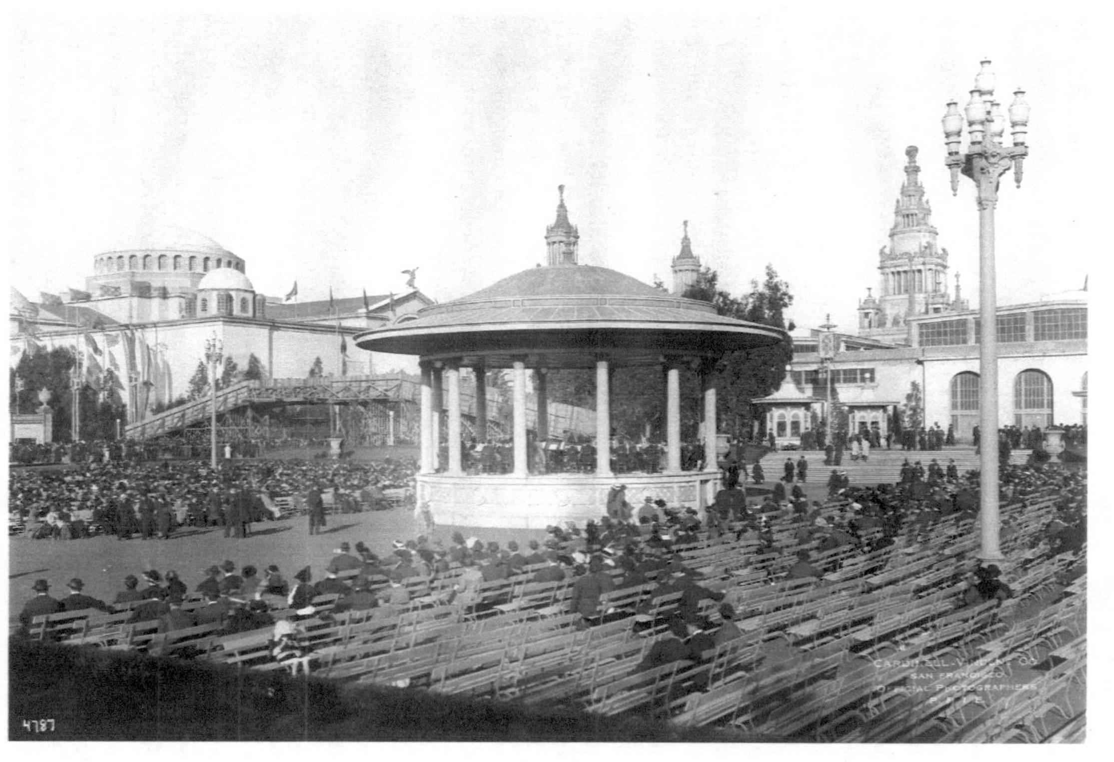

4.2 Musical Concourse at the Panama-Pacific International Exposition, San Francisco, 1915. San Francisco History Center, San Francisco Public Library.

native-born musicians. In 1898 the opening issue of the journal *Musical America* declared, "today the world realizes that there is an Artistic America, a Musical America, an America that teems with aspiration for all that is beautiful and true."[18] Any number of musical leaders in America had long been calling for a renewed American composition, musical training, and confidence in musical capacities; above all, this meant breaking with the post-Civil War infatuation with all things German, Wagner especially. As music critic Homer Moore wrote in 1892, "We can never claim to be the equal of Germany musically while we copy Beethoven and Wagner."[19]

What then was George Stewart doing when he sailed off to Europe? Was he representing a musical culture full of confidence about its own capacities or one still in need of cultural inspiration from abroad; and, if the latter, did the musical inspiration still have to be German? He was, to be sure, looking for European musicians of all sorts, not just German ones, and he brought back a Frenchman, not a German, though not for lack of trying. He had been making his way through Germany's musical centres when war broke out. He managed to get out only in September, in the company of his old friend Amy Beach, who had been enjoying what she called the superior musical culture of Munich for the past three years and left only reluctantly.[20] At the most obvious level, Stewart's efforts indicate what much other evidence confirms, that the image of Germany as the land of music par excellence and of German music as transcending the national to the realm of the universally human still had a strong hold on the mind of music-loving, music-consuming Americans. Such was evident from the earliest days of planning the exposition. In 1912, when the outbreak of a Europe-wide war was not on anyone's mind, a real possibility existed that Germany *and* England, wearied by year after year of expositions and trade fairs, each requiring a gearing-up of the national determination to display their finest wares to the world, would simply decide not to participate. Efforts to forestall such a disaster preoccupied the exposition planners for several years and drew in a number of advocates of German-American cooperation on both sides of the Atlantic. Among them was Benjamin Wheeler, then president of the University of California at Berkeley, who wrote to his friend Theodor Lewald, who was the German official in the Ministry of the Interior in charge of expositional matters, to advise him on the importance of Germany's presence at the Pan-Pacific International Exposition. "I should myself suggest that the whole burden of a German exhibit be laid upon the more ideal products of Germany, literature, education, scientific discovery, music," he wrote. "Let Germany in the Exposition present herself for what she really is and has been in the recent history of civilization ... Germany has all reason to be proud, and to be proud not of her knives and kettles and tin pans, but of her application of science to the arts and uses of life and her development of the arts of beauty and joy."[21]

In the end, Germany as such did not come to the fair, not because of the war but out of suspicion that the expense and bother of it outweighed the economic or political benefits. A number of German exhibitors did come, including the Welte Brothers of Stuttgart, leading makers of mechanical organs and other feats of musical reproduction. Even so, the German arts of beauty and joy, if that is how we want to characterize German music, were on full display via the agency of Americans. And this in turn suggests that the key to understanding Stewart's trip to Europe and the subsequent musical offerings of the exposition must be sought not in who he did or did not bring to the fair but in the very act of bringing, as well as in the places where he put the things he brought there. San Francisco was, of course, a very long way away from Europe in 1915, and certainly none of the millions of visitors who came to the fair over its eight-month run was in any doubt about that, especially considering that the fundamental theme of the event was the transportation revolution that the Panama canal represented, which would, again in the words of President Wheeler, "turn this world inside out."[22] The exposition was at some basic level about bringing things *there*, to San Francisco, not just about people and objects but about the sounds they made, among them the sound of President Wilson opening the fair, heard over that transcontinental phone line. Sounds as much as objects testified to the transformational power of those who moved them, making them magically appear in a different and distant place. It is not without relevance that a significant proportion of the music that people heard at the fair was prominently underwritten by the Pacific Union Railroad in a venue (the Old Faithful Inn) named for one of the quintessential tourist sites that the railroad had created for travellers and placed in the "Yellowstone Park" concession that the railroad managed. Much of the publicity surrounding the coming of Saint-Saëns and of the BSO focused on how they got there and how far they had come. In the case of the latter Stewart himself and much subsequent publicity repeatedly drew attention to the fact that "the Boston Symphony Orchestra comes to the Exposition, making the trip from Boston to San Francisco without stopping over at any city en route. At the close of their engagement at the Exposition, they will return immediately to Boston. No concerts will be given en route, either to or from the Exposition."[23]

To be sure, the organizers had in mind the allure of that phrase "exclusive engagement," but there is more significance to be mined from these preoccupations. Travel bestows meaning, in this case less that of the civilizing mission, spreading European culture all the way to California and beyond, than the simple fact that the bearers of European culture had been summoned and they came. And they came as celebrities, because that is how the organizers wanted them to come and to be, and that is how they literally *placed* them in the exposition grounds. Place, too, bestows meaning, in musical settings as in all others. The Pan-Pacific Exposition did not just scatter bandstands around the exposition grounds – after all, those arrangements merely reproduced, in a larger, somewhat more chaotic and competitive way, the acoustic experience of every public park in Europe, the United States, and the colonized world. Nor did they just put one of their most important musical venues in an enormous restaurant in a hokey mock-up of Yellowstone Park that was located in the so-called Amusement Zone, next to the Grand Canyon and across from the Oriental Village and Somali Land. In an effort to underline, all indications to the contrary notwithstanding, the professionalism of this venue, Stewart emphasized the luxurious musical accommodations: an enormous green room, a fireproof room housing a musical library that could "meet the demands of more than five hundred concerts," lockers for all, and "up to date toilet equipment for members of the orchestra," as well as "a private room with complete toilet arrangements" for the conductors. But beyond all those features, they also built a festival hall even bigger than the Temple of Music in Buffalo or the Festival Hall in St Louis, with an organ on which "a banquet for seventy-five persons sitting at tables could be accommodated" and acoustics so poor that Karl Muck complained it made all orchestras sound the same.[24]

Musical Mixing at the Fair

But that, surely, was the point. The reception and appropriation of European music that the expositions illustrate were a matter of what we might call the demystification and declassing of culture, a process whose dynamic lay not just in acts of displacement but in planned and unplanned interactions.[25] The ensemble of sites and performances in the Marina District of San Francisco encapsulates many developments in European and American musical cultures over the course of the nineteenth century, developments that historian Tim Blanning has summed up, rather dramatically, as the "triumph of music."[26] Through the availability of published scores (represented at the fair in the library of the Old Faithful Inn) and the construction of ever larger and more numerous places for performance, music achieved a kind of omnipresence in private and public life, even before the advent of widespread mechanical reproduction – a sign of the future that was present at the fairs as well. But expositions also illustrate the extent to which this triumph involved, and was indeed the consequence of, a constant toing and froing (not a levelling, not an eradication) across the soft, porous boundaries among nations, social groups, functional domains (church, state, community, family), and cultural hierarchies.

Nowhere was the unhinged nature of musical culture more obvious than in the grand spectacles of and around the festival organ. Organs and expositions go together, it turns out, bound together inexorably by the process of industrialization and its impact on social and cultural practices. The major technological innovations that made the organ more efficient and easier to play, more expressive, and more manageable over the course of the nineteenth century (high-pressure reeds, overblowing flutes, the swell box, the horizontal bellows, combination pedals, pneumatic levers, and, perhaps most important of all, mechanical blowing) seemed timed so as to coincide with one exposition after another. In 1851 a young Englishman named Henry Willis, inspired by the great alchemist of organists Aristide Cavaillé-Coll, built a 3-manual, 70-stop organ for the main hall of the Crystal Palace in London. Its combination pistons, which brought pneumatic action to previously unimagined usefulness, were the envy of all and made organ innovation and display a feature of every subsequent event.[27] New kinds of mechanical blowers were displayed at the International Exhibition in London in 1862, a new, advanced form of tubular-pneumatic action was invented in time for the Paris Exhibition of 1867, Cavaillé-Coll himself installed the latest grand organ in the Trocadéro Palace for the Exposition Universelle of 1878 (the first organ in France custom built not for a church but for a concert hall), and on it went. The behemoth of 1915 in San Francisco, a 4-rank, 117-stop Austin organ, was said to be merely the seventh largest in the world, but putting aside all the one-upmanship, what beyond the competitive spirit itself did these instruments display?

Their bigness naturally draws our attention first: size mattered in these cases. But after the initial impact of the sheer volume of noise a festival organ could produce, noisiness and bigness only begin to account for the appeal and the meaning of the festival organ. The organ was then, as it has always been, the mirror of its time, and those times were marked by big and noisy cities, the crossing of big distances, the noise of big machinery. But aside from size, the notable thing about these organs was the way they controlled all the power at their disposal, shaping it into a musical experience that somehow eluded, or elided, the established categories of musical life. As noted above, the star of the organ recitals at the Panama-Pacific was Edwin H. Lemare; the Englishman had first become famous on his own side of the Atlantic by playing two recitals a day, over a hundred in total, on the one-manual Brindley & Foster organ at the Inventions Exhibition of 1884 in London. Lemare should not be dismissed as a showman equipped with a swell box and overblowing flutes. He occupied, rather, some in-between space in which he was known for his own compositions, his many and widely used transcriptions for organ of orchestral scores from Beethoven to Wagner, and his efforts to popularize the baroque practice of improvisation, with the showman's trick of improvising regularly on themes submitted by members of the audience. Transcriptions themselves represent one of the key musical interactions that the expositions highlighted: a reflection of musical practices as a whole. Their purpose was clear. The inaccessible – whether because of difficulty or expense or simple lack of musical resources – must be made accessible. If an orchestra could not be assembled, then the score could be played by four hands at a piano or, far more thrilling, on one of the great organs that nineteenth-century technical innovations had perfectly equipped to serve as a virtual orchestra. Bands, whether military or commercial, served a similar function, bringing orchestral music not only down from the Olympus (if Olympus it was) of the concert hall but out into the great outdoors, where exposure to these altered versions of universally admired music was all the more easily achieved.

Oddly enough, the effect of the transcription, whether for organ or for band, was often to make something very large much smaller. Transcription is a way of playing with scales, both tonal and temporal, and nowhere was this more evident than in the case of Wagner, whose ubiquity in the repertoires of bands and organists and restaurant or spa orchestras all over Europe and America owed everything to a process of distillation and radical editing. Was the effect of all these things a dumbing-down of culture, a relentless race to the bottom, a bastardized cosmopolitanism that made a mockery of its aristocratic predecessors? The great avatars of the kind of musical experience the expositions contained – from John Philip Sousa to Victor Herbert – did not think so.[28] After the exposition was over, Lemare himself gave an interview to the *Los Angeles Times.* He had been appointed the municipal organist for the city of San Francisco, and the organ had been moved to a new Civic Auditorium. "Old and generally-accepted beliefs that the ordinary human, through lack of education, is unable to grasp music of the highest order, and that none but the musically learned are able to thoroughly appreciate good music, are fallacies," he said. "The public is the final court of appeal as to what constitutes good music, and if it says a composition is good that composition is good." Melody, thought Lemare, was the heart of "the greatest music," and "the musician who pretends to be superior to pure melody, such as that found in the old folk songs, has forgotten the origin of his profession." He continued, "It is not hard to hold the attention of an audience with the organ, for the reason that the less one knows about the music of the organ, *which is essentially emotional,* the better it can be enjoyed." And turning to the key point: "this would not be true of an orchestra because the attitude of an audience before an orchestra of pretension is unconsciously pedantic. Also full appreciation of the wonderful possibilities of orchestral music depends in a larger measure on technical knowledge." "I never play down to my audience," he concluded, "nor do I play so-called popular and ragtime compositions. The public as a whole doesn't appreciate that class of music. It bores, and the organist who persists in playing it will lose the respect of his hearers."[29]

"While Europe is engaged in the greatest war in history ..."

One can scarcely imagine a more effective defence of the *juste milieu* or of the cultural promise of democracy, nor can one quite imagine Lemare saying the same things to an interviewer in France or Germany. But can we be a little more specific about what such sentiments, and such musical offerings, had to do with coming to America as such? As the long nineteenth century came to an end in Europe in 1914 and carried on for this last brief Indian summer in the United States, the Americans knew with certainty what coming to the United States meant. It meant nothing less than the rescue of Europe from itself, the acceptance of the task of saving what the Europeans themselves were squandering on the battlefields of France and eastern Europe. As Charles Warren Fairbanks (Theodore Roosevelt's vice-president) wrote to the exposition organizers in 1915, "while Europe is engaged in the greatest war in history and is destroying the work of centuries, America is celebrating the fruits of peace upon a larger scale than ever."[30] Memoranda, newspaper articles, and all manner of official and unofficial reports concerning the fair dwelt on the theme of beacons of peace in a time of war. By special arrangement, American ships brought exposition wares through the Panama Canal from France, Italy, and even Austria, then carried toys for French children on their return voyage, then returning again, safely shepherded old Saint-Saëns to the fair as the "First Delegate to the Franco-American Commission for the Development of Political, Economic, Literary, and Artistic Relations." These ships were the markers of the displacement of cultural progress and hope from Europe to the United States. So, yes, the fairs were a paradigm of internationalism, and the musicians were among its most eloquent exponents, their national origins and the music they played fully on display but their ability to transcend the tensions among them the essential lesson the Pan-Pacific Exposition taught. From that perspective, the musical highlight was not the incessant performances of Amy Beach's "Panama Hymn" ("We join today the East and West, the stormy and the tranquil seas"), even though her reluctant departure from Munich and her subsequent defence of the Germans as misunderstood were certainly less controversial in 1915 than two years later in 1917. Nor was it Saint-Saëns's fantasia *Hail, California,* with its blending together of the "Star-Spangled Banner," the "Marseillaise," and Spanish themes and its deployment of the combined forces of the BSO, Sousa's Band, the Festival Chorus, and yes, the festival organ. Instead, one could argue that it was the appearance of Fritz Kreisler in the fall, playing concerts that included the works of all nations and accompanied by the near simultaneous publication, in an exclusively American edition, of his war memoir, *Four Weeks in the Trenches.*[31]

Long before the story of the Christmas Truce of 1914 was widely known, Americans could read his account of how Austrian and Russian soldiers, bogged down and cut off from their supplies somewhere near Lemberg/Lviv, came out of their trenches and shared food and tobacco, then went back to shooting each other, albeit in a desultory fashion. Kreisler's memoir unfolds without pathos or drama and ends when he is discharged from the army after receiving serious leg and head wounds in a Cossack attack on his line regiment. "My military service ended there, and with deep regret," wrote this world-famous violinist and composer, "I bade good-bye to my loyal brother officers, comrades, and faithful orderly, and discarded my well-beloved uniform for the nondescript garb

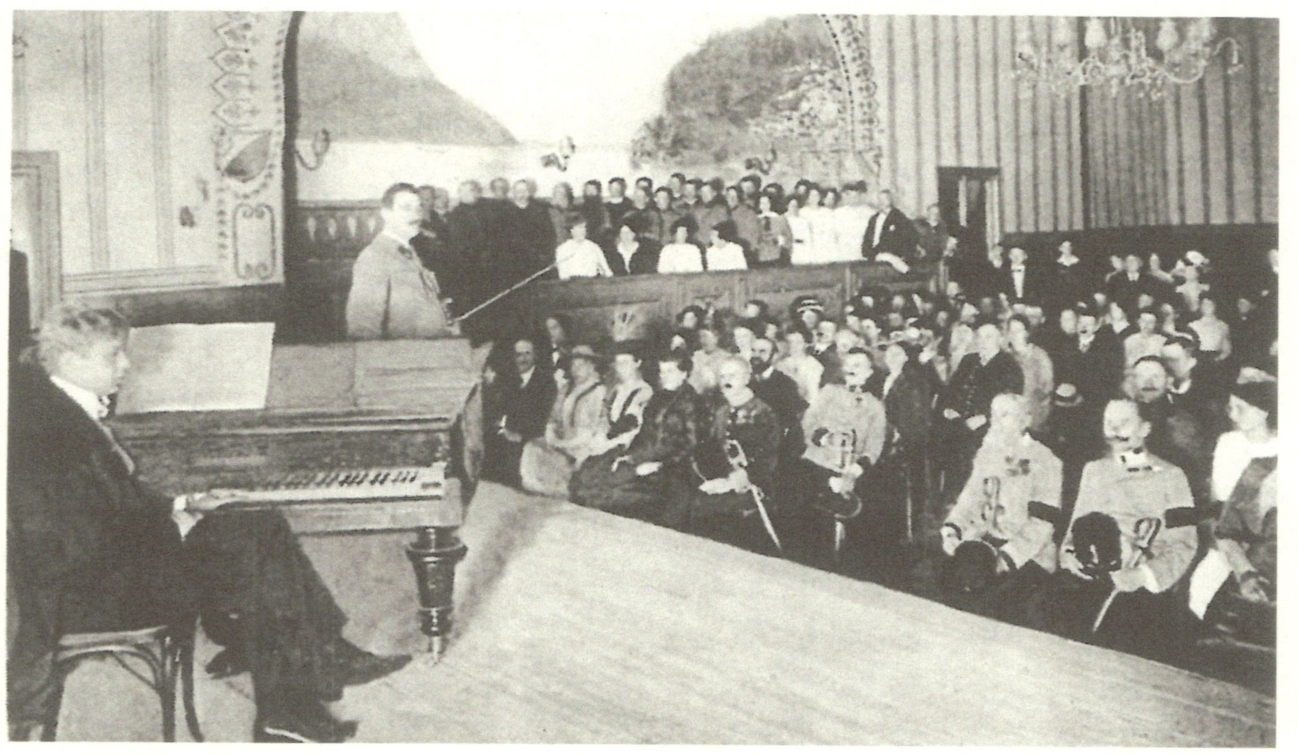

4.3 Fritz Kreisler, concert at Leoben in aid of the Red Cross before his departure to the front. From Fritz Kreisler, *Four Weeks in the Trenches: The War Story of a Violinist.* Courtesy of the Great War Primary Document Archive.

of the civilian, grateful that I had been permitted to be of any, if ever so little, service to my Fatherland."[32] Less than a year later he was standing on the stage of the Festival Hall in San Francisco, performing his signature showpieces "Liebesleid" and "Liebesfreud," a strangely appropriate pairing for the contrasts between Europe and the United States that the exposition sought to embody.

PART II

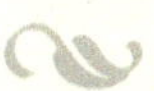

People

Chapter Five

Mendelssohn on the Road

In March 1837 Felix Mendelssohn Bartholdy waited in Frankfurt for the document to arrive from Leipzig that would provide the final legal basis for his marriage to Cécile Jeanrenaud – a formal letter from the city of Leipzig stating that he was both a legal resident and a bachelor.[1] Mendelssohn was an unlikely potential bigamist, given that he had been in the public eye since about age sixteen. But the requirement to prove a settled domicile, a place where one could be known and judged, gestured to something important about the Europe in which Mendelssohn made his living as a musician. That a person born in Hamburg and raised and educated in Berlin should have had a job and a house in Leipzig and have plans to wed the daughter of a family from Frankfurt attests to more than the dispersal of the descendants of Moses Mendelssohn and, by extension, to the Jewish experience in German Europe. It reveals also the nature of a professional musician's career. That particular set of places – Hamburg, Berlin, Leipzig, and Frankfurt – merely scratches the surface of Mendelssohn's musical travels in what would have been, but for his untimely death, a long and peripatetic career.

Travelling Musicians

This chapter's focus on Mendelssohn's life pursues further the subject of an earlier chapter, that is, the cultural work that the centuries of incessant travel by European musicians have performed. As discussed earlier, this work is easy to miss, given its obvious practical purpose in getting musicians to where they will perform or find musical employment. By looking at musicians' travels from a more cultural viewpoint we illuminate how national communities took shape and functioned through cultural exchange, where musicians dramatized the existence of the nation by representing it outside its borders.[2] Such observations fit well within our reigning paradigm of national constructivism, and historians and musicologists now routinely include music among the representational phenomena that have shaped a sense of the national belonging. Stories about nations, just like those about empires and diasporas, involve displacement and "tangled cultural experiences," "impure, unruly processes of collective invention," and continual moving among places and crossing over borders.[3] The travelling musician remains a key figure in our understanding of groups that formed around music-making and found sources of identity in it.

The travel of musicians transmitted knowledge, both practical and theoretical, which in turn made possible the development of new musical styles, instruments, and institutions, all of which themselves became part of a self-sustaining process of continual change in all of its parts – self-sustaining only because of and through and with travel. Travelling musicians also fulfilled social needs: to entertain people, to enhance worship, or to accompany public ceremonials of one kind or another. Over the centuries these three overlapping domains of music-making created the normal ways in which people wrote, performed, and heard music in Europe, and these regularities did not exclude a certain amount of geographical mobility, even though they did not encourage it either. The result was that music-making became less and less an itinerant trade, and musicians were able to settle down in towns and cities and train their children in their profession. Nonetheless, they never entirely gave up the fellowship of the road and its less than respectable associations. In the modern period of nation-states or emerging nation-states musical practices helped to make these imagined communities into actual ones, and the travelling musician became an especially potent representative of national identities that had little to nothing of "official" culture about them. This presents us with a muted paradox. Musical interchange, within and among nations, was certainly all the more rapid and pervasive because of the non-linguistic nature of music. However, the people who engaged in it were not wordless, nor were those who listened, organized, and wrote about performances. Thus, through multiple means, national discourses intertwined with musical practices, not necessarily to the detriment of either – indeed, for most of the long nineteenth century to the benefit of both.

At the simplest level we can say that this intertwinement illustrates a truism, that music is a social practice, as well as a repertoire, and that as a social practice it engaged in European social and cultural development altogether. Still, there is nothing simple about the ways in which music engaged society and certainly nothing merely reflective about this relationship. People made and maintained the international networks that helped to define the national in music. Music was never a definitive boundary among nations, yet through the play of national stereotypes expressed in musical form we find it reinforcing national borders even while crossing them. These ways of thinking about nations defined as much through external relations as internal essences provide us, then, with a way to gain productive critical distance from the kind of nineteenth-century musical idealism that saw the importance of music and indeed of musical travel in precisely its ability to tear down the Tower of Babel and create something transcending petty divisions of language and custom. As cultural historians we are in the business not of labelling such notions right or wrong, naive or disingenuous, but of understanding their relation to actual contexts in which musical practices developed.

National Character in Musical Life

In that spirit Felix Mendelssohn provides a vivid embodiment of the capacity of musical travel to define and strengthen national communities by travelling among them – a community building for which "internationalism" or "cultural internationalism" seems the appropriate term.[4] This is not necessarily a native category, and were one to look for one, the term "cosmopolitanism" might seem a more obvious choice. Many people in Mendelssohn's time used the word *cosmopolitan* to characterize the musical world but often in derogatory terms that referred to a kind of urbane, showy style (of music, of life) associated, above all, with Paris. Take, for instance, the remarks of Ignaz Moscheles, the great Prague-born pianist, close personal friend of Mendelssohn, and his main connection to (and entrée into) London musical life. "Why is it," he wrote to a friend, lamenting the apparent inability of the Parisian public to appreciate the German violinist Ludwig Spohr, "that Spohr cannot arouse any general enthusiasm in this place? Does the French national pride not allow them to give praise to any violinists other than their own? Or could it be that he is too uncommunicative, too detached for the cosmopolitan taste of the Parisians?"[5]

His words reveal the extent to which musicians were acutely aware of national characteristics, especially as they affected the musicians' ability to attract paying audiences. Moscheles suggests two possible reasons that a musician might appeal to the public: first, simply by being of the same nationality – this we can call the chauvinistic or, more charitably, the patriotic appeal – and second, by being a cosmopolitan, which for Spohr, according to Moscheles, would have been a matter of abjuring any national colouring and embracing pure showmanship. Moscheles approved of neither of these musical relationships to nationality.

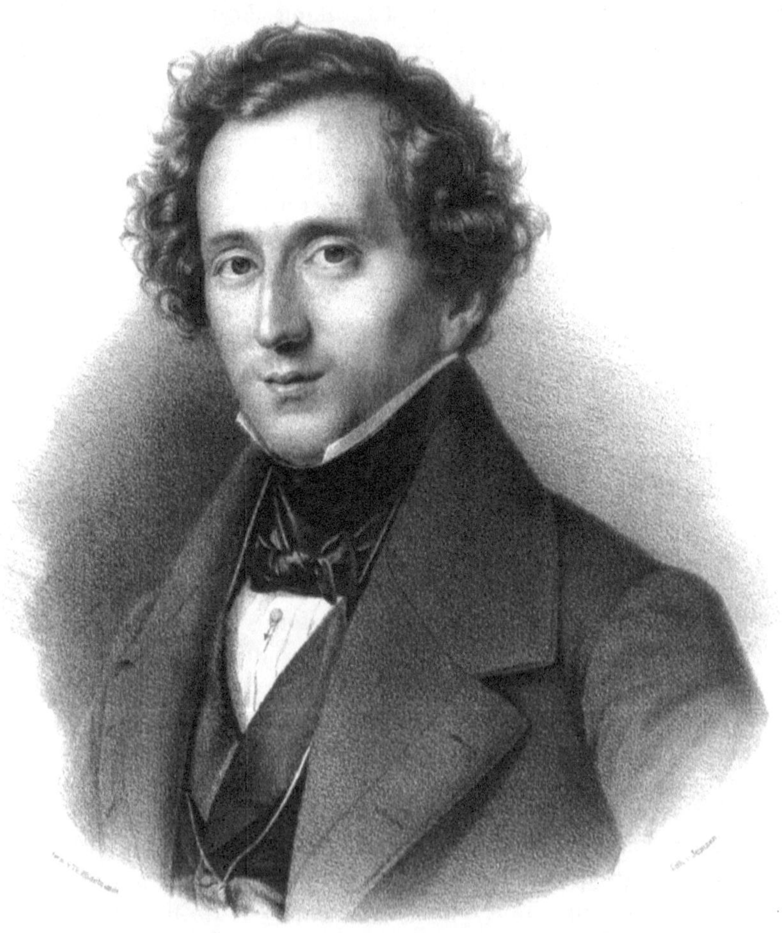

5.1 Felix Mendelssohn Bartholdy, c. 1837. Lithograph by Friedrich Jentzen, from a painting by Theodor Hildebrandt. Frontispiece in the *Allgemeine Musikalische Zeitung* (Leipzig), 1837. Wikimedia Commons.

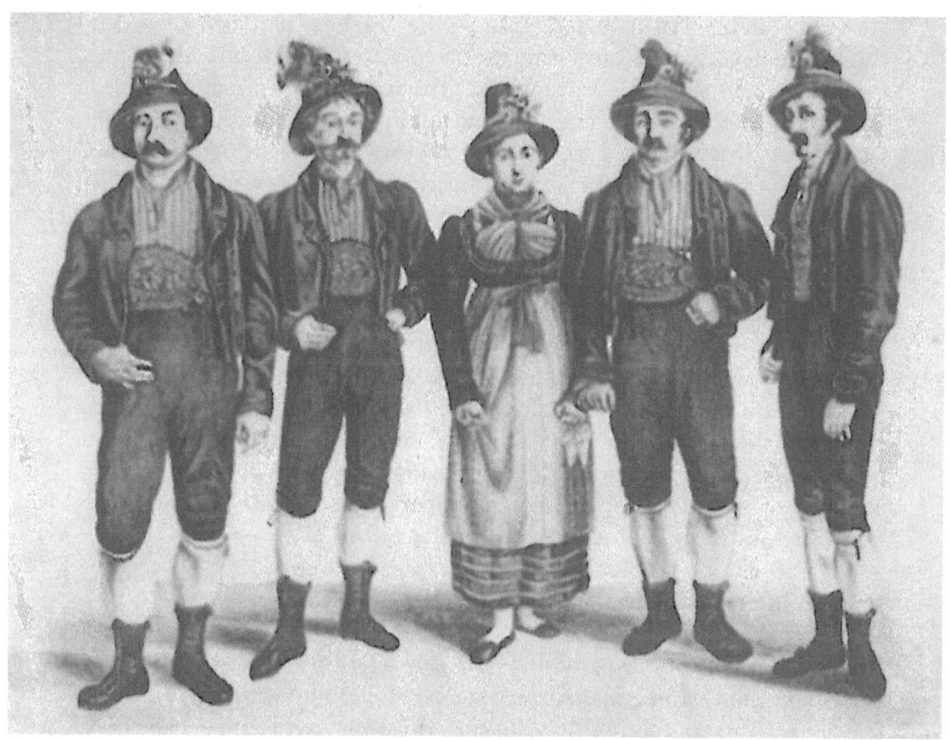

5.2 The Rainer Family of Tyrolean Singers. Lithograph from their English tour of 1827, printed by Vowles of London. Courtesy of the Museum in der Widumspfiste Fügen, Tyrol, Austria.

Hovering behind these two – the chauvinistic and the cosmopolitan – were another two possible relationships to nationality in one's public persona. The first was for musicians, especially touring ones, to represent a distilled version of their nationality – Jenny Lind, the "Swedish Nightingale," for instance, or a family of Austrians from the Zillertal who came to London peddling their Tyroleanism. The Rainer Family ("Geschwister Rainer"), who sought Moscheles's help in setting up concert dates, were the Trapp Family Singers *avant la lettre*, and London society was quite taken with them, their folk songs, and their costumes. Moscheles, invited to Kensington Palace to play for Princess Victoria, wrote in his diary, "The ladies and gentlemen took a friendly interest in my playing, but I think they enjoyed most of all my improvisation on some of the now very fashionable Tyrolean songs, since the Duchess had already invited the Tyrolean singers to her home on two occasions."[6] Moscheles seemed tolerant of this sort of entertainment, though it was not his own mode of musical existence. We might call it the appeal to national character, which was closely related to, in some sense the same thing as, musical exoticism – Spanish dancers, whirling dervishes, gypsy bands, and all the many manifestations that such exoticism could take.[7] Mendelssohn, though deft at incorporating an appeal to national character into his compositions (e.g., his Scottish and Italian symphonies), regarded its use as a marker of personal identity with considerable impatience. In a letter to his family in 1829 from one of the places on earth most prone to exploiting the charm of its musicality, that is to say, from Wales, his exasperation burst forth in the first line, "No more national music!" "Ten thousand devils take all this folksiness," he continued, "in every reputable tavern, a harpist can be found playing some so-called folk melody, which is to say, dreadful, vulgar, badly played junk with a hurdy-gurdy churning out more melodies in the background."[8]

Musical Internationalism and the Anglo-German Symbiosis

There is also a fourth possibility for the relationship of musicians to their nationality, and it is the one that Moscheles and with him Mendelssohn, his close companion in all things musical, represented and strove all their lives to uphold. It involved a definite consciousness of national identity, marked by recognition that one worked within a national tradition of which one was proud. Nonetheless, it also acknowledged the value of other traditions and a commitment to working within an arena of cultural activity and interchange that was at least European in scope (and increasingly North American as well).

This relationship of music to nationality should rightly be labelled musical internationalism, given that the very word *international* acknowledges the existence of the national as the essential unit of interchange. In the majority of cases the people for whom this term is apposite were men and women of broad training and relatively broad horizons, many of whom travelled a great deal among the nations of Europe and beyond. Nevertheless, they felt themselves to be and were perceived as being the representatives of a national tradition. Whenever a widely celebrated musical figure, such as Robert Schumann or Johannes Brahms, worked within a relatively confined geographical area, it was worthy of notice. The fact that they travelled less than had Mendelssohn did not reflect their chauvinism but something more like discomfort, dislike of travel, even existential insecurity. In any case Mendelssohn was a major musical figure who travelled incessantly, exhausting himself in work and work-related travel. The work this travel did, beyond the outpouring of performances and compositions and friendships that it certainly produced, was to consolidate the German musical tradition and musical institutions at home and to strengthen what R. Larry Todd has called "a German-English musical axis connecting Leipzig and London" or what we might call, switching from a mechanical to a biological analogy, the Anglo-German symbiosis.[9]

One of the most striking features of European political and cultural life in the eighteenth and the first half of the nineteenth centuries was the ever more extensive and dense network of ties between the German states and Great Britain. These ties were various, pervasive, and consequential, so much so that the question of why all of them eroded, allowing the two countries to drift catastrophically apart in the last decades before war in 1914, is one of the great questions over which historians have laboured for more than a century.[10] In the formative period in which the institutions, practices, and repertoire of modern musical life took shape, the British and German people were bound together by many dynastic, cultural, religious, and economic ties in which things musical were completely intertwined.

But intertwined does not necessarily mean symbiotic. A symbiotic relationship can take three forms – mutualism, commensalism, and parasitism. These concepts are easily abused; accusations of parasitism, after all, were an essential part of the calumnies later levelled against Mendelssohn by Richard Wagner and his followers. However, the first two less historically burdened terms can be of some use in thinking about the nature of musical ties between two distinct groups of people. It might make sense, for instance, to regard the musical relationship between the English and the Germans as a commensalist one, in which one side benefited from the arrangement while the other was neither harmed nor helped. If one wanted to see it that way, then one would argue that English musical life as a whole benefited enormously from a steady infusion of German musicians and German music into their collective musical life and that German musical life as a whole suffered no harm – moreover, individual Germans made out very well indeed. This trend started in the eighteenth century, when a significant number of orchestral players, together with composers, made their way to the country, sometimes permanently. In the oft-repeated words of Handel's contemporary and friend, Hamburg composer and music writer Johann Mattheson, "He who in the present time wants to make a profit out of music takes himself to England." "The Italians," he continued along the same lines, "exalt music; the French enliven it; the Germans strive after it; and the English give it its due."[11]

In the nineteenth century the numbers of German musicians working in the British Isles also included street musicians, whom Henry Mayhew included in his famous account of London's underclass. As conditions of travel improved, so too did numbers of itinerant musicians, ranging from the great virtuosi and celebrated conductors to the brass bandsmen who came over only for the summer.[12] Mendelssohn himself, of course, travelled to England frequently: ten trips over the course of his life, and every one of them musically significant for him and for his fervent English admirers. In the roughly two decades of sojourning in England he grew from an extraordinarily precocious and talented young man to the dominant figure in English musical life, appearing as pianist, organist, violinist, and, above all, conductor. He shaped musical places ranging from private salons to massive festivals, especially the Birmingham Triennial Festival, which became a key platform for the expression of his eminence and for which he wrote *Elijah* (premiered in 1847).

Counterfactuals are impossible to control, but it is still worth pondering what would have become of the English oratorio tradition without Mendelssohn's contributions of *Paulus* and especially *Elijah*. The least one could say is that he gave a new lease on life to the oratorio by rescuing it from endless repetition, invigorating it, giving it the incalculable effect of the new – the thrill of a premiere, the frisson of his foreignness – as well as the familiarity of his earnestness. The musical public in the nineteenth century did have a tremendous appetite for tradition and historical revival, and one would be hard pressed to find evidence that the English were showing any signs of losing interest in singing Messiah before Mendelssohn came along. Nevertheless, not only did Mendelssohn make historical revival glamorous, but he also became a key figure in transforming it from mere repetition into a living force in musical life. One of the first acts in his conducting career (and in some sense the defining act of his career) had been a revival of a major choral work. J.S. Bach's *St Matthew Passion* is not, strictly speaking, an oratorio; moreover, it never achieved the kind of mass popularity of the oratorios of Handel and Haydn. Nonetheless, its revival signalled a consciousness as essential to the mind of the nineteenth century as was its love of the new, and that was a consciousness of the present and the future engaged in an ongoing conversation with the past, a conversation that simultaneously limited and enriched what was possible. As the music historian Carl Dahlhaus once put it, the "century of revolutions was also the century of museums," a paradoxical phenomenon, the sense of which is an understanding that all that is new today will eventually pass into history, where it will not be dead and gone – quite the contrary – but a guide to all those who come after.[13]

One could argue that Mendelssohn's success in reviving the *St Matthew Passion* in 1829 had effects well beyond the Bach revival itself, already an extraordinarily multifaceted phenomenon. It made it possible, only six years later, for Schumann to write that his musical "attitude" was "simple": "to recall the past and its music with all the energy at our disposal, to draw attention to the ways in which new artistic beauties can find sustenance at a source so pure."[14] From this perspective Mendelssohn's composition of *Paulus* and *Elijah* (and much else, of course) made it clear that elements of the past could be incorporated into new ones, both giving the old a new life and enriching the musical idioms of the future. The German critic G.W. Fink, in an account of *Paulus*'s London premier, wrote that "the work is so manifestly Handelian, Bachian, and Mendelssohnian that it appears as if it really exists to facilitate our contemporaries' receptivity to the profundities of these recognized tone-heroes."[15] Mendelssohn's successful blending of historical and contemporary idioms, of baroque chorale and modern lyrical song, seemed to many reform-minded people (not least his hard-to-please father) the sort of reconciliation they envisaged as the stable yet progressive point between the calcification of restoration and the chaos of revolution.[16] Thus, when Abraham praised his son for solving "the problem of combining ancient conceptions with modern appliances" (as pithy a statement of Berliner reformist historicism as one is likely to find), he was thinking about society and political life as well.[17] *Paulus*'s resonance in English public life was differently shaded, but in all European countries the challenge of reconciling tradition with modern dynamism shaped the politics of culture and the culture of politics. Mendelssohn's music, especially the oratorios, enjoyed their critical and popular success in precisely that field of significance.

Another avenue for answering this unanswerable question of what the English oratorio tradition and English musical culture as a whole would have been without Mendelssohn's contributions to it would be to attempt to place these works in relation to all his other compositional and conducting activity in Great Britain. Here the point to emphasize is that Mendelssohn's example demonstrated that serious instrumental and choral music need not be regarded as separate domains, the latter especially relegated to a slightly lower status as a source of pious uplift for the middle-class amateurs and their audiences. Mendelssohn, unlike any other figure in English musical life, bound together its disparate and at time warring parts. Historians Simon McVeigh and William Weber have outlined the tensions in British musical life in the first decades of the nineteenth century, McVeigh going so far as to call them "culture wars" among the patricians of the Concerts of Ancient Music, the bourgeois and educationally serious Philharmonic Society for orchestral music, and the more evangelical Sacred Harmonic Society's devotion to moral uplift through oratorio singing.[18]

What seems clear, though, is that Mendelssohn's arrival into this contentious scene in 1829 and his subsequent and frequent visits played a major role in calming the troubled waters and creating a remarkable consensus about the kind of music that would be played. The repertoire ranged from chamber music that could be heard both at the somewhat snobby venue of the Musical Union and at the Popular Concerts, which reached a shilling public; a symphonic repertoire that ranged from (again) the highbrowed Philharmonic Society concerts to the gigantic undertakings of the exhibitions and the subsequent Promenade concerts; an oratorio repertoire whose performers ranged across a spectrum of classes and religious tendencies. For most of Mendelssohn's life and for many decades after he died British musical culture was varied but not venomous and had many venues and kinds of performance and a great deal of music criticism and reportage, all marked by a basic acceptance of the value of free markets as the context for artistic, as well as commercial (not that the two were distinct), undertakings. It is difficult to imagine this kind of overall consensus about musical value emerging without the peripatetic figure of Mendelssohn, who was travelling not just to the British Isles from a part of the world whose thought and music were already highly regarded by the British, but also around the British Isles, inscribing parts of it, both geographical and literary, into his very compositions (the "Hebrides Overture," the *Midsummer Night's Dream* music, and so on). Few other figures in British musical life of that period had the geographical and the musical reach of Mendelssohn, and withal he remained a gentleman and a Protestant – both perhaps as essential to his mediating role as his constant movements across space and time.

The case for the Anglo-German symbiosis as a kind of commensalist relationship might then be summed up as follows. From Handel to Haydn to Mendelssohn to Charles Hallé (aka Karl Halle of Hagen, Westphalia) to Max Bruch to Hans Richter, including also the countless forgotten jobbing musicians and street musicians among them, England's experience of both classical and, increasingly, popular music was enriched and shaped by the presence of these musically talented Germans, who often seemed to contemporaries to be compensating for some mysterious failure of the English to be sufficiently musical themselves. Moreover, in some loose sense, this is how the English and the Germans themselves tended to regard the case in the nineteenth century: a matter of compensating symbiosis. In the words of Mendelssohn's admirer and friend Henry Chorley, delivering a series of lectures titled "The National Music of the World," the English had "never produced a great instrumental composer, neither a towering player on any instrument," and a journalist in *The Musical World* suggested that "no one in his senses would think of asserting that we have produced a Bach, a Handel, or a Mozart ... [as] our country grows no such men – they are a distinct race of beings."[19] The English needed the Germans, in other words, and looked to them for musical leadership.

Over the course of the nineteenth century English musicians did from time to time organize to promote their own agenda, as in the case of the founding of the Society of English Musicians in the 1830s. In such moments English musicians made arguments that suggested that they at least thought the relationship of Germans and all foreigners to the English musical scene was closer to one of parasitism than mutual benefit. Foreign musicians allegedly monopolized the salons and the commercial venues alike, preventing English musical talent from ever receiving a fair hearing.[20] Yet no one really followed through on such complaints with any measures of musical protectionism. London in particular became the shining example of what free trade in musical talent, an open market for musical consumption, and the careful infusion of patronage and knowledgeable guidance into the whole scene could produce – that is, a vibrant, varied, innovative range of musical offerings, including the most demanding and excellent as well as the most easily digestible. Still, as late as 1895 a music critic lamented the "almost invariable lagging behind the age on the part of our musicians," whose new works sounded as though they had been written a half-century earlier. Revealing the continuing strength of the Anglo-German symbiosis, he urged his compatriots to "let Mendelssohn's words be ever borne in mind: '... The only things that interest me are new compositions.'"[21]

Nevertheless, to see the Anglo-German symbiosis as a relationship in which all the benefit was to the English and all the travellers were German leaves out any benefit to German musical life that might have resulted from the English enthusiasm for its representatives. Even if we acknowledge that individual Germans gained enormously – in their own compositional and professional development and their financial security – from the English connection, it still remains for us to think about the implications of this relationship for German musical life as a whole, which were considerable. To call this relationship, then, one of mutualism is simply to emphasize its transnational character, where music participated in a wider process of exchanges and circulation of ideas, inventions, policies, goods, and services across and among nations in the nineteenth century. Money, in other words, was not the only thing changing hands between the English and the German musicians and musical publics.

We can see this exchange operating on two levels, one abstract and the other more practical. To consider the practical, first, the clearest case of mutual benefit is the oratorio – the oratorio understood not just as a genre and a set of musical works within that genre but also as a cultural practice. That brings us at least briefly to the figure without whom the entire Anglo-German exchange would hardly have had the weight it did – the artist originally known as Georg Friedrich Händel. As described in an earlier chapter, the first large-scale choral performances of any sort, immediate ancestors of the immense number and variety of choral gatherings in the nineteenth century, took place not on the Continent but in England and grew out of a congeries of Anglican musical rituals that had crystallized by the mid-eighteenth century around the Lenten performances of Handel's new oratorios. In 1784 choirs and choral societies travelled across England to sing *Messiah* in Westminster Abbey. Only in retrospect and only disingenuously could Germans try to claim that there was anything especially German about these origins – the oratorio, as genre and as practice, belonged to the English, and at least two German men were deeply impressed. The first, Johann Adam Hiller, had a varied career as composer, theorist, pedagogue, and impresario, but is remembered mainly as the man who brought Handel back to the Germans. In 1786 he produced and directed the first full performance of *Messiah* in German-speaking Europe, in the Berlin Cathedral, then subsequently in a number of other musical centres in north-central Germany.

At around the same time, an incomparably more famous musician, Joseph Haydn, had an opportunity to make two extended trips to London, where he wrote and conducted new symphonies for his enthusiastic public there. During this happy time for him he was deeply impressed by the English fervour for Handel's oratorios, and he himself attended the last of the huge Handel Commemoration festivals in Westminster Abbey in 1791. "He found," as the great émigré musicologist Karl Geiringer interpreted him, "a whole nation aroused by compositions offered in monumental performances ... [and] desired intensely to write as Handel had written, works meant for a whole nation."[22] This meant, among other things, composing not just for the cultivated aristocracy but also for the large and growing middle class and, geographically speaking, for a musical audience that extended beyond Vienna to every corner of the German-speaking world that published music in the German language would reach. This meant, in short, composing for Germany. So when on his second trip he was handed a libretto in English on the subject of the creation of the world, fashioned from bits of Genesis and John Milton's *Paradise Lost,* he had it translated into German – "clothing the English poem in German garb," in the words of his translator, Baron van Swieten – and set it to music.[23] He then had the text, so artfully matched to the music, translated back into English – the whole procedure being both a metaphor and the actual marker of a unique process, that of the first large-scale work conceived for and written and circulated in the transnational space of Great Britain and German-speaking Europe.

Choral directors and their choruses and audiences in both places duly took up *The Creation,* and each had reason enough to see the work as peculiarly theirs. For the English, the echoes of the English of Milton and the King James Bible, even though compromised by the back-and-forth of the translation process, were enough to prove its essential Englishness quite apart from Haydn's source and site of inspiration in Westminster Abbey, ringing with the sound of Handel's *Messiah.* For their part, the Germans, whether north or south, Catholic or Protestant, regarded Haydn and all his works as their own. Carl Friedrich Zelter, the leader of the first amateur choral society in continental Europe, Berlin's Singakademie, found additional evidence of *The Creation*'s (or rather, *Die Schöpfung*'s) Germanness in Haydn's musical engagement with the legacy of the composer increasingly regarded as the greatest *German* of them all, Johann Sebastian Bach. In words that foreshadow Mendelssohn's own use of historical tradition – and indeed, as his composition teacher, one would be justified in calling this a matter of influence rather than anticipation – Zelter praised Haydn for "noble and clear" fugal work throughout the piece. "The man who has left all his contemporaries behind him, with all his genius and his eternally fresh and youthful richness of invention," he wrote, "is not ashamed to adorn his works with contrapuntal beauties, and as a result, despite all the changes of time and fashion, they will remain immortal so long as music lives."[24]

The amateur choral movement in both Great Britain and Germany was one of the principal and underappreciated supports of transnational exchanges in the long nineteenth century and certainly one of the major sources of reception and dissemination of the Anglo-German symbiosis. Amateur choruses in Great Britain, Germany, and elsewhere came in all shapes, sizes, genders, and places, but dispersed and diverse though they were, they gathered – musically and spiritually – around a common repertoire, at the core of which was Handel, then Haydn, then Bach, and soon Mendelssohn. They also shared a common set of practices, among which the most nationally significant were choral festivals. The number, size, and purposes of the festivals expanded enormously over the course of the nineteenth century, crowding its civic calendars with commemorative and contemporary celebrations of composers, monarchs, events, and inventions too numerous to recount. From the continuous oratorio performances (in a regular rotation of Handel's *Messiah,* Mendelssohn's *Elijah,* and Haydn's *Creation*) that accompanied the Great Exhibition of 1851 to the 3,000 Orphéonistes who descended on London in 1860 for friendly international competition, to the exhibitions of "Welsh choral prowess" displayed annually at the Eisteddfodau, to the chorus of 10,000 and orchestra of 1,000 that gathered in Boston for the National Peace Jubilee and Musical Festival of 1869 (and sang excerpts from Handel, Haydn, and Mendelssohn), nineteenth-century singers left behind an impression of constant motion and tireless enthusiasm.[25]

In German Europe, after Hiller's pioneering but singular festivals, the first in an enduring series of large-scale events began in 1810 in Thuringian Frankenhausen and featured Haydn's *Creation.* In 1818 the repertoire of what would be a long series of Lower Rhine festivals, this one in Elberfeld, centred on Handel's oratorios. This choice did not preclude the performance of oratorios and smaller-scale choral works by other composers – Haydn's *Creation* and *Seasons* chief among them, as well as works by Reichardt, Beethoven, Mozart, Spohr, Weber, and Schneider – in short, oratorical Germans, most of whom were following in the Handelian footsteps. In 1836 the Lower Rhine Music Festival was the site for the premiere of Mendelssohn's own *Paulus,* a work that owed more musically, perhaps, to Mendelssohn's engagement with Bach but as cultural practice owed everything to Handel and the English. *Elijah* is, of course, even more an English work, written for the English, its libretto honed by an English speaker (in contrast to awkward translations of the *Paulus* text), its musical language less Bachian, more Handelian, but, as Todd has written, this was a "historicism blended subtly into the composer's mature style."[26] Mendelssohn was planning to direct its premier in a number of important German musical centres at the time of his death; it never really established itself after that, not to the extent it did in the Anglo-American context. Nevertheless, the English connection had by this time done its cultural work in Germany to the extent that one cannot truly speak of a German oratorical tradition at all but only of an Anglo-German one.

The oratorio and its institutions amount to a concrete example of the more abstract notion of a nation, however construed, benefiting from the engagement of its native-born musicians in a larger world. In addition, that benefit (to come back to our initial query about the work that travel did) was to consolidate what in fact it meant, musically, to be German. Germans, especially, for whom a straightforward political understanding of their national identity was not available, developed a shared culture and sense of common purpose through many different registers – language, religion, economic activity, science, scholarship, art, and music. Not all these senses of Germanness were consonant with each other. Language differences, construed as dialect, continued to bedevil a sense of commonality well into the nineteenth century. Religious differences were a persistent and deep-rooted fault line, and music itself was diverse in its parts. However, for the German musicians who travelled abroad, their nationality seemed much less ambiguous or contested than it did back home. Likewise for those Germans who were reading in the press about their compatriots abroad – Haydn's triumphs in London were widely reported in the German-language press – nationality became clearer from this international recognition. From his first trip to Paris through the rest of his life, Mendelssohn's letters revealed his consciousness of being German despite or even because of his ambivalence about the movement for political unification as such. In Paris the thirteen-year-old was a young champion of Beethoven and Bach, his countrymen; in England, he became the very embodiment of German musical culture.

But there is more to the phenomenon. The concrete results of the Anglo-German exchange gave shape to German national culture – and not coincidentally. After all, the Handelian commemorations in England had been, in William Weber's account of them, *national* celebrations that stabilized the relationship between state, state church, and society; the imitation of them in German-speaking Europe did not produce exactly the same kind of phenomenon – how could it have done? – but it produced something like it, under the changed, more politically fragmented circumstances.[27] The festivals and musical performances, in which

Mendelssohn in his lifetime played such a defining role, were in their own way national celebrations that expressed the relationship between the German musical past and its present and future and sketched out a role for music that made it, as it were, the chief negotiator in relations among localities and individual states, as well as in Catholic, Protestant, and Jewish musical life – at least for a while, because national consciousness changed and with it musical life, though perhaps less than one might think.

The Anglo-German symbiosis or the Anglo-German exchange, whatever we might want to call it, was also crucial in the creation and sustenance of something that went beyond English and German musical traditions and national traits. In writing earlier about the musician's relation to nationality I called that of Moscheles and Mendelssohn – and to them we could add nearly every composer or performer of art music of the nineteenth century (Berlioz, Chopin, Liszt eventually, Verdi, Gade, Grieg, Sullivan, Bruch) – musical internationalism. We might also call it, citing the philosopher Kwame Anthony Appiah, "rooted cosmopolitanism."[28] The cosmopolitan patriot is someone who can imagine a world in which a person is "attached to a home of her own with its own cultural particularities, but taking pleasure from the presence of other, different, places that are home to other, different people." Such a person would also enjoy travel while accepting the "citizen's responsibility to nurture the culture and the politics of their homes." Appiah was talking about a dream of a future beyond national hostilities, but he could just as well have been describing the dominant characteristic of art musicians of the long nineteenth century. The Anglo-German symbiosis was just one relationship within a series of intersecting and interlocking relationships among composers and performers and increasingly also among people who travelled to listen to serious music and to study it at European conservatories (especially German ones). Of course, middlebrow and popular musicians and music consumers also travelled extensively but perhaps to less nationalizing effect (though this is a question to be investigated). The kind of broadly European perspective on the past and future of musical traditions and their importance to the health and vitality of European nations (including those stranded in the Americas) tended to remain the characteristic of art music, that is, music with aspirations to permanence. Among these travellers, Mendelssohn must surely be regarded, in his lifetime and in our own retrospect, as one of the greats.

Chapter Six

A.B. Marx's Cosmopolitan Nationalism

In the past decades the study of nationalism and national identity in the musical culture of the nineteenth century has opened up new perspectives and threatened to close off old ones.[1] On the positive side, as Richard Taruskin noted approvingly in 2006, no one still uses the phrase "nationalism in music" to refer only to a stylistic gesture of folksiness employed by non-German composers, caught in the powerful undertow of German instrumentalism.[2] "Nationalism in music," as Taruskin's own influential entry on nationalism in *The New Grove Dictionary of Music and Musicians* amply demonstrates, is now widely accepted as referring to political purposes as well as stylistic gestures, to contexts as well as contents, to Germans as well as to everyone else.[3] Both musicologists and historians have made important contributions to the recalibration of the terms "nationalism" or "national identity" when used in reference to the musical world. The result has been a heightened sensitivity to the political and the social dimensions of music history and a greater willingness to put the tools of musicology, specifically musical analysis of particular compositions, to work in finding evidence for a composer's political or social awareness, not just for their secret love affairs, their numerological obsessions, or (most commonly) their purely musical designs.

But all this has been achieved at a cost. Few people want to resurrect triumphalist notions about the universality of music by German composers and/or indulge in a complacent belief in the pristinely aesthetic. Yet the attention to national contexts and national identities and the loss of faith in music's universality have worked to obscure the obvious fact of the non-linguistic nature of music, its evasion of what Benedict Anderson memorably called the "fatal diversity of human language" that makes possible and plausible the organization of people by nationality.[4] In the past music's non-linguistic character has helped to justify, among other things, musicology's greater attention to style and genre than to cause and effect, to time period rather than place, and to synchronic rather than diachronic explanation – in short, to the music itself rather than the circumstances of its composition and reception. But its non-linguistic character also underlay an assumption, one could even say an article of faith, that the community of musicians was an international one. Composers might be born in this place or that, and "schools" of composition may have clustered in places, alongside actual buildings where music was performed or taught, but performing and composing musicians were travellers, border-crossers, itinerants in a world where most people in most places and in most time periods have stayed put. Moreover, this belief characterized attitudes towards music and musicians up and down the social scale, low to high. One has only to think of the Pied Piper of Hamelin or the travelling Town Musicians of Bremen to understand how resonant in western folk culture is the image of the musician as a person with the uncanny power to leave a place behind. The internationalism of art music finds a vivid expression in the first pages of Edith Wharton's *The Age of Innocence*: "On a January evening in the early seventies, Christine Nilsson was singing in Faust at the Academy of Music in New York. She sang, of course, '*M'ama*' and not 'he loves me,' since an unalterable and unquestioned law of the musical world required that the German text of French operas sung by Swedish artists should be translated into Italian for the clearer understanding of English-speaking audiences."[5] English-speaking audiences, one might add, in North America.

But now that a great deal of analysis exists on how important national contexts have been to musical life in Europe, it is time to return to the long-assumed transnational character of music and look at it anew as well, from the perspective of a more broadly cultural history. Scholars today have available to them a rich array of concepts by which to analyse this supranationalism, as well as the nationalism, of musical culture in the nineteenth century, and some have already done so.[6] This chapter will consider the figure of Adolf Bernhard Marx (1799–1866), one of the most important musical writers and disseminators of musical knowledge in the nineteenth century. He illustrates how the effort to define the nation necessarily involved a broad engagement with other nations as well.

Marx is acknowledged, though by no means universally admired, as an important music theorist. He is also notorious for his attention to the German tradition, the greatness and dignity of which he advocated in his journalism, teaching, compositional treatises, and books on music for the general public.[7] Nietzsche accused Schumann of threatening German music with "loss of its voice for the soul of Europe and its descent to something dealing merely with the fatherland."[8] One might likewise say of Schumann's contemporary and sometime teacher A.B. Marx that his criticisms of French and Italian music and, more consequentially, his development of a system of musical composition and instruction that placed German instrumental works (Bach and Beethoven) at its centre, marked the descent of musical judgment from aesthetic independence into mere patriotism. But we need to be careful of any uninflected analysis of nationalism's influence on political or cultural activities. As Carl Dahlhaus suggested more than a quarter-century ago, nationalism in the nineteenth century "was seen as a means, not a hindrance, to universality," and further, a "strong national tint" was "not an obstacle to international recognition" but rather "almost always the vehicle."[9] In its context Dahlhaus's observation applied mainly to composers and their music, but the basic idea applies, with modification, to those who wrote about music (Marx was also a composer, though of little distinction). To make sense of the path Marx pursued in recovering the music of the past, reviewing the music of the present, and attempting to influence the musical life of the future, we should place him in the context of Europe as a whole.

Dahlhaus characterized nationalism as "the governing idea" of the nineteenth century," one that had transformative consequences for musical culture, but he also pointed out that "nationalism in fact underwent a profound alteration during the nineteenth century," from cosmopolitan and tolerant beginnings to "haughtily exclusive and even aggressive" endings, and thus the phenomenon needed more consideration than he could give it in a short, provocative essay.[10] The basic narrative line Dahlhaus reproduced is a familiar one, dating back to Friedrich Meinecke's classic *Weltbürgertum und Nationalstaat* (1907). But even if we all agree that the tenor of nationalism at the outset of the nineteenth century was profoundly different than at its close, the premise itself that one way of thinking or being or acting replaced or evolved into another one requires revision. In this context Prasenjit Duara's reconceptualization of the history of China and India outside the categories of "a linear, evolutionary history of the Enlightenment/colonial model" has important things to say to European historians. Pointing to a new kind of narrative of modern China, Duara challenges "the notion of a stable community that gradually develops a national self-awareness like the evolution of a species (History)." We better understand the history of communities, especially national ones, as a process in which "various social actors – often different groups of politicians and intellectuals" redefine the boundaries of community by a "deliberate mobilization within a network of cultural representations." Communities in Duara's analysis are not "well-bounded" but rather are marked by "various different and mobile boundaries that delineate different dimensions of life." Some of these boundaries are hard and cannot be crossed without violating the integrity of the community. Others are soft and easily crossed: "one or more of the cultural practices of a group, such as rituals, language, dialect, music, kinship rules or culinary habits, may be considered soft boundaries if they identify a group but do not prevent the group from sharing and even adopting, self-consciously or not, the practices of another."[11] All communities, he suggests, consist of a combination of hard and soft boundaries, each marking degrees of privilege and inclusion, intolerance and exclusion, and group cohesion and the capacity to change.

The terms Duara proposes for shaping our understanding of national communities help to explain the activities of musicians, music critics, and scholars such as A.B. Marx. Marx formed part of a larger, ill-defined group of intellectuals and would-be politicians, whose activities in the public sphere shaped German perceptions of what they shared only as Germans – the hard boundaries of community – and what they shared as Europeans or indeed as humans – the soft ones. That all such definitions and perceptions were in flux throughout much of the nineteenth century ought to go without saying, though the clichéd view that Herderian notions of national essence, once promulgated, shut down the possibility of a Europe-wide sense of cultural community in Germany has proven strangely persistent. But as Brian Vick has argued, putting Duara's insight into different language, even by 1848 "debate was still emphatically not about the construction of a culturally homogenous nation-state" and functioned "within the porous confines of a national identity still partly open." Hard-boundary making came later: "The oddly, often egocentrically elastic notion of German national character and of broad-based criteria for nationality generally would eventually funnel into the confining flask of a much more exclusivist and assimilationist ideology."[12]

In the case of music such hard boundaries arguably never fully took hold. Thus, both these perspectives help provide a context for A.B. Marx's consciousness of what "his" music, that of Germany, shared and did not share with the other nations surrounding, influencing, and influenced by it. Marx's writings show an awareness of the many different layers of community to which he belonged, ordered conventionally in his writings from the local to the national to the European to the universally human. On the one hand, he was in the business of defining, and thereby hardening, the distinctions among the art music of various European nations. But even while so doing, his participation in a public sphere, an *Öffentlichkeit*, that extended beyond the undefined borders of the German nation, and the ways in which he conceived of his work as an advocate of German music, of Bach and Beethoven in particular, kept these partially hardening boundaries, these "networks of cultural representations," from serving only an exclusive community of Germans. In Marx's writings over the course of his life, an awareness of nationality took place in a world of other nationalities.

Marx in Berlin

Marx's entry into the public sphere took place in Berlin, and his understanding of the meaning of art in society always carried the mark of these beginnings. Marx was twenty-one when he arrived in the city in 1821. Disillusioned with the study of law and looking with admiration on the "many-sided genius" of E.T.A. Hoffmann, he tried composing and writing, while pursuing further musical studies.[13] At the same time he threw himself into the intellectual life of this city of Hegel and Schleiermacher, reinventing himself as the first important exponent of Hegelianism in music criticism. A happy encounter with the publisher Adolf Schlesinger led to his becoming the editor of a new journal with high intellectual aspirations, the *Berliner Allgemeine Musikalische Zeitung* (1824–30). It had been almost twenty years since a music journal of such ambition had existed in the city (Johann Friedrich Reichardt's *Berlinische Musikalische Zeitung*, 1804–6), and in the interim the first sustained episode of political nationalism in Central Europe had taken place. Prussia's defeat in 1806 had imbued commonplace words such as "Vaterland," "Volk," and "Nation" with a politically aggressive and sacralized charge, and a nationalist discourse that promoted the hardest of boundaries between the Germans and the French had matured. The popularity of such rhetoric among urban populations was considerable; no one who frequented the educated circles of Prussian life could fail to have encountered this heightened consciousness of Vaterland. And while the opportunities for political activism diminished, most decisively with the Karlsbad Decrees of 1819, the promotion of cultural unity and national fulfilment through the consumption of culture and the contemplation of history remained.[14]

Marx's Berlin journalism fell within the nation-making project of German cultural exploration. It reveals both why people sought to make firm distinctions among allegedly national cultures as well as the difficulties they had in doing so. His journal became the finest music publication in the city, the mouthpiece of his efforts to raise the musico-national consciousness of Berliners. The Berlin in which Marx arrived had much weaker claims to musical distinction than the much smaller Leipzig, let alone Vienna. It had declined musically during the years of warfare and economic depression and had only one stage of any note, no concert hall, despite a steady growth in numbers of subscription concerts, and entertainment sheets that catered to the local appetite for theatre gossip. Marx's new journal began as it meant to continue, on a sustained note of seriousness – about the life of the mind, about art, and about music among the arts. His themes were few and frequently repeated. He believed that Berlin concert life was in terrible shape: "sunk nearly to the lowest level possible," a junkyard of "one virtuoso after another," possessing only "technical fluency, decked out in fashionable mannerisms." He objected to the performance of only short works or senseless excerpts of longer ones, to the relegation of instrumental music to opera intermissions, to the neglect of unfamiliar or difficult works of known composers or of great works of forgotten composers or of all the work of young, unknown composers. And he objected to gifted performers wasting their talents on trivial pieces and poor performers making a hash of difficult ones.[15] In one setting after another he instructed the reader in the ways of his musical universe, divided between profound and superficial music, between music of lasting value and music of ephemeral pleasure.

So familiar is this dichotomy to us today and so ubiquitous the efforts to deconstruct it, that it takes some effort to appreciate the work that went into its construction.[16] Marx described the task as one of "doing justice to the many artists and artistic accomplishments" that went unrecognized in times marked by the "to and fro of partisan clamor."[17] His calls for free debate on serious issues and his insistence on the need for leaders to sustain a public life of intellectual substance for the people amounted to a critique of political life and the Prussian state overall, especially the moribund public sphere of Prussia's capital. As he remembered them much later in life, Berliners of the 1820s had lacked independence of judgment. They had been frivolously cosmopolitan, liking music because it was fashionable and came from Paris or Vienna, and they had been narrowly provincial, liking music because it was written or directed by people with whom they were comfortable, as in the case of the hoary and, in

Marx's critical view, musically inept director of the Berlin Singakademie, Carl Friedrich Zelter. In both cases becoming national meant becoming independent but not chauvinistic. It meant not dismissing out of thoughtless patriotism the substantial talent and vision of Gasparo Spontini, the Franco-Italian eminence of the Berlin opera scene, and it also meant not rejecting the most recent work (*Euryanthe*) of a celebrated German, Carl Maria von Weber, just because the Viennese had found it boring.[18] Marx wanted the kind of community, then, that he hoped to build through reform of the musical life he conceived of as both national and therefore necessarily progressive.

Moreover, his means of bringing it about – editing and writing in a journal in order to shape public opinion – announced his politico-cultural sympathies as loudly as the particularities of what he wrote. For Marx, as for the liberal, educated Germans who saw themselves as participants in the project of nation-building, the all-important aspect of their work was its publicness. And the publicness that concerned them was not that defined by commerce – quite the contrary, in fact – nor that defined by state authority. It was instead, of course, Öffentlichkeit, the publicness that Jürgen Habermas identified as a space for the exercise of autonomous, rational judgment – a space in which "the mind was no longer in the service of a patron" and "'opinion' became emancipated from the bonds of economic dependence."[19] In theory the public sphere was "a politically and cultural neutral space of communication accommodating many voices," but in practice it meant more than that to liberal Germans, particularly in an era marked by as much censorship as the German states were subject to in the middle decades of the nineteenth century.[20] The vital charge of the public sphere can be felt in Marx's work as well, from the solemnity with which he inaugurated and closed his journal to the critically engaged tone he employed throughout. His journal would represent no faction but would serve as "a forum [*Sprechsaal*] for all, each to find there freely expressed views on artistic matters and on all matters of conviction."[21]

Neither progress, nor freedom, nor the common consciousness that was the essence of nationhood existed automatically. All had to be formed, "from the scattered lives of individuals" through the active moulding, shaping, and expression of public opinion, through activities in the public sphere.[22] And people had to be able, as well as free, to undertake such participation. In the case of music Marx believed that this entailed not just reading his journal but also attending good concerts and working to understand the significance that great and difficult music had in the life of the German nation and of Europe as a whole. When he finally left the editorship, closing down the journal at the end of 1830, he urged his readers to "stay true to the task" of striving towards "pure thinking and pure judgment of music" and expressed his "hope in the progress of art and of the German people."[23]

The *Berliner Allgemeine Musikalische Zeitung* proved only the first in a series of efforts Marx made throughout his life to educate the public and to reform musical life. Leaving behind journalism to preside over musical studies at the University of Berlin, he spent the next decades publishing influential works on music theory and composition that were translated into English and French and found readers in the United States as well. He also composed a great many songs and choral works, edited important historical editions, and helped to found the Berliner Musikschule, which later became the Stern'sches Konservatorium. He became the first to name and analyse the sonata form. He wrote important, thorough, and (to be sure) highly idealized biographies of Beethoven and Gluck. He also worked in a number of ways to promote progressive reforms in music education, arguing as he had done before that the great works of the past could be a "living memory" in service of the "new flowering" of art.[24]

In sum, his writings on music up to the time of his death made technical and general knowledge of music accessible to the lay musical public, inside and outside German-speaking Europe, and in that sense they served what had always been his broader purpose, that of building national communities – in particular his own – through aesthetic improvement. Like many of the nationalist intellectuals who lived through the springtime of peoples, his commitment to *Bildung*, aesthetic experience, and progress did not change as much as is often assumed. In 1855 he was still saying that musical learning could "purify [the learner's] feelings and inclinations without depriving them of their originality or individuality" and that without artistic culture, mankind would "come to a standstill, and relinquish the ideal to which we once aspired."[25] A decade later, in his guide to the performance of Beethoven's piano compositions, he wrote that art offered an alternative to "our workaday lives" and "lifeless industries" – "the promise of another life infused with imperishable fragrance, the life of inner feeling, higher contemplation, great achievements," and "justice and freedom and the well-being of people and nations."[26] To make sense of Marx's views of the German nation in a world of nations is thus to confront a liberal and surprisingly internationalist vision of national community that only the actual experience of nationhood undermined and, even then, never completely in the case of musical life.

Music of the Past and the German Nation

Marx's views about the centrality of the nation to his work of musical reform found a philosophical basis in his Hegelianism, the watered-down A.B. Marxist version of which survived Hegel's death and the subsequent struggles between Hegelians old and young. His efforts to distinguish between the ephemeral and the lasting in musical life reflected his interpretation of Hegel's ideas on the unfolding of human understanding (from the *Phenomenology of Spirit*) more than an engagement with Hegelian aesthetics, which Robin Wallace believes he knew but "chose simply to ignore."[27] Like Friedrich Rochlitz, the Kantian music journalist who sought to overcome Kant's ill-considered dismissal of music, Marx became the Hegelian who used Hegel's ideas to prove Hegel wrong about music's lesser status in relation to the other arts.[28] Whereas Hegel knew little of instrumental music and seemed to have had no notion of musical progress, Marx believed fervently that music did progress, specifically in its ability to express objective ideas and to contribute to the "mature culture of the mind."[29] The worst he could say of a piece of music, German or non-German, was that it provided a "mindless amusement of the senses" and "destroyed [the public's] capacity for more profound, more introspective listening."[30] The best he could say, as when he challenged the Berlin public to prove its mettle by listening to Beethoven's Ninth Symphony, was that a work was "too great, too rich and too deep to be grasped in its completeness and its full grandeur upon hearing it for the first time."[31]

His history of music was thus informed by a broader effort to demonstrate the seriousness of music's place in society, and he did not confine himself to German music. In his scheme each era of European music had a distinctive "consciousness," beginning with the religious era that allowed only writing about technical aspects of music and precluded any "engagement in the free play of ideas."[32] Music in its deepest origins was "sensual play" and became in the hands of the "old Dutch contrapuntists (and their followers in Germany, England, and Italy)," a highly elaborate game to "avoid monotony on the one hand and confusion on the other." Yet in Marx's account of musical progress this "harmless play with tonal forms" had within it the "original and inexhaustible source of art," literally the very breath of life, the "organic necessity of giving vent to our feelings in audible sounds" that would lead eventually to "the revelation of the inner life."[33] Before such revelation could emerge, an antithetical era of "pleasure in life for its own sake" had to follow, marked by "bravura singing and virtuosic performances," all for the pleasure of the ruling elite. Mankind (i.e., Europeans), weary of severity and "prophetic inspiration," sought "to make life on earth more easy and materially comfortable." Art "assumed a more personal, mild, and accommodating character."[34] But now, in his own day, a new era of musical endeavour had emerged, in accordance with the advent of rights and freedom for people in the political world. In it the "free and full life of individuals" began to take precedence over "religious interests" and "court pleasures," and art could become the "common wealth of the entire public."[35]

Marx's musical history was a history of European music in which nations did exist but the basic idea that shaped an epoch transcended national boundaries, affecting each national group equally. Yet Marx's efforts to account for the past of the present provided him ultimately with the larger framework in which he explained the necessity of nations for the future. As Brian Vick has noted, the liberal nationalists of the mid-nineteenth century, like Marx, believed that the course of history brought the advance of culture, from undeveloped to sophisticated institutions, increasingly "infused with spiritual, moral, and intellectual self-consciousness," from "unreflected" communities to national ones marked by a community of mind, a "spiritual national unity" in the words of the philosopher Jakob Fries, which could form the basis of more and more complex and participatory states.[36] For Marx, as for his nationalist contemporaries, the writing of history involved a critique of contemporary political life, and for him, as for them, the choice lay not between a Europeanist cosmopolitanism that was progressive and tolerant and a German nationalism that was exclusive and chauvinistic but between anti-nationalist, even to some extent cosmopolitan, reactionaries and nationalist reformers. Cosmopolitanism, as Marx repeatedly described it, derived from "intellect alone"; it also tended towards frivolity in spiritual and artistic life. As a holdover from an epoch in which the cosmopolitan, nationless aristocracy was dominant, it stifled "all feelings of nationality and independence" and underwrote a "dishonorable indifference ... which has so frequently proved the transparent mask of moral cowardice."[37]

For Marx, writing history served only as a pendant to active efforts to revive the music of the past, in which we see again the view held by contemporary nationalists that nations had to be lived to be real. The music of the past was needed to reform contemporary musical life and with it the nations of Europe. Marx's insistence that all the music of the past had a national character, well ahead of the historical unfolding of the national idea, reflects an unresolved tension between Hegel and Herder in his thought as well as the ulterior motives for his writing. These broad generalizations about history provided a framework for his advocacy of particular individuals who, trapped in the past and forgotten in the present, needed rescuing for the sake of the future.

His first and most extensive rescue mission involved recovering the music of Johann Sebastian Bach for the nineteenth century, a mission in which Marx was, of course, only one of many participants, most in German Europe, including Switzerland, but others in England. Marx came to realize the fullness of Bach's achievement through the work of the much younger Felix Mendelssohn and his early, private rehearsals of the *St Matthew Passion* in late 1827 and 1828.[38] Here, and in the revival performances of 1829, for which he wrote extensive explanatory and laudatory commentary, he discovered "the total vindication of everything this journal has advocated."[39] Marx's advocacy of Bach extended, deepened, and finally concluded the work he had set for himself in shaping public opinion through music journalism. He had long favoured more publication of musical scores from all eras and countries of Europe and had used his journal to draw attention to the availability of such long-forgotten works. The growing interest in Bach's music he considered "one of the most remarkable and profound developments in the cultural history" of music, the "sun of a new day in the fog of our times."[40] As for the *St Matthew Passion* itself, it represented "the full realization of the Ideal of composition."[41] In the progress of musical culture, studying Bach became, for Marx, an integral part of musical reform. To recover Bach was to restore musical life to its properly progressive course of development, out of frivolity, into profundity. In Mendelssohn's work of revival, he saw the sign that "our prediction of a new and more thoughtful period of music" had arrived: "Every word I have written on music, every resistance I have offered to the errors and delusions of our times, finds ... vindication only in the expectation ... of a time when the trumpery of today's fashionable shallowness ... will be cast off."[42] Bach's "importance to German self-understanding" stood now revealed in all its fullness.[43] And the public seemed to have understood, overflowing the performance hall not once but three times. Progress was at hand.

Music of the Present and the German Nation

The Berlin reception of the *St Matthew Passion* expressed for Marx a growing consciousness of German identity itself, because not only had no other nation produced a Bach but no other nation – or at least not the French one – was capable of appreciating him. In the "new and higher period of musical art" that had arrived Germany would no longer be "deprived of its greatest treasure" by its ignorant pursuit of the "lower sensuality of the Italians" and the "soul-less play of the French." Thanks to Marx's journal alone, he implied, the way had been prepared for the public to receive "this greatest work of German music."[44] Such revivals represented "a spiritual armament" in which "the German character" revealed itself "at its best" and in contrast to "French coldness and paralysis."[45] An anonymous contributor was even more explicit on the national significance of an immersion in Bach's work: "for finally the German recognizes the outstanding value of his fatherland and is filled with noble pride." In short, there was "no land in the world today in which true learning and art are more valued and more cultivated than in Germany."[46]

Marx's suspicion of things foreign sits uncomfortably alongside his interest in the music of all times and nations, as long as it was serious and good. It seems to suggest that chauvinism was all there was to Marx and that his effort to distinguish between the ephemeral and the eternal in musical creations amounted merely to an advocacy of the German over everything else. But to conclude this would be to underestimate the instability of the distinctions and boundaries he drew. Marx was not mainly interested in sniping at the Italians or the French, as though he clung to some irrational grudge against them as a whole. This was an accusation levelled against him in his lifetime, and he was always at pains to refute it, particularly in regard to Spontini, whom he praised, in measured ways, throughout his life.[47] He wrote, rather, from a sense of vulnerability to what seemed to him the dominance of Italian, French, and French-sponsored musical forms over everything German composers and musicians had created. As with other nationalists of his era, his view of history emphasized the centrality of struggle in the achievement of progress, and linked to that, the need to defend one's own nationality in an international arena of many nations. What Vick has argued was true of the delegates to the Frankfurt Assembly in 1848 – "the notion that … the German nation … could become the object of foreigners' contempt burned ulcer-like within these fledging national politicians" – characterized Marx as well.[48] The French had not understood or appreciated Bach (Marx had learned that much from Felix Mendelssohn); they did not respect the arc of musical development in central Europe of which Bach formed an essential part; and against all that contempt and indifference German honour and greatness must learn to assert itself. Boundaries must be hardened, to use Duara's terms, though in musical life never to the point of isolation or exclusivity.

Beethoven, of course, was central to this vision of active public engagement in defence of German music and had been right from the beginning of Marx's musical work: "next to Spontini," he wrote of his journalistic beginnings, "Beethoven stood in the forefront" of his labours.[49] Beethoven had moved music to a more advanced stage in its development, as Marx believed, and so he campaigned for more frequent, complete performances of Beethoven's works, especially his symphonies.[50] When in 1825 Berliners were able to hear Beethoven's Pastoral Symphony no fewer than four times, he noted approvingly that the audiences consisted not of "elegant society" with its "Parisian hats and Italian feathers" but of a "gathering of true friends of music and those who had the sense to want to become such."[51]

In a more general sense, Marx hoped that a heightened understanding of the role of nationality in human affairs would lead to greater independence of judgment and the fuller development of individual and national identity for which the times were ripe.[52] Music was crucial to the process of developing oneself and becoming national. His concern for the state of musical affairs in Berlin and in Europe reflected a broader concern for "cultural awakening" among Germans. To improve the capacity to judge music was to strengthen an understanding of what it meant to be German in a world of nations, and Marx's program for the educated public included first learning about all nations' music, not just that of Germany's Bach and Beethoven. He approved of the "greater diversity in the repertoire," which he attributed to "rapidly spreading education" and a "closer community with other nations."[53] He urged Germans to listen to as a wide a range of compositions as possible, from all nations, because musical works "have their true foundation in our time and in the spirit of nations worthy of our attention." "If we wish to understand our times and ourselves," he concluded, we must study them all.[54]

Marx believed also that the educated public understood much less about nationality's influence on music than it did about, for instance, national schools of painting or the differences between French and German tragedy. National differences, he argued, were not just a matter of "incidental traits, styles, or fashions." The truth was just the opposite, thought Marx: "every artist, every nation, and every age has had a peculiar manner in music, as in every other art, and in the conduct of life itself," and this truth has "always been evident to every one at all acquainted with history and man."[55] Both Italians and Germans may have had the

"the gift of artistic creativity," but general knowledge of the world could never advance on the basis of such banal observations. Real knowledge required "the recognition of differences," among the "temperature, the local manners, the mode of life, the state and religious circumstances, and so forth, of ourselves, the Italians, and the French." To deny such differences was to "lose consciousness of one's own intentions and tendencies."[56] To know others one must also understand oneself, and vice versa. An artist, like everyone else, was part of the "ideas and tendencies" of "his time, his nation, and the whole human race," and "every work of art" bore "an impression of a more general nature than that individuality."[57] The thoughtful lover of art appreciated the "boundless diversity" of artistic creations and recognized that "the whole development of language and art, the education, culture, mental condition and feeling" entered into the experience of even a single, simple folk ballad.[58]

Moreover, to be a great artist, Marx thought, one must be the vessel of one's nationality. This attitude had its good and its bad aspects. On the one hand, it underlay Marx's unfeigned enthusiasm for a wide range of composers and artists of all nationalities. He could follow up a lukewarm appreciation for the German singers Anna Milder and Henriette Sontag with an enthusiastic one for the Italian singer Angelica Catalani ("like the sun of her Fatherland"), thus holding himself aloof from the "German-Italian operatic war."[59] He could write frequently about his admiration for Spontini, Paganini, Rossini, Cherubini, and Auber. But at the same time he anticipated, in milder tones, Richard Wagner's notorious attack on Meyerbeer and Mendelssohn for their essential inauthenticity and lack of national character. In Marx's account, both had squandered their rich musical gifts, Meyerbeer because of his eclecticism and Mendelssohn because of his historicism. Meyerbeer, wrote Marx, had been "brought up in the German school," but then moved on to Rossini's style, Scribe and Auber's "scenic contrivances," and finally, back to the German, in the form of Weber's "mode of sound painting," his "delineation of local scenes and characters, and his "popular German tone." Yet despite his "astonishing talents and tact," he lacked one thing – "honesty, the honesty of an artist, which makes him elevate himself to his subject, with all sincerity and faithfulness." If Meyerbeer's sin was to live in too many nations – cosmopolitanism, in other words – Mendelssohn's consisted of empathizing too much with too many time periods, trying to reproduce for each their musical essence. His adoption of the "forms and style of Bach," his effort to evoke the spirits of Sophocles and Aeschylus, not to mention his inadequate imitations of Beethoven, all revealed a further regrettable tendency of the present, "when so many different ideas, opinions, degrees of cultivate etc. divide the people" and "an artist can no longer represent a nation" but becomes merely "the exponent of particular tendencies or interests."[60]

Marx's lifelong engagement with the problem of the nation in music yielded in the end the same conclusion, whether he was writing in 1824 or in 1854 – that Germany's contributions as a nation were underappreciated and to some degree also underdeveloped, both at home and in the world. Here lay the main purpose of his attempt to introduce the nation as a category of analysis in music. Marx, like German music writers before him and after him, observed a lack of balance in musical life, an unthinking preference for Italian music, an unhealthy deference to French musical leadership, and a corrigible ignorance about German music. "A proper cultural life will begin," he asserted, when as many German operas were produced on the stage as French and Italian ones and when singers were given the "knowledge and artistic comprehension" to appreciate "profound German music."[61] Marx also thought that German music was better, not just neglected. If people would only listen to more of it, then this fact would become clear to them too – so he hoped.

To some degree, then, Marx's sense of national identity betrayed the hardening of cultural boundaries and, as Sanna Pederson has noted, Hegel had something to do with this. Marx's disdain for Italian music fell within his quasi-Hegelian analysis of musical progress and the musical future: "Just as surely as we Germans stand intellectually higher than does Italy with its Rossini," he wrote in 1825, so too would Germans eventually demand "a higher music."[62] His references to national differences consistently associated transient pleasures with the Italian national character and seriousness with the German. "The German," wrote Marx, "is too serious, too much inclined to reflection, to be able to apply himself happily and seriously to something that will lead to no results."[63] The Italians, by contrast, tolerated ridiculous operatic plots and dispensed with harmonic development, all for the sake of beautiful melody, and the French, a people "of very meagre musical gifts," were "well entertained by cold, witty conversation pieces," valuing music "only as a superficial accompaniment" to such works.[64] How could it be a coincidence, he wrote in another context, that all Italian composers "dispense with harmony" and "subordinate instrumentation to the requirements of the singing melody"? How could it be accident that the Germans should develop the symphony "to the highest state of perfection," while Italy or France had contributed "as good as nothing" to it?[65] But the Germans were more than serious and instrumentally gifted. As Bernd Sponheuer has documented, Marx also refined a century-long discourse on Germanness in music in which the Germans became the culture that included all others, incorporating the best of all national styles into their own.[66] "German art," as he once put it, "is not exclusive but inclusive of Italian art."[67]

The Music of the Future and the German Nation

The question of national distinctions spoke, finally, to the future of music itself, especially among the Germans, who were the people best equipped to raise music to higher levels – and in turn to be improved by it. Part of this capacity in Germans came from their ability, unique among the nationalities of Europe, thought Marx, to cultivate "an equitable recognition of things foreign," which remained "the honor of our people." But an "equitable recognition" went both ways for Marx; the people of Europe ought also to recognize the greatness of German music. In the lazy listening habits of people Marx saw a vicious circle of incomprehension that threatened to stifle progress in musical life. If people, Germans or otherwise, listened only to Italian operatic music, which Marx considered a dead end in historical development, they would always regard music as merely entertaining. Just as melodic-polyphonic music had been of meagre intellectual value, so too, Marx thought, were "nearly all French and a great portion of our own national melodies, of nearly all Italian and French opera music, of most of our instrumental music, and particularly of our 'drawing room compositions,' which are as shallow and devoid of character as that 'society' under whose patronage they luxuriate and multiply."[68]

The search for deeper meaning in music would fail unless people listened to and played the best music, which lay largely but not entirely within a German tradition culminating in Beethoven. To appreciate the most important music was hard work, requiring education. Over the course of his life, Marx produced a number of texts meant to educate the general public towards just such musical appreciation. Not arbitrarily, the most important audience for his writings outside German-speaking countries developed in England, beginning in the 1840s. Interest in Marx's pedagogy there reflected a broader movement in the United Kingdom "to bring vitality and progress" to a near non-existent musical education in the schools and to rectify what was perceived as a corrigible ignorance about the musical "sciences" among the public as a whole.[69] The determination of a few continentally inclined English musical leaders to alter England's reputation as the "land without music" led them to seek out – mainly, though not exclusively – German music, musicians, and musical scholars. In such a context Marx played second fiddle to Felix Mendelssohn, who by the time Marx's work became known in England had become the dominant representative of the European musical tradition in England. That Marx was a friend of Mendelssohn (much less so than in the 1820s) was known to Marx's English sponsors and was not insignificant. One of his several translators and early supporters was Natalia Macfarren, née Clarina Thalia Andrae, the German-born wife of the English composer and friend of Felix Mendelssohn, George Macfarren. Marx's views about musical seriousness and moral improvement matched well the Victorian sensibilities of the most avid promoters of continental music in England. As Macfarren wrote in the preface to her 1855 English translation of Marx's *Die Musik des neunzehnten Jahrhundert* (*The Music of the Nineteenth Century*), "that music is a moral and intellectual demonstration, capable of exercising an ennobling influence on mankind, is undeniable," yet all the "talent and energy" devoted to it had so far had "but a superficial and devious result, which by no means satisfies the hopes that are fixed on this art as a means of happiness and civilisation." Marx's book, she asserted, "will point out the cause of this insufficiency, and show how the void can be filled up" and thus "must be welcome to every one who has any share in art."[70]

Among the latter, Alfred Novello (1810–96), the founder of a publishing house whose cheap editions of choral works were almost single-handedly responsible for the explosive growth of choral singing in Victorian England, was the crucial figure.[71] Besides the cheap editions, in 1844 Novello took over a short-lived periodical called *Mainzer's Musical Times and Singing Circular*, founded in 1842 by the travelling German musical pedagogue and priest Joseph Mainzer. Under Novello's direction, the *Musical Times* quickly expanded its reach, from covering "important musical performances" and "minor events" especially "with a view to what may be interesting to Choral Societies and Singing Classes" to concerning itself with all aspects of musical life, including, increasingly, music education.[72] A figure like A.B. Marx, in whom an outspoken dedication to social and self-improvement through music combined with an accessible, Teutonically opinionated style, suited Novello's purposes well. In 1854 Novello decided to launch a new publishing venture, *Novello's Library for the Diffusion of Musical Knowledge*, in which he proposed "to reprint a variety of standard Treatises on the Art of Music, written by the most esteemed English and Foreign Masters, at prices which will place them within the means of every student."[73] Marx's *General Musical Instruction*, a translation of his 1839 *Allgemeine Musiklehre: ein Hülfsbuch für Lehrer und Lernende in jedem Zweige musikalischer Unterweisung*, was the second instalment in the series, coming out a month after Novello's English edition of Cherubini's famous treatise on counterpoint and fugue.

Novello also published excerpts from Marx's book in the *Musical Times*, choosing parts of the final chapter in which Marx held forth on the benefits of song ("man's own true peculiar music"), singing groups (by which individuals "will feel themselves more intimately connected with society"), and piano instruction. Marx's advice on the latter was unequivocal: "Sebastian Bach and Handel, Joseph Haydn, Mozart and Beethoven – these are the artists to whom we owe the greatest and most numerous works of art for the pianoforte ... and upon the highest, the vast preponderance in estimation of these five named artists, there is not the slightest question among those who have the least tincture of art."[74] How decisive Marx's instructions were in convincing the English that the main "condition for good pianoforte teaching" was "that the works of those five eminent men shall be considered as the distinguished and governing lessons in the instruction" cannot be determined, though some combination of imported German wisdom and native English inclination gave English musical life a decidedly German sound. Whether that was as beneficial to the English as it was to all the German musicians who found employment in England is another question, though Marx would certainly have said that it was. As he asserted in this, his most widely read book in the English-speaking world, it was "not the possession of great artists, nor of great works of art, which insures to a nation or to its gifted individuals ... the full enjoyment and the highest pleasures of art" but rather "a true artistic education," of the sort he believed he could provide.[75]

Despite bouts of pessimism, he continued to believe that all people, regardless of nationality, could become active, responsible participants in this new age of nations. Responsibility, as far as Marx was concerned, meant seriousness, in particular the effort to understand art at a deeper level. As the years went by and he was repeatedly disappointed by the failure of his own very earnest, very mediocre compositions as well as by the continuing limbo in which German national affairs seemed to hang, Marx indulged in fewer, rather than more, diatribes against the French. He turned increasingly to Mazzinian rhetoric, seemingly outdated even as he deployed it, of nations coming together, each developing towards freedom and self-determination. His major declaration of his musical and artistic principles appeared in 1855, with the publication of *Die Musik des neunzehnten Jahrhunderts und ihre Pflege*, which he published, as he dramatically put it, "under the thunders of cannon, which roll, like the deep voice of prophecy, from Sebastopol even to the extreme edges of Europe." Music, the "most timid of all arts," seemed irrelevant to such martial times, but Marx intended to show its centrality to the present, when mankind has "stepped into the heritage of the last century, that is, the independent, self-conscious life of the people as nations." This heritage, he argued, "means universal brotherhood and the fraternization of all mankind in right, in liberty, in light, and in love."[76]

In the end Marx pinned his hopes on some final achievement of German unity, despite the disappointments of 1848–9. In his memoirs, published in 1865, he wrote gloomily about his "complete helplessness" in the face of the world's indifference to his mission. Yet in a typically Marxian abrupt about-face to mystical optimism, he declared, "but only on the outside!" Some "inner fruit" of all his work would someday come into being, "if only in the invisible treasures of the spirit." He continued, "If one day German opera is ever to achieve a fully satisfactory fulfillment, if the oratorio is ever in our times (in which the church has expanded to embrace a world stage) again to possess complete truthfulness, as it had in the music of Sebastian Bach's St Matthew Passion," then Germany must follow the path of Italy, where people had "finally won the freedom to develop their nationality and with it their moral and artistic powers." Only under such circumstances could the arts flourish.[77]

Still, the "present condition of nations, and more particularly of our German nation" suggested to Marx that "a new spirit of higher self-consciousness, of greater independence, of brotherly union and energetic moral energy" had been "awakened." This spirit, he concluded, "may indeed be stunned, restrained, misled, calumniated, or denied, but cannot be annihilated."[78] That Marx should have adopted such a determinedly internationalist tone at the end of his life suggests the difficulties of regarding even the most overtly German of music critics as someone engaged in the business of cutting off Germany from the rest of the musical world or, even worse, asserting German musical superiority over the music of every other nation. Particularism of the Marxian variety allowed him to achieve a position of universality, since all nations were part of the greater whole of humanity, and people could actively assert their membership in human society through their own national culture and its dissemination abroad. All nationalists, in that sense, sought to get beyond the nation, and Marx was no exception. Like Kwame Appiah's "cosmopolitan patriot," Marx was not unlike Robert Schumann and any number of other mid-century musical nationalists.[79] He lived suspended between the old and the new, avatar of a kind of national identity that allowed him, and others like him, to sustain in musical life the kinds permeable boundaries that seemed increasingly untenable in the life of the state. Anachronistic though this application of twenty-first-century cultural theory to nineteenth-century nationalists may seem, any larger effort to explain how European musical culture did not simply break up into warring national camps in the course of the century will surely founder if we do not acknowledge the existence of this middle, ultimately vulnerable, ground.

Chapter Seven

Schumann's German Nation

In *Beyond Good and Evil* Nietzsche observed that "it is characteristic of the Germans that the question 'what is German?' never dies out among them."[1] Moving from Goethe's "delicate silence" on the matter to Mozart and Beethoven's indifference to it, Nietzsche worked his way eventually to Robert Schumann and the German question. Schumann's "quiet lyricism and drunken intoxication with feeling," he suggested, made him "merely a German event in music, no longer something European, as Beethoven was, and, to an even greater degree, Mozart." On Schumann, he wrote, "German music was threatened by its greatest danger, the loss of its voice for the soul of Europe and its descent to something dealing merely with the fatherland."[2] Nietzsche's observations always represent a provocation, and it is rarely a defence against them simply to call him wrong. At the least, though, it is worth noting that he wrote this passage in the mid-1880s, when the national question was framed differently than it had been three decades earlier. Not only had the conservative or old right long since learned how to turn German nationalism to support their own agendas, but a new right, familiar to Nietzsche through the Bayreuth crowd as well as his sister and her husband Bernhard Förster, was developing a more populist politics of racial nationalism, which repelled him.

Still, the question remains: in the 1830s, 1840s, and 1850s, the three decades of his adulthood, *did* Schumann's commitment to the state of Germany and its cultural health "threaten" the loss of "Germany's voice for the soul of Europe"? How should one characterize, if not Schumann's voice, then at least his attention to the national community? Should we regard him, as Nietzsche ultimately did, as interested only – or mainly – in a narrowly German culture, with deleterious long-term consequences?

Or should we emphasize, as did a recent conference volume, his interest in and openness to the music of composers and cultures of many different nationalities, his reception in France or England or the United States, his enjoyment of his Dutch concert tour – if you will, his cosmopolitanism, or at the very least his identity as a European?[3] This chapter will suggest that neither of these characterizations (the national or the cosmopolitan) is accurate as one choice between two mutually exclusive alternatives. The very notion that we face an either/or situation here reflects the powerfully negative influence of Richard Wagner's polemic in "Judaism in Music" (and elsewhere), a work that attacked cosmopolitanism in the persons of its allegedly most prominent representatives, the Jews of Europe. Wagner, with no great originality, argued for the existence of only two kinds of art – authentic and inauthentic – produced by two kinds of artists: those rooted in a national culture and those lacking one. Wagner offered carefully measured approval of Schumann in that essay, by dividing Schumann's legacy between his "thoughtful and gifted" early career, marked by "plastic bent to shaping," and his later career, when he "visibly demonstrate[d] the influence of the alloy of Jewish essence on our art" with the "turgid blurring of the surface" and "sickliness dressed out in mystery" of his later compositions.[4] If Wagner praised the early Schumann, then surely Nietzsche must deplore him, which he did by praising cosmopolitanism and criticizing aspects of Schumann ("quiet lyricism," "intoxication with feeling") most associated with his compositions of the 1830s and 1840s. The game of either/or was on, with Schumann's reputation a mere pawn in the process.

But regardless of whether, like Wagner, one disdains cosmopolitanism or, like Nietzsche, one claims to admire it, the distinction between a nationalist and cosmopolitan was not so clear-cut then or now. Among other reasons, this is why both Wagner and Nietzsche had to polemicize to persuade. Some theorists of nationalism have suggested, as we saw in chapter 6, that nationalisms, just like processes of nation-state formation, show a great range of attitudes towards the world outside the particular nation in play and that the process of nation-building is neither necessarily homogenizing nor unidirectional, and it has neither identifiable beginnings nor ends. It follows from that observation that historians should write the history of communities, national ones in particular, in terms of how various people were able to define, comment upon, and mobilize a community on the basis of widely varying definitions of that community. Within nations different actors – political, economic, cultural, religious – might have differing conceptions of how national boundaries constrain or define their activities, whether as artists or pious people, as politicians or businessmen. Cultural practices, like economic or religious ones, cross borders easily.[5] In a similar vein theorists of cosmopolitanism have pointed to the existence of what has been called rooted cosmopolitanism, in contrast to the cosmopolitanism of stateless people or expatriates.[6] It shares more sensibilities and practices with nationalists than the polemical use of the term, for or against, would suggest. Immanuel Kant himself, in his essay *Perpetual Peace*, wrote that the condition of world citizenship had its foundation in ancient traditions of hospitality towards peaceful travellers and hence was a condition more of "temporary sojourn" than permanent placeless-ness.[7]

Schumann's Liberal Nationalism

These observations about the flexibility of national sentiments and their compatibility with broader understandings of human community apply to the nationalists in German Europe in the era before national unification. Schumann's entire career fell into a period of transition in the German nationalist movement, and his intense relationship to Germany bore all the markings of a transitional moment – inconsistency, experimentation, and passionate engagement. He belongs within the loosely formed milieu of liberal nationalists of the middle decades of the nineteenth century, the milieu that Nietzsche seems to have had in mind with his category of the "merely German." Like other nationalist intellectuals at mid-century, Schumann's sense of German community and identity lay in his efforts to create a particular kind of community that he conceived of as progressive and necessarily national. This view of national identity as progressive and available to all Europeans characterized what historians have called the party of movement, the advocates of reform, renewal, and even revolution in culture and society. It was European in scope and cosmopolitan in its interest in progressive developments everywhere. And although Schumann was not one of the liberal reformers who gathered in Frankfurt and Berlin to formulate practical answers to the question of "what is German" in 1848–9, one cannot imagine a musical figure more in tune with the political culture of liberal nationalism before it redefined itself in the presence of Bismarck (and that, of course, did not happen until the 1860s). Consideration of their conceptions of nationhood and what they entailed for liberal nationalists helps to specify just how different the community they imagined as the nation was from other kinds of community. Moreover, Schumann's response to much of the musical culture of his time and his understanding of the national community – its potential and its problems – remained remarkably stable over the course of his life, suggesting that however great the shock of the revolutionary events of 1848–9, they did not lead either him or his fellow nationalists to discard hopes for musical and national progress.

Schumann's lifelong association with music journalism represents his strongest connection with the nationalist movement in mid-century German-speaking Europe.[8] In the autobiographical statement he wrote in 1840 in the process of petitioning for the title of doctor of philosophy at the University of Jena, Schumann described his journalistic work in Leipzig as part of the time of movement and change in Europe, a remarkably optimistic view of a period in German public life marked on the surface by autocratic governments and passive subjects. His characterization suggests his consciousness not just of uprisings and artistic ferment elsewhere in Europe but here at home as well. He was reflecting on a growing mood of spiritual discomfort and activism, mainly among a small group of intellectuals – writers, scholars, publicists, and so on – who formed the core of a nascent political-cum-cultural opposition. In literary circles this phenomenon takes the name of convenience "Young Germany," a notion inadvertently encouraged by the Diet of the German Confederation in 1835 (the year Schumann assumed full editorial responsibility for the *Neue Zeitschrift*) when it officially chastised a number of writers for allegedly belonging to a literary cabal. But this sense of things changing and needing to change went far beyond a non-existent literary conspiracy to encompass an extensive, if dispersed, collection of people engaged in reforming public life, of which Schumann must certainly be regarded as part.

Decades ago, insisting on the "single-minded devotion to the arts" of Schumann's work, Leon Plantinga explicitly rejected any parallel between Schumann's work and that of writers such as Heinrich Heine, Heinrich Laube, and Karl Gutzkow, let alone nationalist activists such as Ludwig Camphausen or Carl Welcker.[9] But true though it may be that Schumann, as Plantinga points out, had none of Young Germany's "nihilistic radicalism" and commented only rarely on political events, to separate him completely from a loose fellowship with a reformist oppositional mode in mid-century Germany would be a mistake – again, both before and after the revolutionary events of 1848. After all, Schuman himself claimed "everything that goes on in the world – politics, literature, people – concerns me."[10] We also need to be wary of any effort to draw firm lines between cultural and political nationalism or nation-building.

Such lines impose on this generation a distinction that made only limited sense to them. Nineteenth-century Germans did distinguish between ethnographic and political types of group identity, as we do today, but as one historian has written, "civic and cultural connotations were equally vivid in their minds when they conjured up the image of the nation": for "educated Germans" "the idea of the cultural nation immediately suggested political relations while that of statehood just as surely pointed toward some measure of cultural unity as well."[11]

That said, Schumann's overriding concern was the state of cultural life among Germans, both what they produced and what they consumed. Very early in his life he had written that "true literature, literature, that is, which inspires passion in the soul of the public at large, can never flourish in a land ruled by bondage and slavery."[12] To read the prospectus for the *Neue Zeitschrift,* written in 1834 and consisting in part of a critique of existing musical journals, is to read a critique of Metternich's central Europe, its images drawn from a common store of liberal-reformist objections to the times: "What, then are the few present musical journals? Nothing but playgrounds for ossified systems ... nothing but relics of aged doctrines to which adherence is more and more openly denied, nothing but one-sidedness and rigidity ... None is capable of promoting the true interests of music; none is able to fulfill the just demands made upon it."[13]

Schumann and the Public Sphere

For Schumann, as for the liberal, educated Germans who saw themselves as participants in the project of nation-building, the all-important aspect of their work was its public existence, not its politics, and the nature of the public sphere that concerned them was defined neither by commerce nor by state authority. Jürgen Habermas famously dubbed this domain of activity the public sphere (*Öffentlichkeit*) and defined it as a space for the exercise of rationality and autonomous judgment. In eighteenth-century French salons and English coffeehouses, Habermas argued, "opinion became emancipated from the bonds of economic dependence."[14] In theory, the public sphere was a neutral and accommodating space of communication, but in practice it meant much more than that to Germans. Reading and writing were not neutral activities, in either political or cultural terms, especially in a period marked by as much censorship as were the German states in the middle decades of the nineteenth century. Since the eighteenth century both had worked to question the sovereignty of established authority and even to overthrow it; both were undertaken with deliberation and a sense of purpose and risk. Although censorship eased after the failure of the revolutions in 1848, it did not end entirely; nor did the vital charge of the public sphere diminish. If anything, journalism and associational life became all the more important, given that action in the streets (which liberal nationalists had rarely advocated) had proven so ineffective and misguided.

Schumann was committed to an activist public sphere. This commitment is revealed by the way he took to the printing press with reformist, even revolutionary purposes in mind. The musical times were awry – an arid desert, "from which, even with the best of will, hardly a drop of the sap of life can be pressed" or sometimes, on the contrary, a hothouse of quickly wilting but extravagantly coloured plants – and someone had to do something about it.[15] His sale of the journal to Franz Brendel mainly brought an end to his writing; it is no coincidence that when a moment he perceived to be of overwhelming importance came, that is, the arrival of Brahms on his doorstep, it was to journalism he returned – "new paths" indeed.

Schumann's attitude towards Meyerbeer, who came to symbolize all that was wrong with the musical scene of his day, also turns on the contrast between Öffentlichkeit, the public sphere, on the one hand, and mere publicity or fashion and commerce, on the other. Quite apart from the musical particularities of his compositions, Meyerbeer's sins resided in his commercialism, or to put it slightly differently, in his failure to understand the public as anything *but* a marketplace, wherein value is determined not by the autonomous judgment of the enlightened and free individual but by an irrational clamor of an unthinking crowd. From this perspective Schumann's infamous comparison of Meyerbeer to the "performers in Franconi's circus" and of his opera, *Les Huguenots,* to a "farce at a fair for the purpose of raising money and applause" is philosophically and politically informed, even while anti-Semitic in its undertones.[16] The role that anti-Semitism played in Schumann's political and cultural imagination cannot be answered if one asks the simple question of was he or was he not anti-Semitic. The oft-quoted remark from his marriage diaries ("Jews remain Jews; only after seating themselves ten times will [they] offer a place to a Christian") was a private one, and its power to clarify his attitudes is correspondingly limited.[17] The fact that he wrote it in the context of defending to Clara his tepid support of Mendelssohn on some particular occasion makes it even more problematic. Schumann admired Mendelssohn greatly as man and musician. More to the point in this context, he aligned himself closely with Mendelssohn on the matter of Meyerbeer, whom Mendelssohn also regarded as gaudy and insincere. In any case Schumann's defence of the public sphere as a realm of action peculiarly vulnerable to both commerce and autocracy is unmistakable in his Meyerbeer review. Schumann believed Meyerbeer pursued his musical career too comfortably within the systems of both.[18]

But what exactly was either liberal or nationalist about this conception and use of the public sphere? The liberalism of it is clear enough. These men and women believed in freedom of speech, thought, association, and religion, and the implications of such beliefs for their understanding of the order of things in the world extended far beyond contemporary political life. Liberals believed that the course of history involved the advance of culture, a progress from merely organic institutions to new ones that would be increasingly "infused with spiritual, moral, and intellectual self-consciousness."[19] All had in some way absorbed the Kantian idealist emphasis on the importance of the conscious mind, itself in a sense making the world. And they were nationalists, not because they paraded around with their German flags, but because they shared belief that the advance of culture meant a transition from communities of people based merely on blood ties and extended kinship to communities of people who were self-consciously connected to places and capable of forming more and more complex and participatory states. These collections of people were marked, above all, by a community of mind, a "spiritual national unity," in the words of the philosopher Jakob Fries, who was at the time of Schumann's early career the most famous post-Kantian philosopher and who held a post at Jena, from which, in 1840, Schumann had received his honorary doctorate.[20]

Such communities also represented the eclipse of what increasingly came to be regarded as the artificiality and inauthenticity of cosmopolitanism. The ties it created among people seemed only to reflect privilege and commerce, not authentic communal life. "Cosmopolitan community" was thus an oxymoron, sustainable only by people (aristocrats and so forth) so disconnected from genuine human bonds as to be incapable of full maturity – in Kant's memorable phrase, "the ability to use one's own understanding without the guidance of another." Enlightenment (again Kant: "man's emergence from his self-incurred immaturity"), progress, freedom, and nation thus all belonged together, in an unbreakable bonding – or so it was thought.[21]

But none of these qualities, neither freedom, nor progress, nor the common consciousness and self-awareness that liberals believed to be the essence of nationhood, came into being without effort. Again Fries: "spiritual national unity and personality, a national intellect, are only formed from the scattered lives of individuals through public opinion."[22] National consciousness had to be constructed; it had to be inculcated through activities in the public sphere, through speeches and meetings, through monuments, organizations, scholarship, education, and yes, musical performance. And people had to be free to undertake such participation. Participating in the culture of nationhood took place in public, and the community of the nation in which people believed and which people helped to create was a living one, made real through action and consciousness.

One finds liberal nationalists articulating these underlying assumptions in many different ways – from a belief in local self-government as a school for a national citizenship to advocacy of involvement in associational life of all sorts. The degree to which Schumann shared such assumptions can be found in the texts of many essays he wrote during his years of editorship and afterwards. "Let us not be mere spectators!" he remembered had been their battle cry. "Let us lend a hand ourselves for the glory of things! Let us bring the poetry of our art into honor once again!" To quote again from the journal's prospectus: Schumann wrote that "it seemed necessary ... to create for the artist an organ which would stimulate him to effectiveness, not only through his direct influence, but also through the printed and spoken word, a *public place*, for him to express what he has seen with his own eyes, and felt in his own spirit, a journal in which he could defend himself against one-sided and false criticism."[23]

At the same time, also in common with even the most ardent publicist, writing alone would not be enough to shape public opinion. For instance, Schumann would represent this view by posing a disagreement between Florestan and Eusebius on the usefulness of journalism altogether: "What is a musical paper compared to a Chopin concerto?" asks Florestan, "Away with your musical journals! It would be the victory, the triumph of a good paper, could it so advance matters that criticism would no longer be read."[24] Instead, as it had been for A.B. Marx a decade earlier, the gathering of a scattered community of conscious people also had to be achieved through a new kind of concert programming that would bind together the great artists of the past with those of present and future. The construction of an arc of historical continuity within the conscious national community was conservatism only in our retrospective view. Schumann called it "a sign of the enlightened artistic sensibility of our own era," and as early as 1828 he wrote to a friend that "every question once asked of the past, we will now put to the future, and we shall receive an answer."[25] For the 1848 intellectuals in general, establishing, and then sustaining, these lines of continuity was a way of promulgating the core values that defined the national community, a way to make explicit their criteria for national authenticity.

Schumann, like the liberal nationalist intellectuals, also tended to believe that only the authentic would or could survive; only the authentic was progressive in the truest sense of the word; and all authentic art was, by the very definition of authenticity, *national*, the expression of the most advanced and spiritually whole form of human organization: the nation. As Giuseppe Mazzini, the most famous liberal nationalist of all, wrote in his 1844 *Essay on The Duties of Man*: "The means [of working for the moral improvement and progress of Humanity] was provided for you by God when He gave you a country; when, even as a wise overseer of labour distributes the various branches of employment according to the different capacities of the workmen, he divided Humanity into distinct groups or nuclei upon the face of the earth, thus creating the germ of nationalities." Just as he believed that people who lived in true nations, not "disfigured" by "kings and privileged castes," would exist in a state of "harmony and fraternity," so too did he believe that all progress, in cultural as well as political and economic matters, was possible only when each person, "fortified by the power and affection of many millions, all speaking the same language, gifted with the same tendencies, and educated by the same historical tradition" lived in such nations.[26]

The markedly utopian element in Mazzini's thinking was not necessarily shared, at least not to that extent, by other liberal nationalists of his era. But his tendency to find something inherently disturbing about non-national aggregates, whether in cultural life or, as Mazzini often railed against, in the "egotism of caste and dynasty," did find echoes in many of his contemporaries, Schumann included. To return to Schumann's suspicions about Meyerbeer, his criticisms often centred on the problem of eclecticism in Meyerbeer, that is to say, his lack of a stable national character: "Meyerbeer's extreme externalism, his lack of originality and his eclecticism, are as well known as is his talent for dramatic treatment, preparation, polish, brilliancy, instrumental cleverness, also his considerable variety in forms. It is easy to trace in Meyerbeer, Rossini, Mozart, Herold, Weber, Bellini, even Spohr, in short, all there is of music."[27] Felix Mendelssohn shared Schumann's same cultural habitus, that of an internationally extensive but nationally constituted musical world. As chapter 6 showed, he had similar things to say about Meyerbeer, which likewise reflected the Mazzinian and liberal nationalist distrust of eclecticism as disfiguring and inauthentic. In a letter to a friend written in 1831, three years earlier than Schumann's infamous review of *Huguenots*, Mendelssohn described Meyerbeer's *Robert le Diable* as having music that was "not bad at all": "there is no lack of suspense, the right pungencies are fitted into the right places; there is melody to be hummed, harmony for the educated listeners, instrumentation for the Germans, contredanses for the French, in fact, something for everybody – but there is no heart in it."[28]

A Sense of Place

The search for music that would be heartfelt brings us finally to a consideration of the distinctive sense of place that went along with the construction of the nation through public activity. The nationalists of mid-century central Europe were place-makers, by their activities attempting to redefine Leipzig and Frankfurt and Berlin and Breslau as integral parts of something they called Germany, not just seats of princes or centres of commerce. As I discussed in chapter 2, place can be a hidden dimension in our efforts to write the history of musical culture. In the case of Schumann it is clear that he felt himself to be engaged at mid-century in a struggle over places, some of which had been won over (though always in danger of being lost) and some of which had not. All were significant as sites of change and of resistance to it. The issue was not just people and music but rather people and music in particular places. Musical improvement happened in these places, in cities, which had to be transformed from the places in which aristocrats, philistines, and *Salonmenschen* ruled to the sites of musical and cultural renewal. One could see all this as fairly banal. But at the risk of over-interpreting his geographical consciousness, one might regard Schumann as someone who was in concert with the nationalizing project in trying to remake the map of central Europe from an assortment of commercial cities and *Residenzstädte*, dominated by court and purely commercial musical establishments, into a genuinely national network of true *Bürgerstädte*, cities of autonomous, self-governing, self-regulating citizens. These would be the sites of a new cultural life, neither courtly nor commercial but authentically national, replacing both the old and the degraded new or contemporary. If there was a capital in this mental map (and there really was not, because the mental geography of all Germans, nationalizing or not, was profoundly anti-centrist), it was not Berlin or Frankfurt or Bonn, but

Leipzig. Schumann repeatedly referred to Leipzig as "musically healthy" and by extension other musically healthy places as "Leipzigian." Nor is it coincidence that Leipzig was the centre of liberal nationalism both before and after 1848, the hotbed of discussion and debate, and the site of the rapidly mythologized Battle of the Nations (*Völkerschlacht*) in 1813. This was for most liberal nationalists the ground zero of the nationalist project – the point at which the old Germany came to an end and a new one began.

Schumann's consciousness of this national geography was a constant in his life, and is nowhere better expressed than in his famous comparison of Mendelssohn and Meyerbeer, which begins with words that deliberately evoke the Battle of the Nations and the possibility of the defeat of France and all it symbolized: "Today I feel like a young warrior, who for the first time takes up his sword in a great cause. This small Leipzig, where questions of world importance have already been decided, is called upon to settle musical ones as well. Because here we see meeting, probably for the first time anywhere in the world, the two most important compositions of our time," and so on.[29] Geographically speaking, Meyerbeer was the ruler of a degraded and commercial urbanity, fatally tied to princes and their false glitter, against which a reformist, even revolutionary, movement had to assert a new national urbanity, a nationalizing public sphere. (Revolutions of the nineteenth century were almost always urban affairs.)

In this regard, at least, Brendel's *Neue Zeitschrift* continued to represent a musico-geographical understanding of Germany in sync with Schumann's own. Theodor Uhlig's – and others' – extensive reviews of Meyerbeer's *Le Prophète* in 1850 carried forward, making even more explicit, Schumann's depiction of two musical cultures – an artificial, outdated one and an authentic, progressive one – battling for dominance in the cities of Germany. "A false prophet," declared Uhlig, "stalks through the regions of our disunited and unfree Germany."[30] In the post-1849 era the failure to transform the musical culture of German cities directly reflected the failed effort at political reform, of which the clearest demonstration was the public, ceremonial relationship between Meyerbeer, the court Kapellmeister, and Friedrich Wilhelm IV, king of Prussia and himself a false prophet, once seen as the potential leader of German transformation but now revealed as its most implacable opponent.

Schumann himself, when he spoke privately or wrote publicly about the state of cultural life in Germany after 1849, expressed a sense of discouragement and isolation that one finds in many of the nationalist liberals. The small band of like-minded people who would create a new national community through their activism and example now seemed smaller than ever, the threat of commercialism more widespread, and the power of the established and unfriendly institutions more implacable. "The revolution has scattered us in all directions," he wrote to Liszt, referring to the temporary exodus of musicians from cities under siege and revolutionary disruption.[31] But the phrase also resonates with a sense that all momentum towards the cultural renewal that pre-revolutionary reformists had sought had been lost in the scattering of "genuine music-lovers [*wahren Kunstmenschen*]." "I have long known your zeal in the cause of good music," he wrote to D.G. Otten in Hamburg in 1849, "the news of which is carried, independently of newspapers, you see, by invisible spirits ... Such things *should* be discussed more in the press but rarely are, simply because most writers lack real knowledge or conviction – so things go, and so things will remain." Despite this gloominess, he concluded with one of the stock phrases of the *Burschenschaften*, the nineteenth-century student associations that embodied the revolutionary/reformist zeal of liberal nationalism – "*Verein vorwärts*, forward united, is my greeting to you. We must go forward, never abandoning our effort to bring to the fore all that which we know to be good and true [*gut und echt*]."[32]

Verein vorwärts is not a bad summation of Schumann's public activities in the 1850s. Even if the future seemed at least as likely to lie in the hands of the court favourites as of the "*gut und echt*" *Kunstmenschen*, and even if nothing in his final six years of life suggested that the princes of central Europe were any more inclined to embrace either political reform or a more progressive form of nationally minded cultural patronage, he retained his loyalty to the project of nationhood as conceived in the pre-revolutionary decades. This was a project of consciousness-raising and public activism. Many liberals still hoped it would lead to the reformed world of which Mazzini spoke. Thus did Schumann the German live suspended between the old and the new, avatar of a liberalizing national community that the failure of the revolution had excluded from Germany's future for nearly a century to come. Yet it is worth recognizing the coexistence of a national identity marked by this openness to a larger world, not just out of fairness to Schumann but because any larger effort to explain how European musical culture not only survived but flourished in the age of nationalism has to locate the spaces where exchanges among nations flourished.

Chapter Eight

The Musical Worlds of Brahms's Hamburg

In 2001 a pair of articles in the journal *19th Century Music* addressed what turned out to be an unanswerable question: "Did the Young Brahms Play Piano in Waterfront Bars [in Hamburg]"?[1] Behind the predictable scholarly back-and-forth of "yes he did" and "no he certainly did not" lurked the question of why it matters. Jan Swafford, author of a major Brahms biography and representative of the "yes he did" (he said he did and we have none but circumstantial reasons to think he did not) side of the argument, believed the answer matters because his youthful experiences in sailors' bars in Hamburg, including experiences tantamount to sexual abuse, forever shaped his personality. They tainted all subsequent relationships with women and settled a kind of melancholy pall over his art. Styra Avins, editor and translator of the most extensive English edition of Brahms's letters and a representative of the "no he certainly did not" side of the argument, protests that "a juicy story" should not "overpower the facts"; that Brahms did not grow up in a Hamburg slum at the mercy of drunken sailors and playful prostitutes; that a careful examination of income levels, customs, employment, and (not least) maps suggests the utter implausibility of such a scenario; and therefore we need to seek elsewhere for explanations of his spiritual and musical growth.[2]

But of course Brahms's own life is not the only story in which the issue has relevance, and without attempting to settle the question, one can ask how the controversy illuminates the various and incompatible worlds of musical life in nineteenth-century Hamburg. Whatever the truth may be about Brahms's presence in St Pauli *Lokale,* both Swafford and Avins are able to agree that Brahms himself *wanted* people to think he had spent time in them as a child, indeed went out of his way later in life to tell potential biographers about such experiences. His determined transparency on the issue may reflect unflinching honesty or it may reflect "recovered memory," but to want such "juicy stories" to make their way into his biography seems a refined thumbing of his nose at the good citizens of his native Hamburg. From the perspective of social and cultural history, the controversy points us to one of the defining boundaries within nineteenth-century society, of great relevance to musical life, between respectable society and its disreputable, lower-class Other, inhabiting the slums and dives of an urban life that existed right alongside the parlours and counting houses. Efforts to refute the bar stories, particularly by Brahms's contemporary admirers such as Hamburg scholar Kurt Hofmann, provide a long-echoing reverberation from the nineteenth-century *Bürgertum*'s own efforts to maintain such boundaries. At the same time the controversy reminds us that the unauthorized crossing of class boundaries, whether by Brahms or by any other respectable citizen, is part of what gave his bar stories such piquancy and power.[3]

The controversy also draws our attention to the peculiar indeterminacy of music as a cultural category. Even while serving as a one of the most telling markers of bourgeois identity, music evades straightforward class categorization. It triggers responses in listeners beyond any conscious control, reminding them of other locales and other associations; and it raises tantalizing questions about female and male sensibilities, what counts as work and what as play, the distinctions between high and low culture and between the universalizing claims of art and its links to particular times and places. This chapter focuses only on the middle-class society in which Brahms made music in Hamburg, publicly and privately. Even setting aside the musical venues of popular and working class culture, middle-class music-making in nineteenth-century Hamburg still performed a range of conflicting social and cultural values. It reinforced and crossed in socially acceptable ways a number of categorical distinctions valuable in their stability to the nineteenth-century burgher: male and female spheres; public and private; sacred and secular; amateur and professional; artist and businessman; and local, national, and cosmopolitan.

Hamburg as Music City?

The first task is to establish that there was a viable, even vital, musical life in nineteenth-century Hamburg, rumours to the contrary notwithstanding. Richard Evans wrote in *Death in Hamburg*, that Brahms "was forced to leave the city for Vienna against his will because he was unable to find a decent job" and that "as a centre of artistic and musical life," Hamburg "was completely eclipsed by the much smaller Munich."[4] Brahms himself has something to answer for in promoting this image of Hamburg as a city of unabashed philistines – note how Evans, perhaps unwittingly, echoes the sailors' bars story, the implication being that Hamburg abounded in unsuitable jobs for the unappreciated composer. But then many other commentators also shaped this image of the city of philistines par excellence. Its reputation had not always suffered such indignities. In the seventeenth century Hamburg gloried in its musical culture. One city publisher in 1657 went so far as to print a brochure – *Hamburg's Music, 1657* – with information about the location and the time of services at the city churches "so that one may with pleasure listen to splendid and well-produced music all year round in this great and world-famous city of Hamburg."[5] Regarding the eighteenth century, those in search of local greatness can conjure with figures such as Reinhart Keiser, Johann Mattheson, Georg Philipp Telemann, and C.P.E. Bach. But the general attitude, then and now, regarding Hamburg's musical life in the nineteenth century has been to lament its sorry decline into musical obscurity and mediocrity. Already in 1798, in the first year of its existence, Friedrich Rochlitz's *Allgemeine Musikalische Zeitung*, a periodical published in Leipzig but renowned for its network of correspondents across German-speaking Europe and beyond, reported from Hamburg on the high cost and low quality of its orchestral performances.[6] Another musical journal from the same period reported on the stranglehold of guild musicians over musical life, musicians "who know little of recent beautiful music, who practise less, and who are in some cases completely incompetent in their instrumental work and thus incapable of performing the latest works." The Hamburgers, the same journal's correspondent complained in the following year (anticipating Heinrich Heine's later critique of the city), will spend ten times more money eating in their favourite locale than an evening at a concert would cost, thus clearly demonstrating more care for their stomachs than their ears, and would rather empty their pockets into their stomachs than contribute to filling the pockets (or stomachs?) of a worthy musician or artist.[7]

Such assessments continued to crop up among the national correspondents of nineteenth-century musical journalism and linger on in authoritative texts such as *The New Grove Dictionary of Music and Musicians*, which states baldly that "in the 19th century leading musicians were no longer drawn to settle in the city but merely visited it on their European tours." While noting the presence of "thoroughly competent" musicians such as Julius Stockhausen and Julius von Bernuth, the *New*

Grove echoes Richard Evans's evaluation of musical life – the appointment of such men, it argues, "pales into insignificance beside the failure to keep Brahms in Hamburg."[8] Thus does the history of musical life demonstrate its loyalty to the "Great Man" school of historiography, and thus is musical life in nineteenth-century Hamburg consigned to historical marginality because all the Great Men came and went, while only the *Kleinmeister* stayed.

But there are other ways to assess musical life in the city that seems so unceremoniously to have ejected Brahms from its gourmandizing midst. (Of course, even that assessment has something dubious about it: in early 1859 Brahms premiered his difficult Piano Concerto in D Minor to stony silence and rather vigorous hissing in the acclaimed musical city of Leipzig; a few months later he performed it to a packed and wholly appreciative audience in Hamburg – so much for the image of an unsophisticated public unappreciative of its native son.)[9] We might consider the nearly seven decades from the founding of a *Gesangverein* (Singing Society) in 1819 to the establishment of a star-studded subscription concert series under the professional auspices of the Berlin Wolff agency in 1886, as the great era of *bürgerliche Musik* in Hamburg.[10] This was an era dominated by a plethora of voluntary associations, some continuous in their existence, many coming and going with the times, all of them devoted to the practice and promotion of music in the private and public places of Hamburg. To date, we still have too few local studies of this kind of musical world. By creating the cult of genius and canonizing a set of musical works suitable for performance over the ages, the musical writers and scholars of the nineteenth century did much to obscure the workings of music in their own societies and to consign subsequent generations of scholars to endless search-and-discovery missions for forgotten genius or overlooked masterpieces. Without denying their importance, I would like to suggest that Great Men as such, their presence and their absence, do not tell us much about the musical life of a place like Hamburg. We can slightly shift the perspective and say that the admiration of genius and the pious maintenance of canonical musical works of past geniuses were part of what this nineteenth-century world of middle-class music-making was all about. But it was also about the creation of a certain kind of subjectivity – a sensibility formed by musical performance and listening.[11] And it was about redefining the place of the sacred in a modern world, a process conventionally called secularization.[12] Finally, it involved maintaining a community at the local level, the national level, and perhaps also the European level through the cultural practices of music.

Bürgerliche Musik

Most would agree that the great transition in the musical practices of Europe was from institutional church and court music to the modern concert, and most would probably place this transition as having taken place gradually over the course of the eighteenth century and rapidly after that. It happened faster in Hamburg than elsewhere, spurred by the absence of a court and the demand for consumable, entertaining culture on the part of a commercial class with money to spend. Already in 1678 Hamburg had a public (compared with court) opera company, the first of its sort in German-speaking Europe, and one whose popularity overcame religious objections to its existence. The shift of the principal site for music-making from Hamburg's churches to various public, secular places accompanied the declining political influence of church musicians. This shift could have influenced J.S. Bach's decision not to come to Hamburg in 1721, and it was reflected in Telemann's dual role as head of church music and director of the opera. Though the assertion may be disputed, Hamburg musical chroniclers claimed for the city the distinction of the first public concert in Germany, in 1761. By the 1770s the city seems to have offered a number of public concerts of sacred and secular music, not least by Bach's son C.P.E. Bach. In 1780 the city fathers even considered allowing concerts to be held on Sundays; they rejected the idea, only to approve it a mere seven years later.[13]

By 1819, when the Gesangverein, the first long-lived bourgeois musical association in Hamburg, was founded, the church as an institutional support for music-making had reached so marginal a status that various lovers of religious music felt it necessary to undertake the task of maintaining and promoting it themselves, outside the auspices of the churches as such. This development fits the definition of secularization (now rapidly waning in influence) proposed by Bryan Wilson as "the process whereby religious thinking, practice and institutions lose social significance." More illuminating, though, is the observation of Lucien Hölscher that the German educated middle class increasingly loosened its ties to formal, institutional churches without at the same time de-Christianizing.[14] In Hamburg, an almost exclusively Protestant city (92 per cent as late as 1890), the churches and parishes formed a vital part of the organization of public life and education. The Senate governed them (even after the official separation of church and state in 1870), and pastors and parish politics played a significant role in the political careers of Hamburg's leaders. Yet, as Richard Evans reports, "in the years 1880–4 fewer than 10% of the Protestant population of Hamburg attended communion, the lowest proportion in Germany."[15] Evans is concerned mainly with the de-churching of Hamburg's working class, but the decline in church attendance seems to have characterized all levels of society. If not a loss of faith, then certainly a reconfiguration of its expressions and institutions had occurred and, in the case of music, an effort to relocate the musical practices that institutional churches had once sustained. The full name of the group founded in 1819 was the Gesellschaft der Freunde religiösen Gesangs, and its founders declared that the tercentenary of the Reformation in 1817 had been their inspiration. The original members of the Gesangverein first gathered a year later in September 1818 for a two-day musical festival held at the great St Michael's church in Hamburg and dedicated (still) to the Reformation's 300th anniversary. They performed Handel's *Messiah* and Mozart's *Requiem*, both apparently without cuts. Professional musicians and "*kunstgebildete Dilettanten*" made up the chorus and orchestra, in that blending of amateur and professional so characteristic of the musical voluntary associations, and the favourable reviews and full houses so moved the performance organizers that they drew up statutes for a less ad hoc, more permanent singing association.[16]

The Gesangverein turned out to be the longest-lived but not the only such group in Hamburg during the era of bürgerliche music: A.G. Methfessel founded a men's *Liedertafel* (reportedly out of the remnants of the Hanseatic Legion) in 1823, and in 1829 he founded a second oratorio society. In 1840 Carl Voigt founded the Caecilien-Verein, an a cappella group mainly devoted to religious song; in 1855 a specifically *Bach Gesellschaft* was formed. After that came the founding of a second a cappella group called Euthymia; Brahms's friend Karl Grädener led a *Singakademie* (Singing Academy); and Brahms for a short while had his Frauenchor. Despite the variety of singing associations that existed in Hamburg and in some cases their performance of secular music, the phenomenon of singing associations and the great enthusiasm of nineteenth century Germans for choral performance represented the musical expression of nineteenth-century re-confessionalization, that is, a recasting and reinvigoration of religious practice. At the same time, they reveal an important means by which women moved relatively easily into public roles in society. Women played an active role in the choral movement throughout Germany – a role sanctioned by its close connection to redefined religiosity and its corresponding separation from the morally dubious space of the stage.

The association on which the Hamburg Gesangverein modelled itself was Carl Friedrich Fasch's Singakademie in Berlin, established in 1791 for the purpose of practising (and only occasionally singing in public) the sacred music no longer performed in Berlin's churches.[17] One of the founders of the Hamburg Gesangverein was the composer Louise Reichardt, daughter of the Berlin composer and writer Johann Friedrich Reichardt and a former member of the Berlin Singakademie. Admiring contemporary accounts described her as like a nun in her composure, good works, and pious devotion to "classical church music."[18] Her leadership of the Gesangverein took a form closer to that of patron saint than director and lent the group its religious yet non-church aura. As in the case of the Berlin Singakademie, public performance was not the prime reason for its formation but was instead the "communal practice of religious songs" (*gemeinschaftliche Uebung des religiösen Gesange).* It gathered an initial membership of seventy-one people and committed to one public concert per year, on Good Friday. Nevertheless, the singers practised once a week, all year long on Thursday evenings from 7 to 9 o'clock, warming up with chorales and hymns and meeting at first in someone's large house and later in a music store.[19]

Over the years the Hamburg Gesangverein carried on more or less as it had begun, rising in member numbers, changing its leadership occasionally, and retaining its devotion to religious music. Although it lost all its scores in the great fire of 1842, the society recouped, rebuilt, renamed, and remained throughout a reliable feature of the Hamburg musical landscape. Its annual performances from 1845 through 1889 constitute a list of canonical large-scale oratorio and Passion music in the German tradition – and, of course, it was the activity of such groups that made these works canonical, from Bach's *St Matthew Passion* (from 1868 the work most frequently performed) to Handel's *Messiah* (a close second) to Bach's *St John Passion,* to Handel's *Judas Maccabeus,* to Mendelssohn's *Elijah* and *St Paul,* to more obscure works such as Meinardus's oratorio *Luther* and Graun's *Tod Jesu.*[20] Groups did not need to practise all year in order to sing pieces as familiar to them as Handel's *Messiah* would have been, so we must look beyond the rehearsal needs for a particular performance in order to explain the routines of the groups such as this one. Their emphasis on regular practice without regard to how long it actually took to be ready for a performance suggests the importance simply of gathering and singing together in something like liturgical practice – and they sang a much greater variety of music in practice than they did in performance.

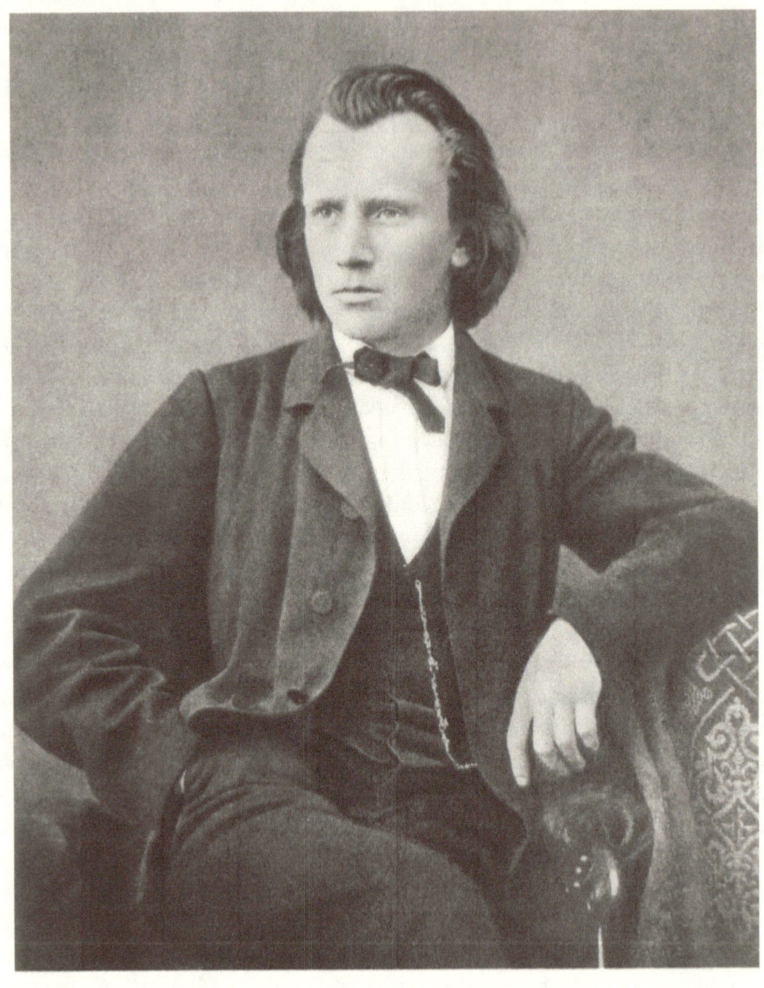

8.1 Johannes Brahms, c. 1866. Photographer unknown. Wikimedia Commons.

But their commitment, come fire or epidemic, to the annual performance, their participation in large-scale regional musical festivals, and the very nature of these oratorios as an amalgam of religious and concert music all suggest something more public and secular. So do such performance-related concerns as the quality of soloists, the reputation and fund-raising potential of the music director, and the submission of these events to the application of critical judgment in the form of concert reviews. The religious sensibility such practices reveal was adaptable, pervasive, and remarkably well channelled into alternative organizational forms, and it brings us back to the question of re-confessionalization in the nineteenth century. If, as some historians have argued, mere or sheer belief began to take precedence over institutional markers such as church membership and regular church attendance in the definition of who was a Protestant, a wide variety of ways to demonstrate belief or simply express it remained available.[21]

Take, for instance, Brahms's Frauenchor, which consisted of about forty mostly young, unmarried women and came together in 1859 after his successful concerts there had produced something of a Brahms cult, especially among young unmarried women.[22] Brahms conducted them in works he wrote especially for them, works of an explicitly or quasi-religious flavour such as his *Marienlieder*, which were settings of folktales of the Virgin Mary. The Frauenchor performed only a couple times and only in churches. It attests to a kind of unfocused religious sensibility, closely linked to sentimentality and romance and existing in the space between private and public life in which sentiment, romance, and personal religion flourished. Within this space unmarried girls such as those in the Frauenchor had considerable freedom to come and go, to call extra rehearsals, and to fantasize about Brahms himself. They even took trips into the countryside with Brahms in tow. This Frauenchor, like choral societies in general, created new ways to engage with religious ideas in their artistic manifestations, independent of the time and space of established churches' own institutions.

Local, National, and Cosmopolitan

Placing choral societies in the context of recasting German Protestantism in the nineteenth century in turn reminds us of the importance of Protestant culture in the process of nation-making as well. Protestantism had long provided a powerful set of origin stories, heroes, and national virtues (seriousness, hard work, honesty, etc.) for German nationalists to draw upon, and choral societies had been one of the major vehicles for disseminating the cultural myths and values of Protestant Germany. But German Protestantism was only one aspect of the national implications for the remarkable proliferation of choral societies in nineteenth-century Germany, before and after unification.[23] Contextualizing only Brahms's choral works, Leon Botstein writes that "German-speaking Europeans before and after 1871 used culture as an explicit form of political expression" and "allegiance to things German was maintained in large measure by that curious combination of private and public: the singing group, the Liedertafel, and the Singverein."[24] To bring this larger story back to Hamburg, the whole array of musical associations in the era of bürgerliche music expressed the city's status as a place of dynamic interplay among local, national, and cosmopolitan identities. James Sheehan has divided eighteenth-century culture into parallel worlds with little significant interaction – one courtly and cosmopolitan, one oral and local, and one literary and embryonically national.[25] By the beginning of the nineteenth century these three worlds had begun to develop into one national culture incorporating, reordering, and subordinating the local and cosmopolitan elements. Cities were the primary site of these developments, and the musical associations helped to make it happen.

No single organization fully expressed this dynamic interplay of place identities. Returning briefly to a group like the Gesangverein, we see that its personnel; its situation in the everyday rhythms of the working week and the liturgical year; its mutual relationships with musical businesses, teachers, and families all express its localness, its Hamburg identity. But at the same time it participated from the outset in national choral events, compared itself to and communicated with similar groups in other cities, and most strikingly maintained a near total adherence to the choral works of German composers – or perhaps more accurately, of composers regarded as German (e.g., Händel/Handel, who in Hamburg seems to have been regarded as virtually native). One can also make a case for the Gesangverein's cosmopolitanism if we regard it in its relationship to the other musical groups with which it worked and shared both membership and audience. Foremost in this regard was the Hamburg *Philharmonische Gesellschaft* (Philharmonic Society) founded in 1828 by a number of the same people who a few years earlier had founded the Gesangverein. The Philharmonische Gesellschaft, more than any other single organization, became the centre point of bürgerliche music in Hamburg, the point where all lines crossed and identities cohered. Its founding protocol described it as an association for the sponsorship of winter concerts, in which "the performance of symphonies and outstanding overtures by professional musicians" would take place and in which "local and out-of-town artists would have the opportunity to be heard by the educated public [*gebildeten Publikum*]."[26] Until its role was usurped by professional concert management after 1889, it sponsored an orchestra, largely made up of professional musicians, for a yearly concert series, often with featured soloists from out of town, and helped to organize charity concerts and musical festivals in conjunction with the amateur singing groups of the city, especially but not exclusively the Gesangverein.

The group was not filling a vacuum. Hamburg did have its *Stadttheater* (city theatre), located since 1827 in a building in the centre of the city designed for it by Karl Friedrich Schinkel, and the theatre had a resident professional orchestra, headed by Karl August Krebs. Just the year before the founding of the Philharmonic Society, Krebs himself had initiated a yearly concert series and also provided instrumentalists to play with visiting virtuosi, as needed. Between the Philharmonic Society concerts and those under Krebs's direction with the Stadttheater orchestra, dozens of professional soloists or virtuosi came through Hamburg before 1889 – all those with whom we are familiar – Jenny Lind, Clara Wieck Schumann (nineteen times), Franz Liszt, Ferdinand and Louise David – and a hundred more hardly known at all today. Of these travelling artists a little fewer than half were German; the rest came from Italy, France, Scandinavia, Poland, Bohemia, Moravia, Bessarabia, Russia, Holland, Hungary, England, Spain – in other words, from all across Europe. Before Liszt and after him as well soloists did not take it upon themselves to provide the sole entertainment for an evening but simply served as the ticket-selling highlight of the occasion, so each one of these visits involved local musicians and relied on the patronage of local audiences. Seen from one perspective (that of, e.g., the *New Grove*), the musical weakness of the city revealed itself in this reliance on outside talent for its musical edification, but matters appeared different to members of the cultivated circles of Hamburg society. The music lovers of the city, with the indefatigable Josef Sittard as their main spokesman, regarded the frequent comings and goings of musicians as a sign of their city's vitality, prosperity, and taste, manifested in their cultivation of the finest music the world had to offer. That said, what the visiting virtuosi performed often depended on where they were from, in that curious way that educated people of the nineteenth century, self-styled cosmopolitans or otherwise, expected people to conform to their national character. An Italian singer such as the soprano Carlotta Patti was known for her "trills, staccatos and passage work," which one Hamburg critic compared to "the ringing of little silver bells," and thus the audience expected her to sing excerpts from Italian opera (and were not disappointed). A German tenor such as Julius Stockhausen sang Lieder. Many of the piano virtuosi, in addition to their own pyrotechnics, would perform a Beethoven sonata, and the local critics often judged the artistry of the pianist based solely on its execution.[27]

In 1842 Berlioz wrote to his friend Heine about his visit to Hamburg shortly after the devastating fire that destroyed much of the inner city:

> Now for your native town of Hamburg, that city desolate as ancient Pompeii, which yet rises powerfully from its own ashes, and bravely stanches its wounds ... Certainly, I have only praises to bestow upon it, for it has grand musical resources, singing societies, philharmonic societies, military bands etc. ... The Kapellmeister Krebs fulfills his functions with talent and a strictness that is excellent in a conductor. He helped me with great good nature during our long rehearsals ... An excellent performance, a numerous, intelligent and very cordial audience made this one of the best concerts I ever gave in Germany ... After, two musicians close to my desk touched me deeply by these simple words, spoken under their breath, in French, "Ah monsieur, notre respect, notre respect!" It was all the French they could muster ... Krebs alone displayed a curious reticence in his opinion. "My dear fellow," he said to me, "in a few years your music will be known all over Germany. It will become popular, and that will be a great misfortune! What imitations it will provoke, what a style, what absurdities! It would be better for art that you had never been born!"[28]

Berlioz's anecdote invites us to consider how in the end one regards the whole travelling show of artists who came through Hamburg over these years. Krebs's response harks back to the eighteenth-century argument that Germany constituted a musical crossroads, a mixing point – an attitude that one still finds in Wagner's writings and reflected the kind of insecurity about national culture that Krebs's remarks embody. However, the main point of the Berlioz visit and those of all the other musical travellers is that, despite its reputation for being an outlier and a freak in German history as a whole, Hamburg reflected a German-wide pattern in musical developments, and that pattern was one of local organizations sustaining local, national, and international musicians performing overwhelmingly German instrumental works. (The pattern is different for opera, of course, where the repertoire was far more international.) The repertoire of the Philharmonic Society, with its emphasis on large symphonic works and overtures, consisted of works by Beethoven, Mozart, Cherubini, Hummel, Beethoven, Spohr, Rossini, Weber, Mendelssohn, Beethoven, Mozart, Beethoven, Beethoven, Mozart, Beethoven, Mozart, Romberg, Weber, Cherubini, Spontini, Beethoven, Beethoven, Haydn, Mozart, Beethoven, Haydn, Romberg, Rossini, Mendelssohn, Beethoven ... and so on. In the realm of instrumental music, German composers dominated "the most British city on the continent."[29] Yet participating in musical life did not compare to surveying the battlefield at Sedan, despite Schumann's famous and half-wistful comparison of Beethoven to Napoleon. After all, what was regarded as German music did not correspond to the borders of 1871; even after 1871 musicians made little effort to pretend a conformity to those political arrangements. But more than that, participating in musical organizations in Hamburg meant combining a localized sense of musical competence with an appreciation for musical genius wherever it appeared – in a Hamburg-born musician such as Brahms or Louise Japha, in a Leipzig-born musician such as Clara Wieck Schumann (who over the course of her long career performed fifty-five times in the city and in an 1840 letter to her fiancée Robert Schumann had sung the praises of the city, natural and musical), or in a Frenchman such as Berlioz or a Hungarian such as Eduard Remenyi. It meant acting locally in a cultural field that was universally practised and on which German achievement could be regarded and celebrated as peerless.

Conclusion

How, then, should we understand the era of bürgerliche music in Hamburg, as well as elsewhere in Germany? Certainly, it was a time when a firm consensus on what constituted German music triumphed, a consensus that reflected the combined efforts of music critics, writers, and professional and amateur musicians and music lovers in associations in every German town and city. The degree to which the music of the "great German masters" dominated the everyday practising and listening of these groups in Hamburg is striking, even if not wholly unexpected. Yet the cultural meaning of that consensus is more complex and interesting than some triumph of nationalism and national identities. Moreover, there were decent jobs in music to be had in Hamburg, even if a young and rather inexperienced Brahms did not get the one he wanted in 1862, that of first co-director of both the Gesangverein and the Philharmonische Gesellschaft. The directorship went to Julius

Stockhausen, whom the association leaders thought would prove to be a better fundraiser and administrator. And who is to say they were not right; sustaining the musical life of a city as was not then and is not now only a matter of cultivating, or hiring, genius. Brahms went off to Vienna, where he did direct a Singakademie; he returned a number of times to Hamburg and in 1889 received from Bürgermeister Carl Petersen an *Ehrenbürgerschaft* or honorary citizenship, which Brahms accepted, saying it was "the finest honour and greatest joy that I could have received from mankind."[30]

PART III

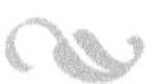

Public and Private

Chapter Nine

What Difference Does a Nation Make?

Art culture in one guise or another has been so important to German thinkers, poets, and everyone else who has defined nationhood that to ask how the political consolidation of a German nation in 1871 made a difference to cultural undertakings within this new nation is to risk simply restating something obvious.[1] This chapter takes a generalizing approach to the topic, providing an account of musical culture before and after unification. Those who regard unification as having had a major impact on German culture tend to see the changes as all for the worse. From their perspective unification produced only artistic stagnation and repression. A second tendency, generally less coherent but perhaps truer to life, regards unification as having had both stimulating and stultifying consequences throughout cultural life, though at the same time acknowledging, in the words of Françoise Forster-Hahn, that the creation of the German nation-state was a force for change "lying beneath the surface" of artistic trends and creations.[2]

This chapter tries to bring to the surface some of the assumptions that shape our study of art culture, and music in particular, in their German context. One may immediately object that culture means too many things and that use of the word fails to acknowledge a distinction between works of art and ways of life. But the Germans under review here, contemporaries or late avatars of Herder, seem almost to invite such an encompassing definition of their *Kultur*, which included everything from creating to thinking to living. Friedrich Nietzsche, in his "untimely meditations" written shortly after German unification, wrote that culture was, "above all, unity of artistic style in all the expressions of the life of a people." This unity ought to be present for the German, he suggested, in "every glance he casts at his clothes, his room, his home, every walk he takes through the streets of his town, every visit he pays to a fashionable shop, in his social life ... [in] his manners and deportment, in the world of our artistic institutions, of our concerts, theatres and museums."[3] I will not try to examine the difference that political unification made or did not make to all these things, but I will consider music in the context of ways of living or, to be a little more precise, in the context of ways of organizing and interpreting it.

Musical Culture before 1871

The history of German musical culture in the seven decades before political unification begins with a new and invigorating self-consciousness about music's importance and ends up with a great deal of complacency among music-consuming Germans. If we compare Friedrich Schiller's treatise of 1795, *On the Aesthetic Education of Man*, with the speeches at the centenary celebrations of his birth, or E.T.A. Hoffmann's essay on Beethoven's Fifth Symphony in 1810 with speeches on the occasion of the 1870 Beethoven centenary celebrations, then we must conclude that German culture suffered a catastrophic constriction in these decades, abandoning a vision of art as the expression of human wholeness in order to embrace a diminished vision of art as the embodiment of Germanness and its purported unity. But this trajectory from cosmopolitan humanism to self-regarding nationalism captures only one aspect of the history of the musical arts in the years from 1800 to 1870. Alongside an increasing insistence on music and the arts' role in national unification, these decades saw the transformation of the institutional and commercial circumstances of music making in central Europe and an accumulation of musical compositions that assured its full, even leading, participation in a "cultural flowering" that has no rival in German history, either before or since. As early as the 1760s (much earlier, in other words, than what Friedrich Meinecke called the glorious "classical decade" for German literature from 1795 to 1805) German-identified composers were producing the music and the interpretation of musical meaning that together laid the foundations for the institutions of music that shaped musical life up to and beyond German unification.[4] And although no uniformity of style or genre and only the most general commonality of ethos characterized all this music, these decades nevertheless stand as a tentative whole, as the period in which Germany's existence as a musical nation became more than the fantasy of an isolated few.

The Ideal of the Aesthetic Community

To the extent that we can identify a general attitude characteristic of those who cultivated the music and the arts in this period, it consisted minimally of a belief that aesthetic experience enabled human beings to live fully, freely, and, morally. Intellectual self-cultivation alone could not achieve such an end, nor could everyday life in the established patterns of family, church, work, community, and state. Aesthetic experience, the creation and appreciation of beauty, encompassed all of life, especially those ineffable aspects of it that a purely rational view of the world could neither perceive nor explain, and at the same time it expressed man's freedom in a world that did not make sense. We usually call this view of the world and of art's place in it "romanticism." But the term is less important than the thing itself, which as Isaiah Berlin overstated, consisted of "the first moment, certainly in the history of the West, when the arts dominated other aspects of life, when there was a kind of tyranny of art over life."[5] The pursuit of art, whether by people who hoped to make a living from it or by amateurs, began to take on a new aura at the end of the eighteenth century. Whatever we call that aura, it surrounded the philosopher Kant, the writer Goethe, the musical journalist Friedrich Rochlitz, the composer Beethoven, and every civil servant who ever joined an amateur choral society and every young woman who studied the piano, alongside self-proclaimed romantics and flouters of social convention such as Friedrich Schlegel.

Schiller's essay *On the Aesthetic Education of Man*, written in its first draft as a series of actual letters to a benefactor, the Duke of Schleswig-Holstein-Augustenburg, and then published in 1795 in Schiller's own journal, *Die Horen* (for the Greek goddesses of the seasons), provides the fullest defence of art's simultaneously moral and humanizing capacity. Schiller was thirty-six years old at the time of its publication, and more than a decade after his sensational debut as a dramatist with *The Robbers* he was still struggling to make literature – art – his career. The *Aesthetic Letters* expressed Schiller's understanding of what had gone wrong with the world and what might be done to heal it. Much had been achieved in the past century in rousing man "from his long indolence and self-deception" and in "demanding restitution of his inalienable rights." Yet though it seemed that for the first time in centuries there existed "a physical possibility of setting law upon the throne, of honoring man at last as an end in himself," this hope was in "vain," for this "moment so prodigal of opportunity" found "a generation unprepared to receive it." Instead of a full realization of freedom, passions overcame judgment, reason tyrannized feeling, the "cultivated classes" lacked all conviction, and the lower ones, filled with passionate intensity, "hasten[ed] with ungovernable fury to their animal satisfactions."[6] Art, in contrast, entailed the free play of all human capacities in its creation and appreciation. Beauty itself was nothing other than "freedom in appearance" and, through "aesthetic education," art, which gave beauty substance, had the potential to make this unprepared human material ready for freedom through the peculiar autonomy of art. Aesthetic experience, as T.J. Reed has characterized Schiller's thought, could liberate and liberalize people, both as individuals and as members of communities.[7]

Schiller's treatise was not a work like Goethe's *Sorrows of Young Werther* a generation earlier, which seemed to express for all literate Germans the essence of what it was to be German. Nor was it like Fichte's *Addresses to the German Nation* in 1807, which came eventually to impress Germans profoundly, not least as patriotic legend. Goethe said of Schiller's *Aesthetic Letters* that "they'll oppose him now, I'm afraid; but in a few years they'll be plundering him without acknowledgement," and his observation holds true even today.[8] For Nicholas Boyle, Goethe's biographer, Schiller's aesthetic treatise was "the founding document of a new age in German culture." It appropriated religious terminology for the creation of a secular theology of art inspiring ethical conduct and making possible human self-formation (*Bildung*) as a new kind of salvation.[9] Schiller's treatise and Goethe's *Wilhelm Meister's Apprenticeship*, published just a year later, showed that enlightened principles could survive political revolution gone bad and that acts of creation, of art and self, provided the path to human wholeness.

Over the next century many, perhaps most, Germans involved in the creation and appreciation of music shared a sense of moral purpose. For some it was based on this orientation to the arts that Schiller articulated so ambitiously. But for many it probably reflected a more general sense of music's moralizing capacity, deriving from the age-old entanglement of music in the practice of religion. The sense of urgency, characteristic of Schiller's treatise and of announcements such as Friedrich Schlegel's that "the right moment for an aesthetic revolution" had come, faded. Satire and some cynicism followed, and the "application" of his ideas to actual educational projects missed subtle distinctions and psychological insights.[10] But when a musical man of letters such as Friedrich Rochlitz wrote of music as "a means toward the perfection and the ennobling" of humans, a "bridge across which one passed from sensuality into freedom," or when a pedagogue like Nina D'Aubigny wrote of how "every day shows us the influence of the Muses" drawing out people's "intellectual and moral powers," or when the designers of Leipzig's new concert hall for the Gewandhaus Orchestra inscribed on its architrave the words "*Res severa est verum gaudium,*" all were participating in the aesthetic community of Schiller's imagining.[11] Critics such as Heine may have found it isolated in its disdain for reality and cowardly in its retreat from an unfree social world. Later historians such as Meinecke accused its members of being unable to "accommodate the concrete forces of history" because they felt "too free, too lofty to enter readily into the restrictions of actual life."[12] But all such criticisms accepted the idea that art and music mattered in the world and must not exist for their own sake alone. The aesthetic community may have dwelt in the imagination, but its manifestations encouraged experiences of togetherness and apprehensions of immortality as essential to its members as those of the equally imagined community of the German nation.

Experiencing the Arts

One historian of nineteenth-century artistic life has described the process by which institutions formed in the arts as "congealing," and although the image is not beautiful, it does suggest the paradox of regularity in the means by which people had exposure to what they increasingly believed to be the freest of human endeavours.[13] One can follow this process of standardization across a spectrum ranging from the grandly public to the intimately private and find throughout remarkably durable modes of experiencing art. Most of them have survived into our own times and, though embattled and revised, they are still recognizable. For the arts the distinction between public and private came to mean something reasonably clear to people in the nineteenth century. Monuments, museums, concert halls, symphonies, statues, and large-scale paintings clearly belonged to a public culture, accessible, if not free, to all; singing recitals, amateur theatricals, four-hand piano music, and genre paintings belonged to something or somewhere more private and personal. Yet despite the seeming clarity of such boundaries, artistic culture in the nineteenth century reflected also their porousness – or artificiality. Cultural activities took place along a continuum, and even the most private ones shaped the most public, and vice versa. The princely courts maintained a significant role, the nature of which evades the distinction altogether, and the marketplace, the great mediator and binder, affected all.

The most public of nineteenth-century creations for art consumption were the hundreds of new buildings dedicated to sustaining the aesthetic community and improving the individual within it, from museums to opera houses, concert halls, theatres, and libraries. Of these the art museums were the grandest and largest. But new buildings for music-making were not far behind and shared the same goal as that articulated by the architect (and sometime designer of opera sets) Karl Friedrich Schinkel, that of providing "worthy nourishment" for those learning to regard art "as one of the most important areas of human culture."[14] The more popular and the less ambitious the cultural form, the less it seemed to matter how or where the public consumed it, but the creators of new concert halls, opera houses, and theatres for plays, operettas, and less elite forms of music making also sought to make the building express the significance of what it contained. In the case of concerts the process of institutional "congealing" in the nineteenth century involved the creation of a mighty ritual around the passing moments of musical performance, which could actually take place in a wide range of settings. The formal public concert had its beginnings in the urban sociability of the eighteenth century, and in the nineteenth century it became the centrepiece of German musical culture. First in major centres like Vienna, Berlin, and Leipzig and soon after in most cities, the concert took on its now familiar aspects: some kind of hall with seating usually arranged facing a stage; the rejection of overt theatricality in the dress of the performers or the decoration of the stage; the applause for the arrival of the principal musicians; silence during the performance and applause afterwards and only after an entire work had ended.

Like the museum, the concert existed to display the work of art to the advantage of the public and to educate listeners in the fullest possibilities of serious art. In 1835 Franz Liszt made the comparison explicit by calling for the establishment of "an assembly to be held every five years for religious, dramatic, and symphonic music, by which all the works that are considered best in these three categories shall be ceremonially performed" then placed in a "musical Museum."[15] The concert, like the museum preserving some otherwise vanished spirit of the past into the present, embodied the historical consciousness of the nineteenth century alongside its admiration for individual genius, of the present and past. The recognition that an autonomous musical work existed, worthy of preservation and repeated performance, emerged in the late eighteenth century and became stable in the nineteenth. As pedagogue Bernhard Natorp described them, sounding a Schillerian note, well-designed concerts could supplant "all inauthentic music" and allow "true music, the music of the heart" gradually to "spread itself more generally," to "flow over into schools and churches into the workshops of laborers, into the cottages and fields of the farmer," and finally to "make humans more human," "tearing them from the animal condition of torpor."[16] Despite its talk of workshops and farmhouses, such rhetoric suggests that the ideal concert was not an egalitarian event. It demanded of the listener a certain level of training and attention, a philosophical commitment to artistic autonomy, and an emphasis on the musical score and its complexities as much as on the musical performance. Concert performances came to be judged as more or less perfect realizations of the intentions of the composer, as he (mostly) set them down on paper for posterity. The most prestigious concert programs deliberately contrasted their programming to that of the middlebrow potpourri model of musical bits and pieces and instead performed major works in their entirety. Beethoven's symphonies constituted the core of this repertoire, with concerti, soloists, large choral works, and smaller orchestral pieces orbiting around them. A regular schedule of public concerts of large and difficult works required well-trained musicians in formal organizations. In the course of the nineteenth century cities and states thus founded or cobbled together professional orchestras, their members drawn mainly from court and opera orchestras but with a more standardized – and larger – array of instruments and a more businesslike organizational structure.

Public buildings, professional ensembles, and public events do not, however, exhaust the means by which music "went public" in the nineteenth century. Every sphere of artistic activity, music being no exception, flourished in close connection with the expansion of reading and writing and with the increasing complexity of the public sphere. This amounts to a truism in the case of literature, of course, with the sheer number of published works increasing and literacy rising, but music criticism and reviews, biographies of great musicians, printed versions of popular opera libretti, and a myriad of musical instruction manuals expanded in number alongside the growth of a literary public. Writing about music appeared not just in general-interest periodicals but also in increasing numbers of specialized journals, which first emerged in the cities of north Germany, especially Hamburg, Leipzig, and Berlin. From the last years of the eighteenth century on, journals such as Friedrich Rochlitz's *Allgemeine musikalische Zeitung* (General Musical Newspaper) and writers such as E.T.A. Hoffmann, A.B. Marx, and Robert Schumann explained to the public why and how to appreciate music. Writing shaped a German musical public that lasted after any given performance ended, mitigating what Kant had considered the merely "transitory" effect of music on the mind. The teaching of musical judgment – how one should make distinctions among different compositions, what kind of language was appropriate to the passing of judgment – could also form a substantial part of a periodical's raison d'être. Consequently, a music-attentive public emerged, larger than the overlapping circles of musicians, music critics, and scholars. In the 1850s and 1860s the heated controversies over the merits of Johannes Brahms versus Richard Wagner reflected public engagement in what amounted to expert discussions of musical style. At the same time publishers of the less ambitious entertainment sheets, such as Leipzig's *Newspaper for Elegant Society*, conveyed information about musical and artistic happenings just sufficient to allow one to hold one's own in polite conversation. By making cultivation into something that could be acquired almost as easily as a fashionable piece of clothing, the entertainment sheets did not so much foster a society of bluffers as, like their high-brow counterparts, create common knowledge about cultural life.[17]

Taken as a whole, the print culture of music formed an integral part of the growing market for music in all genres and venues. Whether in the form of sheet music for playing music at home or in the form of concert and theatre subscriptions, the musical marketplace replaced and supplemented the older sources of support from high-born patrons and church establishments. In this new artistic world of market forces print culture served several functions. It disseminated information about music – performances and performers – to its new consumers. Closely related, in its efforts to teach judgment and promote good taste, writings for the lay public tried to bridge the gap that threatened to open up between musicians-as-professionals, committed to an aesthetic of expressive autonomy, and music lovers-as-consumers, interested in seeing or hearing what they liked. The nineteenth-century musical world bequeathed to us a lasting image of the artist as misunderstood genius and the bourgeois art lover as rich philistine. But even while a creative genius like Schumann proposed to wage war against the degraded musical tastes of his countrymen, he chose the culture of print as his medium and, in a gesture of Schillerian optimism about the possibility of cultural wholeness, founded the *Neue Zeitschrift für Musik* in 1834.[18] Some musicians of the nineteenth century may have felt themselves in opposition to society as a whole, but the ideal of the aesthetic community and the reality of the market demanded of them, as well as of art's consumers, the effort of communication. Their communications with their publishers also suggest the extent to which they knew and wrote for a living audience, not for posterity.[19]

Public performances and journals also lead us away from the most public aspects of nineteenth-century artistic culture towards private life. The salons of the urban patriciate created semi-public spaces with their own quasi-formal rituals of performance, conversational or musical. Under the cover of sociability people tried out ideas and compositions, performing not just for each other but also for an imagined audience of the educated and refined. At a less socially elite level were the voluntary associations, which grew rapidly in number after 1800, to the point that by mid-century most cities in German-speaking Europe had several musical associations, including amateur orchestras and chamber music groups, mixed-voice choirs, and men's glee clubs. Salons and music clubs point to the phenomenon of the artistic amateur, "a lover of the arts," as Goethe wrote in 1797, "who not only observes and enjoys them but also wants to take part in their practice."[20] The first half of the nineteenth century saw a flourishing of amateur artistry, mainly among the educated urban elites. The singing organizations tended to be based either on the model of Berlin's Singakademie, founded in 1791, or on that of Carl Friedrich Zelter's patriotic *Liedertafel*, founded in 1809. Singing and instrumental groups typically included amateur and professional musicians, often had professional directors, and wrote statutes for themselves declaring their devotion to the higher aims of artistic pleasure.

Amateur artistry of the nineteenth century flourished in art, drama, and literature as well, taking place both in and out of the public eye, with and without paid professionals, but its relation to both publicity and professionalism remained in a state of permanent vexation. Sometimes, theatre amateurs did stage productions in restaurants and taverns, and amateur painters displayed their work. But the branch of artistic amateurism that established the most prominent and honoured place for itself in the public sphere was music, and mainly choral music (most amateur chamber and piano music stayed in the bourgeois music room). Choral societies did not automatically take to public performance: Zelter's Berlin Singakademie, for instance, remained the most famous and least often heard of its type, turning to regular public performance only after the enormous success of its revival of Bach's *St Matthew Passion* in 1829. Other such groups performed once, at most twice, a year, often at Easter or Christmas, though they increasingly served as the chorus for professional concert performances of works such as Beethoven's Ninth Symphony or Mozart's *Requiem*. What really pushed choral singing into the spotlight in Germany was the invention of a new and characteristically German form of aesthetic experience, that of the regional music festival. G.F. Bischoff established the first one in 1810 in Thuringia, in cooperation with the composer Ludwig Spohr. It involved a large amateur chorus, orchestra, and audience from the surrounding towns and cities; Haydn's *Creation* was the highlight of the first day, Beethoven's Fifth Symphony of the second. By the time of the founding of the German Reich in 1871, regional festivals all over Germany – from a Hanseatic one in the north to the Lower Rhine Music Festival to gatherings in Bavaria, Saxony, and Silesia – had gathered tens of thousands of participants.

The flourishing of amateurism accompanied the increase in professional opportunities for artists, neither inhibiting the latter nor itself diminishing because of, for instance, the growing number of touring musicians. It reflected the potent coming together of sociability, aspirations to a higher cultivation, and new technologies of print, keyboard, and mass production. Professional artists and other gatekeepers of an elevated culture did express concern about its consequences. At the beginning of the nineteenth century Goethe found in their striving towards art an aspiration that might be useful to the progress of art, yet at the same time he worried about the dilettantes' lack of intensity and originality. The artist, he thought, "makes the rules" or "gives them to himself," in short, he "commands the times," while the dilettante, as an avid learner of rules and a plagiarist at heart, expecting recognition for the mere expending of effort, only followed them.[21]

Yet as became increasingly clear, an important source of income for artists themselves lay in teaching the rules to everyone else. The new music conservatories, master classes, and apprenticeships (including those in military bands) all trained the professionals, but very little training in music took place in schools, thus leaving open a wide field of play for the spread of private instruction. Not all such opportunities fell into competent hands. Publishers produced scores of dubiously helpful manuals for learning how to play an instrument or sing, and instructional charlatans proliferated, alongside sellers of cure-all tonics. Johann Bernhard Logier of Kassel, for instance, an underemployed trumpeter, invented a device for the keyboard called the "chiroplast," which tried to do for piano-playing what Hargreaves's spinning jenny had done for cotton thread: produce large amounts of the desired product in the shortest possible time by mechanical means. Logier's advertising materials promised that any person of "ordinary capacity and ordinary industry" through his new methods would quickly become "capable of emulating Corelli, Handel, Haydn, and Mozart."[22] Still, most teaching of music to children or artistically awakened adults took the more conventional form of tutoring in the home. If music journals regularly lamented the poor quality of private instruction or the misery of piano recitals, the trend towards such forms of private enjoyment of the musical arts continued strongly throughout the century. The word *Hausmusik*, or the playing and learning of music in the home, first appeared in the press in 1837 in Schumann's journal; by 1880 several journals and hundreds of musical medleys and song collections, and piano veterans beyond number had gathered in its service.[23]

From the simple piano collections of German dance music to the grand portico of Berlin's Staatsoper, artistic culture permeated the most private to the most public of nineteenth-century places. It became a matter of pride and identity for the bourgeois household and the princely state alike to cultivate the arts and to display the various tokens – a piano in the parlour, a statue in a public square, concert rooms in a public building – of its presence among them. Nietzsche, as we saw at the outset of this chapter, regarded such pride with derision and such culture-mongering as incoherent. We might instead recognize in people of this era a state of chronic aesthetic indecision. For what did not emerge in the first seventy years of the nineteenth century, despite much heated debate, was any agreement on where the boundary lay between true art and mere entertainment or decoration. It was clear enough that Beethoven's later quartets, being far too difficult for amateur performance, must then indeed be art, but not even those who adhered to the most sacralized, most emphatic definition of art could dismiss as trivial fluff every opera by Rossini. For the nineteenth-century music lover, serious and light, like public and private, represented a spectrum, a range of possibilities, not a dichotomy. Theatres and opera houses offered a variety of dramas, from grand opera to operetta; concert halls reverberated with more than symphonies; restaurants hired musicians to play everything from Haydn to Johann Strauss, senior and junior. In short, the period from 1800 to 1870 brought about a vast expansion in the possibilities for musical appreciation, in the places one encountered music, and in the forms it took. Given the burden of choice this placed on those who wished to experience music, it is not surprising that contemporary writings, even before Nietzsche's harsh words, reflected so much anxiety about taste and judgment. As music became autonomous and the musician became a freely creative individual, so too did the observer, the listener, the buyer, and the student become adrift in a state of aesthetic independence.

Musical Culture after 1871

Little of this great array of institutions and practices changed dramatically after 1871. For many Germans of 1871 the whole question of how political unification might affect German culture would have made little sense. The pressing question about culture and the arts was rather the reverse: how had this great victory of politics and arms itself emerged from the past and ongoing achievements of German *Kultur*? As the previous section suggested, German speakers, especially middle-class literate ones, had long been living in a nation of sorts, actual to them in the various ways they cultivated literature, theatre, visual arts, and music, in the clubs they joined and the newspapers they read, as well as (more abstractly) in the way they understood themselves as they travelled among and related to non-Germans. The cruder answers to the question of how Bismarckian unification might have emerged from this *Kulturnation* are notorious, from a geography teacher claiming that victories had been made in the German classroom to countless and forgettable paeans to "proud soldiers of the line" marching into battle singing "Die Wacht am Rhein."[24] The theologian David Strauss, who many decades earlier had scandalized and fascinated the reading public with his miracle-debunking *Life of Jesus,* offered his own explanation in 1871 in a book called *The Old and the New Faith: A Confession.* In it he championed science as the new faith, rationally demonstrable in the evidence of historical progress shown in the German victory over France. "During recent years," declared Strauss, we "have participated in the liveliest way in the great national war and the construction of the German state, and we feel ourselves profoundly uplifted by this turn, as glorious as it was unexpected, in the history of our much-tried nation." "Our knowledge of nature," he claimed, the "writings of our great poets," and "the performances of the works of our great composers" were "a stimulus for the spirit and the heart, for the imagination and the sense of humor, that leaves nothing to be desired." "Thus we live," he concluded, and "go our way rejoicing."[25]

Repelled by such complacency, Nietzsche replied, as we saw above, with his first untimely meditation deriding cultural philistines, and it is worth noting that he began it by excoriating the "destructive delusion" that victory on the battlefield in 1870–1 had represented the triumph of "German culture," which "must therefore now be loaded with garlands appropriate to such an extraordinary achievement." Victory, said Nietzsche, had arisen from "stern discipline, natural bravery and endurance, superior generalship, unity and obedience in the ranks, in short, elements that have nothing to do with culture."[26] Yet the notion of cultural victory, accompanied by its even more pernicious companion, the notion of cultural superiority, persisted throughout the Second Empire and on into the Great War, manifesting itself in enormous accumulations of paintings; large-scale, loud compositions; festivities; buildings; and, above all, a veritable infestation of monuments, featuring many German musicians among them. Berlin's Tiergarten alone had monuments to Mozart, Beethoven, Haydn, Wagner, and Albert Lortzing.

Unification and Cultural Stagnation

Just as the triumphalism of historians of the Prussian school, who saw German unification of 1870–1 as the right and inevitable culmination of all German history, found its counter-narrative (still a Prusso-centric one) in the Wehlerian model of a *Sonderweg* or specially arrested development, so too has cultural triumphalism produced a counter-narrative of arrested cultural and artistic development. Nietzsche had already identified the culprit as the person who "bears with him everywhere the triumphant feeling of being the worthy representative of contemporary German culture."[27] These Germans lived parasitically off the greats of the past (Goethe, Schiller, Beethoven), parodying them to the point where no new creation was any longer possible: "'All seeking is at an end' is the motto of the philistines."[28] The failings of this notional category of Germans have formed the centrepiece of all subsequent accounts of what went wrong. Gordon Craig, for example, disposed of the entire unification period in one sentence: "The victory over France and the unification of the German states inspired no great work of literature or music or painting."[29]

More recent accounts of this German philistine treat him less ruthlessly, but the diagnosis is the same. Wolfgang Mommsen's consideration of culture and politics in the German empire began pluralistically, positing the existence of multiple "cultural milieux" within the new Germany, from aristocratic at one end of the social scale to working class at the other, with a Catholic milieu thrown in to account for the first major cultural initiative of the new Germany – its effort, known as the "struggle for culture" or *Kulturkampf*, drastically to reduce the power and influence of the Catholic church in Germany. But in fact the only milieu seemingly worth discussing at any length was the "dominant" one, that of "middle class and Protestant" culture – Nietzsche's concern precisely. Mommsen argued that middle-class culture, once in "close partnership with constitutional liberalism" and dedicated to ideals of aesthetic humanism and artistic autonomy, turned quickly and easily to focus "on the Imperial throne as the symbol of the new nation." In so doing, it tied itself to a state apparatus and personnel at best indifferent to the "artists, writers, composers, and scholars themselves" and at worst actively promoting lifeless, sycophantic, and aesthetically bankrupt "official" culture. "By about 1880," concludes Mommsen, "in contrast to the situation in France, German culture had become stalled." By 1900 the situation had, if anything, worsened. The "influence that the general public" (i.e., the middle-class and Protestant middle-class one) "exerted over cultural matters steadily declined," and "the loose symbiotic relationship between cultural and nationalist attitudes," along with the general depoliticization of the middle class, "prepared the ground for a particularly aggressive form of cultural imperialism."[30]

There is some truth in this version of cultural development, particularly after unification. In Ulrich Scheuner's words, art became a "state function [*Staatsaufgabe*]" after 1871, serving as a "weight-bearing pillar of the idea of the state": "without doubt the official care, cultivation, and organization of the arts in the Kaiserreich reflected a growing state determination" to control artistic expression by means of a concerted *Kulturpolitik*.[31] Although funding of the arts remained in the hands of the individual states and a number of them jealously guarded their powers of cultural policy-making, the general phenomenon of state sponsorship of key projects and institutions, facilitated and supported by nationally conscious middle-class committees and associations, describes much of cultural production across Germany after 1871. Prussia and other states spent their money on designing and constructing public buildings and monuments, on preserving and making inventories of historical buildings and works of art (music included), and on supporting educational institutions such as art schools and music conservatories. Painters such as Anton von Werner produced enormous canvases depicting the triumphs of the Prussian-led German state. Ambitious building projects, such as the creation of grand new public spaces and buildings in Strasburg and a new university in the Prusso-Polish province of Posen, projected an image of the new and confident nation, rooted in the past, oriented to the future.[32]

In many, if not most, of these activities, the obvious predominance of a "historical" style, along with a gate-keeping insistence on tried-and-true technical training in elements of the craft such as perspective and anatomical accuracy in painting or rules of harmonization and voice leading in musical composition, gave creative endeavours a stultifying aura of conventionalism and traditionalism. Scholars since Nikolaus Pevsner, in his classic *Pioneers of the Modern Movement from William Morris to Walter Gropius* (1936), therefore have averted their eyes in horror from all the monumental buildings, the paintings of monumental events, the monumental spaces, and so on, as representations of a lesser aesthetic value, backward looking and stale at best or looking forward only to the repulsive historicism and monumentalism of National Socialism at worst.[33] Thomas Mann, in his brilliant, difficult, profoundly ambivalent essay "The Sorrows and Grandeur of Richard Wagner," looked back at the nineteenth century more in sorrow than repulsion. Reflecting on the taste for large-scale works such as Wagner's, he wrote that the bourgeoisie of the nineteenth century was "equivocal" and "laughable" in its attachment to "liberal ideas of reason and progress," "crass" in its materialism, and absurd in its "willful love of mere largeness," its "taste for the monumental and standard, the copious and grandiose." They made their aesthetic choices, he accused, "as though size in itself were the natural attribute of morality."[34] Such teleologies of disaster are, of course, *Sonderweg* thinking at its most direct. Even a relatively recent summation of imperial German culture notes that "it would be wrong to dismiss all the cultural products of the post-unification period as pompous and overblown *kitsch*" and acknowledges that it is "doubtful whether the official art and architecture of the Empire will ever be regarded with much affection.[35]

The Question of German Identity

The music of the period cannot be so easily absorbed in a narrative of stagnation at the hands of officialdom and its sycophants. But it is still true for music, as for the other arts, that no one engaged with them seemed able to ignore the question of German identity, and after 1871 that preoccupation very often was accompanied by more than a whiff of triumph and complacency. German identity intruded itself into every discussion about a concert, building, or exhibition, every production of a new opera or play. Nevertheless, Frederick's flute compositions to the contrary notwithstanding, musical life did not and could not conform to the German borders established in 1871. It seemed fitting that the intellectual leader most insistent on the Second Reich's legitimacy as a cultural as well as a political expression of the German nation, Heinrich von Treitschke, was almost completely deaf by 1871. The new boundaries of German nationhood failed to make sense of the German musical heritage for anyone literal minded enough to ask whether Mozart – or, heaven forbid, Beethoven himself – must now be considered an Austrian musician and not a German one at all.

The most notable feature, then, of "German" musical life after 1871 was the continuity of established ways of talking and performing and thinking about German music across what one might expect to be a great and momentous divide. People did not trouble themselves to settle the non-issue of whether Mozart was German in the 1871 sense of the term, and institutional life followed suit. Orchestral concerts and choral societies continued to show a distinct preference for the works of German-speaking composers, whether Thuringian (Bach), Hanoverian (Handel), Rhenish (Beethoven), Salzburger (Mozart), or Hanseatic (Brahms), but for all the chauvinism implicit in musical activities it was a *grossdeutsch* chauvinism, indifferent even to the claims of Prussia as dominant power and Berlin as capital city. Wagner had tried to evade the politics of unification altogether by putting his own musical capital in the middle of Bavaria, or the world as far as he was concerned. More prosaically, the first journal dedicated to professional music scholarship was a joint German-Austrian venture, the *Vierteljahrsschrift für Musikwissenschaft*, edited by Friedrich Chrysander in Hamburg, Philip Spitta in Berlin, and Guido Adler in Prague, then Vienna.

But even if what Wagner called the "true meaning and peculiarity of the German essence" could derive from a Germany larger than Bismarck's Reich, German music could not be entirely sealed off from the rest of Europe and the world.[36] German musicians in the imperial period worked in a field of tension between their desire for international cultural exchange, on the one hand, and for an authentically German art, on the other. The search for true Germanness in a world of nations also exposed a series of further tensions that found expression in the arts and cultural institutions of these years. First among these were religious tensions. Nineteenth-century Germans were profoundly divided on the question of religion's place in their rapidly changing society. These divisions came out explicitly in the "cultural struggle" of German liberals against Catholicism in the 1870s, but before and after that conflict, an undercurrent of cultural anxiety reflected the possibility that there could be no single German culture because of these confessional divisions. The confessional divide also expressed itself, not surprisingly, in efforts to represent the sacred in visual, dramatic, and musical forms. Brahms regarded his *German Requiem* of 1867 as speaking to the experience of all humanity, but this intention did not prevent the work from receiving over the next decades (with a few exceptions such as Protestant Leipzig, where audience response was tepid) a warmer reception in largely Protestant areas than in Catholic ones, and abroad, from being performed more frequently in largely Protestant countries than in Catholic ones.

The question of religion reflected an even more general questioning of the hold the past had upon the present. The Wagnerians disliked Brahms's *Requiem* because they regarded it as old-fashioned and stylistically regressive, and its admirers underscored this quality by praising its "*Bach-Protestantisch*" contrapuntal writing.[37] Nietzsche's second "untimely meditation" on the "uses and disadvantages of history for life" extended his lament about Germany's lack of cultural vitality to the question of historical consciousness, an excess of which he believed had inhibited people's ability to live and create. Critics other than Nietzsche worried that too many artistic works relied on historical precedents to the point of lifeless conventionality. But many artists and consumers of music regarded the past as the only sure guide in society's march forward. Ambivalence about both tradition and modernity formed a subtext of much musical activity and creation.

The relationship of music to political and social life after 1871 inevitably raised one final, encompassing set of questions, which lay behind music criticism, programming, education, and publishing. Who were the musical leaders in society: musicians, scholars, critics, or even a more self-consciously modern category of commercial producers and sponsors? Who could or should participate in musical life? Did music have a role to play in the collective life of the nation? And if it did, then was it celebratory and affirming or critical and interrogative? As musical styles and schools developed and collided in the rapid pace of cultural activity after 1871, these questions received no clear answers. Not even the most optimistic observer could have found in these decades the "unity of artistic style, in every expression of the life" of the German people, that Nietzsche had seemingly (but cryptically) endorsed. But amid the "chaotic jumble of styles" he derided as the pedants' modernity, Imperial Germany sustained a musical life that created as many glimpses of the future as homages to the past.

Musical Support Systems

The foundation of the German Empire in 1871 left much in the way of cultural organization intact but at the same time improved certain practical conditions for national musical endeavours. As to the first, cultural policy remained decentralized and in the hands of individual states and municipalities. It constituted one of the more vigorous survivals of particularism in German Europe. Particularism and decentralization did not necessarily produce backwardness and provincialism in cultural affairs, although critics were always quick to find both. One English observer of Germany in the 1870s wrote that "*Kleinstädterei*, or the niggling government of petty princes," with its "consequent narrow views and interests, place-hunting, and stagnation of culture," was "the bane of Germany."[38] Its consequences after 1871 were less dire than that. For one thing, the persistence of a pattern of dispersed cultural organization generated local pride in the offerings of a state or city's cultural institutions. This in turn led to perpetual competition for the best conductors and the best orchestras – or, in other artistic domains, the best international art exhibitions or the best permanent art collections. Cultural activists, especially in the area of music, often had only limited interest in political borders, because the German culture that they sought to nurture had much to lose, both as a historical tradition and as a continuing project, from too much attention to political borders. The German General Music Association (*Allgemeiner Deutscher Musikverein* [ADMV]), founded in 1861 in Weimar as the first national music society in Germany, sponsored annual music festivals that alternated among different German and German-speaking cities and established a number of scholarship funds for which many more Germans than the residents of Bismarck's Reich were eligible to compete. Arnold Schoenberg of Vienna was a recipient of an award from the ADMV's Beethoven-Stiftung, established in 1872.

The decentralization of German culture and the arts across the great divide of unification in 1871 reflected two distinct processes in play, the continuation of each of which sheds a different kind of light on the question of unification's significance or lack thereof. The first consisted of what Abigail Green called "particularist state-building" and was accompanied by, among other things, the active promotion of cultural activities such as museums and art collections, monument building, and festivals involving music, costume, dance, and drama.[39] Preservation of the German states after 1815 meant, in Green's analysis, that they had to reinvent themselves "as modern states," and that in turn meant taking a firm grasp on cultural and artistic life as much as or even more than on armies and foreign policy. The Saxon government in 1857 supported increased arts funding on the grounds that Saxony should "surely continue to lead the way for her larger German neighbours, as she has done so gloriously in the past."[40] The wish to "continue to lead" did not fade away in 1871, nor did the institutional arrangements that reflected and encouraged them. Green concludes that "the underlying belief in a cultural nation that transcended political boundaries changed surprisingly little" after 1871.

Confining our view to the question of state sponsorship of culture and the arts, we see that unification's nearly non-existent effect on concepts of cultural nationhood meant that individual states went right on sponsoring artistic and cultural projects intended to celebrate their own monarchy or state traditions. The stimulating effects of so many different localisms in competition with each other, along with a general expansion of commerce, wealth, and tax receipts, meant that more and more money was spent on artistic undertakings. Funds for projects ranging from grand new buildings to band music in the town park also came from a wider variety of sources, with an inexorable shift to bourgeois patrons and audiences and to public coffers, at the state and civic levels. Just as significant was the presence of private, non-state sources of funding even for public projects. Voluntary associations, for instance, played a crucial role in music as well as in the visual arts, helping local orchestras, conservatories, theatres, and art museums in their ongoing activities; raising subscription funds for big projects such as monuments of composers; and organizing amateur performance groups for public performances. Little of this was new. Concert associations and choral societies had been around for decades, the opening up of court concerts and princely museums to a paying public had its beginnings in the eighteenth century, and the transformation of civic cultural institutions into joint ventures between taxpayers and wealthy local citizens had long characterized the cultural life of commercial cities such as Hamburg and Frankfurt. Further, churches now provided only meagre patronage of new music, which reflected changes in church independence going back to the decline of the Holy Roman Empire. In sum, the imperial period saw the final consolidation of a complicated and more or less functional system of densely interrelated but dispersed cultural institutions.

But unification changed some of the basic conditions of making music as a profession. The biggest changes occurred with the further integration of cultural activities into the commercial market, with mixed consequences for artistic autonomy. Works of art became products for sale in a marketplace of art galleries and auction houses, music publishers and concert series. Musicians could potentially make enough money to remain independent of governments and wealthy patrons. Or they could, as many feared, become as co-opted by the market as they had been controlled by the courts. The range of commercial opportunities for musicians was considerable. Johannes Brahms (1833–97), one of the first composers to earn a comfortable living from his compositions' royalties alone, composed a lucrative line of Hungarian dance music for amateur pianists. In his early, impoverished years Wagner wrote short articles and prepared piano reductions of opera scores for the Parisian publisher Schlesinger. For their part the directors of cultural institutions showed increasing ingenuity in their search for commercial revenue and private donations. The greatest innovator of all may have been Wagner, whose long march through the nineteenth century's monied institutions, in search of funding for his Festival Theatre (*Festspielhaus*) at Bayreuth, took him from traditional royal patronage (King Ludwig II of Bavaria) to the more impersonal patronage of the new German national government (an appeal to Bismarck, who declined the honour) to an even more novel scheme involving Wagner clubs (*Wagnervereine*), established around Germany and the world chiefly to raise funds for Bayreuth.[41] Germany's complex arrangements for the maintenance of culture and the arts did make artistic innovation on a grand Wagnerian scale difficult. But the very difficulties Wagner encountered in his epic quest for money reveal the norms – and the limitations – of his time. In the jaundiced view of George Bernard Shaw, the "energetic subscription-hunting ladies" of the Wagner clubs soon triumphed over Wagner's own "fabulous and visionary" experiment to "keep the seats out of the hands of the frivolous public and in the hands of earnest disciples." As "an attempt to evade the ordinary social and commercial conditions of theatrical enterprise," Bayreuth, concluded Shaw, "was a failure."[42]

Legal changes that came about as a direct result of unification had major repercussions for the music profession. The removal of restrictions on the practice of trades meant that a baffling array of regulations and privileges, which had lingered on in the localized worlds of German home towns and states, disappeared, and this in turn led to high numbers of publishing houses, theatres, concert societies, and skilled craft associations. Unification of the postal system and changes to censorship legislation made the dissemination of written matter quicker, cheaper, easier. This phenomenon had consequences in all branches of cultural life, not just in literature, because journals and feuilletons had long been a crucial part of the cultivation of music and painting, popular science and amateur archaeology, and so on. Standardization of copyright legislation stabilized notoriously insecure professions like writing and composing, while at the same time the elimination of timeless copyright made possible the proliferation of cheap editions of "classics" of German literature and music.[43] Such developments worked particularly well in strengthening the position of German music publishing, not just in Europe but also in the world. In the course of the nineteenth century, musicologist Albrecht Riethmüller has suggested, the music publishing industry "burgeoned into an enormously powerful and prosperous motor – internationally positioned for success, benefiting from protectionist practices, energized by both domestic creative potential and rampant nationalism, and eager to contribute to national prestige." Unlike literary publishing firms, music companies were not "hampered by the troublesome aspect of translations" and thus enjoyed "unencumbered access to the international" as well as the domestic market.[44]

The Divisions of Musical Germany

George Bernard Shaw's juxtaposition of ordinary conditions and visionary projects hints at a division of European culture into two categories of unstable definition – the high and the low, the serious and the frivolous, the avant-garde and everybody else. Shaw was not alone in viewing the cultural scene dichotomously. Many commentators defended the fortress of art from incursions of triviality and trash. More recently, musicologist Carl Dahlhaus suggested that the great dividing line in nineteenth-century culture lay between a strong and a weak concept of art, on either side of which lay two kinds of artists and audiences.[45] The strong concept of art hearkened back to Schiller's aesthetic community by regarding art as a serious undertaking. An advance guard of creative artists constituted an elite few able to move beyond the conventions of the time and conquer ever more demanding artistic heights. It was up to audiences to follow. On the other side were those who regarded art as entertainment, diversion, and pleasure, who valued transparency of meaning and ease of consumption, and who expected little staying power from the objects of their artistic attention, given that repetition of such work would inevitably produce boredom.

But to illuminate the great variety of ways that people actually participated in musical life we need a finer set of distinctions. Overlapping but distinct circles of musical activity characterized Imperial Germany. First, all the arts, not just music, attracted amateur practitioners and developed new ways to involve art lovers. Urbanization, technology, and a continuing adherence to the elevated goals of self-cultivation combined to make more art available to more people. The legal end to timeless copyright in 1867 meant that music and book stores became awash in the works of Goethe and Beethoven, Schiller and Mozart, the promotion and consumption of which provided a satisfying way to express one's national identity. With the shift in piano manufacture from craft shop to factory by mid-century and the consequent development of standardized types, the production of pianos increased eightfold in Germany between 1870 and 1910, and their cost was halved. The piano came into its own as the centrepiece of middle-class cultivation not in the first half of the nineteenth century, as people sometimes imagine, but in its later decades. The commercial production and availability of other instruments increased also. The genre of Hausmusik, or simple compositions for amateur players, became the profitable foundation of many music publishing houses. These firms oversaw an explosive increase in the sheer amount of available printed music up to a high point around 1910. Anthologies with titles like *Deutsche Hausmusik aus vier Jahrhunderten* (German Music for the Home from Four Centuries) included easy instrumental and vocal pieces and piano reductions from both popular operas and canonical symphonies of the great German masters. The importance of the "piano in the parlour" for middle-class sociability, for the persistence of an idealist view of art's edifying effects, and for the growing certainty among ordinary Germans about Germany's special musical gifts can scarcely be exaggerated.

The people who participated in the amateur artistic activities of Imperial Germany were also among the most avid students of the past, early and persistent consumers of the historical scholarship that assembled a genealogy of German artistry across the centuries. The repertoire of serious musical amateurism was historical in orientation, and associations of amateur musicians had been among the pioneers in the recovery of the German musical baroque. But hand in hand with a nationally inflected reverence for the past went an openness to contemporary artists and composers, especially those who saw themselves as contributing to this tradition. Of these, Hamburg-born Brahms was uniquely able to combine profound musical language with accessibility to performance and understanding. Obsessed with his late entry into a musical tradition of near-unapproachable greatness (he famously spoke of hearing the footsteps of the giants who came before him), Brahms paid homage to it with works that sought to extend the models from the musical past. A direct consequence of his historical interests was his continuing attention to genres such as the string quartet and the piano sonata. In an era that saw chamber music moving increasingly out of the salon and private drawing room and into the concert hall, Brahms composed a number of chamber works dedicated to the serious musical amateurs who were his friends and supporters. The piano, instrument par excellence of the amateur musician, also stood, in Leon Botstein's words, "at the very heart of his compositional genius."[46]

In addition, Brahms composed hundreds of *Lieder* or art songs, another musical genre central to serious music-making in the home and small gatherings. The *Lied* was a genre closely linked to German identity through its integration of the texts of Germany's poets with the music of its composers. In developing the Lied beyond what previous German composers had already achieved, Brahms and his younger Austrian contemporary Hugo Wolf (1860–1903) helped to shape the culture of feeling and subjectivity that marked middle-class participation in the arts. Its characteristic milieu was not solitude but intimacy, between the keyboard and the vocal lines of music, between pianist and singer, and between performers and their audience. The Lied thus expressed a German community constituted through close communication, and its ubiquity in the middle-class household created a commonality of experience as crucial to national consciousness as visits to large public monuments or participation in the popular historical parades.

The performance of a Lied formed the central subject of the most often reproduced painting at the turn of the century. Titled "Billet outside Paris" (*Etappenquartier vor Paris*) and completed in 1894, its painter, Anton Werner (1843–1915), was the director of the Royal Academic Institute for the Fine Arts in Berlin and already famous for his depictions of the proclamation of the new German empire at Versailles (also frequently reproduced in postcards and prints for the drawing room). "Billet outside Paris" illustrated a scene from the Franco-Prussian War, now some two decades past. Like all Werner's work, this painting had a cinematic realism to it, with the artist's characteristic attention to every detail of décor and uniform. Set in a rococo drawing room of an occupied French chateau, its focal figure was a Prussian officer, standing by a piano and singing a Schubert Lied to the accompaniment of another officer. The spontaneous house concert (*Hauskonzert*) evoked the intimate culture of the German home, which the soldiers' valour now combined with military tradition, elevating both to a national monument of German greatness and contrasting its ineffable substance to the material superficiality of the French society in which it now resounded.

Amateurism also took more public, less domestic forms. Increasing numbers of choral societies, orchestras, and brass bands filled the schedules of performance halls and city bandstands to the bursting point. Dresden, the third-largest city in Germany, boasted fifty male choirs, and even the new industrial city of Ludwigshafen had more than twenty amateur choral groups. Typical of all such groups was the *Singverein Ludwigshafen*, whose director, the grammar school teacher Jakob Gutwein, kept them on a steady diet of "folk songs and the easier art songs," rehearsed "to stand up to the most exacting criticism."[47] In industrial areas, a distinctive culture of mine and factory bands and choruses developed. The Saarland's coal and steel industries generated nearly fifty such organizations at the high point in the decade before the war, with links both to factory music associations elsewhere in Germany and to middle-class musicians in the Saarland's cities.[48] The repertoire of bands and choruses consisted of works from both the past (the oratorios of Handel, Haydn, Spohr, and others) and the present. Max Bruch (1838–1920), a composer now remembered only for his violin concerto, enjoyed tremendous success in Imperial Germany because of the many works he wrote for amateur choruses. The public rapturously received his first great success, *Frithjof*, an un-Wagnerian oratorio based on a thirteenth-century Icelandic saga.[49] The oratorio, old and new, became an important form of religious expression in Imperial Germany, no longer linked to religious services but nevertheless representing a modernized piety, all the more pervasive for being freed from traditional sacred spaces. Bruch himself wrote fourteen sacred oratorios. Brahms's *German Requiem*, the texts for which he drew not from the Latin requiem mass but from Luther's translation of the Bible, offered contemplation of this world's sorrows and consolation to those who grieve. Its debut in Bremen in 1868 and its progress through the choral societies of Germany, Switzerland, England, and the Netherlands – all places with choral traditions that paralleled Germany's own – established Brahms's reputation as a major composer.

If Goethe was right that amateurs were merely following the "tendencies of the times," then amateur involvement in culture and the arts, even though widespread, remained dependent – for repertoire, for instruction, for directors and conductors, for the prestige that amateurs hoped to absorb second-hand – on two other circles of artistic activity, all of which were shaped by professional artists and their creations.[50] These circles can be characterized as the serious, including the musical avant-garde, and the light or entertainment music. Of these, the most commanding arena of artistic activity was that of the serious artistic establishment. It consisted of music conservatories and master classes, prizes and scholarships, opera houses, orchestras, the theatres that housed them, and reviews in newspapers often hand in hand with scholarship in universities.

Disparaged by its critics, as we saw earlier, for being little more than rule enforcers, the artistic establishment of Imperial Germany seemed old beyond its actual years, which were not always that numerous. This was particularly true in the case of musical life, the institutions of which had hardly reached adolescence when they came under attack for being hidebound and conservative. The concert and its rituals and the canon and its composers had early modern precedents, but their defining characteristics had been established only in the middle decades of the century, as we have seen. All reflected a new seriousness, not an old one, and an ongoing process of canon formation and professionalization. After 1870 the leadership of German orchestras was firmly in the hands of a new breed of conductors, who commanded their increasingly large forces like generals in a war on fashion and superficiality. The first full-fledged music conservatory in Germany, Felix Mendelssohn's Leipzig Conservatory, dated back just to 1843; the Berlin Philharmonic, soon the epitome of the serious music ensemble, was founded only in 1882.

Meanwhile, music scholarship too had been preoccupied with German masters of the past for some time, not just following German unification. Scholars had embarked on one of its greatest achievements already in 1851, with the new Bach Gesellschaft's inauguration of its massive effort to publish a complete edition of Bach's works, an effort completed in the 1880s. Choral societies purchased the choral works, chamber music groups the chamber works, and piano teachers everywhere took advantage of a new, though perhaps not better, edition of *The Well-Tempered Clavier.* The Bach edition resonated throughout the community of composers, critics, scholars, and amateur musicians. Brahms, for instance, received the first volume as a Christmas gift from Clara Schumann in 1855 and thereafter subscribed to the complete series. Further critical editions of the works of a single "German" composer followed with the complete works of Handel (begun in 1858), Mozart (begun in 1876), Schubert (begun in 1883), Beethoven (begun in 1884), and Lassus (begun in 1894). These critical editions became, in effect, the musical community's version of monument mania, and starting in the last decade of the nineteenth century they even took on the very name *Denkmal* (monument). In 1889 the *Denkmäler deutscher Tonkunst* was launched with an edited volume of Frederick the Great's compositions for flute, presented to his descendent, Wilhelm II, as a means to flatter and simultaneously draw attention to the need to preserve musical "treasures" in published editions. Wilhelm, impressed with the "patriotic and artistic goals" of the undertaking, duly subsidized future volumes. But his gesture was by no means essential to the overall success of this kind of musical scholarship, which had long relied more on the activism of music lovers than on the patronage of state or aristocracy.

Although the concert repertoire became overwhelmingly historical in the course of the nineteenth century, with the symphonies of Ludwig van Beethoven (d. 1827) at its heart, serious orchestras did not close their lists to new compositions. The death of Beethoven had led to a crisis in the composition of large-scale instrumental works, as composers faced the impossibility of either ignoring or imitating him. The Ninth Symphony in particular, with its introduction of vocal music and words into the symphonic form, seemed to call into question the whole future of purely instrumental music. Wagner claimed it marked the end of the symphony as a vital musical form and proceeded to infuse the operatic form with his inimitable version of the music of the post-Beethovenian future. But after relatively small-scale symphonic composition in the middle decades of the nineteenth century, Brahms's First Symphony, premiered in 1876, took the symphonic tradition (four movements and an old-fashioned array of instrumental forces) and made it once again the centrepiece of the established concert. His ability to fuse tradition with profound innovation demonstrates that the musical establishment of Imperial Germany was not an inert and backward-looking set of institutions incapable of either encouraging new creative energies or recognizing new talent. Nevertheless, without the unbroken musical ties between the Austro-Hungarian and German Empires, the strictly German scene would have been unimaginably poorer.

Unlike art and literature, the progressive forces in music tended to work within these established institutions, not in artistic communities in city and countryside. Another way to reconceive the nature of musical life in Germany after German unification is thus to see not cultural stagnation but the ongoing development of settings in which musical innovations could develop; the ground for modernism in music was provided, in other words, by the very striving to absorb and move beyond the musical language of the past. Beethoven, of course, was the first great representative of what would later in the nineteenth century be called the avant-garde, followed in succession and self-consciously by Robert Schumann, Brahms, Wagner, Richard Strauss, Mahler, and Schoenberg. The musical avant-garde, if one can even use the concept, was hardly touched by the phenomenon of the secession movements that so defined the visual arts. Richard Wagner, for instance, could be seen as Imperial Germany's first and most important avant-garde artist, breaking all rules, musical, social, and otherwise – a veritable one-man secession movement, cutting loose from existing musical and theatrical institutions to build his own centre at Bayreuth, which he organized according to all his own rules of tonality, architectural design of theatres, social conduct at performances, and professional expectations of performers. Yet even while his music dramas continued to enact a radical challenge to existing politics, society, and religion, he became the cultural focus of a radically anti-Semitic and racialist movement, which sought to exclude and to shut down much that was vibrant in Imperial Germany's cultural and artistic life. The musical avant-garde after Wagner thus found little to inspire or sustain them in the Bayreuth ruled over by Wagner's widow Cosima. Wagner's influence, enduringly important in purely musical terms, lost its revolutionizing potential to the suffocating cult of one man's genius. Major new developments in the Austro-German musical world tended, as before, to come to fruition in major centres of cultural production – Vienna, Munich, and Berlin chief among them.

By far the largest and most lucrative amount of music in Germany was made neither by the avant-garde, nor by the establishment, nor by the multitudes of amateurs, but by musicians performing under the banner of entertainment, diversion, and pleasure, unaccompanied by claims to moral edification. Few of these music-makers sought or achieved immortality, and the idealism inherent in the concert repertoire contrasted with the status of entertainment music as commodity. "Light music of quality," as one music historian has dubbed it, had its spiritual home in the Vienna of the waltz-composing Strauss family and the Paris of Jacques Offenbach's operettas.[51] It was performed by professional musicians in venues consistent with its easy-going nature – in restaurants and parks, at spas, in ballrooms and theatres, in popular concert series that provided an alternative to the Beethoven-based repertoire of the symphony concert. The ubiquitous military bands of the nineteenth century were not commercial, but they also performed essentially "light music of quality" and were a much-loved feature of Sunday afternoons in the public gardens. A significant portion of the opera repertoire fell into this category as well, extending beyond operetta into less intellectually ambitious offerings in the formal opera houses. Even Wagner's music dramas, the whole point of which was to elevate dramatic music beyond an evening's diversion and into the higher realm of the symphonic, became a paradoxical kind of middle-brow entertainment for the paying public, especially in regional opera houses with their countless performances of *Lohengrin* and *Tannhäuser*. The bridal chorus from *Lohengrin* began to define the bourgeois wedding ceremony, and it was a rare brass band, whether made up of miners or middle-class civil servants, that did not perform some simplified version of "Siegfried's Rhine Journey."

Conclusion

To regard as important all the cultural developments since 1871, from copyright laws to the Berlin Philharmonic, does not require that one throw out the old notion of a German *Kulturnation* in existence long before 1871, opting instead for the view that national cultures take shape only after state consolidation.[52] Nor does such regard rule out the possibility that unification made little fundamental difference; the important institutions and tendencies may already have been in place and unification just could have strengthened them, in the case of German musical self-regard to an unpalatable degree. The kind of difference unification made would seem, then, to depend on who, what, and where in the culture-producing community we are considering. If the creation and maintenance of a national culture to go with a national state would seem to matter more to writers, critics, statesmen, educators, impresarios, demagogues, audiences, and amateurs than to the artists themselves, then presumably we have to blame only our own reliance on language in making such abstractions explicit. The existence of a nation-state after 1871 did affect how people encountered and understood art of all sorts, but this was conditioning of a tenuous sort, as often irrelevant as it was significant to the sustenance of artistic and cultural life.

Chapter Ten

Men with Trombones

In 1941, interned in a German camp for enemy aliens, P.G. Wodehouse wrote a satirical short story on German plans to conquer England by parachuting brass bands all over the country: "It's the one thing England dreads," says Wodehouse's Hitler, "One hundred thousand parachutes, each dropping a man with a trombone."[1] This frivolous tribute to German military musicians relies for its comic effect on the discordant companionship of war and music: the former violent, destructive, causative, and consequential; the latter expressive, distracting, soothing, emboldening but with a limited capacity to effect change. And yet they are deeply entangled.[2] The essential affinity between war and music is order and control: music is organized sound, and even as it arouses the unruly passions and emotions, it disciplines them as well. A "a well-conducted war," wrote Ernst Jünger, "is like a great symphony."[3] To understand the dynamic role of music in society we should regard it as part of a continuum of disorder and order, war and peace. Music seems uneasily poised along this continuum. Its emotional power is undeniable, but its meaning is unfixed, its impact unclear.

In the modern world, military music and its rituals in public life embody these ambiguities. For historians they suggest how music nationalized public space, reinforced national solidarities, and confirmed national stereotypes in a world, increasingly, of nations. But at the same time the proliferation of military bands in nineteenth-century Germany complicated social and musical hierarchies and introduced new areas of tension into civil-military relations, even as the bands were providing large amounts of what one historian has called "extraordinarily beloved military music" in parks, streets, and other public venues, and states were trying to use them to forge close bonds between soldiers and civilians.[4] Military bands also played a significant role in the rituals of modern internationalism, from stage-managed competitions to its politics of representation during visits of foreign heads of state or at world's fairs. Across national lines they shared a considerable body of musical knowledge – of instruments, composition, and training – and (perhaps more surprisingly) of repertoire. Military bands illustrate Christopher Bayly's observation that "nation-states and contending territorial empires took on sharper lineaments and became more antagonistic to each other at the very same time as the similarities, connections, and linkages between them proliferated."[5] They provided a banal but ubiquitous experience of national belonging. Their purpose, and perhaps their achievement, was to tie individual sensations of sound and rhythm to collective identities.

Military bands may seem an unlikely place to find such fundamental kinds of social action and communication.[6] Yet because of their tremendous growth in numbers and popularity since the mid-nineteenth century, they provide an unexpectedly varied array of practices and controversies to explore. Their ubiquity alone requires explanation. By the last decades of the nineteenth century men in uniform performed in parks, marched in streets, accompanied civic occasions, and sometimes went to war. They were a pervasive aspect of the soundscape of modern life. Some twenty or more military bands, large and small, performed regularly in Berlin alone, and other European capitals were not far behind.[7] Over the course of the century the numbers of military musicians grew rapidly, and military bands improved the quality of their music-making, pioneered the use of the many newly invented or improved wind and brass instruments, and extended the range of their repertoire to include reams of new works and transcriptions of the repertoire of compositions we associate with civilian musical life. Brass and wind bands became difficult to categorize in musical hierarchical terms; they played marches and fanfares, potpourris drawn from the world of opera and operetta, and – at their most ambitious – versions of entire Beethoven symphonies. As their numbers and performances grew, the bands also delivered this varied repertoire to civilian life, their reach extending into provincial centres that lacked symphony orchestras or opera companies of their own.[8]

People of the nineteenth century mainly took this noise for granted, commenting on it in memoirs as though it were something that had always been part of their collective life, a background noise with mostly pleasant associations. As histories of military music have emphasized, the phenomenon of instrumentalists accompanying men to war stretches back as far as humans have fought each other. Henry George Farmer's popular history of military music, written in the early twentieth century, found evidence of its presence among our "pagan forebears" as well as among more "civilized peoples." Peter Panoff, writing in 1938, thought all peoples "equal in their love and enthusiasm" for military music and had always practised it.[9] In the form of the military march and trumpet call, military evocations are common in western music, woven into works of instrumental and operatic music, serious and light music alike. For musicologist Frank Heidlberger, the "distinction between the notion of 'military music' on the one hand and 'art music' on the other ... is both phenomenologically and historically false."[10]

Yet the role that military music came to play in collective life in the nineteenth century did represent something new, in number and quality of a different order than what had come before because of the expansion of armies on a mass scale and the penetration of military ceremonies and ritual into society. Military musicians continued to function much as they had for centuries: they provided battlefield commands with trumpet and horn calls. They reinforced the discipline of military life, with music to march by and music to signal the start and the end of the day, and of garrison routine or service in the field in between. They accompanied military rituals: funerals, formal troop reviews, and ceremonies of celebration and commemoration.[11] They made audible the discipline and the prestige of the troops they accompanied. But little by little, the musical ambitions and activities of these ensembles came to exceed their functionality and so their significance in the societies that sustained them changed as well.

Wilhelm Wieprecht and the Reform of Prussian Military Music

No single person was more important to this process, or more exemplary of the changes it entailed, than the Prussian bandmaster Wilhelm Wieprecht, the man whom Hans von Bülow dubbed in 1858 the "*l'état c'est moi* in Prussian military music."[12] Wieprecht was a civilian and came from a civilian musical background. He was born in 1802 in Aschersleben in Prussian Saxony, a garrison town that was absorbed by the Napoleonic Kingdom of Westphalia in 1807 and remained in French hands until 1813, when the Prussians recovered it and made it the seat of a light cavalry regiment (the 10th Hussar Regiment). His father was a former military trumpeter who became the director of the city music institute upon leaving the service in 1807, just before the French arrived. He was a highly competent musician but seems to have wanted his son to do better for himself and so encouraged him to study the violin, along with the wind and brass instruments that made up town ensembles. In 1819, having received his qualifying certificate as a town musician, young Wieprecht set off, in his words, "to see the world," that is, to find a musical post in a larger setting.[13] He settled first in Dresden. There, through family connections and the help of Carl Maria von Weber, music director of the Dresden Royal Opera (and an exemplar of composers who integrated military topics into "civilian" genres of operatic and symphonic music), he was able to further his studies of the violin and clarinet. In 1820 he left for Leipzig, where he obtained a position with the famous Gewandhaus orchestra and played for city and opera musical ensembles, sometimes as a violinist, sometimes as a clarinetist. During this time he studied with the great virtuoso trombonist of the day, Karl Traugott Queisser and perfected his mastery of the other brass instruments as well. One senses a restless ambition in Wieprecht, a determination to do more than find a settled place in the existing musical arrangements of the day. These were in a parlous state, caught somewhere in that extended transitional phase of the *Sattelzeit*, when early modern ways – and older instruments themselves – were gradually disappearing, shifting, and changing.[14] Among the most important aspects of his musical education in Leipzig was extended contact with Friedrich Rochlitz, the learned editor of German Europe's most important music periodical, the *Allgemeine Musikalische Zeitung*. Through Rochlitz, Wieprecht saw a "new world" opening up to him and came to understand that "without knowledge [*Wissenschaft*], one will never be able to grasp the spirit [*Geist*] of music."[15]

When Wieprecht moved to Berlin in 1824 to join the royal opera ensemble as a violinist, he became an agent who was moving this process forward, not just a single person trying to adjust in unsettled times. Wieprecht interpreted his life in such terms, subsequently describing the epiphanic moment in 1824 when he heard "for the first time" a "full infantry band": "I was seized by a feeling that I have never been able to describe. Was it the rhythm, the melody, the harmony, or the fusing of all these different elements that moved me so profoundly?"[16] Perhaps it was also the possibility of escaping from the musical rut in which he found himself, missing the musically more vibrant orchestral and educational opportunities in Leipzig. Military music was not a novelty for him – his younger brother was a member of the military band that brought on his stroke of insight. Nor was it in any sense a step up in the musical world. His father, after all, had tried to elevate his son out of precisely this workaday world of bandsmen in service. Yet, at least in retrospect, this ambitious twenty-two-year-old still recognized in the musically unassuming military band a vehicle for social advancement: "And when I heard the band play the overture to Mozart's *Figaro*, I came to the firm decision that I must devote my life to military music ... Here was my calling, here was a musical endeavor in which I could soon achieve something worthwhile."[17] The child of the eighteenth-century father was turning himself into the modern man of music, a person for whom striving and excelling, talent and ambition, not fitting in and settling down, were becoming the watchwords of the era.[18]

Still, though Wieprecht was trained in the instruments that constituted a military ensemble, the military musical establishment of the time did not take advice from minor court violinists.[19] Looking around among the well-appointed Berlin military ensembles, he noted that the cavalry units had particularly "miserable" bands, and so he found a trumpet corps attached to a lowly dragoon regiment and offered his services to the commander, who accepted them. A typical regimental band at that time was small, ranging from about seven to fifteen instrumentalists and dominated by woodwinds, not brass. Extra musicians were added for special occasions – percussionists and Turkish crescent bell (*Schellenbaum*) players – and every regiment also had signal musicians (fifes, trumpets, and drums) for marching and battlefield command and control.[20] A musical chain of command hardly existed within the bands, and before the 1820s officials showed little concern for the musical excellence of the ensembles, despite the efforts that had already been made by musicians such as August Heinrich Neithardt to transcribe overtures of Mozart and Beethoven for these small wind ensembles.[21] Musical ambitions that did exist were restricted to the competent execution of the military ensemble's duties, much as Johann Sebastian Bach, a century earlier, had sought to provide his new employers in Mühlhausen with "well-ordered church music." These duties had long included the provision of small performances for the commanding officer and his staff, and in 1819 Frederick William III, an admirer of military music, had appointed Georg Abraham Schneider, his new music director of the royal theatre, to serve, as had many Prussian court musicians before him, as the overseer of all Prussian military music as well.[22] But this was a only a gesture, or perhaps a faint echo still sounding from the era when Frederick the Great had appointed his leading court musician, Johann Joachim Quantz, to keep an ear attuned to the small military bands as well. Neither Schneider nor his king promoted centralization or systematic organization, training, and practice of all military ensembles.

Despite his own stated wish merely to create "a well-organized military music," Wieprecht's life work consisted of changing the status quo and making military bands a more prominent part of public music-making.[23] His story represents the possibilities of careers opening up to talent in the early nineteenth century, yet it is still extraordinary to find a civilian musician managing to use the vehicle of the status-conscious Prussian military musical establishment, or of any military band, to fulfil his ambitions. For Wieprecht change began with new instruments. The decisive invention for brass instruments was the mechanical valve, first patented by two German instrumentalists (both from Breslau in Prussian Silesia), Friedrich Bluhmel and Heinrich Stölzel, in 1818.[24] It made possible the playing of more sophisticated music on instruments long recognized as the most effective for music performed in the open air, and it therefore presented immediate benefits for the improvement of military music-making. Yet someone had to want to transform regimental bands into significant musical ensembles. Wieprecht was not the only such person nor was Prussia the only country in which such persons could be found. In 1827 the Munich correspondent for the Leipzig *Allgemeine musikalische Zeitung* had noted his amazement on hearing the trumpet corps of the Bavarian Royal Cuirassier regiment playing music with "modulations and chromatic transitions," rather than the "so-called extracts" he was used to hearing from military bands.[25] In Berlin Wieprecht had encountered an initial unwillingness to consider the new instruments, and only after demonstrating the splendid qualities of a valved trumpet could he convince the commander of the Prussian Garde-Dragoner-Regiment to buy some. In 1829 he was invited to Breslau to train their cavalry bands to play the new instruments and then, having at last caught the attention of the king, he proceeded to re-instrument the prestigious guard regiment bands of Potsdam as well, replacing trumpets, adding cornets of all ranges, replacing bass trombones with the new bass tuba, which, as he reported, "I invented together with the court instrument maker J.G. Moritz."[26]

By 1838 the old king had appointed him Schneider's successor as director of Musikkorps des Garde-Corps, the most prestigious of all Prussian military ensembles. Wieprecht, on his own initiative, made the position an even more powerful one and held it until his death thirty-four years later. He used it to bring the entire array of Prussian military ensembles into a single system of expanding numbers and types of instruments within progressively more complicated ensembles (signal corps, trumpet corps, horn corps, full infantry regiment), and for these groups he then created musical arrangements of the extant corpus of military marches and miscellaneous other works, with different versions carefully calibrated to the varied sizes of the ensembles.[27] A common criticism of military bands in the first decades of the nineteenth century was the poor quality of their repertoire. Vincent Novello, the English music publisher, travelled around Germany and Austria in 1829 and was disappointed to hear the royal military bands in Munich play only "harmonies of the poorest common-place description," "arrangements from Opera Airs by Rossini and his imitators," and miscellaneous pieces "of the usual trashy waltz kind."[28] From this perspective Wieprecht's achievement was to add many more musical works to the wind ensemble repertoire – including at least fifty of his own marches and overtures and about sixty of his transcriptions of overtures and symphonies from the orchestral repertoire. All of this relentless effort worked to make art music (he was most admired for his transcriptions of the Beethoven symphonies) an increasingly prominent part of the military band repertoire.[29] The ensembles of the Wieprecht System became bigger, louder, and more like orchestras in their expressive range. Eventually, he created full military orchestras that included stringed instruments as well. As for the soldier-musicians, he made them practise harder, and he worked, mostly fruitlessly, to persuade the Prussian monarchs to support conservatory training for military bandleaders.[30] He improved their pay and supported their right (when off-duty) to perform for weddings, town ceremonials, and local choral societies and theatre productions. In the 1840s he travelled extensively in the German states and continental Europe, gathering knowledge of other military musical practices and more or less proselytizing for his own system.[31] In the decades that followed he was asked to advise countries from Turkey to Guatemala for help in reforming their military bands.[32]

Changing Aspects of the Civilian and Military Musical Profession

By the end of the century and in a process confirmed by German unification and extended with the expansion of the armies of the German states, the foundations he had laid supported a German-wide military musical establishment of some 560 bands, employing altogether about 17,000 musicians and reaching every state, province, city, and town in Imperial Germany.[33] Underlying the work of this enterprising civilian musician were structural transformations in society that contributed to the far greater presence of military music-making in modern life. The labour market for musicians had changed drastically since the eighteenth century, as Wieprecht's own career illustrated. The disappearance of guilds as regulators of musicians' employment and defenders of professional musicians' privileges in towns and cities had created what was in effect a musical proletariat of jobbing musicians, some with a settled residence and regular employment but most with neither. The "independent" (*freistehende*) musicians found short-term employment providing dance, civic, church, funeral, and wedding music; they became supernumerary members of civilian bands or orchestras when extra musical forces were required; and they worked mainly without contracts and hence were subject to every kind of exploitation and economic insecurity.[34] In Bavaria the abolition of guilds was followed by the establishment in 1838 of requirements for the licensing of musicians that could be both onerous and expensive, particularly for itinerant musicians.[35] The Allgemeine Deutsche Musikerverband, which was founded in 1861 by Franz Liszt and Franz Brendel with the dual aim of promoting contemporary music (primarily of the New German School variety) and of supporting musicians, made sporadic and mostly ineffectual attempts to help these unaffiliated jobbing musicians, but was unable to exert much influence. Employment exchanges proliferated in major cities but were mainly just a more organized form of exploitation.

At the same time two unrelated processes of expansion accelerated and intensified this dual dynamic of opportunity and conflict within a musical proletariat. The first aspect concerns the Prussian army, and later the armies of the other German states, which grew significantly as part of its modernization, especially after 1862, and with it grew the number of musicians in military service. Unregulated musical academies established in the nineteenth century by professional musicians as another way to make money churned out young musicians who were often drawn to musical employment in the military upon finishing their training. After their military service they could receive a "civil benefits certificate," which gave them preference in obtaining jobs in public service, working as postmen, railway workers, or town clerks.[36] Once in such a position many continued to earn money in their off-duty hours as musicians and, indeed, could receive preferential treatment in hiring in that function as well. In 1910, for instance, the Württemberg Ministry of War received a request from the mayor of Neckarsulm for help in filling the post of the town's music director, explaining that it was the "wish of the citizenry to obtain a capable military musician."[37]

In post-Napoleonic Bavaria the establishment of the *Landwehr* or citizens' militia in 1807 led to a tremendous expansion of small military brass and wind bands all over Bavaria, supported in part by the royal budget and in part by commanding officers. Bavarian King Maximilian I Joseph regarded them as particularly important for winning over the population in newly acquired crown lands such as Franconia.[38] In Nuremberg people would have heard military bands constantly and everywhere – their reveilles and taps, their parades and concerts, and their presence in popular restaurants and dance halls. Already in 1833 the local civilian musicians were registering complaints about unfair competition from soldier-musicians; the only result seems to have been an 1835 regulation that forbade members of the military from offering private instruction to civilians.[39] Meanwhile, as the military function of the citizens' militias diminished, their musical ensembles still flourished, blowing horns and beating drums for every kind of local event and contributing to the establishment of the small brass band as the quintessential ensemble of Bavarian local culture.

The Bavarian case provides an intense example of military music's extensive presence, but elsewhere as well, military bands became more tightly woven into the fabric of local life in peacetime. In the Prussian army the so-called music commission officers, who provided oversight of the military bands within individual regiments, and regimental band leaders also acted as unofficial hiring agents, setting up local gigs (weddings, restaurants, theatre ensembles) for their musicians and taking a cut of the proceeds. Prussian military musicians did receive regular paychecks from the army, but most military musicians were paid less than regular soldiers, earning barely enough to support an individual, let alone a family.[40] The ready availability of military musicians for casual musical labour thus further exacerbated the difficulties of independent civilian musicians.

Opportunities for supplementing soldier-musician income were available only because of a second aspect of nineteenth-century expansion: the growing demand for middlebrow musical performances at spas, at restaurants, and in parks with bandstands newly built to accompany the leisure and weekend hours of urban people with agreeable "light" music of quality.[41] Military bandsmen appeared in such venues both in uniform (in "official" performances) and out of it. Their performances thus formed part of a larger marketplace for the consumption of music, exploding in productive output over the course of nineteenth century. It included publishers, composers, transcribers, instrument-makers, uniform tailors, and not least, civilian performers, both amateur and professional. And its expansion conditioned not only the nature of military-musical contributions to public life but also the increasingly tense relations between professional civilian musicians and their military counterparts.

Kindling His Genius upon His Times: Military Bands, Nationalism, and Militarism

Such developments provide a broad context for understanding what Wieprecht did with the military musical ensembles. To understand the nature of his and his reforms' relationship to these societal changes, we might compare Wieprecht to the figure of Jacques Offenbach, as interpreted by Siegfried Kracauer in his unconventional biography of this nineteenth-century, middlebrow, musical hero. Kracauer called his study the "biography of a society," and in it he attributed Offenbach's success to his "feel for congruency." "Just at the time he was making his first public appearances," Kracauer wrote, "the Paris that was to adopt him as its own, the Paris of the Boulevards, was coming into being. His environment leaped to meet him, and he kindled his genius on it."[42] So too did Wieprecht show an extraordinary capacity to kindle his genius upon his own times, and in his remaking of the Prusso-German military musical establishment we see the creation of musical practices and common musical experiences that had resonance and repercussions well beyond improvements in the wind bands themselves. These practices provide us with a "social history of the imagination," in which collective life comes "out into the world of objects" where people can experience it and we can study it.[43]

Wieprecht's music-making, like the military itself, was nothing if not "out in the world." Hector Berlioz wrote of military bands in Berlin that "one would have designedly to avoid them not to hear at least some, since at all hours of the day … they are passing through the streets."[44] Wieprecht had a talent for using his bands to lay claim to public space. Berlioz saved his fullest description for a performance arranged in honour of his visit by Wieprecht himself, the "head bandmaster" who commanded not "regimental musicians" but "regiments of musicians," each of them "favoured by nature with indefatigable lungs and lips of leather." As was true of his contemporaries, what struck Berlioz most about Wieprecht the bandmaster was not his extraordinary organizational talent but the dramatic public spectacles he produced. The one he witnessed in 1843 involved a brass band of 320 players, concealed behind a curtain and becoming audible as they launched into Berlioz's overture to *Les*

Francs-Juges – played with brass instruments rather than strings and with "marvelous exactness" and "furious fire."[45]

Enormous performances by massed military bands were by then the Prussian bandmaster's signature. What Berlioz experienced was meagre compared with Wieprecht's first demonstration of bands in a grand order of battle – a performance in honour of the 1838 state visit of Czar Nicolas I, for which Wieprecht assembled 1,200 musicians, from 32 military bands, with an extra 200 drummers. Along with Prussian marches this giant ensemble played the Russian *Zapfenstreich*, followed by what Wieprecht called the "Russian national hymn" – "*Ich bete an die Macht der Liebe*," a poem by the eighteenth-century Protestant Pietist Gerhard Tersteegen, set to music in 1822 by the Russian Orthodox composer Dmitri Bortniansky.[46] It was an elephant of a performance, assembled by Wieprecht out of disparate parts – Prussian military marches, aspects of camp routine, a dash of Russian Orthodoxy, a dollop of German Pietism. It took place in daylight in the courtyard of the Berlin Palace with a crowd of civilians attending. They were, according to a contemporary newspaper account, "enraptured."[47]

In 1843 Wieprecht travelled to Lüneburg to organize and direct a mass concert for the armies of the German Confederation; this event took place at night and brought together some 1,300 musicians from the military bands of the states of German Confederation. It included – another Wieprechtian flourish – 600 torchbearers spelling out the initials of the monarchs of Prussia and Hanover and 48 men shooting off flares, which ascended into the night sky in coordination with the firing of 14 cannons. He repeated much of this *grosse Nachtmusik* for the 1845 visit of Queen Victoria to Coblenz, this time forming a "V" with his torchbearers and playing what Wieprecht called the English "folk song," "God Save the King." Around 1856 he wove everything together – torches, marches, fanfares, a "serenade" (usually his own transcriptions of art music for wind band), presentations of arms, troop reviews, prayers, and anthems – into what came to be called the Prussian *Grosse Zapfenstreich*.[48] In the retrospective gaze by which new-made ceremonials become traditions, this spectacle gradually became a ritual and still, despite the controversy it has caused in contemporary German society, exists today as the "highest form of military recognition" in the Federal Republic of Germany, reserved for the retirement of a German chancellor, president, or defence minister, as well as military officers of the highest rank.[49]

Already by the 1840s, then, military bands had become a spectacular form of music-making in the open air. The meaning of all this sound

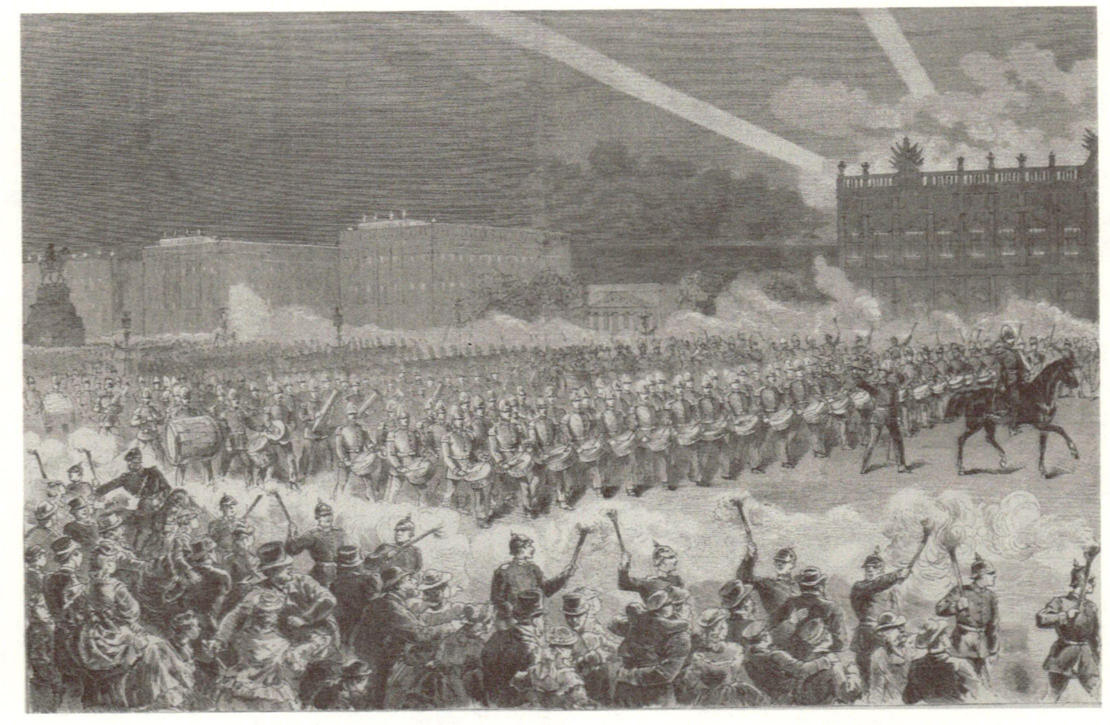

10.1 The Prussian Grosse Zapfenstreich in Berlin, 1872, on the occasion of the "Meeting of the Three Emperors," Wilhelm I of Germany, Franz Joseph of Austria-Hungary, and Alexander II of Russia. Friedrich Kaiser, *Leipziger Illustrierte Zeitung*. AKG Images.

is nevertheless elusive. Wieprecht seems to have seen himself not as a preserver of traditions but as an impresario of state display in the modern mode. His writings come back repeatedly to the "effect" (*Wirkung*) of his spectacles and how best to achieve them with all the forces at his command.[50] Even before the 1848 revolutions this Prussian civilian was already providing an answer to his state's need for new forms of public display and popular legitimation, and the Grosse Zapfenstreich, which reached a stable form shortly after the revolutions, was his most important ceremonial creation. Its chief characteristics were slow, deliberate tempos, choreographed movements of groups, massed crowds of spectators, hymns and prayers and ordering of ranks, accompanied by torches in a flare-lit night. Such ceremonies both nocturnalized and theatricalized power.[51] They enacted the dignity of the state in daytime and nighttime and quite often in the presence of foreign visitors.

Yet the aesthetic influences that shaped his spectacles had their origins not so much in the Prussian military or musical past as in those of the greatly mistrusted French, their state, and their revolution.[52] Revolutionary fetes had demonstrated to a watching world the stunning effects to be achieved by massed brass and woodwind instruments playing out of doors.[53] Here the military band first glimpsed its future, separated from court ceremonial and camp life, directed towards an audience of all. Just as important, the Wieprechtian spectacle took the aesthetic of French grand opera out of doors, evoking the distant past of Louis XIV and his Italian-turned-Frenchman Kapellmeister Jean-Baptiste Lully. Lully had been in charge of military as well as court music, and he first developed the stylistic features of the military march itself, albeit for the useful purpose of moving massed groups of singers (as soldiers, priests, the triumphant, and the defeated) on, off, and around the stage.[54] His operas, moreover, had been the total work of political art; in the words of the seventeenth-century moralist Jean de la Bruyère, they held "the mind, the eye, and the ear equally in thrall."[55]

In 1825, a century and a half later, another Italian-turned-Frenchman, Gasparo Spontini, came to Berlin as the celebrity music director of the Prussian State Opera. He was a composer of a transitional form of opera, with echoes of Lully, Handel, and Gluck and foretastes of the fully realized grand opera of Meyerbeer and Auber soon to come. Already in *La Vestale* in 1807 he was handling mass tableaux of soldiers and citizens accompanied by military-like music. The opera was an enormous hit and was eventually performed in Berlin, as in every important European city. He followed it with *Fernand Cortez, or the Conquest of Mexico*, in which the military-musical aesthetic could not have been more overt, and in Berlin (with the help of E.T.A. Hoffmann) he premiered a new version of his 1819 Parisian flop *Olimpie*, featuring an unlikely tale of a daughter of Alexander the Great, caught between the warring kings of Greece and Macedonia. And there in 1824, in Spontini's orchestra pit, sat young Wieprecht, bored and restless in his second-string assignment but watching and learning nevertheless.[56]

Many decades later, in June 1871, the triumphant German armies marched for hours through the streets of Berlin, led by the newly crowned German emperor with Bismarck, Moltke, and Roon and accompanied by scores of military bands. Wieprecht helped to plan this grandest of military spectacles but was too ill to participate in it; he died a year later.[57] But because of his reforms the military bands were ready to assume the role for which he seemed to have intended them, that of making visible and audible the existence of the nation, out in the open air for anyone to see and hear. In the decades after Wieprecht's death and German unification the military musical establishment became an increasingly significant part of culture and society across Europe and the Americas. For us the spectacle of their growing size and popularity offers new insight into long-running debates concerning the relationship between war, nation-building, and the militarization of society in this era of expanding armies and intensifying nationalism.[58]

Since its foundation at the triumphal close of three wars, Germany had been the model of a nation forged in and by war. Heightened nationalism was the consequence (more than the cause) of Bismarck's wars, and it solved a problem that Germany, like all nation-states, faced, that of achieving what Arjun Appardurai has called large-scale, "full attachment" to the nation, a "surplus" more "libidinal than procedural," and achieved often through the violence and predations of war.[59] What historians – and some contemporaries – identified as "militarism" and "militarization" in the nineteenth century were broad social and cultural processes. The military made concerted efforts to adapt and insinuate itself into all levels of civil society, and civil society obliged with increasing approval of the military, evident even before the wars of national unification.[60] The "theatricalization" itself of military parades and reviews, especially after 1871, represented a "modernization" of traditional festival culture, a phenomenon that Jacob Vogler calls "folklore militarism," binding together the state, the military, and the people.[61] After 1871 men joined veterans' associations in droves, and as the decades went by and actual veterans became a distinct minority within such associations, what

Thomas Rohkrämer calls "sentimental militarism" began to yield to outright war enthusiasm and "Hooray patriotism."[62] Meanwhile, paintings and postcards, poems and stories gave a "war-happy" (*kriegfreudig*) flavour to the nationalist cast of mind among the educated middle classes.[63]

The public response to military bands would seem to fit seamlessly within this militarized nationalism in the German Empire after 1871 – and to a large extent it does. Stepping into the world of military band music is to confront continuities of authoritarianism and bourgeois spectatorship, tactics of repression, indoctrination, and populist enthusiasm – all present in uniformed bandsmen playing a Wieprechtian transcription of Beethoven's Fifth Symphony and his "Yorkscher Marsch" in the park on a Sunday afternoon.[64] In this tableau, we confront Frevert's "nation in barracks" with a vengeance, so much so that even Germany's great musical heritage seems clothed in Prussian blue. But at the same time, it is important to emphasize that in the immediate aftermath of German unification the enthusiasm for how it was seemingly achieved (war) was inextricably bound up with satisfaction at national unity itself, forged by military prowess and soldierly courage. Band performances inspired and sustained the consciousness and the pleasure of belonging to the entity the band represented – in this case the nation – and a similar everyday nationalism was part of the message of most civilian bands, whether those of town, school, or workplace.

Hans Heinz Stuckenschmidt, writing in the 1930s about generations of collective experience, asked whether "hand on heart, who among us was not, when a youngster, filled with excitement at the sound of military music, who among the lovers of music has not been affected by its elementary rhythms and clear melodies?"[65] Across the turn of the nineteenth century attending band performances became a central part of the experiences that habituated Germans to living in their new nation-state. The Wieprechtian system of military bands had been the musical counterpart to the efforts of the military reformers around Scharnhorst to bind the army more closely to society, and if the armies themselves were the "training school" for the nation, then the bands were its music.[66] Military bands played in the near constant military parades and at veterans' association festivities. Their influence extended into other areas of civilian life where cultivation of military and national values was of central importance. For the festivities of shooting associations (*Schützenvereine*) brass bands were indispensable.[67] For those seeking to save working-class youth from bad influences (especially Social Democracy), brass bands formed an integral part of youth associations, youth centres, and the Young Germany League's continuation schools, all dedicated to providing settings to develop working-class physical fitness (in part through paramilitary exercises) and to purvey patriotic education.[68]

Even better, this was music that could be shared by soldiers and civilians. In the national soundscape bands did more to produce a consistent and common experience across the German states and regions than did army service itself (a more complicated phenomenon and one limited to men). Wieprecht had improved Prussian and influenced all German military music by harnessing for his purposes the political, commercial, and industrial forces transforming musical life as well as all else, from new instruments to new music to new venues and new audiences. The repertoire Wieprecht had developed out of opera and symphonic music was German, indeed international, in scope, and one of the characteristics of the famous and much imitated Prussian Army March Collection of 1839 was that not all its marches were Prussian in origin.[69] The bandsmen, like the army itself, wore distinctive uniforms marking their identity as Bavarians, Saxons, Prussians, and so on, and each had marches and flags with specific regional identifications. But the melodies, rhythms, and instrumentation expressed a common set of regional traditions increasingly recognized by all Germans. Military bands did more than provide a musical performance of the nation in arms. They enacted the nation's sense of its past, extending lineage and honours back through the military victories and rulers commemorated in the march repertoire itself. The Army March Collection of 1839 resulted from a royal decree in 1817, which ordered that a collection of "good army marches" be published for use by regimental bands. Bandmasters and civilian composers alike quickly began adding to it.[70] Prusso-German, *kleindeutsch* history of a particular sort is enclosed in these volumes, and the fact that many of these marches have enjoyed an unbroken performance history up to the present – the "*Badenweiler*" (allegedly Hitler's favourite), the "*Fehrbelliner*," the "*Hohenfriedberger*," the "*Königgrätzer*," to name just a few – represents a form of historical continuity that is impossible to ignore.

Military Bands in Transnational Perspective

The expanding presence of military bands in Germany as in all western and westernizing societies over the course of the nineteenth and twentieth centuries speaks to the wide resonance of the cultural and political experiences they provided. The military ceremonials of the Wilhelminian Reich and the French Third Republic adopted similar modes of public spectacle, and all Europeans and Americans heard a great deal of military band music in the latter half of the nineteenth century in the streets, theatres, and parks of their cities and towns.[71] Proponents and producers of military music everywhere began to write about it for the public, establishing journals for and about military music and contributing to general interest publications such as Ernst Keil's *Die Gartenlaube*.[72] Jacob Adam Kappey (1826–1908), a Prussian Rhinelander who learned his trade as military musician in the bands of the Wieprechtian reform era, took his skills to England, as did so many of his fellow German musicians, and eventually he became head of one of the prestigious marine bands. In 1894 he published perhaps the first history of military bands, in which he claimed that this "music of the open air" was the "music of the people." It had been, he lamented, "passed over with almost contemptuous indifference" by historians who "revelled in descriptions of the grandeur of ecclesiastical compositions, of the music of the princely palaces or the royal playhouses" and seemed "ashamed to mention the poor cousin who found inspiration in the open air or 'went a soldiering.'" Yet, he continued, "most of our orchestral music of the highest class originated in that class of music which struck its roots into the hearts of the uncultured people."[73]

Here was a historical perspective with which to conjure. Kappey's account of military music made it the centre of human music-making of all kinds and thereby domesticated it. Less indirectly, other writers on military musical affairs made a case for its importance in the civic life of nations and localities. According to French journalist Oscar Comettant, on the occasion of the 1867 International Military Band Competition at that year's World's Fair in Paris, "Regimental musicians have become an essential part of our civic life, a necessity for every person." The essence of the case such writers made was emotional: for Comettant the "enthusiasm with which people meet these bands speaks to their usefulness."[74] This kind of music – out of doors, at night, woodwind and brass, men in uniforms – had the power to bind people together. It could "lift and strengthen" the hearts of soldiers and civilians alike.[75] It could do for civilians what it allegedly did for soldiers by conveying "that generous exaltation, that sublime intrepidity" that "made heroes and assured victory" and uniting them "in service to a single purpose, lightening their cares and fears, distracting their thoughts from death and the grave."[76] The very form of the military march provided a short musical meditation on war and peace, through its alternations between two tempi, one insistent and brisk (the military march proper), the other more lyrical and peaceful (the trio section). John Philip Sousa once irreverently characterized these two styles as the roast beef and ice cream of march music, but even though he introduced a great deal more playfulness into the genre, his marches still ended with the final definitive cadence that sounds like – and is meant to sound like – the clicking of booted heels.[77] In any case, the discipline of the musicians was the discipline of the exercise grounds and drill, and for Wieprecht, who was after all a civilian in (band) uniform, that meant his bands had to be as excellent musically as the Prussian soldier was militarily.

The evolution of military bands provides us with a history of old or expansive empires as well as modern nations, of internationalism as well as nationalism. To call military music a project of the nationalizing nineteenth century should not obscure the significant role it also played in sustaining bonds of allegiance in Russia, Austria-Hungary, and Ottoman Turkey, let alone in dramatizing the imperial presence in British, French, and eventually German colonies.[78] In the comic, darkening atmosphere of *The Radetzky March*, Joseph Roth's 1932 elegy to the Habsburg Empire, the weekly performances of the military band in the provincial outpost presided over by District Commissioner von Trotta are a reminder of victory in the past, a routine of resistance to change, and a doomed effort to make the *Radetzky March*'s inevitable return to the tonic a guarantor of meaning in a world of lost illusions, homesickness, and decay.[79] In more far-flung places brass bands, both military and missionary, were the dominant form of western musical expansion, the musical differences among them so negligible as to make them, in the words of ethnomusicologist Robb Boonzajer Flaes, "a virtually identical musical formula": "The idiom of the Western brass band," he writes, "is one of the first forms of worldwide standard music."[80] Famously or infamously, the first western music heard in Japan in the Meiji period was that of Commodore Perry's military bands in 1853, "the best bands in the Navy," as Perry dubbed them. Within a decade every western state had brought in their military bands: a British military band in Yokohama in 1864; a Prussian band accompanying Count Eulenburg, the leader of Prussian East Asian Expedition, to his residence in the same year; French instrumentalists arriving to help build brass instrument factories; and the German-trained English bandsman John William Fenton staying on to help train new Japanese bands.[81]

If military bands of the ancient, medieval, and early modern periods expressed a kind of aristocratic cosmopolitanism, then their descendants in the modern period are exemplars of the transnational and global circulation of cultural and military practices. As noted earlier, European

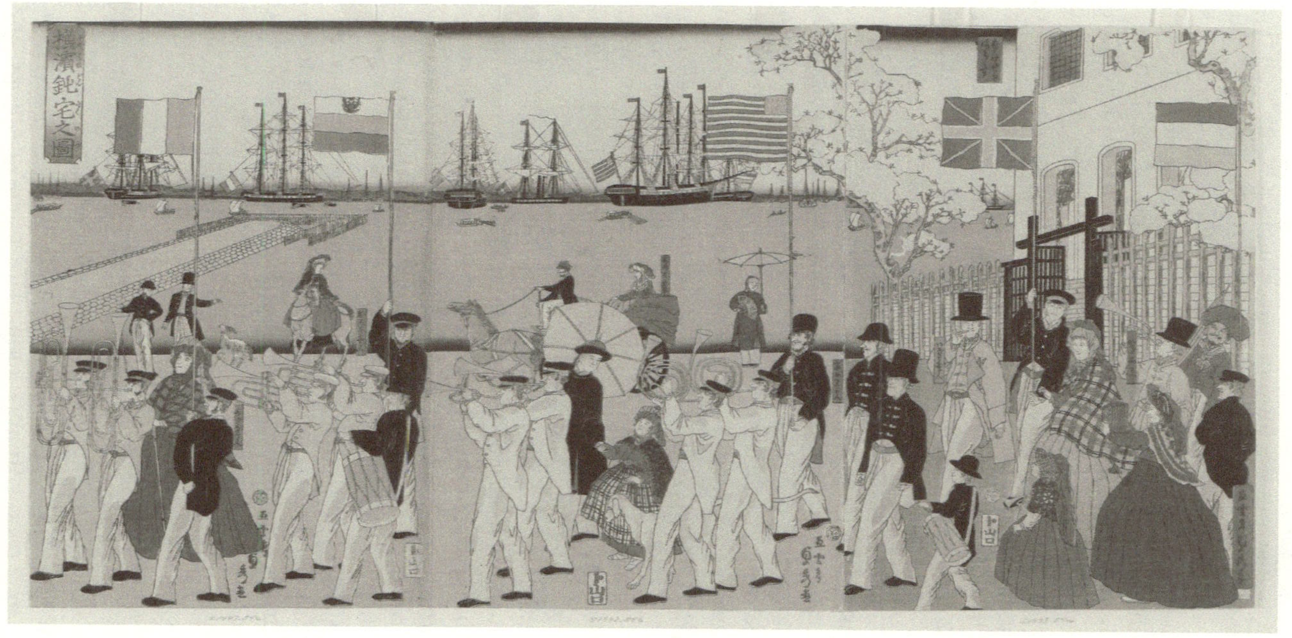

10.2 A brass band parades along the waterfront in Yokohama during Treaty-Port Japan, 1859–72 (Sadahide). Arthur M. Sackler Gallery, Smithsonian Institution, Washington, DC. Gift of Ambassador and Mrs William Leonhart, S1998.54a-c.

military music, particularly in the form of marching bands, drew on the Mehtarân tradition of the Ottomans, integrating its instruments and rhythms into its compositions, especially after the Ottoman incursions into Habsburg Austria and Hungary in the late seventeenth century.[82] After 1828 the situation was reversed: the destruction of the Janissary Corps under Sultan Mahmoud II threw traditional Ottoman military music into disfavour, and the sultan brought in a European (Giuseppe Donizetti, elder brother of the opera composer) to organize a new, more western musical establishment as part of the modernization of the state and the army.[83] The Ottoman Turkish influence was only the most exotic of the transnational aspects of military music.[84] Although each national tradition had its own marches, innovations and improvements in one country's bands tended to circulate quickly across borders. The Wieprechtian System was the most portable of all, designed as it had been to make possible uniform musical practices among the many branches and regional customs and ceremonies of the Prussian armed forces. In England after mid-century it became common, in rough parallel to the importation of German conductors and instrumentalists, to hire German bandmasters, especially from Prussia; at one point in the 1880s, three out of four of the bandmasters of the Royal Marine Bands were Germans.[85] Transcriptions of operatic and symphonic music, by Wieprecht and many others, were published and circulated widely, becoming an international commodity in which the national coloration of the products were a large part of their appeal. For instance, Wagnerian marches adapted from the music of his operas were a particular favourite in France.[86]

Military bands present an especially ambiguous case, travelling across the soft boundaries of cultural life and reinforcing the hard ones of states and their armies. That ambiguity itself came into focus at the international events that proliferated in the six or so decades before 1914. Wieprecht's finest hour, in his own and his admirers' estimation, was when he led the Prussian military band to victory at the first-ever International Military Music Competition at the Paris World's Fair of 1867. The event, and the world's fair that hosted it, were welcomed as the pursuit of national rivalry by means other than war. Something of that mood was reflected in the warm reception Napoleon III gave to Wieprecht, then later to his victorious bandsmen.[87]

Nor had Wieprecht ever been alone in his love of the musical spectacular. Once established, such self-consciously big events – sometimes in the form of what were called "*concerts monstres*," sometimes in the form of parades and band competitions – took place often in Europe and the Americas under the batons of civilian as well as military bandleaders. These events escaped from the confines of concert halls and opera houses, expressing not just national pride but the palpable sense of growth and progress that marked the nineteenth-century bourgeois consciousness. Here was music for modern people, big and ambitious, like cities and industries; here was music for nations with their large and modernizing armies and navies. All subsequent world's fairs, and many other international events besides, included large contingents of military brass bands. The monster concerts could not have existed without brass instruments in general and the participation of brass bands, especially military ones, in particular. The most famous of the monster concerts were choreographed by the showman conductor Louis Jullien in London between 1845 and 1852, and many musical entrepreneurs, from Glasgow to Buenos Aires and from Moscow to Philadelphia, spent the rest of the century vying to gather the most choristers, the most trumpets and tubas and trombones, and the most grand pianos, for the edification and amusement of the public. Although their repertoire varied, it was the nature of this musical beast that all concert directors favoured music involving great outbursts of sound, and whether massed military bands, regional orchestras, and amateur choral groups performed Handel's "Hallelujah Chorus" or Verdi's "Anvil Chorus" or "God Save the King," they all sounded very loud. Irish-American bandleader Patrick Sarsfield Gilmore's International Peace Jubilee of 1873 included eight military bands, each the leading representative of its country.[88] Theodore Thomas, the German-born founder of the Chicago Symphony Orchestra and music director for all the musical events at Chicago's White City Columbian Exposition of 1892, sought out "all the famous military bands of Europe" in order to bring them to the United States for the extravaganza.[89] George W. Stewart of Boston, the music director of two American world's fairs, regarded bands as more important than the highbrow material: in planning the 1915 Pan-Pacific Exposition he wrote that "instead of serious symphonic compositions to be rendered in a solemn temple, and of interest but to a limited cult, there should be great military bands playing in the open, and playing music that would appeal to all classes – not trash for that purpose, but good, popular compositions."[90]

We are not so distant from the nineteenth century, either in our sonic expectations or in our valorization of competition in every domain of human activity, as to lack some basic understanding of the appeal of such music-making. The monster concerts were not bigger versions of conventional concerts but something new – a musical counterpart, perhaps, to factories, the biggest buildings of the industrial age, in which high levels of technical sophistication, temporal coordination, and human skill came together in spectacles that "alternately dazed and enraptured" their auditors and observers.[91] In their enthusiastic modernity, moreover, they demonstrated the close relationship between industry and nation. These industrial-era concerts promised that the modern culture of time and space would produce awe-inspiring, even sublime experiences, in which people would feel carried beyond everyday limitations. Of course, sometimes they did produce only noise. One commentator noted that the failure of Gilmore's chorus of 10,000 to sing either in time or in tune with the thousand-plus instrumentalists, organists, church bell ringers, anvil strikers, and soldiers firing artillery provided unexpected pleasure to an audience at the 1873 "International Peace Jubilee," who were more barraged than entertained. Gilmore's Gesamtkunstwerk reminded him of "volcanic eruptions, cyclones, and earthquakes – all very grand and impressive, but not of any benefit to the surrounding country."[92] In any case, sheer sensation was the main point, and Gilmore, in his determination to include thundering cannons and clanging bells in all performances, was by no means the only performer, in the Americas or Europe, for whom the soundscape of modern life demanded musical experiences that might somehow reach crescendos of noise that exceeded even those of the battlefield.[93]

Military Bands and Civilian Music-Making

What follows from these general observations about bigness and brass bands is the conclusion that Wieprechtian band reforms illustrate the extent to which nineteenth-century militarism also involved the military adapting itself to civilian life, even taking on what we might call, in the case of the military bands, civilian attitudes and civilian forms of behaviour. Wieprecht's treatise on how to achieve "a well-ordered military music" emphasized the need for "mildness" on the part of the director: "music-making can only prosper under a mild regime: not military force but fundamental instruction is required to awaken the love and enthusiasm for (ensemble) music, without which the practising musician will only ever bear the stamp of musical training, not its essence."[94] His reforms had little to do with military necessity and, by the time the size and ubiquity of military bands had become an issue in the late nineteenth century, even their defenders had ceased to say much of anything about their importance on the battlefield. Everything that Wieprecht achieved in recalibrating the military-musical complex worked to attach it more firmly to the emergent, rapidly evolving national and civilian musical culture, "kindling his genius" upon it. The expanded repertoire he created represented an antidote to the always threatening tedium of march music and made possible more ambitious, varied, and frequent public performances. He took the music that the new audiences for opera and concert life were listening to and made it possible for a much broader range of ensembles to play it. He took the standards of musical craft that were taught in music schools and conservatories and sought to make military musicians train and play to them. He took the music celebrated as most profound, most important, most German and made it accessible in the hinterlands. One contemporary claimed that "his concerts have the character of a popular festival [*Volksfest*]: Wieprecht reconciles all parties; reactionaries and democrats applaud him equally."[95] His reforms affected civilian music-making as well, such that at some point it becomes impossible to say whether military music was pacified or civilian music was militarized.

Wieprecht had made his bands seem essential to musical life even if they were not. Non-military musicians came to see them in that way, even to benefit from them. In his later years Richard Wagner suggested that his expectations for the performances of his works were based on his "knowledge of the circumstance that in every important city in Germany a strong and well-staffed corps of musicians, namely those belonging to the military, were ready to combine with the theater musicians and make up sufficient musical forces to perform *Tannhäuser*."[96] At the same time musical ensembles less ambitious than those performing Wagner operas experienced the advantages of large numbers of trained military musicians in circulation. Any provincial orchestra or second-rank touring opera company was able to perform because such musical forces could provide reinforcements. Wieprecht's reforms also indirectly stimulated the amateur brass band phenomenon, which increased enormously after 1870, first among firemen, then among miners and factory workers, and all of these bands generated from the workers themselves. Management rarely sponsored brass bands; they resulted from the efforts of men who had perfected their instrumental technique in military service and now adopted Wieprecht's model of the brass band (the numbers, instruments, and repertoire) to shape their factory-based ensembles. The typical Kapellmeister of a miner's band was a former military bandsman, as were many of its members, and they all wore uniforms, some with fezzes that seemed to invoke the "Turkish music" of the past, others with Prussian *Pickelhauben*.[97]

Even women musicians might be said to have reaped some modest rewards from the ubiquity and popularity of brass and wind bands. Musical women of the nineteenth century fell into two categories. Women from bourgeois or aristocratic families studied, composed, performed, and organized music in the private and semi-private sphere of salons and music rooms; and women who were born or married or made their own way into the hybrid class of artist-musicians were able to pursue public musical careers, even as married women with children.[98] Those of the latter category were usually singers, sometimes pianists, occasionally violinists, violists, and composers, and almost never conductors, cellists, string bass players, or woodwind and brass players. The reasons for such a professional profile are not surprising in light of prevailing gender norms, not to mention the chronic shortage of opportunities for musical employment. Music-making is a physical process, and every effort of women to use their bodies to make music met with some objection, couched in moral, religious, or biological terms. In the early nineteenth century too much singing was said to be harmful for young women.[99] Likewise, blowing into a mouthpiece, even one so delicately formed as that of a flute, allegedly distorted the face in unattractive ways as well as being obscurely immoral.[100] Brass instruments were suitable only for strong men – like those regiments of musicians whom Berlioz credited with "indefatigable lungs and lips of leather."[101] Added to such difficulties, the nineteenth-century debate over the adaptation of valved brass instruments had further established horn-blowing, preferably the so-called natural horns and trumpets (without valves), as an activity fundamental to man the hunter at his most primal. Concerns about diminishing the "masculinity" of the trumpet and its embodiment of elemental forces of the earth itself (metal, in other words) also informed resistance to the valved trumpet, especially in military circles.[102] Wieprecht himself, champion of valved brass instruments, explained that his bands had "let go the good old instruments that earlier generations bequeathed to us in one respect – the invention of valves – which we used in order to preserve the original essence of the instruments."[103]

Despite all this undergrowth, or perhaps because of the opportunities for transgression it made possible, the last decades of the nineteenth century were marked by a growing number of women's brass bands in Germany and Austria-Hungary. Bearing names such as the Ladies' Trumpet Corps "Stefanie" and Hermann Brandt's Ladies' Trumpet Corps and String Orchestra, these ensembles were commercial enterprises, and they made music in large restaurants, spa towns, dance halls, and outdoor

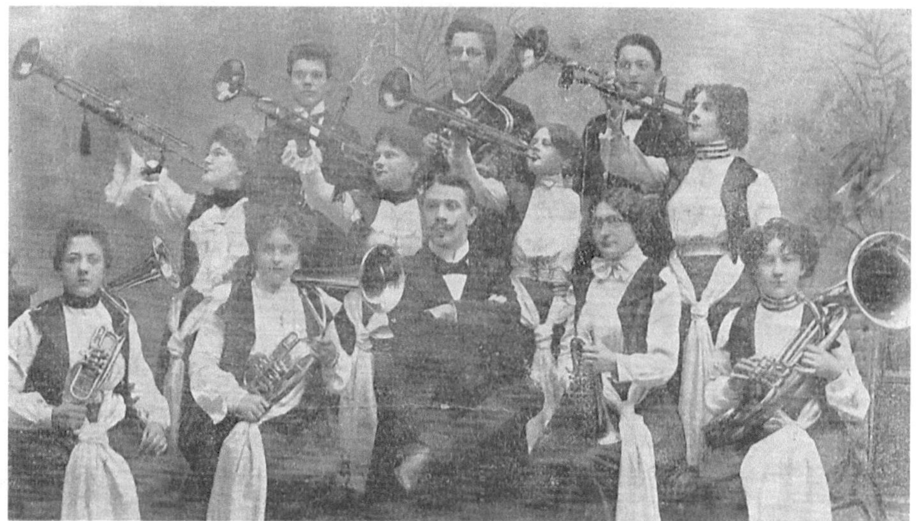

10.3 Ladies' Trumpet Corps "Stefanie" (Damen-Trompeter-Corps "Stefanie"), 1909. Courtesy of Mike Brubaker, http://temposenzatempo.blogspot.ca/2011/10/postcards-of-german-ladies-orchestras.html.

beer gardens, in short, in many of the same venues where the local military band would also perform. They also played the same eclectic mélange of light music favourites, in which marches, polkas, and waltzes proliferated.[104] The large number of surviving photographs attest to their novelty appeal – women in uniform, playing herald trumpets, bugles, tubas, saxophones, and drums, dressed in the kilts and tam o'shanters of the Janietz Elite Ladies' Brass Orchestra; the orientalist fezzes of Otto Iboldt's Ladies' Trumpet Corps "Diana"; or the dirndls of the Ladies' Brass Orchestra "Tannhäuser." By such mild provocation, women performers manipulated the meaning of military music, not so much challenging it as having a bit of fun with its paraphernalia. At the same time, of course, their bands testify to the sheer presence of what they were so obviously *not*, that is, men with trombones wearing regimental uniforms.

But novelty acts aside, the pervasive cultural influence of the military bands had a cost, and in the minds of some struggling civilian musicians, they were the ones paying the price. The growing prominence of the military in Germany after 1870 also meant that it was "watched, judged, praised and reprimanded," and its "rules, performances and communication structures ... [were] publicly analyzed and debated" as never before.[105] In this context the practices of military bands became a focus for civilian musicians' resentment of how the military bandsmen were taking their work. The life of a jobbing musician, whether civilian or military, was difficult wherever one sat and whatever one wore. Either in draughty, leaking bandstands or hot, smoke-filled taverns and dance halls, on parade grounds or spa grounds, in uniform or mufti, they all tended to be underpaid and overworked, up late playing and up early practising or travelling. All had inadequate provisions for sickness, family, or retirement, and all had problems with instruments, contracts, and employers.[106] Even while leading orchestras and opera singers enjoyed a growing prestige in European society, the social standing of civilian musicians employed in less prestigious musical activities deteriorated significantly. Even while military musicians enjoyed enthusiastic crowds and praise in the popular press, military expenditures for their upkeep barely kept up with their growing numbers, and indeed budgets were calculated to take into account the money they could earn on the side.[107] Such conflicts between civilian and military musicians during the last decades of Imperial Germany ended up in the Reichstag, where the civilian musicians' trade associations demanded restrictions on what they deemed unfair competition, subsidized by the government itself.[108] The Reichstag eventually passed minor restrictions on the off-duty employment of military bandsmen, just enough to anger both sides in the conflict.[109]

Meanwhile, the conflict was also aired in a war of pamphlets, journal articles, and books. For those sympathetic to the concerns of civilian musicians, the notion that military bands could adequately represent the people of music – the heirs of Bach, Beethoven, and Brahms – formed the nub of the matter. In 1909 Hermann Eichhorn, a well-known musician and widely respected authority on the history and performance of brass instruments, published a polemic called *Militarism and Music*, in which he argued that the proliferation of military bands had disfigured German musical life. Following a long opening section in which he laid out the history of military music in unflattering terms and analysed the structural changes in musical life that had made civilian musicians so vulnerable to them, he characterized the military bands as parasites living on the creative geniuses of the past and preventing the development of creativity in the future. They had, he charged, a "ruinous influence" on cultural life.[110] Defenders of military music, such as Alexander Pfannenstiel, a prominent figure among veterans of military bands, tended to fight on the same grounds that Eichhorn had marked out. Rather than suggesting that the bands made an essential contribution to warfare, they argued instead that they provided employment and musical training for music-loving Germans who would otherwise not receive either. Military bands, wrote Pfannenstiel, exposed people in the hinterlands to music of the "pre-classical, classical, romantic, and modern era"; the "concert activity" of military bands had been responsible for the "popularization of the masterworks of Richard Wagner." How could choral societies and amateur theatricals perform without the local military bands? Where would the population be without their frequent concerts? It was, in fact, the civilian musicians who lacked "artistic seriousness and ambition," not the military musicians, who catered to the "musical needs" of the German people "to the highest degree."[111]

One could regard this protracted controversy over the role of military bands in society as a struggle for the soul of Germany: men in evening dress on the one hand and men in uniforms on the other. But the reality was that all the men, and a great many women as well, were fighting for the same thing, for "Haydn, Mozart, Beethoven, Schubert, Mendelssohn, Schuman, Brahms," for Wagner and the "recent works of Bruckner and Mahler," for "all the other works, the overtures, orchestral suites, romances, rhapsodies, fantasias, concertos for solo instruments," and all the medleys, potpourris, popularizations, and pastiches conjured out of them, every note of it all expressing what it was to be German.[112] As Pfannenstiel's pamphlet announced, this was a "cultural question" (*Kulturfrage*), a question of how best to preserve and promote something that all sides considered valuable beyond debate. It is easy to see the small step from this consensus to the war of "culture" versus "civilization" that broke out just months after Pfannenstiel's pamphlet, with military bands in full array as soldiers marched through German cities and towns to the railway stations where more bands were playing. This chapter has suggested how it was that military bands came to play such a central role in the affairs of the nation, as well as to show how intertwined this history was with that of other countries that had much in common with the Germans. Had war not broken out in 1914, as it well might not have, this entangled history of German music, the German military, and the world would have developed differently and we would have regarded its nineteenth-century origins differently as well.[113] As it happened, though, the choice Wilhelm Wieprecht made in 1824 to abandon the opera orchestra pit for the parade ground carries a burden it cannot possibly bear.

Chapter Eleven

Women's Wagner

From the beginning of Richard Wagner's public career, women were crucial to his successes and to his ability to survive his many failures, reversals of fortune, and periods of poverty, exile, and public opprobrium.[1] They were his most enthusiastic audience and his loyal supporters. The prominent women in Wagner's life have received considerable attention among Wagner scholars, and some have themselves been the subject of books.[2] Mother and sisters, wives and lovers, daughters, granddaughters, and great-granddaughters, well-born and wealthy admirers, patrons, singers, and even the female characters who play such a prominent role in his music: all have a presence in the Wagner legend and the Wagner literature. It is hard to think of any other male artist whose life and reputation have been so intimately, abundantly, and colourfully bound up with the women in his life. Challenging though it may be to bring these women out from behind the Wagnerian shadow, to grant them lives beyond the marriage script or the erotic plot, and to allow them to illuminate histories other than his, it is that much harder to find the voices of the women who had no personal connection with Wagner. Yet women of his times and since have encountered, admired, rejected, and absorbed his music and allowed it to affect their lives, even if only in small, momentary ways. This chapter gathers a few such scattered voices in order to illuminate a neglected aspect of the reception of Wagner's music. It shifts our gaze to people who were on the margins of the Wagner phenomenon, by virtue of their role as listeners and their gender. It does not aspire to a systematic survey of Wagner in the female imaginary. It consists only of soundings to measure the depth of the Wagnerian effect at various moments from the mid-nineteenth to the mid-twentieth centuries. In these moments we might see possibilities for understanding why Wagner elicited such strong reactions, from women as well as from men, and what those reactions might tell us about the role of music in the psychosocial drama of gender roles and emotional and moral regimes in transition. In his tortured coming-to-terms with him in 1933 Thomas Mann suggested that Wagner, just like Rossini and the other Italian composers he derided, had used his musical art "to captivate and subjugate bourgeois society throughout Europe"; "Was it not that element of the delicious, the sensual-pernicious, sensual-consuming, heavily intoxicating, hypnotically caressing, the thickly and richly padded – in a word, that supremely luxurious element in his music – that drew the bourgeois masses into its arms?"[3] Perhaps Mann was right, but the variability of the responses to Wagner and the variety of ways people describe them attest to the instability of musical meaning, even as they testify to myriad musical pleasures.

How Women Encountered Wagner's Music and What They Heard

The musicologist Rebecca Grotjahn has made a model effort to understand the musical sensibilities that infused everyday life by examining one woman's *Nachlass* of piano scores in search of the practices and preferences of an amateur musician of the early twentieth century. Her subject, Lucia König, referred to herself as a *höhere Tochter*, possibly ironically and perhaps because she never married. The term, as Grotjahn writes, usually denotes a "girl from a good home with a sheltered upbringing who has learned to draw, speaks some foreign languages, knows something of art history, and has some training in piano playing, and yet does all these things not for their own sakes, but rather out of boredom."[4] In English, one would say a well-brought-up young lady. For Grotjahn, who knows König only through her piano scores left behind after her death and the memories of a much younger neighbour, the evidence of this music indicates diligence in practising and a "self-determined way of life," in other words a great deal more than the effort to alleviate boredom. König had a decided preference for piano transcriptions from opera and operetta. The well-worn pages of the "Grail Narration" from *Lohengrin* and "Senta's Ballade" from *Der fliegende Holländer* (both to be found in her several volumes of the Ullstein Verlag's *Musik für Alle* opera excerpts for piano and voice) further attest to how frequently she played Wagner.

To Lucia König, I would like to juxtapose Virginia Waite Strait, an American woman born in the same year (1898), a middle-class Pennsylvanian of Lutheran ancestry (the name Waite had been Wecht generations earlier), musically active in the small town of Huntingdon as a piano teacher, a church organist, and before her marriage a high-school music supervisor.[5] Virginia Strait, my grandmother, probably knew Wagner initially through the local concert society's performance of symphonic excerpts and, like Lucia König, through piano transcriptions for solo and four-hand performance, such as the "*Spinnlied*" from *Der fliegende Holländer* or the prelude to *Die Meistersinger*. The piano recitals she organized twice a year for her students would often end with a pair of her most advanced students playing these works. One of the happiest experiences from her young married life in the 1920s and 1930s was her annual trip with a music-loving friend to New York City, where the women would attend concerts and go to the Metropolitan Opera, mostly to hear Wagner. These were years of prosperity followed by economic hardship but throughout the Met continued to sustain its program of Wagner operas, most of which it had premiered in the United States before the war. My grandmother continued to go to New York to hear them or to listen to the Met radio broadcasts that had begun in 1931. She heard the astonishing vocal partnership of Kirsten Flagstad and Lauritz Melchior on at least one of these expeditions, perhaps in *Parsifal*. Certainly, attending the Met performance of *Parsifal* was one of the great musical experiences of her life, one that she spoke of with remembered awe. Like Lucia König, she left no written accounts of these experiences, but she did hang a portrait of Wagner in her front hallway, the only musician portrait on her walls.[6] Her daughter remembers that her mother had a particular passion for Wagner's music, sustained over the course of a long life of teaching, performing, and listening to many other composers as well.

What would we learn were we able to know more than such external facts about these women's relationship to Wagner and his music? Writing about someone is a form of appropriation of that person, of claiming authority over him or her, and just as I am appropriating Lucia König and Virginia Strait for my purposes, so we can say that they appropriated Wagner for theirs, by collecting, performing, teaching, and listening to him over a long period of time. In each of these actions there is scope for negotiation and even opposition on the part of these audiences of listeners, readers, and interpreters; each heard and understood Wagner from her own cultural background and personal experiences. These are the truisms of reception theory. In the case of Wagner we find ample evidence of what Umberto Eco called "aberrant decoding," interpretations by audiences that may be at odds with what the author intended or in Wagner's case insisted upon in his many writings and stage directions.[7]

Cosima Wagner herself was the first aberrant decoder, despite claiming precisely the opposite. As historians of the reception of cultural works, we are interested not just in how such acts of decoding are aberrant, but in why they are, what purposes are served, and what needs are fulfilled by these individual wanderings in and around a work of art.

In the case of women in the crucible of modernity, the central question concerns what Laurence Dreyfus has called "the erotic impulse." Dreyfus believes that the centrality of sex for Wagner and his operas has not been sufficiently acknowledged. Other scholars, including Eva Rieger, the premier interpreter of Wagner's women, if not of women's Wagner, make similar arguments.[8] Laurie McManus has developed a more historicist approach to how sexuality infused these works. Writing about "the rhetoric of sexuality" in the middle decades of the nineteenth century, she calls it a discourse concerning sensuality (*Sinnlichkeit*) more than a discourse concerning the sexual pleasure that dare not be spoken of and thus haunts the emotional world conjured up by Dreyfus.[9] Still, the central point is the same. That we need to insist on so obvious a point more than a century and a half after people first heard this music is itself testimony to the lingering influence of Lucia König's and Virginia Strait's sensibilities, particularly in the way we put into words what we hear, that is to say, metaphorically and always inadequately.

Of course, many people experienced Wagner's music only in the versions delivered by sheet music transcriptions and LPs. In these, his evocations of sensuality did not necessarily dominate. From the first piano transcriptions in the nineteenth century to the many record albums such as *Orchestral Highlights from Wagner* or *Theo Adam Sings Wagner* or *Toscanini Conducts Wagner* in the twentieth century, music publishers and record companies presented a package of Wagner's greatest hits, which ranged from the boisterous (the prelude to Act III of *Lohengrin*, the prelude to *Meistersinger*) to the naturalistic (the "Forest Murmurs" from *Siegfried*) to the yearning (extracts from Act II of *Tristan und Isolde*) to that mixture of yearning and piety (the Grail story from *Lohengrin*, the Good Friday music of *Parsifal*) that Nietzsche found so sickening.

Even in these forms of bowdlerization-via-excerpt Wagner could still deliver a powerfully sensual experience for his listeners, providing a dramatic, theatrical version of the joy, intensity, and irresistible force of the human sexual drive. Nevertheless, we need more nuanced means than Dreyfus provides for interpreting intense reactions to the sexuality in Wagner's music. Dreyfus posits only three categories of reaction: admiration and awe; condemnation and horror; and an avoidance of explicit discussion that fluctuated between "euphemism in treating the obvious" and a pointed evasion that for Dreyfus implies discomfort or repression.[10] The last two categories are the most problematic. The category of outraged critics reduces the reasons why people objected to Wagner's influence to the shopworn cliché of straitlaced Victorians, and the category of "euphemizers" encompasses such a range of nuanced human responses that it is meaningless. More important, there are reasons why people resorted to euphemism and talked around a subject. To use circumlocution was not merely a matter of prudishness or cowardice, and both men and women, defending or resisting social expectations or doing both at the same time, had reasons to choose their words carefully. They also lived under a different emotional regime than does a person of the early twenty-first century, understanding and expressing their emotions in ways that may have been perfectly clear to themselves but seem merely evasive to us.

Amy Fay: An American Musician Abroad

Critics could also be supporters. The most straightforward of Wagner's critic-admirers was Amelia Muller Fay (1844–1921), the American concert pianist and conductor whose published correspondence from her youthful experience of studying music in Germany was an immensely popular, often reprinted work in the genteel tradition.[11] On her mother's side Fay was a member of a distinguished and musical New England family. Her sister married the German-American Theodore Thomas, conductor of the Chicago Symphony Orchestra, and she (like her eight siblings) received serious musical training from childhood on. She arrived in Germany in the immediate run-up to unification, witnessed the triumphal return of the Prussian troops to the new capital of a united Germany, studied with a succession of leading pianists, from Carl Tausig to Franz Liszt, and attended great numbers of concerts, observing the personalities and talents of Joseph Joachim, Clara Schumann, Anton Rubinstein, and many others, including Richard Wagner.

She expressed her responses to Wagner's music in ecstatic terms, consistent with her enthusiasm for a great deal of the music she heard in Germany but a degree or so more effusive. On hearing a concert performance of the "Ride of the Valkyries" she wrote of imagining one could "really see the spectral horses with their ghostly riders": "it produced the most unearthly effect at the end … and I was perfectly enchanted with it." Describing "Walther's Traumlied" from *Die Meistersinger*, she wrote, "you must begin in a dreamy way, as if you were in a trance, and then you must gradually become more and more excited until you end in a grand gush of passion." She was "perfectly carried away" with the overture to *Tannhäuser* – "all other music pales before it in passion and intensity."[12] Her longest disquisition on his music came after hearing strains of his "Kaisermarsch," coming from an orchestra some distance away as she toured the town of Gotha. The disembodied nature of the sound led her to a surprisingly sensual account of all his music:

> Wagner's melodies are so heavily and intoxicatingly sweet, that they are almost narcotic. His music excites a set of emotions that no other music does, and he is a great original. It has the power of expressing longing and aspiration to a wonderful degree, and it always seems to me as if two impulses were continually trying to get the mastery. The one is the embodiment of all those vague yearning of the soul to burst its prison house, and the other is the cradling of the body in the lap of pleasure. I always feel as if I should like to swoon away when I hear his compositions. Then his harmonies are so strangely seductive, so complicated, so "grossartig," as the Germans say, and so peculiar! Oh, I have an immense admiration for him!"[13]

It would be too simple to conclude that Fay was rebelling against her family of Episcopal divines or was a starry-eyed naive. Describing his command of the orchestra in a concert at the Berlin Singakademie, she wrote that "his whole appearance is of arrogance and despotism personified." Acknowledging that he had a "great many enemies here [in Berlin]," she writes, "perhaps his character has something to do with it, for he has set all laws of honour, gratitude and morality at defiance all his life long." She continues: "It is a dreadful example for younger artists, and I think Wagner is depraving them." "In this country everything is forgiven to audacity and genius," she concludes, "and I must say that if Germany can teach *us* Music, we can teach *her* morals!"[14] Still, weighing in on the "quarrel over Wagner" that was engaging the "whole musical world, "she wrote that "I am on the Wagner side myself. He seems to me to be a great genius. – Pity he is such a moral outlaw!"[15]

Luise Büchner: A German Advocate of Women's Education

Luise Büchner (1821–77) disapproved of Wagner's morals possibly even more strongly than did Fay and without her insouciance, but hers is at the same time a more complicated response, perhaps because she could not take the detached view of an American visitor. Büchner was an early leader of the German women's movement, an ardent advocate of equality for girls and women in the sphere of education, and a pioneer in creating opportunities for young women to work. In 1877, shortly after the grand opening of the Bayreuth festival, she wrote a passionately critical essay called "A Woman's Reflections on the Ring of the Nibelungen." Her concerns for the progress and status of women were so inextricably mixed into assertions about the improprieties in Wagner's *Ring* – "Such crudeness, such lack of any decency is nowhere to be found as one finds it here in the nineteenth century on a German stage, in front of an elite public of German men and women!" – that we cannot simply label her a disapproving, outraged bluestocking.[16] Büchner was also one of the earliest examples of a woman who had once loved Wagner's music but declined to love it all. "I too was born in Arcadia," she begins, "that means that I too once rhapsodized over Richard Wagner."[17] In this display of erudition, hard won by self-study – a man's education having been denied to her by social norms – Büchner quotes the first line of Schiller's famous poem "Resignation" in order to draw attention to the fleeting nature of pleasures.[18] In the poem the soul of a man who has recently died invokes the Latin tag "*et in Arcadia ego*" to remember the joys of his youth and lament the vista of eternity he sees before him in which memories of past pleasures give more torment than comfort. Eighteenth-century Pietist understandings of eternal truth and Christian hope are juxtaposed to epicurean pleasures, though in the form of the poem the moralizing message also might be said to undermine itself, the sweetness of Arcadian memory lingering even after death. Büchner thus remembers her "sentimental education" in the Flaubertian sense: Wagner had offered her lessons in emotional intensity and pleasure in earthly beauty and, with some of his music, he still did.

Like Louise Otto-Peters (1819–95), her fellow women's advocate and a more ardent and untroubled supporter of Wagner, Büchner claimed adherence to Wagner's radical legacy. She described poring over his written works on musico-political reform and admiring his earlier operas. "What German heart does not beat more quickly," she wrote of listening to *Tannhäuser* and *Lohengrin*, when encountering the "truly poetic material of the ancient tales and histories," "brought to life through a music that is always new and astonishing."[19] She became disillusioned with his approach to the relations between the sexes with *Tristan und Isolde*, which escaped her worst criticism only because she thought its words nonsensical and its music incomprehensible. Her denunciations of the Ring

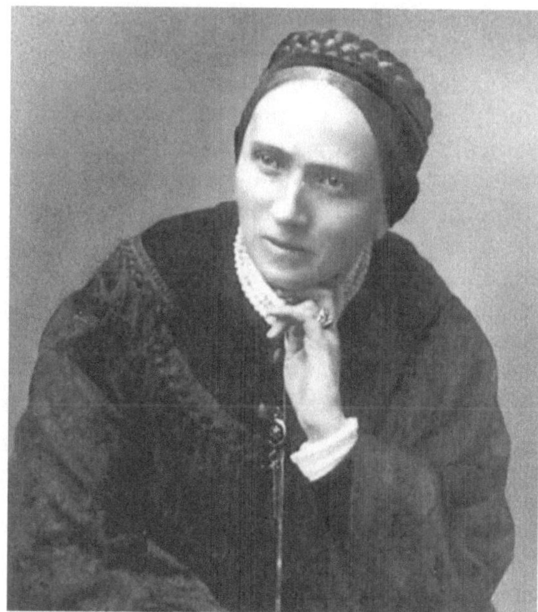

11.1 Luise Büchner, c. 1870. Photographer unknown. Wikimedia Commons.

Cycle were much harsher, not least because she objected to the hype surrounding it, a hype that she thought concealed the social and moral transgressions at its heart.[20] She seemed to suggest that Wagner deserved her criticism because he had asked for it, demanding so much of the public's attention that it could not be ignored. But this was no "music of the future," she concluded; indeed it undermined everything she had tried to achieve for the young women of the future in terms of education and influence.

George Eliot: Mary Ann Evans and German Music

Others also objected to the hype. Mary Ann Evans (1819–80 – better known by her pen name George Eliot), that stern and serious admirer of things German, travelled to Germany in 1855 and spent a good deal of time in Weimar, where she and her lover George Henry Lewes had frequent contact with Liszt and attended his performances of *Lohengrin*, *Der fliegende Holländer*, and *Tannhäuser* in the Weimar theatre. She was never so taken with Wagner as Büchner had once been and never regarded him as a figure of great importance to German culture. Both she and Lewes disapproved of the way that recent restorations of the Wartburg Castle, undertaken by Carl Alexander, the Grand Duke of Saxe-Weimar-Eisenach, had favoured a reconstruction of the minstrel hall featured in Wagner's *Tannhäuser* over attending to proper display of the desk and manuscripts of Martin Luther. For Lewes this indulgence of contemporary fashion was "a symbol of the intellectual condition of Saxe-Weimar."[21] For both Eliot and Lewes German culture above all meant Goethe, along with a host of other writers, philosophers, and theologians. Among musicians she admired Liszt enormously, but as Lewes wrote to a friend in 1870, "The Mutter and I have come to the conclusion that the music of the future is not for us – Schubert, Beethoven, Mozart, Gluck, and even Verdi – but not Wagner – is what we are made to respond to." Wagner's music, he wrote in 1872, "remains to us a language we do not understand."[22]

Nevertheless Eliot knew and appreciated the serious music of her time, and in her novels she infused her prose with musical and sound motifs. The words that describe them mediate with great skill and sensitivity between two ultimately inexpressible realms of inner experience, those of the senses and those of the emotions. So it cannot be said that she lacked an emotional investment in music. Still Eliot seems to have been disappointed by Wagner, the magus of emotional intensity. Writing of the Weimar performances, she described the declamation of *Lohengrin* as "monotonous" and the "situations trivial or disagreeable" and "dwelt upon fatiguingly." She thought *Der fliegende Holländer* and *Tannhäuser* had good passages, but she "ventured to say" that his work "fails in one grand requisite of art and that is contrast."[23] In 1877, when Wagner made his third and final trip to London to conduct a series of concerts at the Albert Hall, Eliot and Lewes attended a party for him at the house of his admirer, the German-born musician Edward Georg Dannreuther. Eliot met Cosima Wagner there. She came to admire Cosima, who reminded her of Liszt, though at the same time Eliot spoke plainly about her lack of sympathy with the Wagners' anti-Semitism. The two attended a performance of *Siegfried* together. Cosima subsequently told Hubert Parry, the young composer and Wagnerite, that Eliot had "wept plentifully over the heavenly scene between Siegfried and Brünnhilde."[24] We learn about this reaction through the medium of two fervent Wagner admirers, Cosima and Parry, the latter of whom recorded it in unpublished diaries, which have since been mined by scholars for just such details of musical life. This account doubly distances us from Eliot herself, and so it probably tells us little about her actual response to the music-drama. However, it does tell us something about the conventions of female emotionality in the presence of this music – romance, arousal, and transcendence all mixed together in unstoppable tears.

Ricarda Huch: A Restless Höhere Tochter

It is still possible that Eliot became more rather than less enamoured of Wagner's music as she grew older. The opposite – initial enchantment followed by growing distrust – was the case for Ricarda Huch (1864–1947). She was two generations younger than Eliot (who was old enough to be her grandmother) but still a child of the nineteenth century and, like Eliot, a woman who conformed to and rebelled against its expectations in equal measure. By the 1920s Huch had become a formidable figure in German letters, a true *grande dame.* She was the author of a much admired two-volume history of the flowering and decline of German romanticism (published in 1899 and 1902); a three-volume history of the Thirty Years' War (Germany's *Grosse Krieg*, published, uncannily, in 1912–14); biographical studies of disparate figures such as Garibaldi, Luther, and Bakunin; as well as historical novels, plays, and poems. In 1924, on the occasion of her sixtieth birthday, her older contemporary Thomas Mann published a *Glückwunsch* that anointed her "not only the leading woman of Germany" but "probably of Europe also."[25] In 1926 she became the first female member of the writers' section of the Prussian Academy of the Arts and shortly thereafter won the Goethe Prize, again the first woman to be so honoured.

In 1886, however, Huch had much more in common with Lucia König, a hôhere Tochter like herself, than with Thomas Mann or previous Goethe Prize winners such as Albert Schweitzer or Sigmund Freud. She was the middle one of three children in the family of a wholesale merchant who was absent for long periods of time on business trips to Porto Alegre, Brazil. Ricarda was raised by a sad and withdrawn mother and an energetic grandmother. Like her older sister, she was educated adequately but not extravagantly. Because of the family's precarious financial situation, she was not sent away to a fancy boarding school, but like every höhere Tochter, she learned to play the piano. Several members of the extended Huch family were serious about their musical avocation, but Ricarda seemed to have engaged no more intensely than the average *Bürger* with this most German of the arts. When she was fifteen, her older sister married their cousin, a melancholic, unconventional lawyer,

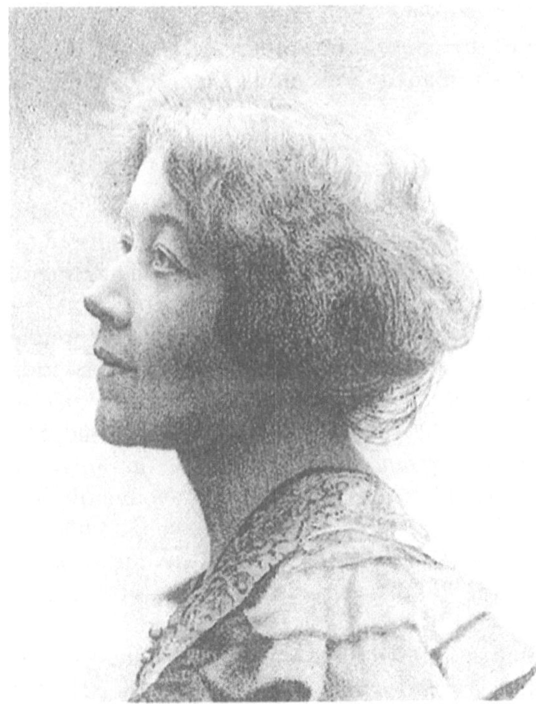

11.2 Ricarda Huch in 1901. Johann Lindner, etching from photograph. Wikimedia Commons.

amateur geologist, and pianist named Richard Huch. When she was sixteen she fell in love with him, and at some point in the next decade the two – Ricarda and Richard – became lovers, exchanging passionate letters and meeting secretly. By 1886 the situation had become untenable, a more or less open secret in the family. Ricarda's sister demanded that she leave Braunschweig and cease to have any further contact with Richard. So on the last day of 1886 she left for Zurich, where she spent the next decade of her life, working first to complete the *Abitur* (secondary school), which no gymnasium in Germany would have allowed her to do, then enrolling in the University of Zurich as a student of history and philosophy, earning an advanced teaching certificate with the highest possible score. Shortly thereafter she completed a doctoral dissertation titled "The Neutrality of the Swiss Confederation [*Eidgenossenschaft*], especially in Zurich und Bern, during the Spanish War of Succession." This impressive series of educational accomplishments, even more so given that she was a young woman on her own, living on minimal funds in rented rooms, yielded predictably minor rewards – a clerical position at the city library and a teaching position (German and history) at the Höhere Tochterschule in Zurich, an educational institution for girls such as she had been. But she had a lively social life, an ongoing and passionate exchange of letters with Richard, and, above all, she began to write: first short stories and poetry (under the pseudonym Richard Hugo), then dramas on historical themes, novels of real and invented historical characters, and short historical narratives.

She also went to the opera. Between 1892 and 1897 she attended every Wagner opera that was available (*Der fliegende Holländer, Tannhäuser, Die Meistersinger von Nürnberg, Tristan und Isolde,* and *Der Ring des Nibelungen*). Such thoroughness might suggest that she was a devotee. Considering also the vaguely incestuous nature of her forbidden relationship with her brother-in-law, with a name so close to her own and a shared first name with the Richard of Bayreuth, the whole situation had more than a dash of the Wagnerian about it. Yet her letters from Zurich to her lover/brother-in-law tell a more complicated story of attraction, ambivalence, and self-control. The letters are copious and expressive – the affair was over, but the letters nevertheless perform in highly dramatic language the experience of longing, forced renunciation, and endless love, intertwined with accounts of work and friendships.[26] The first reference to Wagner finds her planning to attend a performance of *Tristan und Isolde* and writing in an Isolde-like postscript, "Do you know, I could have been married to someone else for ten years and you would only have to make your voice from far away and I would immediately be at your feet, as though I were a part of you."[27] In the end she was unable to go to the performance.

A few months later, though, she reported to Richard that she had attended a performance of *Die Meistersinger* on the previous day, just as he had – though not on purpose, she assures him, and she did not much like it, "too contrived" (*ausgeklügelt*). Nevertheless, her awareness of the profound disjuncture between their simultaneity in time and unbridgeable separation in space and circumstance produced in her "a choking, gagging feeling in the throat, whenever I think of our situation." Rebuking herself for her difficulty in focusing on her studies, she finds also that

> alongside that, a wild desire for fame grows daily in me. That is the only thing that will save me. When I hear music, for instance yesterday in the theatre, I always feel that I am about to cry and I long for verses or poetry of any kind as one might long for a person, it feels so terribly empty and desolate

> within me. And then sometimes I think that this must be because of my age, and that thought makes me raging mad. I would not have thought that I would find this completely motionless life so difficult to bear. I live among so many artless, upright, conventional people and relationships and usually trot along with them, and then sometimes a kind of wildness stirs in me, I don't know, perhaps something like what stirred in Achilles when he dressed in girls' clothing or in an ancient pagan god in the Christian heaven. And just then the thought crosses my mind that I am a wild horse that has been captured and that has freed itself and has galloped off across the steppes, which stretch out into the distance beyond what the eye can see, and when I think of that, I immediately begin to cry. I am so terribly weary of everything, what is to become of me?

She cannot accommodate herself, she writes, to this "barren life of servitude" or suffer any more the "unbearable weeks and months."[28] Four hours later she has mastered herself, asserting her formidable intellectual powers to understand her distress. Her "paroxysm of rebellion has passed," she reported to Richard, and she galloped no more as a wild horse of the steppes. Instead, "I trot along now as before." Thinking back to a performance of Bach's *St Matthew Passion* she had heard only a fortnight earlier, she calls it "the most beautiful music that I have ever heard, nothing has made such an impression on me as it has."[29]

May we give Wagner credit for stirring her deeply and Bach for calming her down? Such a characterization conforms, certainly, to a common view of nineteenth-century female sexuality – the raging force of sexuality repressed, where Wagner is the instrument of its arousal and Bach, no less, the instrument of its suppression. But such an explanation reduces to cliché a complicated response. Starting with *Die Meistersinger*, Wagner's operas increasingly disappointed Ricarda. *Die Meistersinger* may be "eminently witty" (*eminent geistreich*), she wrote, "but it overreaches the task of the music" (*aber die Aufgaben der Musik überschritten*). In her next letter, apparently explaining her views in response to Richard's intervening defence of it, she again acknowledged it to be "keen, comprehensible, humorous, and above all witty" (*fein, sinnig, humoristisch und hauptsächlich sehr geistreich*), but for all that, it remained confined in its little medieval, *bürgerlich* world. The setting of the drama stimulated her historical interest, but Sachs's passionate monologue on the pathos of renunciation and resignation seems to have left no impression.[30] One wonders whether she expected more eruptions of feeling such as she had experienced momentarily but memorably in the theatre at *Die Meistersinger*, perhaps primed for it by what she had heard about *Tristan und Isolde*. If so, she was consistently disappointed or maybe even prepared to resist her emotions. *Tannhäuser* was merely "wonderfully beautiful" (*wunderbar schön*) and *Der fliegende Holländer* passed through the narrative of her week's activities without further comment.[31]

In February 1893 a performance of *Die Walküre* caused her to declare, "I'm increasingly uninterested in Wagner." "It is a great pleasure," she wrote, "but not a musical one." The music of Wagner, she asserted, "is thought music" (*Gedankenmusik*), an ambiguous term, to be sure. The "empty zest for motifs" (*hohle Motivlust*) of "completely unmusical people" unmasked the music's fundamental problem, which was that the whole consisted of mere contrivance, the piecing-together of "meager" (*ärmlich*) motivic parts. "Mosaic-like" was her final, dismissive judgment. A few months later a performance of *Rheingold* was "horrible" (*schrecklich*) and this time she declared, "I'm not thinking about Wagner any more." By comparison with Brahms, whom she loved "more and more," and Mozart, whose *Don Giovanni* she considered "divine music" (*göttliche Musik*), Wagner was "fraudulent" (*schwindelhaft*). And she returned time after time to Bach, especially the *St Matthew Passion*. In contrast, Wagner (*Götterdämmerung*, in this case) "can only cause conflict."[32]

Two aspects of Huch's long engagement with music are worth noting: the self-conscious and purposeful involvement as emotional experience and the trajectory of disappointment with Wagner because of his failure to provide such experience. To be sure, every generation, every group, and every individual describes this emotional relationship to music through their own idioms and experiences. In the case of Huch music offered her something beyond the everyday – a heightened apprehension of reality, a trigger that brought her insights into her own churning emotional life, release, and ultimately control. In the long account of her experience listening to *Meistersinger*, she mentions her longing for fame as escape from the circumstances that confine her, but fundamentally she longs for poetry, for a fuller apprehension of the world than her family, friends, and even her studies seemed to be offering her. In the future she imagined herself as a poet and writer, she saw the escape from the dread of weightlessness and suffocation to which she refers frequently in her letters to Richard. Poetry as a way of being offers the promise of intense existence. She seeks but does not find such intensity in Wagner's operas, but they still draw her back again and again, only to be further disappointed.

Marianne Weber: Wagnerian Pan-Eroticism

Intense emotional experience and what Max Weber in irritation called "Wagnerian pan-eroticism" (*wagnerischen Pan-erotismus*) attracted both men and women to Wagner, but perhaps especially for those, including many bourgeois women, for whom the open expression of sexual desire was socially and psychologically fraught.[33] As in the case of Büchner or Eliot, we should not be surprised to find no explicit reference to the sexual currents emanating from Wagner's music, or if it is to be found, then it is *between* the lines of how people remembered or wrote about it and not explicitly *in* them. Dreyfus refers to the rhetoric people resorted to in describing Wagner's effect on them, a rhetoric of nobility, depth, profundity and uplift, as "so lofty that they are rarely seen to peer down onto the facts of fleshly love named by more courageous literary libertines."[34] But such a judgment concerning people's silence in this case is doubly unwarranted, first because of the anachronistic expectations of sexual openness embedded in it and second because explicitness is not the same as honesty.

Still, when Huch described herself as a wild horse or when Charlotte Teller's heroine Frederica in her novel *The Cage* sits in a dark hall listening to an orchestral version of the "Ride of the Valkyries" and "felt herself, struggling, breathless, to get higher and higher … and felt strong and vital, astride a horse of Valhalla," the physical counterpart to emotional longing becomes almost explicit.[35] Horses have been a cultural code for carnality and sexual desire for centuries in the west, and Huch was not alone in expressing her physicality by feeling herself to be a horse. Marianne Weber's marriage to Max Weber (Marianne, 1870–1954; Max, 1864–1920; both contemporaries of Huch) constituted an excruciatingly prolonged exercise in celibacy and sexual frustration. In 1902 she wrote to her mother-in-law from Rome, where she and Max were supposedly relaxing, that she needed to return home to their old routines and their distracting effect, "since otherwise the unfulfillable desires – I mean, the specifically female ones – take on unpleasant dimensions." "My nerves," she lamented, "despite everything that enthralls me, are like bolting horses": "in these matters, it is like the horse that got used to starving on the very day it died." The experience of attending *Tristan und Isolde* within such a marriage was disturbing for both Marianne and Max: she wrote that days after the performance, they were "still reeling from the impact of *Tristan* – probably the loftiest and most powerful transfiguration there can ever be of the 'earthly' = *erotic* … an intoxicating liquor."[36]

Women – and there were many – who wrote this way, in high emotional ecstasy, created a "Women's Wagner" and identified fully with their own version of him. They illuminate a realm of female sensibilities in which Wagner was the screen on which they projected their interior lives and their exterior ones: in the former the need for profound experience and in the latter the need for active, effective lives. Joseph Horowitz has catalogued many similar expectations of emotional intensity and emotional liberation among the women who flocked to Wagner operas in turn-of-the-century New York; he calls the phenomena "proto-feminist."[37] Such music was both an opportunity to feel intense emotions and to learn how to experience emotional intensity in one's life outside the opera house. Charlotte Teller's heroine, returning to her room after the searing experience of the concert, feels it to be "a place from which she had been gone a long time."[38] Such experiences were both private and public, and that was the beauty of them: in the space of the theatre and during the time of the performance, with lights down and all silent except for the performers, a person was free to enjoy whatever fantasies or emotional adventures – or boredom, frustration, longing – in the protected space of the theatre. Peter Gay observed many years ago in *The Education of the Senses* – the first volume of his path-breaking *Bourgeois Experience* trilogy – that the nineteenth-century "bourgeois experience included a substantial measure of sensuality for both sexes, and of candor – in sheltered surroundings."[39] He used the evidence of people responding to performances of *Tristan and Isolde* and *Walküre* to support his case.

M. Carey Thomas: College President and Closet Wagnerian

Candour, but in sheltered surroundings: that was surely the key point for women. M. Carey Thomas (1857–1935), first dean and second president of Bryn Mawr College, was a closet Wagnerian. The child of a prominent Quaker family in Philadelphia, she retained the Quaker commitment to equality, education, and social justice but came ultimately to hold views on religion and art that were wholly unacceptable to the orthodox Quakerism in which she was raised. In the case of the former she became increasingly agnostic; in the case of the latter she fell head over heels in love with Wagner's music. All music and theatre were held in deep suspicion by Quakers; opera was the worst and Wagner's works beyond the pale. Thomas came by this love in the course of her education, each step along the way driven by her ambition and immense curiosity about the world. She left

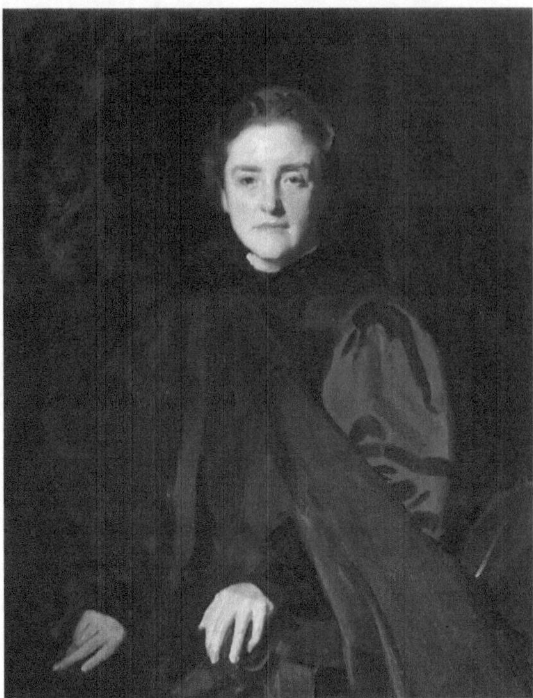

11.3 M. Carey Thomas, official portrait as president of Bryn Mawr College, 1899, by John Singer Sargent. Wikipedia Commons.

Philadelphia as a teenager to attend a Quaker boarding school in upstate New York and later Cornell. After earning her bachelor's degree, she tried to obtain a graduate degree first at Johns Hopkins, then at the University of Leipzig, leaving each institution in turn because they refused to allow women into graduate seminars or to grant them doctoral degrees. Finally, she went to the University of Zurich (as would Ricarda Huch a decade later), where she earned a doctorate in linguistics, summa cum laude. There decades earlier Wagner had written his most important treatises on music and art and "found the intellectual and financial freedom to be able to put his theories into compositional practice."[40] In Zurich Thomas probably heard Wagnerian opera for the first time and deepened her knowledge of music, theatre, and the visual arts. Wagner became her life's private passion, experienced discreetly while she pursued her public life's work – leadership in the struggle for women's rights, especially their right to an education as complete and rigorous as any a man could pursue.

As her biographer Helen Horowitz writes, Thomas is "a baffling subject because she had to hide so much of herself from public view."[41]

Returning from Europe to lead the newly established Bryn Mawr College, she served as dean, then won a narrow vote in the board of trustees to become president, a position she held until her retirement in 1922. It was a return to the childhood milieu that she had not so much fled as grown out of. The Quaker board of trustees included several cousins, her uncle, and her father, and everything she did in her activist, energetic career she did in the knowledge that her decisions and her behaviour needed to conform at least publicly to their moral and anti-aesthetic strictures. Thomas had already made the decision not to marry. "Knowing that marriage would end her autonomy," writes Horowitz, "she forced herself to dampen her attraction to men and turned to women for her life's loves."[42] Emotionally intimate female friendships were expected and supported in the nineteenth century, and whatever further intimacies her relationships with Mamie Gwinn and Mary Garrett involved, no one knew or wanted to know. Far less acceptable was Thomas's love of the arts, and so she did not go to the opera, the theatre, or even art galleries, where she might be seen. In her public persona she also set out to make Bryn Mawr as different from a höhere Tochter finishing school as possible. She transformed Bryn Mawr into the most intellectually rigorous institution of higher education for women in the United States; its entrance exam was as tough as that of any college in the United States, its seminar system was modelled on the Germanic Johns Hopkins model, and no concessions were made in its curriculum to the softer liberal arts of literature, modern languages, and the arts. Greek, Latin, and mathematics were the order of the day, and the likes of Wagner had no place in the course of study over which she presided for nearly forty years.

Yet we know from her correspondence that Wagner was extraordinarily important in her interior world. She spent many summers in Europe where she could attend as many performances as she wished, and she went to New York for opera as well. In 1891 she heard *Tristan und Isolde* at the Metropolitan Opera, directed by Anton Seidl, the charismatic Hungarian conductor late of Bayreuth, who had arrived at the Met in 1885 and soon had American audiences swooning in ecstasies of Wagnerian emotion – or so the newspaper accounts suggested. Thomas, for her part, wrote to her companion Mary Garrett that it was "the most glorious of all Wagner's operas, flawless from first to last, the most triumphant rhapsody of love ever." Like Teller's Frederica, she describes the "rapturous, soaring, heavenly high, winging thro. the Empyrean, without a touch of earth, all human emotion sublimated into godlike passion & longing panting & throbbing thro. thousands of memories of the splendid things of seas & stars and plains and marble & pictures & poetry until all together are blended into one in the rapture & fire of the music." One can only imagine what would have been the response had Thomas stood up at the Haverford Friends meetinghouse and spoken even a hint of how the Spirit had found her and moved her. She seems to have been very aware of what dangers she risked by pursuing her double life of bluestocking educator by day and Wagnerian by night. In another letter to Garrett, she wrote that the experience of both *Parsifal* and of *Tristan and Isolde* was to be "carried away" and to be "utterly lost to everything else": "I think I should be capable of anything mad and impulsive after a week of Tristram – & there wd be the rest of one's life unlit with Wagner to repent in."[43] Yet in its way Wagner's music was her link to the inner light that illuminated the life of a Quaker, revealing the wonder of human existence and the path to joy.

Virginia Stephen: Agnostic Pilgrim in Bayreuth

Consider the contrast to Virginia Stephen (1882–1941, later Woolf), who in 1909 was in her twenties and keeping house with her brother Adrian in Fitzroy Square, London, when the two of them took a trip to Bayreuth – a not uncommon pilgrimage for English people of their class and educational background. They attended performances of *Parsifal, Lohengrin,* and *Götterdämmerung*. Virginia struggled to make sense of them. Her biographer Hermione Lee considers this period of her life as one of "enfranchisement." "This was when they all established a truthful way of speaking," writes Lee, "when they began to talk freely of homosexuality and 'copulation' ... and were shedding the inhibitions of the past."[44] They were, as Peter Gay suggested, candid with each other in their private circle. But one did not publish writings with that degree of candour, or at least Virginia Stephen did not, and so her account for the London *Times* of her "Impressions of Bayreuth" in 1909 makes no reference to Dreyfus's "facts of fleshly love" and adopts the tone of the quizzical detachment of a writer who is struggling with the problem of how differently words and music do their work in the world and on the individual.

To be sure, she was writing about Parsifal and Lohengrin, not Tristan and Isolde or Siegmund and Sieglinde. Nearly two decades later, in her novel *The Years*, published in 1937, Wagner's music appears as all grandiloquence and aggression, the Wanderer going "on and on," Siegfried bounding and shouting, hammering and brandishing.[45] But in 1909 Virginia is "stirred" by it and baffled by the inability of language to describe an art that "is so much alive that it fairly suffocates those who try to deal with it." She suggests that the music of *Parsifal* "lays a weight upon the mind" and "one feels vaguely for a crisis that never comes, for, accustomed as one is to find the explanation of a drama in the love of man and woman, or in battle, one is bewildered by the intensity of a music that continues with the utmost calm and intensity independently of them." Yet the impression it makes is "deep and perhaps indescribable." "Puzzled we may be," she writes of the "change from the Temple of the Grail to the magic garden with its swarms of flower maidens and its hot red blossoms – too violent a break to be bridged conveniently," but our puzzlement stems from the phenomenon of the music itself, which "has reached a place not yet visited by sound." The music "is intimate in a sense that none other is; one is fired with emotion and yet possessed with tranquility at the same time." "It may be that these exalted emotions," she continues, "which belong to the essence of our being, and are rarely expressed, are those that are best translated by music." Yet she also acknowledges that anything she writes will ultimately fail to account for its effect on its listeners: "Perhaps music owes something of its astonishing power over us to this lack of definite articulation ...When the bows actually move across the strings, our definitions are relinquished, and words disappear in our minds."[46]

The emotional surrender that Wagner's music seemed to demand from her was not entirely pleasant: "Enormous is the relief, and yet, when the spell is over how great is the joy with which we turn to our old tools again."[47] Paul Hindemith later expressed this fleeting efficacy of music more baldly when he wrote that the "emotions released by music are not *real* emotions ... if they were they could not change as rapidly as they do."[48] The trajectory of disappointment that marked Huch's experience of Wagner has faint echoes in Virginia Stephen's. Perhaps we could speculate that, for many people, expecting a great wave of emotional sensations, Wagner did not deliver as promised or, just as plausible, this "Nordic sorcerer," this "crafty old magician," as Thomas Mann called him, had woven his spells and immersed them deep into the emotional intensities of his world, but the spell did not and could not last.[49]

Women's Wagnerian Activism

The trajectory of disappointment, and the futility of the emotional experience that Wagner provided, suffuses a short story by Willa Cather (1873–1947), published in 1904 in *Everybody's Magazine.* It is called "A

Wagner Matinee" and is a story, characteristic of Cather's oeuvre, of a woman who had once been a music teacher but married and moved to the harsh lands of the west, where all the gentility and refinement were worn out of her. In the story she has come across thousands of miles to Boston to visit her nephew, the story's narrator. He takes her to hear the Boston Symphony Orchestra, which is performing a program of selections from Wagner's operas. The audience, our narrator tells us, "was made up chiefly of women." The music awakens her from something like a catatonic stupor. The nephew watches her closely throughout, this burnt-out shell of a person: "Had this music any message for her?" She is silent, gripping the armrests and weeping "quietly but continuously" through the concert. "It never really dies, then, the soul," observes the narrator. The story ends with her breaking down completely and sobbing, "I don't want to go, Clark, I don't want to go." But of course she has to, returning to the "gaunt, moulting turkeys picking up refuse about the kitchen door."[50]

Rather than conclude on this note of Catherian despair, we might consider finally what women did with this emotion, or to put it otherwise, how they channelled the emotional energy that Wagner evidently brought into their lives into purposeful action. Women made considerable efforts to integrate their Wagner into the bourgeois households of Europe and the United States, in ways that deserve to be seen for what they were – claiming a place of their own, indeed a crucial role, both midwife and mother and patron and guardian, in the cultural life of their time. Women exerted their organizational and integrative efforts particularly strongly on behalf of Wagner, from the patron associations (*Patronatsvereine*), in which women like Marie von Seiditz were dominant forces, to the Richard Wagner Federation of German Woman (Richard-Wagner-Verband Deutscher Frauen), founded in 1909 as a foundation to support visits to Bayreuth for deserving music students without adequate means; from Laura Langford's efforts on behalf of Anton Seidl in New York to the efforts of my grandmother and many like her, playing his music for their students, studying the Leitmotifs ("meagre" though they may have been) and introducing their children to Wagner via storybooks based on the fairy tale and medievalist worlds his operas dramatized. My grandmother gave her young daughter, already studying the piano, a copy of Angela Diller's "arrangement" of *Siegfried* into the form of a children's book. It featured woodcut illustrations by the pioneering graphic novelist Lynd Ward and abundant musical examples, from the motives of "Nature," "Forest Murmurs," and "Magic Fire" to "Love," "Peace,"

"Happiness," and "Faith" at the end, accompanied by the sentence "Siegfried and Brynnhilde were very happy together."[51]

For such women the Wagner whose music they listened to over and over again, played at commencements and convocations, at weddings and funerals, in recitals and symphony concerts, as well as in metropolitan and provincial opera houses, underwrote a great range of satisfying activities. Far outside the Bayreuth circle of family and followers Wagner became a kind of all-purpose composer in the private and public lives of his admirers. He had composed what was regarded as noble, uplifting music well suited to the ceremonial life of modern times: *Tannhäuser*'s "Pilgrim's Chorus," the "Prelude" to the second act of *Lohengrin*, the "Bridal March" of *Lohengrin*, the "Prelude" to *Meistersinger*, the "Valhalla" and "Siegfried's Rhine Journey" music of the *Ring*. But he had also written music of swirling, passionate emotionality that was like no other.

Women could assimilate both of these musical modes, the public and the private, into their lives without needing to declare their bohemianism or their sexual liberation, either of which would have been too high a price, too great a commitment. In the short "Prelude" to *Middlemarch*, George Eliot wrote of the "blundering lives" of women in whom "ardour alternated between a vague ideal and the common yearning of womanhood" and "here and there a cygnet is reared uneasily among the ducklings in the brown pond, and never finds the living stream in fellowship with its own oary-footed kind."[52] In a similar vein Henry David Thoreau wrote in *Walden* of "lives of quiet desperation" in which an "unconscious despair is concealed even under what are called the games and amusements of mankind."[53] It is tempting to regard the named and nameless women for whom Wagner's music was important as unhappy in their lives, finding the solace of fellow suffering if not fellowship in the endless night of Isolde. But this supposition would be just as wrong as regarding them as prudish Victorians. They were able to assimilate their adventures in what Mann called the Wagnerian kingdom of subliminal knowledge into their everyday lives, thereby adding some dimension to them, both personal and public, that they found meaningful. Again in Mann's words, they could experience "the hours of deep and solitary happiness amidst the theatre throng, hours filled with frissons and delights for the nerves and the intellect alike, with sudden glimpses into things of profound and moving significance, such as only this art can afford."[54] What M. Carey Thomas wrote about listening to *Lohengrin* perhaps expressed the experience of many women: it made her "feel a little like my real self."[55] In this, women were not so different from men.

Chapter Twelve

Hausmusik in the Third Reich

The phenomenon of *Hausmusik*, homey and familiar by definition, is a well-known one, and its main twentieth-century outlines have been explored in a number of works.[1] This chapter considers the culture space that a long-standing tradition of Hausmusik had established in German life and how that space was reoccupied and redefined between the world wars of the twentieth century. As was mentioned in earlier chapters, Hausmusik – the playing of music in the household or in company with amateur music lovers in semi-public settings – had existed at the centre of *bürgerlich* life throughout the nineteenth century. It was the domestic counterpart to concert life, and although different in scale and degree of difficulty, it was connected to more public forms of music-making through common assumptions about music's place in national culture. Yet in the 1920s and 1930s Hausmusik acquired a new set of champions who sought to define it in opposition to bourgeois culture, that portmanteau of a legacy from the "bourgeois century." The rhetoric of these self-conscious redeemers of music in the home reflected middle-class disillusionment, along with a good deal of hypocrisy and mendacity. It also reflected a curious need to rewrite the past history of Hausmusik. That need is what requires some explanation.

The interwar promoters of Hausmusik wrote about moral reform and national regeneration through amateur music as though the nineteenth century had not been filled with middle-class people engaged in that same effort, even at times using the same language. This repackaging of a conservative, old-fashioned, middle-class phenomenon like Hausmusik into something allegedly new, revolutionary, and not middle class at all can tell us much about the uses of culture and everyday life under Nazism. Hausmusik's rhetorical and organizational place within the Nazi regime illuminates the ways that Nazism attempted to build a unified culture out of the diverse, at times fragmentary, elements of middle-class life in the Weimar period. The study of Hausmusik's interwar significance reveals two kinds of limitations within cultural life. The first is the limited degree to which cultural phenomena can constitute an autonomous sphere of social activity in the political circumstances of the twentieth century, and the second, conversely, is the limited degree to which politics can control culture. The latter is a somewhat old-fashioned view, but not an unwarranted one.

Hausmusik in the Nineteenth Century

We can begin by considering the question of genealogy, that is, what is Hausmusik and who says so. A definition articulated early in the Third Reich in the *Zeitschrift für Hausmusik* (Journal for Hausmusik) called it "all music which for reasons of its instrumental settings, its degree of difficulties and its nature [*Wesen*] can be aspired to be played by the musically active amateur [*Laien*], alone or in small circles of singers and players."[2] Its genealogy, as put forward in the 1920s and then the 1930s, was simultaneously continuitarian and catastrophic. The story tended to begin somewhere around 1600, when music was said to have formed an organic part of daily life, with composers and players barely distinguishable from people as a whole and a kind of musical spontaneity obtaining in town and countryside, in "family, community, state and church."[3] These halcyon days lasted perhaps even through the early nineteenth century, depending on the writer. Some, like Friedrich Blume, located the catastrophic break with this past late in the nineteenth century; others placed it much earlier, perhaps when the first person of liberal persuasions picked up a violin. In any case the diagnosis was the same. Music had become cut off from people, alienated, and now existed only in the form of hyper-sophisticated modernism and sentimental junk – "*gedankenlose Schlemmerei und gesinnungslosen Snobbismus*" was Blume's phrase.[4] The suggestion was that its main practitioners of music had been selfish individualists concerned only for their own reputation, and their stomping grounds had been the massive concert hall and the institutional arrangements that sustained it.[5]

As the rhetorical juxtaposition of continuity and catastrophe demands, Hausmusik before the fall was different than Hausmusik after it. Until the Nazi seizure of power made all things seem possible and the rhetoric even of Weimar-era enthusiasts took a decidedly fantastic turn, most of those who wrote on the fate of Hausmusik felt that only a modest and limited recreation of earlier times was possible, largely through the organization of new associations. It went without saying that these associations, complete with their journals and manifestos, had more in common with their own times than with bygone days. In any case the prevailing rhetorical stance was that things were in a bad way, thanks to a nineteenth-century legacy only worsened by war and creeping Americanism, and that winning back some cultural ground for a healthy Hausmusik would be an uphill struggle.[6]

Before further identifying who said such things and why, it might be worth considering how accurate their depiction of both past and present really was. Because amateurism as a social and cultural phenomenon has not garnered the same scholarly attention as professional cultural activity, it is surprisingly tempting to take such pronouncements at face value. Minus the moral outrage, the diagnosis of amateur decline followed by late Weimar-era renewal continuing into the Nazi period has seemed on the face of it plausible.[7] But is it? Measuring such activity is, in the absence of sustained research into the question, a somewhat inferential process, but inference suggests no such catastrophic break with the patterns of early nineteenth-century amateurism ever took place. No one doubts the vitality of associational life in its first phase of development in the first decades of the nineteenth century, or the widespread presence of musical associations and music making in the home in that first flowering. As Andreas Schulz has written, the widespread engagement of city burghers in music-making in the home and in organizations such as amateur orchestras and amateur drama groups represented an important part of the social construction of the German middle classes and continued across the divide of the Napoleonic wars – which did not, in any case, seriously disrupt the development of city life in Germany – on into the 1840s.[8] Other measures, such as the growing affordability of keyboard instruments and the increasing quantity of sheet music, likewise paint a picture of the widespread presence of music-making in middle-class households and in amateur organizations such as *Liedertafel.* Of course, there were the carpers and the complainers as well, those who felt the looming threat of "mere entertainment" and invented the category of serious music in order to lament its decline after the death of Mozart, Haydn, or Beethoven. The origins of modern musical criticism, as Bernd Sponheuer and others have argued, is closely linked to the simultaneous definition and defence of some higher version of music against some lower.[9] But for those actually engaged in

Hausmusik, the first half of the nineteenth century was, objectively speaking, a marvellous time.

Did catastrophe come later perhaps? Certainly the civil unrest of 1848–9 disrupted associational patterns in German cities, but again, a number of recent scholars have shown the rapidity with which even explicitly political associations re-established themselves in the 1850s, a decade once seen to have been marked by quietism and retreat.[10] Cultural groups, at least in the cities that have been studied (such as Mannheim and Leipzig), were not slow to follow and often led the way.[11] What Thomas Nipperdey called a second stage in association-building developed in the 1850s and 1860s and formed the backdrop to *Reichsgründung*. Musical activities in the home and in the semi-private settings of associations had their own reinvigoration, new figures coming to the fore and new waves of publication and fashion in home performance taking shape.[12] Four-handed transcriptions of symphonies, opera overtures, and virtuoso compositions became popular, as did simplified versions of popular operatic themes, potpourris of dance and entertainment music, and piano or simple two-instrument variation compositions on well-known themes.[13] Music in the house followed music in the concert or opera hall and at least made it possible to enjoy the remembered thrills of concert performances in a different setting. Hausmusik also constituted an essential practice in the emergence of a modern piety that was just as widespread but less "churched" than traditional piety.[14] The nineteenth century saw belief made individual and religious experience made private, the intense domestic cultivation of Christmas, Bible study, and prayers for all domestic occasions being the outward markers of this shift. Hausmusik accompanied that transformation every step of the way.[15]

Of course, not everyone thought that Hausmusik should encompass such a wide range of musical genres, from Christmas carols to show tunes, and the post-revolutionary period brought a new wave of cultural criticism, similarly concerned with the boundaries within the overall phenomenon of Hausmusik between morally elevating and morally depressing music, healthy and unhealthy music, and what truly educated and what merely entertained. But the existence of such screeds confirms only that the issue of boundaries between high and low culture and between amateur and professional remained unresolved. Rhetoric is not the same as reality and can mislead – and may well have misled the Hausmusik Jeremiahs of the 1920s. In any case the writings of several of the most prominent spokespeople for Hausmusik at mid-century were suffused with nostalgia for the previous generation. Wilhelm Heinrich Riehl's

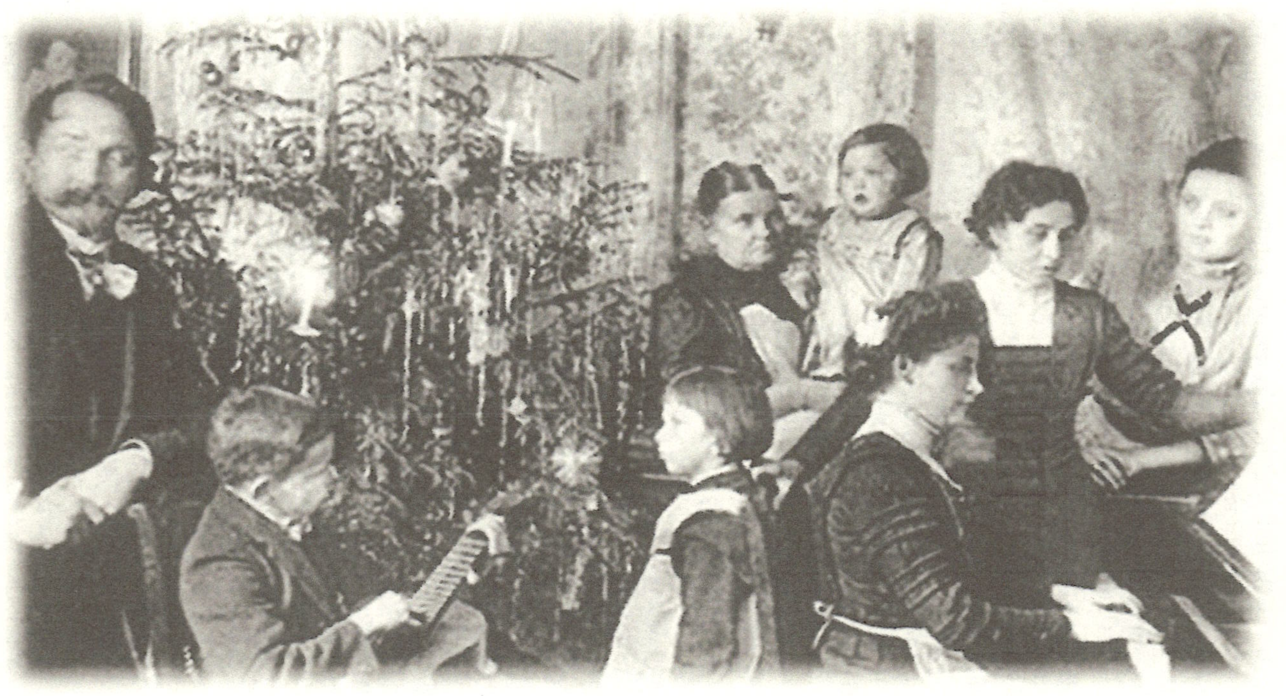

12.1 A family gathered around the piano and the Christmas tree, c. 1900. From the collection of historical Christmas photographs of Werner Abresch. Courtesy of the Boss Verlag

lamentations are both typical and unusually eloquent and memorable – and were highly influential in the 1930s.[16] Riehl, one of those energetic nineteenth-century polymaths, was both cultural historian and sociologist and both enthusiastic musical amateur and author of many novellas on musical themes as well as of several long essays (three books' worth) on music history, aesthetics, and criticism.[17] He had decided opinions on what we now call the social history of music, though in his time his effort to write about music in relation to social life was virtually unprecedented. In common with his more sociological opinions, these musical ones were mainly gloomy. Lamentation for a lost balance to life and an elusive intimacy between the people and their own culture suffuses his writings, whether his subject was the family, the landscape, the *Bürger* class, or music. Riehl greatly admired the *Vormärz*, and wrote a serious of essays on its minor lights. These "jovial musicians [*gemütliche Musikanten*] from the good old days," all of them "good and true souls, sturdy fellows ... personally cheerful, harmless, and each in his own way, a lovable human being," evoked the sound, "not completely faded away," of those "musical evenings which were celebrated in the houses of our grandfathers, where an amateur string quartet sawed away at a light, intelligible, and merry quartet, and trios and sonatas were played, where the friends of music drank the mild wine of such Hausmusik, in order to refresh themselves and stimulate their spirits."[18]

Riehl's reference to the "houses of our grandfathers" provides an important clue to the psychology, if not the chronology, of such nostalgia, both in his time and later when we encounter it in the twentieth century. Modern people, as Reinhard Koselleck has shown most subtly, use history to obtain a vantage point on the present. A defining characteristic of modernity is the belief that we live in a time of change and that the future will inevitably be different from both the past and the present.[19] Nostalgia is the concomitant of such perceptions; it is the sense that such change involves (to use Goethe's phrase) dispersion and loss, as well as progress and gain. A further aspect of this modern sense of time that deserves our attention is the tendency of nostalgia to attach especially to memories of home and home life. In contemplating the home, cultural critics almost irresistibly move from personal experience of dispersion and loss to societal breakdown. It is not just that one has left the childhood home oneself; all childhood homes are not what they were, are lesser and colder places. This is why one finds lamentations about family decline even in periods later considered to have had strong families and why one finds a rhetoric of decline and loss in nearly everything that one reads, from Riehl's time onward, about the music of the house and home. In contrast to what Riehl had experienced as a child in a small-town bürgerlich household, he regretted, often and in print, that the times in which he lived as an adult were dominated by large concert halls, prima donnas, virtuosi, and prancing maestri. Riehl accused his contemporaries of having replaced the "mild wine of such Hausmusik" with the unhealthy "brandy of opera and salon music, which stupefies and feverishly excites" us. This was a world dominated by Richard Wagner, whom Riehl volubly and publicly despised and whose circus of artificial music, artificial drama, and artificial Germanness at Bayreuth symbolized everything that had gone wrong in the relationship of music to the German people.[20]

Unsurprisingly, those who resurrected Riehl's reputation in the 1930s made no mention of his antipathy, even though it was an integral part of his sense of musical crisis. The ghost of this antipathy seemed to haunt Hausmusik enthusiasts of the 1930s in their struggle to reconcile their musical goals with those of the Nazi state. However, to continue, with the question of Hausmusik's fate in the nineteenth century, we need to look not just at what Riehl said but at what he and a number of other contemporaries did. Riehl ushered in what we might tentatively identify as a third stage of amateur music-making in the nineteenth century, a stage marked by a greater emphasis on folk motives and folkloric groups and on singing and youth participation than had existed in earlier stages. Riehl himself put together several *Lieder* collections, including a number of his own compositions. Other contemporaries, such as August Reissman, author of a widely read book on the "organization and cultural meaning" of Hausmusik, likewise attempted to reinvigorate musical instruction in both house and school.[21] We cannot say for certain whether they achieved the moral improvement towards which their efforts were ultimately directed, but most scholars would agree that amateurism as a whole enjoyed an expansion in the latter part of the nineteenth century, that associational life in general expanded in quantity and social reach, and that new strands of associationalism – such as the youth movement and singing organizations larger than the old Liedertafeln – joined the already existing scene.[22]

Hausmusik in the Weimar Republic

The Great War, of course, disrupted many such activities, but the point of this tour through the nineteenth century is to suggest not only that rumours of Hausmusik's demise were greatly exaggerated but also that by around 1925, when we encounter the first Weimar Jeremiahs, a pattern of Hausmusik invigoration and lamentation was firmly established. It was as predictable as any cultural phenomenon can be that yet another wave would wash ashore. The only difference this time around was that the political backdrop refused to remain a backdrop. Instead, more intensively of course after 1933, politics intruded to set the agendas, sharpen the rhetoric, and create a whole public facade of unity and centralized common purpose out of what was historically, and perhaps essentially, fragmented and dispersed phenomena.

One of the first signs of such pointed political purpose came with the formation in 1923–4 of the *Finkensteiner Bund*, a group of young, nationalist Germans, radically alienated from the Weimar system and committed to an ill-defined program of "musical renewal ... as a powerful branch of German renewal." They embodied a familiar type of right-wing activism with loose ties to a host of other anti-Weimar organizations.[23] The Finkensteiners, as they called themselves, were most closely linked to the Sudeten German movement, which was to play such a fateful role in 1938. (Finkenstein was a little town in North Bohemia.) The "idea of Finkenstein," as one enthusiast called it, demanded an "unrelenting struggle against everything trivial, common, and superficial [*seichte, gemeine, oberflächliche*]."[24] Music, properly understood and performed, was "the soul's renewal and promised the "inner liberation of the people's essence."[25] The Bund produced a journal, *Die Singgemeinde,* published by the Bärenreiter Verlag and edited first by Heino Eppinger, then by Konrad Ameln, until it was merged in 1933 with the journal *Musik und Volk*, an organ of the *Reichsbund Volkstum und Heimat* (Bärenreiter Verlag continued to publish it). It espoused a fairly windy series of propositions about the importance of choral singing, of German music in general, and of early music of the sixteenth through eighteenth centuries in particular, culminating in J.S. Bach. From its denunciations of *Virtuosentum* to its careful drawing of lines between concerts (bad) and "musical evenings" or "choral singing evenings" or "instrumental evenings," and so on (good), between dilettantes (bad) and amateurs (good), the Finkensteiners acted out a musical version of that revolt against the nineteenth-century bourgeois liberal fathers that Peter Gay saw as so defining an element of Weimar culture.[26] One can follow its main activists more or less easily into the Third Reich: Ernst Sommer, for example, declared the Finkensteiners "political soldiers of Adolf Hitler" already in 1932.[27] And while the Finkensteiner Bund as such ceased to exist during the process of *Gleichschaltung*, the group's redeployed members could rightly consider themselves a primary source for much of the National Socialist rhetoric on music making in the home and among amateurs.

Yet we cannot fully appreciate the essentially rhetorical nature of the Finkensteiner victory in 1933 – the triumph not so much of its music-making as of its spin on it – if we do not consider the larger spectrum of amateur practices in the Weimar period. As Pamela Potter has pointed out, the material and intellectual circumstances of the 1920s in Germany combined to encourage both old and new forms of musical amateurism. The publication of literature for home piano playing continued to flourish. The proliferation of books, guides, and music for amateur string quartets and other small-scale ensembles attests to the popularity of such forms of music-making, even if the numbers of actual performances are impossible to count. These guides ranged from the serious to the comic, from Wilhelm Altmann's *Handbook for String Quartet Players,* published in 1928 as a comprehensive guide to easily playable works for the committed amateur, to an anonymous (its author was in fact a lawyer named Franz Anton Ledermann) comic masterpiece, first published in the *Berliner Tageblatt* in 1924 and thereafter reportedly "passed from hand to hand among musical amateurs" and finally published as a pamphlet in 1936. It was called in its English version (published in 1938) "See You Again at the Double Bar: A Contribution to the Natural History of the Amateur Quartet."[28] The 1920s also saw the beginnings of a new market in old instruments like the soon-to-be-ubiquitous recorder, cheaper and quicker to learn than more formal modern instruments and soon attracting a linked production of music geared to the amateur player. Magazines for every conceivable amateur musical specialization flourished: on singing at home and on instruments such as the guitar, the lute, the zither, the violin, the mandolin, and the recorder. Of these publications surely the least prepossessing was called *Der Harmoniumfreund: Zeitschrift für Hausmusik und Kunst.* It catered to the owners of home organs and included pieces such as why a harmonium made a wonderful Christmas present or how regrettable it was that professional musicians looked down their noses at this humble, eminently useful instrument.

The difficulty in analysing Hausmusik in the Weimar era, in fact, lies in determining which spectrum best describes this variety. Should one order it along a spectrum of political to apolitical, conservative to democratic, aesthetic to commercial, high to low, or sublime to silly? How one categorizes it has consequences for how one assesses the subtle and not-so-subtle shifts after 1933. For the most articulate segment of the Hausmusik community, the distinctions most worth maintaining, both in print and in practice, were between the serious and frivolous manifestations of Hausmusik. We see this not only in the fulminations of the Finkensteiners against the "widespread musical dilettantism that nibbles on technically simplified versions of genuine art" but also in concerns about inadequate musical education and inaccurate historical understanding, voiced in essentially apolitical publications such as the *Collegium Musicum: Blätter zur Pflege der Haus- und Kammermusik.*[29] The act of drawing such distinctions can easily be over-interpreted as a political move on the part of anti-liberal ideologues. But such politics did not dominate Hausmusik as a whole before 1933. Politics aside, the distinction between serious and frivolous allowed certain groups in a crowded landscape to stake out their own territory, to define their own identity, to win supporters and move merchandise. Nor should it be forgotten that, certainly in the *Collegium Musicum,* the distinction reflected a high level of involvement on the part of musicologists, in particular of experts in the interpretation of old music, who were in the Weimar period actively seeking connections to the general public: again, according to Potter, "musicologists wielded far more influence in the amateur arena than in education, professional issues, or politics."[30]

Hausmusik in the Third Reich

The distinction between serious and frivolous functioned in a number of ways and was not particularly problematic in political terms until the National Socialist seizure of power in 1933. But what had previously represented an impulse to self-definition and musical progress in pluralistic social and political circumstances (the *Collegium Musicum,* for instance, articulated high Enlightenment values such as accuracy of scholarship, "free exchange of opinions," and constructive criticism) changed to a prescriptive (though largely unenforced) demand for dominance of a certain type of Hausmusik in the drive to social and political uniformity after 1933.[31] As the Finkensteiners became absorbed into the Reichsbund Volkstum und Heimat and the *Collegium Musicum* abandoned both its sober intellectualism and its Latinate moniker, becoming simply the *Zeitschrift für Hausmusik,* the overall aspect of the public face of Hausmusik became thoroughly National Socialist. A certain amount of effort, particularly in the pages of *Music und Volk,* went into rewriting the history of Hausmusik in the Weimar Republic, in order to emphasize its straining towards the "national renewal" of 1933 and to make ever clearer its distance from its nineteenth-century bourgeois origins.[32] Even more

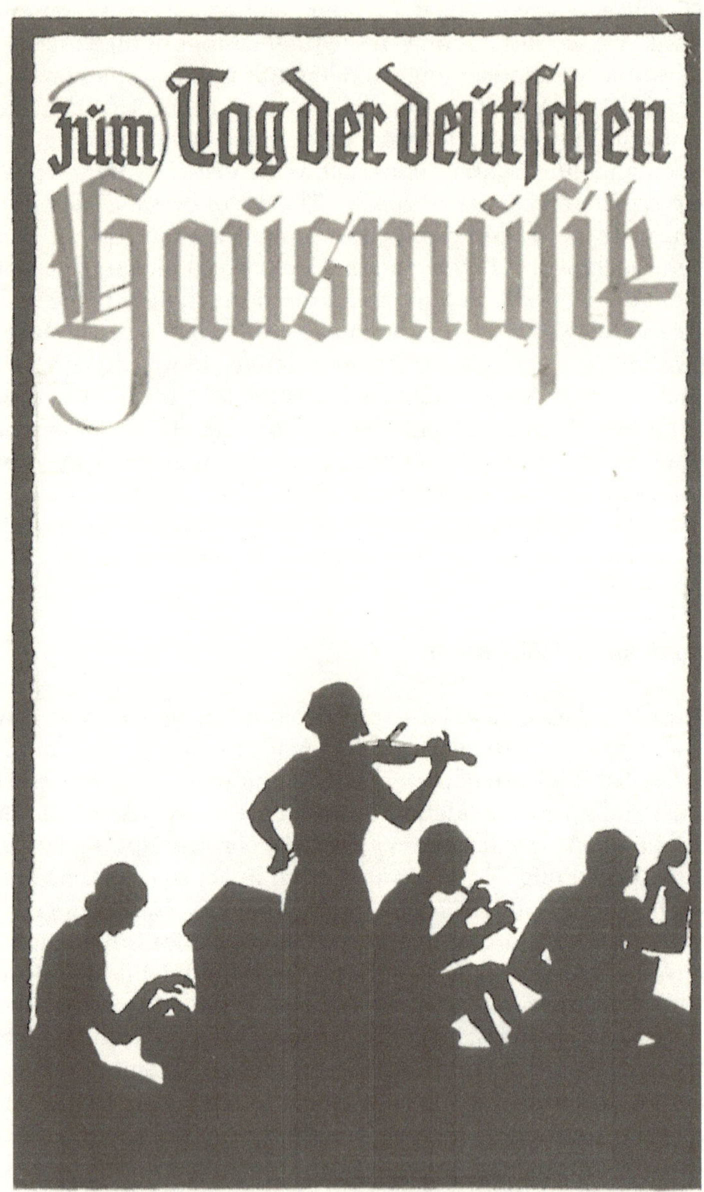

12.2 Postcard for the *Tag der deutschen Hausmusik*, 1938. Author's property.

effort went into triumphalist declarations of Hausmusik's now reformed and re-centred place in German life, into analyses of the Nordic essence of Bach's instrumental music and other such reinterpretations of the repertoire, and into more or less convoluted explanations of the organizational paths that various Hausmusik practitioners were following in the new Reich. The new era also brought showy demonstrations of the spirit of national unity now informing the performance of music in the home. These so-called Days of German Hausmusik ultimately came under the direction of the Working Community for Hausmusik (*Arbeitsgemeinschaft für Hausmusik*), part of Goebbels's creation, the Reich Music Chamber (*Reichsmusikkammer*), and continued as an annual event well into the war years.

In all of these writings the serious-frivolous distinction lingered, transformed into the distinction between politically acceptable and unacceptable – or more pragmatically, as the distinction between what could appear in public as Hausmusik versus what remained strictly unofficial and, if not sanctioned, then not officially encouraged. The Gleichschaltung of Hausmusik was, in other words, something of a victimless crime. More to the point, the very nature of the process of Gleichschaltung – its penchant for ideological pronouncements, its drive to centralization and a terrible simplification, its need to mark the process by ostentatious public display, and, most perplexingly to the reader of its texts, its oxymoronic rhetoric that everything has changed/nothing has changed – favoured the more highly organized elements of any civilian activity. Nazification worked most easily on those who took themselves most seriously, on the educated, the rationalized, and the institutionalized segments of the population. In the case of Hausmusik, Gleichschaltung worked most effectively on those who had sought to reform it, whatever their previous political allegiances.

But rather than dwell on the ample evidence of changes resulting from conformity to National Socialist doctrine or the equally extensive evidence indicating no changes at all, either in the pages of the periodicals or in the types of music published for the amateur or indeed in the actual playing of music in the home, we may turn in conclusion to the muted and dispersed evidence of dissatisfaction in the Third Reich and what its presence tells us about the role of Hausmusik under this version of totalitarianism. Short of checking Gestapo records for arrests of rowdy recorder players, we can find a species of discontent and petty point-scoring against rivals present in the Nazi Hausmusik periodicals. Such low-level dissidence almost always reflected a sense of unease with

Nazi centralization and monumentalism, an unease that one finds also in regionalist, Heimat circles. Reviewers often expressed reservations, for instance, about the annual Hausmusik extravaganzas. Fritz Jöde welcomed the 1933 Day of German Hausmusik (*Tag der deutschen Hausmusik*) as evidence that the Germans had one again become a "singing people" (*singendes Volk*), but he warned that there were dangers in such events and that too much publicity and carrying on in large public groups threatened the very essence of Hausmusik. A few months later Herbert Just concurred. Hausmusik was a private thing, he suggested, not really suited to "public propaganda" (*öffentliche Propaganda*), but that said, what a marvellous thing to see all these young people together, but *that* said, all the publicity meant that people were paying just a bit too much attention to "technical perfection" and that was tending to "overstep the bounds of genuine *Hausmusik.*" Moreover, here and there he was sure he heard a bit of salon music, not really *echte* Hausmusik, and a virtuosic youngster or two seemed to have snuck into the proceedings, and so on.[33] Such complaints persisted throughout the lifespan of the Hausmusik periodicals without ever becoming more pointed. Often they took the form of complaints against other Hausmusik organizers, who were accused of having no understanding of the "movement for renewal" (*Erneuerungsbewegung*); if they had understood the movement, so it was implied, they would not be staging such mass events. At other times the target lay outside the Hausmusik circles themselves, in the wider world of concertizing, opera-going, musical professionalism, and the star system. Once Goebbels himself came in for direct criticism, but overall the style of complaint was sideways and evasive, weaving back and forth across the musical landscape, seeking to establish its own credentials without making any powerful enemies.

That we encounter such muted evidence of discontent at all signifies two things: first, that Hausmusik experienced the same dynamic of self-coordination that has been well analysed in the historical literature. Ian Kershaw has drawn our attention to the concept of "working toward the Führer" in the speech of a second-rank ministry official. It meant promoting doctrines that one felt the Führer would have liked, fitting oneself in, and clamouring for space in the limited attention span of the Nazi leadership.[34] Grumbling in this context was a sign of feeling neglected and resenting those who were getting the attention. Such discontent also reveals how very low were the stakes in this particular corner of the Third Reich. The politics of Hausmusik was wide and shallow. It included a highly developed rhetorical commitment to the new regime and sense of importance combined with very little alteration in the actual practices of home music-making. One can read between the lines, as well as in the advertisements and sales of instruments, a persistently private form of music-making, the political significance of which remained as negligible as it had always been. An optimist could call it the failure of National Socialism fully to control private life. A less rosy view of this persistent sameness would say that it attested to the complexity of the social formations over which the National Socialist state presided. In the Weimar period right-wing nationalists regarded such complexity as a sign of social fragmentation and hence of a crisis that only the formation of a *Volksgemeinschaft* would overcome. But of course not even a police state like the Third Reich could so easily turn back the multiply interconnected processes of modernization. For some historians the National Socialist regime succeeded in transforming this complexity not into solidarity and consensus but instead into isolation, atomization, and finally the community of the air-raid shelter.[35] From this perspective the phenomenon of Hausmusik was simply too widespread, too various in form, too dispersed in its sites, and too disorganized in its impulses ever to transform into a unitary phenomenon under the control of the state.

The least rosy view of such persistent sameness in the practices of Hausmusik – the same practices as in Weimar, the same complaints, albeit re-articulated and re-centred – holds that the Third Reich was a regime in which conformity to racial doctrine bought one a fair amount of room to differ and diversify and complain on other, essentially insignificant matters. We could state this final view even more strongly: grumbling and privatism on the Hausmusik front deflected attention from the real horror of it all, or indeed made the horror palatable. Saul Friedländer has famously noted in his reflections on "kitsch and death" that the presence of kitsch – "the pinnacle of good taste in the absence of taste" – in the National Socialist era, far from being an irrelevancy, reinforced the regime's larger mechanisms of death. Likewise, Peter Williams wrote in regard to the German organ reform movement in the 1920s that "unbelievable though it may now seem, playing Telemann's recorder sonatas came to have a hidden political agenda."[36] But do we really need these stunning, ultimately insupportable theses to make sense of phenomena such as Hausmusik? This chapter has tried to cast doubt on such assertions of hidden agendas, not in defence of amateur musicians but in deference to those areas of German life where change was unavoidable, direct, and brutal. We do not necessarily understand the mechanisms of death better by studying them where they did not operate; nor do we understand politics better by finding it everywhere. We may indeed feel that *frisson* that Friedlander describes, as we juxtapose the harmonium with the Albrechtstraße SS torture chambers, but did the harmonium player feel it – and if she or he did not, then what have we learned? The story of Hausmusik before, during, and after the Third Reich is a story that sheds light on the many strands of musical culture present in modern Germany and on the peculiarly vital role of music as a whole in German national identity. We do not need to make greater claims for it than that.

Chapter Thirteen

To Be or Not to Be Wagnerian in Leni Riefenstahl's Films

Musically speaking, there is no talking people out of their belief that Richard Wagner composed the score for the Third Reich.[1] We can find plenty of reasons for the persistence of this belief, not least in the unacknowledged influence of the anonymous sound editors who have chosen to score nearly every modern documentary on the Second World War with excerpts from Wagner preludes. The frequent use of the adjective "Wagnerian" or the phrase "Wagnerian *Gesamtkunstwerk*" (total work of art) to characterize the aspirations of those who choreographed public life in the Third Reich also owes something to Walter Benjamin's suggestion that the "logical result of Fascism is the introduction of aesthetics into political life."[2] Thus, for instance, one finds a recent textbook on the Holocaust referring to Hitler's development of his "own vision of politics and power" while inspired by Wagner's "huge casts, imposing music, exaggerated passions, and powerful depictions of Germanic myth."[3] Never mind that his only opera with a "huge cast" (*Rienzi*) was not based on Germanic legend, or that the Ring Cycle's sources were not mythological in the Greek sense or Germanic in any modern sense, though Wagner perhaps regarded them as both. And whether one regards the passions expressed by his dramas as exaggerated does depend on one's experience of life. But nowhere does the myth of the Third Reich as Wagnerian prove more influential than when it shapes impressions and interpretations of Leni Riefenstahl's Nazi-era films. *Triumph of the Will* and *Olympia* are routinely identified as Wagnerian Gesamkunstwerk or assumed to use Wagner's music as their scores.[4] As Ray Müller put it to Riefenstahl in his documentary *The Wonderful, Horrible Life of Leni Riefenstahl*, were not the scenes of massed people in *Triumph of the Will*, "teilweise wie eine Wagner Oper?" – at least in part not like a Wagnerian opera? His question was clearly designed to elicit the answer "yes," which Riefenstahl declined to provide. Although it takes no effort to discover that Herbert Windt, not Wagner, wrote the score, the suitability of the term "Wagnerian" to describe the music used in these films is rarely examined.[5] Yet we must examine it if we are to understand the character of the musical scores, their place in both German musical tradition and contemporary film music, and their contribution to the films' overall aesthetic and moral-political appeal.

The study of fascist, and specifically Nazi, aesthetics has come a long way since Benjamin's brief, suggestive remarks from the 1930s. We now have a detailed portrait of cultural activities in the Third Reich, and scholars of film, music, art, and dance have made considerable efforts to link the picture that has emerged to the findings of historians on matters of everyday life, coercion, and conformity in the racial state. For Linda Schulte-Sasse, writing in 1996, providing a more detailed portrait required an "epistemological reversal" that rejected the view that Nazi films were "of interest only as propaganda" and instead pointed out their ambivalent, contradictory character. Nazi-era films were not simply the conveyor belts of political ideology, but multivalent art forms that could "harbor, transform, exceed, and undermine political ideology."[6] A few years later, in 1999, Lutz Koepnick argued for the interdependence of politics and consumption in the cultural works of Nazism. He suggested that "the charismatic power of public mass events and the lures of privatized consumption" worked together in Nazi-era films, art, and musical productions, both to mobilize the population behind the regime and to isolate individuals in the dreamworlds of leisure culture.[7] Both Schulte-Sasse and Koepnick regarded the Nazi aesthetic as working to create illusory states "of reconciliation, coherence, wholeness" (Schulte-Sasse) or "a utopian unification of modern culture" (Koepnick). And just as historians have urged us to turn away from the obvious (Gestapo headquarters) and towards the everyday (neighbourhoods, local networks of acquaintances, business, the family) in order to understand the workings of conformity in the Third Reich, so too have scholars of film and media urged us to turn our gaze away from the oh-so-obvious works of Leni Riefenstahl and her fellow propagandists if we are to make sense both of the regime's astonishing popularity and, connected to that, of its lack of aesthetic homogeneity.

Yet productive though these interpretive moves have proven to be, they have not necessarily led to a better understanding of Riefenstahl's work. Koepnick, for instance, still relies on the trope of Riefenstahl as

Wagnerian: he uses phrases such as Gesamtkunstwerk, a "carefully choreographed spectacle of ethereal bodies and geometrical shapes," theatricality, "glorified gestures of surrender and idealized figurations of death," all Wagnerian in their ultimate point of reference. He sets these images against a more realistic picture of "the stuff dreams were made of," that is, "racing cars, radios, Coca-Cola, swing, and Hollywood-style comedies."[8] Riefenstahl's work itself remains in Koepnick's revisiting of fascist aesthetics where it was before his return trip took place; he simply suggests that we now see it as only part of a more complex whole, not the quintessence of the whole. Its enactment of "homogenizing ritual" made it the foil to the strategies of banal entertainment and consumerist isolationism that the regime pursued simultaneously – strategies that broke "the bonds of old solidarities" and hence prepared the now "atomized individual for the auratic shapes of mass politics."[9] But what if the films themselves contained all these elements, the banal as well as the auratic, the deliberately ordinary as well as the hypertrophied ritualistic? What if, taking a cue from a not uncommon undergraduate response to *Triumph of the Will*, her work is boring and repetitive – or in the word of Brian Winston, reviewing the 2001 DVD release of the film, "turgid"?[10] This chapter will consider Riefenstahl's own (limited) interest in music as well as the work of her chief musical collaborator, Herbert Windt, in order to recover something of the appropriation and the appeal of the everyday that was present even in these products of a person with a highly dramatic, indeed self-dramatizing, aesthetic sensibility.

Riefenstahl and Music

Although Riefenstahl herself neither composed nor selected the music for her films, her own relationship to music is relevant both for her choice of composer for the film scores and for her substantial involvement in coordinating sound and image in the final product. In both matters implicit assumptions about the cultural significance of music are revealed and help us to analyse the overall effect of the films. Nothing in the interviews Riefenstahl gave or in her memoir suggests that she ever regarded music as anything but instrumental. Punning aside, her evident indifference to a long German tradition of taking music seriously on its own terms reminds us that an individual's attitudes cannot be reliably deduced from their social class or milieu. Riefenstahl's membership in the German educated middle class and having a youth graced with the obligatory run of piano lessons did not instil in her any strong tendency to regard music as especially profound, especially expressive, or especially German. In her banal telling, both she and her brother had "a love of art and of all things beautiful," but "with the piano as with painting, I had some talent but not enough," and further, "I lacked the passion that I felt so deeply for the art of dance."[11]

Dance is, indeed, the key to Riefenstahl's relationship to music, in her life as in her films. Her exposure to classical music came almost entirely through her involvement with dance, and her responses to music can be described only as kinesthetic. Music was of value to her insofar as it inspired or enabled her to move. The only contemporary composer she discusses in her memoir is Ferruccio Busoni, the German-Italian virtuoso pianist, composer, and champion of musical modernism, who worked in Berlin in the decades before the outbreak of war in 1914 and returned to Berlin after the war to teach composition. Riefenstahl encountered him in the 1920s, at a musical salon in Berlin, and wrote about how she spontaneously danced to his piano playing. This response allegedly enchanted him to such an extent that he composed a short piano piece to accompany her dancing, personally sending a handwritten score to her with the inscription "For the dancer Leni Riefenstahl, Busoni." This "Valse Caprice" "eventually became one of my greatest successes," wrote Riefenstahl.[12] Likewise, her early training in dance, at the Grimm-Reiter School in Berlin and later at Mary Wigman's celebrated school for modern dance in Dresden, involved her in constant interaction with music, though strictly as accompaniment to dance exercises and performances.[13] During the period of her transition to film-making, she insisted, diva-like, on having a piano and pianist (Herr Klamt) available to her while on location in various mountain lodges, so she could keep up her dance training, and she likewise graciously accepted a gift of a grand piano from the lovesick Arnold Fanck in order to have a fully equipped dance studio back home in Berlin.[14] In all these quasi-musical anecdotes the piano (and pianist) is literally and figuratively the instrument of her ambitions as a dancer and dancer-actress.

The music Riefenstahl heard and used in the course of her early training and career also reflected practical considerations. Her own choices of musical accompaniment during her brief career as a solo dancer and choreographer reveal what one comes to expect of Riefenstahl even in her later, more celebrated career as filmmaker – elements of genuine innovation and moments of brilliant inventiveness, combined with aesthetic conventionality, even predictability, and an ambivalent relationship to the modern. An exponent of "the modern dance in Germany," as critic André Levinson described the scene in 1928, she reflected both the synchronistic views of the relationship between music and dance and the ambivalent attitude towards modern music.[15] Even in quintessentially modern studios like Mary Wigman's the use of modernist music was exceptional. Modern music's growing rhythmic complexity and irregularity was part of the problem. All the exponents of modern dance in Weimar Germany were, directly or indirectly, disciples of Émile Jaques-Dalcroze, whose "eurhythmics" posited a natural connection between music and the movements of the human body through the medium of pulse or rhythm. The desirable, "natural" relation between music and dance was thus one in which the musical pulses controlled the bodily movements, and a perfect synchronization was the ideal to which dance aspired. Yet, as Dalcroze himself discovered, the body could not "naturally" accommodate the irregular, rapidly shifting rhythmic texture of much modern music.

Harmony, or rather the move away from western tonality into atonal or twelve-tone music, posed a further aesthetic problem for dancers. Many of the exponents of modern dance in Germany had their roots in the anti-materialist, "life-reform," sun-worshipping milieu of *Körperkultur* and believed that through dance, indeed through physicality itself, modern men and women could recover a harmonic relation to the world, even the world of industry and the machine. Although the more adventurous exponents of this ideal found precisely in atonality the promise of a new harmonization of the world, most dancers, by no means indifferent to the preferences of the paying public, remained wedded to the more familiar expressiveness of nineteenth-century romantic music. Nor were musicians so cheap to hire or instrumental ensembles so simple to assemble or the music of living composers so easy to obtain that dancers, even famous ones like Wigman, could afford music accompaniment beyond what a single pianist could produce. Surveying more than 200 concert dance programs from across Europe in the first decades of the twentieth century, Karl Toepfer found a "strong preference" for a list consisting mainly of nineteenth-century romantic composers, including Grieg, Schumann, Chopin, Tchaikovsky, Brahms, Schubert, Mozart, and Dvořák.[16]

Notably absent from the list is Richard Wagner. "Scarcely any dancer," writes Toepfer, "showed the boldness" of Janine Solane, who in 1932 debuted as a solo performer with a lengthy dance set "entirely to the music of Wagner."[17] The problem here was probably musical rather than ideological, for many a dancer, with Rudolf Laban leading the way, had felt powerful affinities with Wagner the dramatist, Wagner the theorist, Wagner the anti-Semite and cultural nationalist, and Wagner the vegetarian life-reformer.[18] But the music itself, whether because piano reductions of it were unsatisfactory or because it was simply too modern in harmonic, melodic, and rhythmic terms, did not settle easily into the dancers' repertoire. As for Riefenstahl, she proved to be entirely mainstream in her musical choices, choreographing her solo dances to the music of, among others, Schubert, Chopin, Tchaikovsky, Grieg, and Mikhail Ippolitov-Ivanov.[19]

Chopin, for instance, provided music for a languid piece, all drifting veils and imploring, come-hither arm gestures, which she called "Traumblüte" (dream flowers) and modelled on Anna Pavlova's famous "Dying Swan." Along with her "Dance to the Sea," set improbably and with considerable originality to Beethoven's Fifth Symphony, "Traumblüte" proved to be the vehicle by which Riefenstahl first reached the broader film-going public.[20] Both dances were featured in Arnold Fanck's 1926 film, *The Holy Mountain*, in which Riefenstahl appears in her first credited role as the dancer Diotima. The trope of "Beethoven Hero," so powerfully represented by the Fifth Symphony in particular, may account for why Fanck, and presumably Riefenstahl, thought this strangely disjointed introductory sequence – in which shots of Riefenstahl perching on rocks and undulating madly on the beach are intercut with shots of crashing waves – formed a suitable introduction to a movie about mountains. Riefenstahl herself, never loath to draw attention to the heroic physical demands required of those who would make movies, later recalled how a lone violinist was "lowered down the cliff by a rope" in order to provide what could only have been the merest snippets from the Fifth, so that she, engaged in "horribly difficult dancing on the slippery rocks in that wild surf," might somehow synchronize movement, music, and waves.[21]

Leni Riefenstahl's early musical experiences reveal, then, a person whose musical choices seemed to have been dictated mainly by a feel for what was the norm in the circles in which she worked and, perhaps, by a preference for music that somehow enabled what she called her "own urge" to "surrender completely to the rhythms of the music."[22] Just as her musical choices traversed a comfortable terrain of classical music already well integrated into the European soundscape and dance world and just as her dancing occupied an aesthetic middle ground within the modernism of expressionist dance, so too did her understanding of how one could integrate sound into the visual world of the film develop neither behind nor ahead of the rapidly emergent conventions of film music.

Fortunately for her, she found in Herbert Windt someone with the musical imagination that she seems to have lacked.

Herbert Windt and Film Music

In 1929 Riefenstahl acted in her first sound film, Arnold Fanck and G.W. Pabst's *The White Hell of Piz Palü*, and in 1931–2 she worked on *The Blue Light*, the first film she directed and also, of course, a sound film, scored by the veteran composer of the silent era, Giuseppe Becce (who was already something of a specialist in Alpine films, including *Piz Palü*). In 1932 following the successful debut in Berlin of his opera *Andromache*, Herbert Windt received from Ufa his first commission to compose music for film, the much ballyhooed *Morgenrot* (*At Dawn*; directed by Vernon Sewell and Gustav Ucicky), a "magnificent epic from the annals of German history," according to the pre-publicity, and a "film for the German people."[23] This was followed by a number of other film commissions, which established Windt's reputation as one of the few serious composers in Germany able to make the transition to film music. In 1933 he and Riefenstahl were brought together, exactly how is unknown, so that Windt could assemble the film score first for *Victory of Faith* (*Sieg des Glaubens*) and then, in short order, using much of the same material, *Triumph of the Will*. Riefenstahl turned to Windt in 1936 to score *Olympia* and again in the 1950s to adapt d'Alembert's operatic score as well as to compose a substantial amount of new music for her *Lowlands* (*Tiefland*) project – such was the collaboration between the two. Riefenstahl later had a few words of praise for her collaborator to offer, and Windt for his part made some equally diplomatic and brief expressions of admiration for "Leni Riefenstahl, who has a 'sixth sense' about what is right in musical matters."[24]

What strikes one first about their collaboration is its timing. It occurred right at the beginning of the sound era, when filmmakers and musicians alike had to rethink the relationship of sound to image in technical but also in aesthetic and theoretical terms.[25] By the time the first sound film was made in the United States in the mid-1920s, film-makers had already begun to commission original scores in order to improve the fit between film and sound. Although an improvement on earlier methods of providing music for film, which had relied on compendia of musical snippets organized according to recurrent themes (life, death, love, terror, etc.), the new film scores tended still to consist of a string of musical fragments.[26] The Italo-German film composer Giuseppe Becce, perhaps the prime exemplar of this phenomenon, learned early on how to imitate the music of Richard Wagner in film scores, initially because permission to use Wagner's actual music, or after 1913 other people's recordings of his music, proved too expensive. Becce, whose one and only role in front of the camera was as Wagner himself (in a 1913 biopic of the composer), also became his musical stunt double, composing hundreds of film scores *á la mode wagnerienne.*[27] He, and many others like him, created the illusion that musical fragmentation could contribute to continuity – or, in knock-off Wagnerian terms, endless melody and, above all, a Gesamtkunstwerk.

The principle by which musicians composed their original score was overwhelmingly that of parallelism or manufactured synaesthesia. In its simplest (or most idiotic) form, this was called "Mickey Mousing" – a descending glissando accompanying an actress down a staircase, for instance.[28] Parallelism could also take more sophisticated forms, but in all cases, wrote Hanns Eisler and Theodor Adorno, there had to "be some meaningful relation between the picture and the music," and the "actual inventive task of the composer is to compose music that 'fits' precisely into the given picture."[29] In any case, most composers never got past conceiving of music's relation to image as some more or less subtle version of the silent film accompanist's rendition of Grieg's "Hall of the Mountain King" while the villain appeared on the screen.[30]

At the same time the presence of recognizably "classical" music in film scores, even if in bowdlerized versions, gave rise to what Pierre Bourdieu has called "classification struggles," in this case in the form of confusion and consternation over whether the music in films was indeed serious music or, more likely, just entertainment.[31] Writers in scholarly musical periodicals, for instance, lamented the degeneracy, declining standards, and generally degraded position that music held in the world of film. Such discussions provide further demonstration, if it were needed, of the pervasiveness of an increasingly widespread nationalist paranoia in the interwar period. Discussions of film and its music, like many other cultural discourses in the years after 1918, easily took on nationalist, even *völkisch* nationalist tones, with denunciations of Americanization, of Jewish influences, of racial mixing, and of any number of other manifestations of degeneration and decline increasingly attached to the particular issues of how one set music to images on the silver screen.

Placing Leni Riefenstahl and Herbert Windt in the midst of these rapid, even dizzying transformations in social relations, cultural meanings, and political power structures would seem, nevertheless, to be a straightforward task. As we have seen, Riefenstahl herself brought a more or less uninflected version of the synaesthetic, or synchronic, ideal to her film work from her experiences as a dancer. In the ongoing debates about how representational music should be Riefenstahl would seem an unlikely candidate to find anything amiss in the musical codes of the silent film era. All her biographers, interpreters, accusers, and defenders agree that her overriding concern was with the composition of the visual, not the aural, world; in that sense she was more than comfortable with an early film culture characterized by what Kathryn Kalinak has identified as "the transcendent power of the image and the dependence of the soundtrack."[32]

But then one must reckon with Herbert Windt, the man in the shadows. Before turning to the relationship of music and image in the films that were, at least in that aspect, their joint creation, we need to take some measure of the talents and musical values he brought to this work. As indicated earlier, Windt represented a different kind of musical figure than Giuseppe Becce.[33] Before the war Windt had come to Berlin to study piano at the Stern'sche Conservatory, one of the oldest and most important music schools in Germany. He had been there only a few months before he had had his fill of formal studies and sought instead a position as assistant music director (*Hilfskapellmeister*) at Max Reinhardt's Deutsches Theater. With similar restlessness he volunteered when the war broke out in 1914 and was assigned to a Hussar regiment. He was horribly wounded at Verdun in August 1917, his face partially blown off and an arm permanently damaged. By the time he emerged from multiple efforts at reconstructive surgery, he resembled one of the veterans in a George Grosz painting; he had minimal use of his arm and was thus forced to abandon all hopes of a career as a pianist or conductor. He decided instead to become a composer.

Back in Berlin Windt's compositional efforts in the 1920s were neither so successful as to allow him to give up working as a theory teacher and journeyman orchestrator, nor so unsuccessful as to make him turn to another profession altogether. A number of his compositions were performed publicly and received respectful notices. One, "Andante Religioso," even won him a place at the Hochschule für Musik in the composition class of Franz Schreker, whose operas were breaking new ground in their explorations of polytonality and timbre. Through Schreker, Windt fell in with the "Berlin Group," mostly young composers, self-conscious modernists, and active publicists for the "new music."[34] Never entirely comfortable in this particular vanguard, he nevertheless continued to work in what was a recognizably modernist aesthetic, identifying more with Richard Strauss, "the true father of the modern," than with Arnold

Schoenberg.[35] In 1928, around the time Riefenstahl was performing her heroic best in her first major hit (*The White Hell of Piz Palü*, 1929), Windt embarked on what he hoped would be his own defining opus, *Andromache*, based on an original adaptation of Racine's play. At this point in their lives the aesthetic distance between Leni Riefenstahl, glamorous star of melodrama on the silver screen, and Herbert Windt, mutilated minor composer of excruciatingly earnest music, could hardly have been greater. Yet they were drawing closer.

The decision to attempt an artistic breakthrough as a composer of operas, in the tradition of Strauss, Schreker, and yes, inevitably, Wagner, was a bold one on Windt's part. It required a statement of artistic intent. He published it in 1932, at the time of the opera's premiere under the great Heinz Tietjen and Erich Kleiber at the Deutsche Staatsoper in Berlin, arguably the most prestigious site in all of Germany. "I will never belong to those self-consciously 'new' composers, who want at any cost to be 'modern,'" he wrote in the *Blätter der Staatsoper* (Notes from the Berlin State Opera, a journal for serious opera lovers); "on the other hand, I am not such a reactionary that I would ever undervalue the expanding musical language created by modernism, or ever neglect to make use of those elements of modernist musical language where I think they are appropriate and justified."[36] Despite receiving a gratifying amount of attention and some respectful reviews, *Andromache* did not turn into a major breakthrough for Windt. But the opera – or perhaps his decision at this time to join the Nazi party – did bring him to the attention of those conservative nationalists through whom he received his first major film commission to score the overtly nationalist film *Morgenrot*. Almost overnight he became a composer of film music, most but not all, in the heroic mode. *Morgenrot* led to a commission to compose large choral set pieces, for Richard Euringer's *Deutsche Passion 1933*, one of the first of the *Thing* (assembly) plays, those ultimately unsuccessful efforts to create an authentic German theatre embodying the *Volksgemeinschaft*.[37] This in turn led to his involvement in the party films with Riefenstahl and many more commissions to score propaganda, documentary, and feature films in the Third Reich (despite what he later called "artistic differences" with Goebbels). He received no honours from a state notoriously fond of bestowing them and was turned down for positions such as membership in the Kultursenat, circumstances that weighed in his favour during post-war denazification proceedings.[38]

If the rise of Nazism and the sound film coincided in felicitous ways for Herbert Windt, making him (in those days at least) a rich man, his writings on the subject of film music conveyed a clear refusal to regard his work as in any sense mere entertainment. On the question of the musical score's illustrative function Windt stood, ironically but not surprisingly, much closer to a left-wing modernist like Hanns Eisler than to Giuseppe Becce or the dozens of other workmanlike compilers of film scores. Deriding the notion that music should either obey the visual action, like a well-trained dog, or fill in visual lulls or transitions with compensatory sound, Windt described his work as one of creating a "dramatic counterpoint" to the visual image, which would widen and deepen the import of what was happening on the screen. Likewise, on the question of the use of serious or classical music in films Windt expressed his opposition. The film score should be an original work, created by a single artist and complete in itself, not a strung-together series of excerpts from the grab bag of the musical past. As the debate about the status of film music unfolded in the Third Reich, mostly ignored by the serious music community, Windt and a few others like him articulated an ambitious agenda for film music, one that staked a claim to a status equal to that of operatic music.[39] Windt, then, was a man who neither wanted to compose, nor had the reputation of composing, music that would be mistaken for anyone's but his own.

The Music of *Triumph of the Will*

The score for *Triumph of the Will*, which contains about twelve minutes of Windt's own music in a little over two hours of film, does not overwhelm the ear as fully as the visual images overwhelm the eye. It is, of course, the nature of film, even the sound film, to make a primarily visual impression, and people have observed and analysed this effect since its earliest days.[40] Nor can one any longer experience the film without being conscious of the hand of Riefenstahl, the "wonderful, horrible" Leni Riefenstahl, in its making. She, after all, gets prominent billing in the film credits and Windt gets none. To be sure, some have found something musical in the rhythmic movement of images, a metaphorical kind of music, to which Riefenstahl herself often laid claim. Martin Loiperdinger, in a similar spirit, calls it a purely musical film ("*ein reiner Musikfilm*").[41] Still, what the music contributed to the overall effect of the film seems to most observers a relatively minor question, and the bulk of a very bulky scholarly literature on it concerns its visual composition. Riefenstahl once articulated what we might call the "hundred per cent rule": "I always take every precaution," she said in a 1966 interview with Michel Delahaye, "so that the sound and the image never total more than a hundred percent." If the image is "strong," then the "sound must stay in the background." And the converse was also true, although, as she herself implied in the interview, the visual usually took precedence.[42] Besides expressing her disdain for the "Mickey Mousing" phenomenon, this statement also points to the clearest yet most overlooked aspect of the difference between her total works of art (if that is what they were) and Wagner's. For Wagner, despite his attention to costume, theatre design, set design, and movement, the music always came first – and remained when all else was gone.

Those who have written about the score have tended to regard its contribution to the film as essential. After all, the case for the potency of the whole Wagner-Hitler nexus in shaping the nature and destiny of the Third Reich depends on the music: no music, no Gesamtkunstwerk. In short, the analysis of the music has been driven by the point people have wanted to make about the film overall. People have expected to hear Wagner in the score and, *mirabile dictu*, so they have.[43] The recent work of Reimar Volker on Windt's propaganda films, in which analysis of the music of *Victory of Faith* and *Triumph of the Will* forms the opening piece of a larger argument about Windt's contribution to the aesthetic footprint of Nazism, is an exception. Concerning Windt's twelve minutes, expanded and repositioned from the eleven minutes of music he composed for *Victory of Faith*, Volker makes a two-part case for its crucial role in the film as a whole, one comparative (mainly to *Victory of Faith*) and the other cultural-political.

First, compared with the earlier film, which was cobbled together in a more slapdash manner under greater time pressure (and which Riefenstahl essentially disowned), the musical score of the *Triumph of the Will* showed growing skill on the part of Windt in deploying music to heighten the intensity of Riefenstahl's visual drama and to add additional layers of cultural resonance. Riefenstahl's decision, for instance, to begin *Triumph* with the famous airplane-over-Nuremberg sequence received in Windt's score a calm, expansive, quietly magisterial accompaniment, in which the string, woodwind, and brass parts work together to create the smooth and unified texture of the music. As the spires of the city and the marching columns of the faithful gradually appear below, the music moves without overt drama into Windt's instrumental version of the party's *Horst-Wessel-Lied* (or *Die Fahne Hoch*). It does not take up a marching rhythm and thus sounds unlike the song as routinely sung by SA or Hitler Youth units, the male voices thumping along with the boot-stomping movement of the singers; it does not, in other words, trivialize the troops below. But Windt does begin subtly to raise the level of tension in the music by orchestrating the familiar melody in contrapuntal style, a subdued but distinct brass section taking the lead role and the strings echoing and very slightly elaborating their notes. All of this, as Volker argues, emphasizes the "mythological-sacral" position of the plane and its passengers vis-à-vis the people and city below and, with the introduction of the *Horst-Wessel-Lied*, identifies the airplane's passenger (if anyone was wondering) as the leader of this movement.[44] It contributes, then, to the transformation that takes place between *Victory* and *Triumph*, from stodgy documentary to skillfully crafted drama – in Volker's terms, from "*Dokument*" to "*Erlebnis*" (experience). "Identical music used in conjunction with identical filmic content," he explains, served in *Victory of Faith* "simply to differentiate one scene from another" but in *Triumph of the Will* "through a more adroit placement of the music viz. the images, it takes on a dramaturgical function: individual moments of a very rapid sequence of images are prepared and accented through the music and iconographic elements of National Socialism are branded."[45]

The same, deft placement characterizes the music Windt composed for the scenes of Nuremberg in the early morning: streets empty, sun rising. This scene and its music opened *Victory of Faith* but in *Triumph of the Will* take place after the arrival, after the procession through the streets of Nuremberg, and after the night rally in front of Hitler's hotel. The music reworks the "*Wach auf*" chorus from the third act of Wagner's *Die Meistersinger von Nürnberg*. But Windt's use of Wagner, even as it highlights a difference between the two films (one that was really Riefenstahl's doing, not Windt's), is more essential to the music's resonance in the context of 1934. Placed as it is in *Triumph of the Will*, the music introduces the rally day itself, and the cultural-political import of the choice of Wagnerian quotation – the single authentic Wagner quotation in the whole film – would seem too obvious to require explanation. In 1933, on the occasion of the first production of *Meistersinger* in Bayreuth after the Nazi seizure of power, Goebbels had claimed it for Nazism, as the work "in the entire music literature of the German people" which stood in closest relationship to "the spiritual and intellectual [*seelischen und geistigen*] forces of our times."[46] The quotation of the "*Wach auf*" chorus signalled both a claim to cultural continuity, not only with Wagner's nineteenth century but with the whole panorama of the German past evoked in his drama, and a call to new awakening.

But the quotation is not literal. Windt's orchestration of the theme stays close to Wagner's but it is not a copy. The entire quotation radically reduces the volume of the Wagner original, including the bold two-note opening of the "*Wach auf*" chorus. In the opera these notes reverberate as a veritable shout from the assembled people of Nuremberg in the form of a perfect fourth in the key of G major. In Windt's version these notes barely register, emerging gradually out of near silence as the quietest of a two-note phrase from the horns. In it and in the brief passage that follows Windt also slows down the tempo to match the movement of the camera over waking Nuremberg, evoking the equally tranquil image of Wagner's lyrics about the sound of a nightingale calling out of the deep forest and echoing over mountain and valley as the night ends. But, as Volker further argues, the cultural resonances of the "*Wach auf*" quotation are not confined to Wagner. By association with the two words themselves – *Wach* and *auf* – the canny listener could be reminded of a sixteenth-century hymn, present in most Protestant hymnals of the modern period and particularly beloved of National Socialists, who often sang it during Nazi festive occasions. This was Johann Walter's "*Wach auf, wach auf, du deutsches Land, du hast genug geschlafen,*" (Awaken, awaken, oh German land, you have slept long enough), a hymn that probably has its origins in the period of the Peasants' War. The opening two notes of the hymn are, like Wagner's "*Wach auf,*" a rising fourth. A rising fourth also characterizes what Volker identifies as the "Signal Motif," the horn fanfare that appears at many points in twelve minutes of Windt's own composition. This fanfare, along with the *Horst-Wessel-Lied*, the aural counterpart to the swastika, are the two most persistent elements of his score. The means by which Windt weaves these and less prominent motifs in and out of the music, sometimes in counterpoint, sometimes in congruence with the rapidly shifting camera angles, all attest to the skill of his scoring of Riefenstahl's visual creation.[47]

Finally, Volker makes clear the distinction between Windt's motivic work and Wagner's. Far from replicating Wagner's own texture of overlapping and intersecting signifiers, which comment on, deepen, and sometimes foretell the action on the stage, Windt's motifs are simple phrases that at their most dramatic merely highlight an image on the screen. There is no Hitler, Goebbels, or Göring motif or even an SA or a German people motif; nor do any such signifiers interweave and comment upon each other as they do in Wagner's orchestral writing. Windt, as Volker explains, was not so much a Wagnerian, with that term's suggestion of a monomaniacal discipleship, as he was someone whose techniques of phrase development and patterning signal the combined influence of Bruckner, Wagner, and Strauss. In other words, he was more influenced by the avatars of a loosely similar, late Romantic maximalist style in which he had been trained since his earliest compositional classes. To those who hear in Windt's various fanfares and other brassy passagework the echoes of Siegfried travelling down the Rhine or Hagen summoning the Gibichung (not a good precedent in any case) or even the people of Nuremberg gathering on the festival field, Volker points instead to Windt's recent work on the Euringer *Thingspiel*, which in its "mythologizing of National Socialist iconography" represented a more closely fitted and more immediate precedent to the National Socialist festival of the party rally.[48]

Volker's careful musical analysis provides a more nuanced and accurate account of how Windt's music worked and what politico-cultural meanings it actually evoked in *Triumph of the Will*. But two additional perspectives are needed if one is to make any judgment, speculative or otherwise, about the overall effect of the film score. The first concerns the limitations of musical analysis. Even while pointing to some of the more idiotic things recent scholars have said about the "Wagnerian" music of *Triumph of the Will*, Volker rightly acknowledges the significance of such misconceptions for the reception history of the film, an insight that informs Scott Paulin's similar discussion of the seductive appeal of the Gesamtkunstwerk idea to film theorists.[49] And as is now well known, the Third Reich had its own Wagner problem. We could characterize it crudely as the large emotional gap between Hitler's love of the music dramas and the public's indifference to them. The literature on Bayreuth is filled with quasi-comic anecdotes about Nazi officials practically ordering soldiers on leave to fill the uncomfortable wooden seats of the Festspielhaus for five-hour performances. In light of such stories the government's subsidizing of tickets to Bayreuth looks less like official approval than an act of desperation.[50]

It would seem, then, that musical analysis, crucial though it is in illuminating one kind of truth about the score, has limited explanatory power in the context of what the untrained ear might have heard. Yet we may have some access to that notoriously unanswerable question. As I indicated earlier in this chapter, there *was* a way in which the general public experienced a quasi-Wagner through the crossover media of film and radio. Versions of Siegfried's horn call, for instance, abounded on the radio and in both silent and sound film scores that were assembled by the Giuseppe Becces of the music world. Even those who explicitly wanted *not* to invoke the spirit of Wagner did so. In 1924, for instance, Fritz Lang released two silent films, *Siegfried* and *Kriemhild's Revenge*, the screenplays for which had been written by Thea von Harbou and were based not on

Wagner's *Ring des Nibelungen* but solely on the *Nibelungenlied* of c. 1200. Seeking to avoid the unavoidable, he asked his friend Gottfried Huppertz (who subsequently wrote the score for *Metropolis*) to undertake the task of writing a musical score. But the point is that the effort to disengage from Wagner proved ultimately futile. Not only did the use of brass instruments in Huppertz's score summon up Siegfried's Rhine Journey from *Götterdämmerung* but when the films were released in France, Italy, and the United States, local organizers simply used their own musical scores to accompany the films, all of which were overtly Wagnerian, characterized by the same kinds of creative imitations of Wagner of which Becce had been the pioneer.

So, his own intentions aside, Windt's fanfare music evoked these film music conventions just as powerfully, perhaps more powerfully, than the serious music learned in composition classes or the would-be serious music of the Thingspiele. As I argue in chapter 2 of this volume, place makes a difference in how we recover the cultural meaning of music. From that perspective the sounding of the Windt fanfare in a movie theatre rather than in a concert hall or outdoor Thing amphitheatre aligned it with different musical associations than those perhaps intended by its composer. In that perspective also, one cannot help but think that Windt was a man who somehow managed to have his cake and eat it too. On the one hand, for trained and serious music listeners, in his time and ours, the deftness of his quotations of and references to Wagner and the skill of his blending together musical themes that were evocative but original to him forced the knowledgeable to concede his stature as a serious composer. This was clearly important to Windt, who had limited respect for most movie music and particularly detested the vulgarity of dropping pieces of classical music into musical scores.[51] On the other hand, for the general public, familiar with the sound of movies, his score *sounded* more than a little bit like other movie scores, and one can imagine people enjoying the pleasure that the middlebrow cultural consumer would feel in making a simple chain of associations – Nuremberg, Wagner, Meistersingers; horn call, Siegfried, Wagner; and so on.

But associations made in this way, by reference to popular media and easily digestible snippets of high culture, do not, returning to Koepnick's analysis, necessarily work to break "the bonds of old solidarities," or prepare the "atomized individual for the auratic shapes of mass politics."[52] They instead constituted gestures of familiarity, which made the new and still unfamiliar rituals of the Nazi regime seem to emerge seamlessly out of the past. Doris Bergen has written that "on the one hand, Hitler revolutionized Germany, but on the other hand, the ways in which he did so seemed undramatic to many participants and observers at the time."[53] This observation applies to the music of *Triumph of the Will* as well, especially to the seventy-odd minutes of music in the film that Windt himself did not compose. In the technical language of film, much of this music was diegetic, that is, one hears it as part of the narrative, as the sound of bands, occasionally glimpsed, accompanying marching, rallying, waving, speech-making, and the like. For most German listeners, who probably understood the oscillations in film scores between diegetic and non-diegetic music only intuitively, the great preponderance of diegetic over non-diegetic music in *Triumph of the Will* only increased the familiarity of this new world. Diegetic music as such is generally considered to heighten the illusion on the part of the spectator of being actually inside the world of the film, but when the diegetic music is as well known as most of this was, it also works in the opposite direction, locating the action of the film in the everyday, experienced, real world. Or, to put it yet another way, music that unmistakably comes into the world of the film from the surrounding culture brings with it what Roger Hillmann has called the "cultural memory of other contexts."[54] In the case of the diegetic music of *Triumph of the Will* these were powerful memories indeed.

The film's diegetic music falls roughly into three categories: folk songs, German military band marches, and National Socialist *Kampflieder* or battle/official songs. But even these distinctions are at best permeable boundaries, easily crossed. Even though the Hitler Youth song, "*Vorwärts, Vorwärts*" (Onward, Onward), was the joint creation of the organization's leader Baldur von Schirach (lyrics) and Hans Otto Borgmann (tune), its simple, hobby-horse-like melody had the nagging familiarity of a half-remembered nursery song or a children's camp song.[55] Likewise, *Horst-Wessel-Lied* or *Die Fahne Hoch*, which in Nazi lore was the sole creation of Horst Wessel himself, represented one of the countless reattachments of familiar melodies to new words, in this case a marine reservists' song, "*Vorbei, vorbei, sind all' die schönen Stunden*" (Gone, gone are all the wonderful times) about the battleship *Königsberg*.[56] In the case of the military marches themselves, from the "*Badenweilermarsch*" to the "*Yorcksche Korps Marsch*" to the "*Husarenmarsch*" (connected to Windt's own wartime regiment), they consisted of something like a review of old favourites, comparable to American listeners hearing the "Stars and Stripes Forever" or "The Battle Hymn of the Republic" or "Dixie" or even "Yankee Doodle Dandy."[57]

The importance of military band music in the everyday of German life cannot be measured but neither is it easily exaggerated.[58] In the *Kaiserreich,* Sunday band concerts constituted a well-loved fixture of leisure practices of many classes, and before the war the military musical ensembles of Germany had an international reputation. German military music was a source of both pleasure and pride for ordinary Germans. The reduction under the Weimar Republic of the number of bands from 560 to a mere 160 was thus extremely unpopular.[59] After 1933 the gradual return of prosperity and, of course, the commitment of the new regime to German remilitarization benefited the military bands directly and dramatically.[60] *Triumph of the Will* captures this resurgence and through the musical score tells a story of continuities and new beginnings.

Two especially beloved and culturally resonant pieces of music had prominent places in the score. The first, the *Grosse Zapfenstreich* (Grand Tattoo or Grand Taps), is seen and heard played by the Musikkorps of the Leibstandarte Adolf Hitler, the largest of the military ensembles of the Third Reich, arrayed under Hitler's hotel window during the night rally. In *Triumph of the Will* this rendition represents a modified version of a Prussian ceremonial dating back to the sixteenth century. An ordinary "tattoo" or "taps" signified the end of the day (the striking of the taps, or the shutting down of the liquor supply), but the elevated, nineteenth-century form of the Grosse Zapfenstreich, performed only in the presence of the monarch himself, represented a military version of evening prayers or calling down God's blessing on the work of the army.[61] Its function in this context as a serenade to Hitler at once transgressed and appropriated its traditional use, thereby carrying a meaning that would have been obvious to the German public: Hitler was now, since he became president on 19 August 1934, the head of state, and, more important in light of the internal tensions that shortly before the 1934 party rally led to the murder of SA leader Ernst Röhm, the Führer had also made himself supreme commander of the army and heir to a Prussian military tradition in which he himself, of course, had played no part. The music is thus the aural equivalent to a poster from the period showing the overlapping heads of Frederick the Great, Bismarck, Hindenburg, and Hitler, with the caption, "*Was der König eroberte, der Fürst formte, der Feldmarshall verteidigte, rettete und einigte der Soldat*" (What the king conquered, the prince shaped, and the field marshal defended, the soldier has rescued and unified). The music that accompanied Hitler's review of the Reichswehr conveyed the same message, by which class, regional, and even chronological

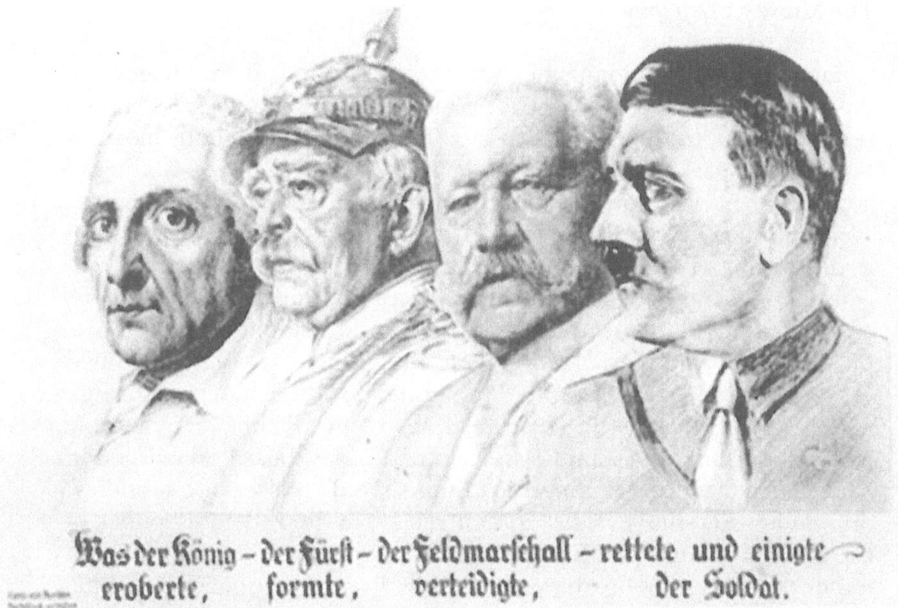

13.1 "What the king conquered, the prince shaped, and the field marshal defended, the soldier has rescued and unified." Postcard, 1933. Hans von Norden. Deutsches Historisches Museum, Berlin.

boundaries all dissolved into the present of the Volksgemeinschaft and *Führerstaat.* At that point in the film we hear a quiet march version of what is perhaps the best known of German soldier songs, "*Ich hatt' einen Kameraden*" (I had a comrade). The melody and lyrics (by Ludwig Uhland) of this song dated back to the Napoleonic wars and had taken on nearly unbearable resonance in the slaughter of the First World War. Hitler, reviewing the regular army soldiers to this most familiar of music and most evocative of lyrics, embodies the German people's ability to mourn their losses in the war and, in a filmic moment that demonstrates as clearly as any the ability of the Nazi movement to appropriate the past as well as the future, to gain strength from them. Here, then, more powerfully than could be achieved by loose adaptations of Wagnerian themes, one finds music working, in Windt's formulation, to heighten the sounds of the everyday.[62]

The Music of *Olympia*

Compared with the dominance of the vernacular and the diegetic in the music of *Triumph of the Will*, Windt's music for *Olympia* sounded more modern, more up-to-date – a dash of tonally ambiguous modernism here, a sparkle of Hollywood glamour there. Windt received more acclaim for his work on this film than on anything else he did, and the same could be said of Riefenstahl. At the same time their collaboration in the making of the final product of the film was more substantial, a circumstance acknowledged in the opening credits. And yet, like *Triumph of the Will*, *Olympia* labours under misapprehensions about its alleged propulsion "by the Wagnerian score of Herbert Windt," variously described as "heroic-lyric" or marked by "false grandeur."[63] Such accusations go at least as far back as the 1958 hearings of the Filmbewertungsstelle (loosely, the Board of Film Classification, a review board established in 1951 allegedly to determine which films should receive state subsidies) on whether to refuse certification for release in the Federal Republic of Germany of the two-part film. Complaining that the music was "laid on too thick," the review board wrote critically about the suspiciously "stimulating effect" of the film, "ultimately achieved through an intrusive and purposive symphonic score which blares into the ears of the spectator almost unceasingly."[64]

One hardly recognizes the score or the soundtrack in such a description, yet just like the phantom hearings of "Siegfried's Rhine Journey" in *Triumph of the Will*, the impressions tell us something important not just about spectators' expectations but about cultural contexts that shape our hearing. Riefenstahl herself argued with vigour and partial accuracy against the accusation of musical intrusiveness. Rightly pointing out that much of the soundtrack was filled with such diegetic sounds as Richard Strauss's Olympic hymn, Werner Egk's special Olympic fanfares, sports commentary, crowd shouting, and various national hymns at the awards ceremonies, she described Windt's score itself as "purely background music."[65] Of course, it was more than that, or rather more effective than that, as Riefenstahl herself acknowledged in less politically fraught circumstances. What Riefenstahl and Windt achieved together in the coordination of music and image in *Olympia* was both the solution of specific practical problems and the heightening of experience that Windt identified around the time of the film's release as his main aesthetic goal. Both these elements of the film's scoring come through in the still impressive coordination of music to image in the marathon sequence. As is well known, Windt had originally written this music in 1936 to accompany the German radio broadcast of the marathon to fill in the gaps in the necessarily discontinuous and uneven coverage of the long race. Characteristic of his ambitions for film music, he had come up with a high cultural solution to this problem that was essentially one of keeping people interested (i.e., entertained) while not very much happened. He composed a three-movement orchestral suite, which had a short, quick first movement (in other words a scherzo), a long, extended middle movement, and a last triumphalist finale. In the film the coordinated and the contrapuntal possibilities of such a three-movement design came into their own. At the outset Windt's music seems literally to be pacing the runners, driving them on, a characteristic that has led some commentators into the interpretive dead end of dubbing it "fascist" in the bossiness and regularity of its rhythmic patterns. But in the most effective parts of the whole marathon sequence the runners' legs seem to move slower and slower (in the famous basket shots, from the heads of the runners) and yet the music rushes on faster and faster, not with bombast or blaring trumpets but with all the more effectively relentless, increasingly frantic strings, joined finally by brass and wind instruments, until the whole sound resolves itself into silence, then a diegetic trumpet fanfare as the lead runner (from Japan) enters the stadium for the final lap. At the time, Windt described this visually contrapuntal music as the runner's "mood, his flight of ideas, his spirit, his will, his driving idea," elevating itself "over the body which begins to tire," the music "flying before him and pulling the body further on."[66] If there is indeed something National Socialist about the movie and its music, then it lies not just in modernist archaisms, gleaming bodies, and feats of strength – traits that, as many post-Sontag commentators have pointed out, can be found in sporting culture the world over, then and now – but in the musical drama of this triumph of the will.

To return to where this chapter began, then, the generations of spectators and critics who have heard in the music of Riefenstahl's films something profoundly attuned to the regime whence it emitted have not been wrong. Yet to limit our understanding of this fit between art and society to various elaborations on Wagnerian themes is to draw the wrong conclusions about the effect and the appeal of this music. Both Windt and Riefenstahl brought to their collaboration musical experiences that encompassed a much broader range of musical life than the term "Wagnerian" could possibly encompass.

Chapter Fourteen

Saving Music

Music is "about becoming," said Daniel Barenboim, "it's not the statement of a phrase that is really important, but how you get there and how you leave it and how you make the transition to the next phrase."[1] We might say the same thing about Germany as a collective entity, in a state of becoming where the now of it matters less than all its yesterdays and tomorrows, less than how it understands those yesterdays and uses that understanding to navigate into the future. But then again, perhaps we should resist the analogy, because, after all, the assertion of some deep current of affinity between German identity and music amounts to one of the most persistent claims that Germans have made about themselves over the years. Since the eighteenth century writers have been exploring this connection and wondering aloud if there isn't something even providential about the German relationship to music. Nor have the Germans been alone in noticing this. A conviction that there is something special about the conjunction of music *and* Germans has informed, for good or ill, the concert schedules, travel plans, career decisions, institutional reforms, public and private spending, movie scripts, and innumerable other things, even government policy (in the case of the post-war occupation of Germany) and all of non-Germans, for at least 100 years, if not longer.

Music as Cultural Citizenship

Given the foregoing, music would appear to be the key to something in modern German history, and I would like to suggest in this chapter that this "something" is continuity. The many-faceted relationship of Germans to music has worked for a very long time to cement Germans together and to create a sense of community, of belonging. The outcome of such processes is what we might call "cultural citizenship." Music surely ought to be regarded as a crucial contributor to cultural citizenship, that is, to membership in a community defined by culture. But what that in turn says about political citizenship, about a sense of awareness of being a member of a political community, whether it precedes it or follows it or depends on it in any significant way, would require a different essay. What follows is instead an account of the way that music has served as a marker and a method of continuity in twentieth-century Germany especially – a crucial element in a search for things that persist in the face of fragmentation, integration, disintegration, catastrophe, and starting over. Yet to the same extent that for so many years music has been caught up in the German sense of cultural kinship, to just that extent is its current capacity to serve as a carrier of the past and a source of collective identity compromised. This is the paradox of the collective identity of Germans, expressed in a particularly wrenching way in the case of music. Regarding collective identities especially, like the collective life to which they give meaning, there really is no starting over; there is just carrying on. Yet the stronger the links of any aspect of German culture to the past, the more suspect, guilt-ridden, and hence unbalanced that carrying-on can be.

On the surface nothing has been simpler over the course of the past century than for Germans to reaffirm, again and again, just how enduring is their special relationship to music. If the Germans before unification in 1871 engaged in a lengthy process of cultural definition, musical life being one of the most important arenas of their activity, then the Germans after unification tended more towards repeated assertions of a cultural identity now supposedly achieved, assertions that built in volume and intensity to the awful clamour of the Third Reich. The point of transition, from tentative explorations of music's meaning for the Germans to more confident, less subtle statements of an unassailable superiority, is, of course, difficult to determine. Many people assume that Wagner is to blame for the change. But the reality is more recalcitrant. German writers had already begun the attempt to define the nature of Germanness in music in the early decades of the eighteenth century, and by the nineteenth many believed that Germans held a unique place in the history of music, developing music's spiritual and introspective qualities far beyond any other nation, to the point that Germans alone had awoken all peoples to "the highest meaning of humanity."[2] No one could say precisely what Germanness in music actually was, neither composer and flautist Johann Joachim Quantz in the eighteenth century nor philosopher Theodor Adorno in the twentieth nor anyone in between. In what Wagner called his "final word upon the sadly earnest theme" of "what is German," he declared the issue "more and more puzzling" and himself "unqualified for further answering of the question."[3] But the question was unanswerable because it was the wrong question. The continuity in German musical life consisted not in a quality demonstrably present in music itself but in a kind of ideology or "national cultural myth," as Bernd Sponheuer has called it, and beyond that in a relationship, at once cultural, intellectual, social, and political, authorized between Germans and music by the myth. Germans, so it held, understood the deeper sources of music more fully and intuitively than others. Hence, the German nation had brought forth an unbroken chain of musical compositions more universal in their impact than that of any other nation and musical leaders who had a role to play in not just Germany but the world. Wilhelm Dilthey expressed the general view of educated people in many nations when he wrote in 1906 that "with Bach and Handel, mastery over the art of inwardness and profundity passed from the romantic nations to Germany, and we have retained this mastery up to the present day."[4]

The Weimar Republic

After defeat in the Great War, the appeal of such visions of continuity, bound together with a sense of peculiar virtue in matters far deeper than the transitory fortunes of the world, increased enormously. The first post-war period presents us with a society-wide commitment to music as a kind of guarantor that despite travail and tribulation something essentially German still survived. As the musicologist Hans Joachim Moser wrote, "if Germany has *one* area and *one* profession that wield absolute influence, despite all of the enmity and distance we face in the world, these are German music and the composer … one must not allow this noble, truly peaceful weapon to rust from lack of use."[5] One did not have to be a right-wing nationalist to indulge in such comforting visions; one could easily persuade oneself that the assertion of musical superiority represented a rejection of German militarism. In early 1919 Arnold Schoenberg wrote to a friend that the most important task for music education was "to secure the ascendancy, rooted in the people's endowments [*Volksbegabung*], that the German nation has held in the realm of music." His own twelve-tone system, he asserted two years later and with greater notoriety, itself would secure this ascendancy for the next 100 years.[6] At the other end of the political spectrum, the conservative nationalist composer Hans Pfitzner held superficially similar ideas about retaining German musical superiority, though not through radical innovations that might emulate the revolutionary spirit, if not the musical style, of a Beethoven or a Wagner. Pfitzner favoured fierce attacks on all challenges to the great tradition: in responding to a call from Ferruccio Busoni for a new era of compositional innovation, he wrote in 1917 that "German music is not just some kind of cerebral sport, but an art we love; and when the spirit of one of our great masters is willing to appear before us, we should receive him accordingly, should call him 'Prince' or 'Father.'"[7]

Although Schoenberg came to see how little legitimacy his own musical leadership had in the eyes of many of his countrymen and Pfitzner never achieved quite as much recognition as he thought he deserved, the Weimar Republic experienced an enormous range of musical activities, many of which drew inspiration from the idea of this Volksbegabung, or special German endowment for music. For instance, the larger project to which Schoenberg had alluded, that of the reform of music education, became one of the lasting achievements of the Weimar Republic and at the same time an achievement deeply rooted in more than a century's worth of thinking about how to preserve and maintain Germany's musical gifts. Leo Kestenberg, a Social Democrat and musician who led the reconstruction of Prussia's music education in the public schools, made important practical efforts to improve the professional competence of school music teachers, inspired by the idea, originating in the days of Humboldt and Prussian reform, that active involvement in music belonged at the centre of a German humanistic education.[8] Music-making also flourished in branches of the German youth movement, in homes and voluntary associations, in new movements focused on neglected historical instruments such as the recorder (*Blockflöte*), and in reinvigorated or expanded music festivals. Pamela Potter has estimated that the number of Germans involved in amateur choral singing alone numbered around 2 million.[9] The publication of literature for home piano playing flourished, and books, guides, and music for amateur string quartets and other small-scale ensembles attested to the popularity of such forms of music-making, even if the numbers of actual performances are impossible to count. Magazines for every conceivable amateur musical specialization were started: singing, guitar playing, piano and organ playing; even the mandolin had its own periodical. And alongside this remarkable expansion in musical amateurism in the Weimar years a more evident kind of continuity of German musical life also asserted itself in concert halls, conservatories, opera houses, publishing houses, and, increasingly, the broadcasting of the canon of great German composers in new media such as radio and film.

The Third Reich

Much of this musical activity, as well as the underlying sense of musical mission, survived, unscathed and even strengthened, throughout the Second World War. A number of scholars have explored the institutions and ideology of music in the Third Reich, and their scholarship emphasizes the continuous nature of musical cultivation and the fact of institutional survival in the face of political upheaval. Aspects of German musical life long in the making made both possible and attractive the forms of accommodation, participation, and support that characterized musicians' relationship to Nazism in power. The Nazi administration of German musical life raised the professional status and economic security of musicians and saved groups such as the Berlin Philharmonic from looming financial ruin, often by use of the same mechanisms (an obligatory musicians' union and the like) that excluded Jews from Germany's musical life.[10] Amateur musicians, for their part, found their string quartets and recorder evenings absorbed into important-sounding umbrella organizations such as the *Arbeitsgemeinschaft für Hausmusik* in the *Reichsmusikkammer* and now could look forward every year to the "Day of German Hausmusik," which continued as an annual event well into the war years. To be sure, a few people warned that too much publicity and performance mania threatened the private essence, the inwardness, of the Germans' love of music.[11] But such criticisms were muted and inconsequential. As long as they were not Jewish, musicologists, professional musicians, and even the more avant-garde composers found they could live with a regime that interfered far less in musical affairs than it did in the visual arts and film. In a situation where the local church choir seemed to have enough autonomy to fight off efforts to purge hymns of all references to the Hebrew God and an ardent Nazi like Herbert Gerigk could allow that in the right hands even atonality had a place in new German composition, it was little wonder that people chose to regard music as one part of German life that would never change, except for the better.[12]

Stunde Null

In the final years of the war and the first years after it Germany experienced a destruction of institutional and individual life so fundamental as to leave no aspect of German society unaffected. Considered objectively, it would be foolish to deny the break in the history of German music that 1945 represents. Yet it has remained possible for a surprising number of people, recounting those years, to do something like that. In trying to determine just what kind of break the *Stunde Null* (Zero Hour) amounts to in German musical identity, we inevitably encounter in both institutional and individual memories the continual reappearance, like some hardy perennial, of the image of music in the ruins. The exact form of this image, of course, varies. In the case of the Berlin Singakademie, arguably Germany's first and finest amateur choral society, nearly every official post-war publication – 175th anniversary Festschrift, 200th anniversary Festschrift, short histories, commemorative programs, even flyers one can pick up in a Berlin tourist office – makes some mention of the group's performance on 14 April 1945 of Brahms's *German Requiem.* Director Georg Schumann assembled his chorus of lamentation literally on the edge of the ruined shell of the Berlin Philharmonic Hall, the boom of advancing Soviet artillery audible in the not-so-far distance.[13] Examples of the special place music holds in the collective imagining of German life do not come any more dramatic than that. Individuals remember amateur string quartets that kept meeting throughout the war years and resumed again when the war was over, perhaps with some minor change of membership – not for nothing was one of the most popular guides to organizing your own string quartet called "See You Again at the Double Bar." Or they remember huddling in basements listening to music over the radio or, just as common, trying to make music of their own with a couple of recorders or a makeshift chorus or a cobbled-together instrumental ensemble. The Frenchman Edgar Morin remembers walking through the ruins of Berlin in July 1945 and hearing a Beethoven sonata broadcast from a loudspeaker by the Brandenburg Gate.[14] Radio stations up and running again by June 1945 with a playlist of German classics, pianos rescued from collapsing buildings, symphony orchestras patiently reassembling instruments and players scattered in a bombing raid: the "survival stories" of twentieth-century Germans have a steady undertone of musical experiences, mediating, binding, connecting tales of disruption and loss.[15]

After survival came rebuilding, and after rebuilding came reuniting. All of them had a soundtrack, shifting from German requiem and

Götterdämmerung to Beethoven and Bernstein, the kiss embracing the entire world, the cry of freedom, and Rostropovich playing Bach's unaccompanied cello suites atop the Berlin Wall. Once again, accompanying these moments, made the more memorable by the familiarity of the music, was the persistence of music-making of a more mundane variety, the carrying-forward of music pedagogy in both Germanys, the resumption of all types of concert life, the state subsidization of more orchestras per capita than in any other country, and the lengthening waiting list for tickets to Bayreuth. Richard Jakoby, writing in 1997, described a music scene "so vast that it can hardly be defined": more than 8 million people actively engaged in amateur music-making in Germany, another 80,000 professional musicians, a further 300,000 people working in the music industry, 92 publicly subsidized theatre orchestras, 50 publicly subsidized symphony orchestras, 70 chamber orchestras, 34 nationally ranked music conservatories, 1,000 local public music schools, 1,000 local private music schools, and so on.[16] W.H. Sebald, in his effort at writing a "natural history" of the destruction of Germany, found himself studying experiences so harrowing that postwar Germans, he thought, had been literally unable to say anything about them. But people could talk about music, remember it and listen to it, making who knows what connections along paths of experience not necessarily accessible to words.

Thomas Mann, Music, and the German Problem

If much of this discussion seems excessively romantic or Schopenhauerian or simply abstract, then it should. For, as Marshall Sahlins has said, culture is the way we change, and Germans changed after 1945 within a cultural tradition that since the early nineteenth century had understood music in ways that *were* romantic and soon Schopenhauerian and that placed music among the human creations that contained an important element of the non-rational and instinctual, the transcendent and ineffable. Many held a wholly Schopenhauerian attitude towards music, believing it the evidence of a reality inaccessible to us through cognition or sight. Perhaps the existence of such views about music made it easier to recruit music to the psychic task of making whole a shattered past; perhaps, as Nietzsche once wrote with a sincerity impossible to trust, music simply made life not a mistake.[17] Leaving aside such metaphysical penumbra, we do need to attend, more prosaically, to the evidence of fracturing and discontinuity that challenges any affirmation of a German identity made whole through music and that indeed constitutes a restatement, in a minor key, of the music-in-the-ruins motif. Some of this evidence stares us in the face, like the eternal recurrence of Wagnerian controversy or the process of denazification. Other disruptions are more subtle and perhaps more the effect of academic debate than its cause, like the efforts of scholars to scrutinize musical scholarship in the twentieth century. Yet further evidence of disruption comes to us in a transformation of the claim with which we began, the one that linked Germans and music like French and fashion, now transformed into a disturbing juxtaposition of beauty and atrocity, music and murder – a new German cliché, as it were, the representative figure of which is the piano-playing German soldier in Steven Spielberg's *Schindler's List.* Altogether, it becomes plain that the musical identity of Germans, like any other facet of life, persists through participation in a larger process of cultural and political disruption and transformation.

It is time, surely, to mention Thomas Mann. Any attempt, such as this one, to provide a view from afar of the past century's intertwining of musical citizenship and German history, needs to acknowledge Mann as someone who represents more than just an important or influential contributor to the discussion. He was really the founder of the discussion itself, the one who determined both the terms and the stance of the discussant, which, with variations, obtain to this day.[18] The stance is that of a person engaged and even compromised, yet distant, often literally: as he said in his address to the Library of Congress on 29 May 1945, "I stand here before you, a man of seventy … of patriarchal years … swept from the remotest nook of Germany, where I was born and where, after all, I belong, into this auditorium, on to this platform, to stand here as an American." The terms are laden with characteristic Mannian paradox and irony: again, from the address at the Library of Congress, "the German problem" was "the enigma in the character and destiny of this people which undeniably have given humanity much that is great and beautiful, and yet have time and again imposed fatal burdens upon the world."[19] Mann's purpose, as Hans Vaget has expressed it, was to ask "what if the origin of the German catastrophe was not some obvious evil but rather some generally esteemed good." What if there are not two Germanies, one good and one wicked, but, as Mann asserted in his 1945 address, "only one, whose best turned into evil": "wicked Germany is merely good Germany gone astray, good Germany in misfortune, in guilt, and ruin."[20] In *Doctor Faustus* Mann attempted, again in Vaget's words, to make music the "crucial factor" in tracing "Germany's slide into catastrophe." The novel was his "unsparing reckoning" with a "far-reaching concatenation of music, politics, and German identity," which even by the time of his famous/infamous 1933 address on Richard Wagner, the event that precipitated his exile, had preoccupied him as no other aspect of the German people ever had.[21]

Mann came to believe that what the Germans as a people did best – that is, to commune more deeply and thoroughly than any other group with the "irrational forces of life against abstract reason and dull humanitarianism," to glorify "the vital in contrast to the purely moral" – gave them "a deep affinity to death" and along with that, inevitably, a strong susceptibility to the "hysterical barbarism" of Hitler, which led to "a spree and a paroxysm of arrogance and crime" that was now finding, he said in 1945, "its horrible end in a national catastrophe, a physical and psychic collapse without parallel."[22] From such a perspective one could hardly find any comfort in being a member of the same national culture (the borders of which could seem almost as expansive as Hitler's Reich) that produced Bach and Mozart and Schubert, let alone Beethoven and Wagner, whose demonic genius was arguably more in evidence. Mann himself never suggested that after Auschwitz Germans should not listen to Beethoven. But his legacy is a sense of unease attendant on every emotional experience of German music, not just the Tristan experience of sinking into the oblivion of Wagner's night but also the experience of being moved by a Beethoven symphony or a Schubert *Lied* (those "miraculous" products of German culture, as Mann saw them). This sense of unease, I would argue, lies behind the now common practice in concert programming of juxtaposing (neutralizing?) Beethoven's Ninth Symphony with Arnold Schoenberg's *A Survivor from Warsaw* (1947).[23] The unease was evident when, minutes before a performance of Beethoven's Ninth was to begin, an eminent orchestral conductor reminded a choral group of which I was a member that Germany was the land that produced not only Beethoven and Schiller but also Auschwitz. It is evident when the German soldier in the film *Schindler's List* sits down to play Bach's prelude from the English Suite in A minor while his comrades – as he himself had done a minute earlier – round up and brutalize the Jews of Cracow.[24] And it is evident, with the additional shiver of being true to the historical record, when the HBO film *Conspiracy*, a carefully accurate depiction of the Wannsee Conference, ends with Adolf Eichmann listening to the endlessly beautiful String Quartet in C Major of Franz Schubert playing on the phonograph.

Denazification and German Music

In none of these examples is the nature of the connection between German music and German mayhem spelled out so explicitly as in Mann's wartime writings, yet in them Mann's legacy, of refusing to separate the highest of culture from the most hideous human actions, persists more influentially than through his essays themselves. But there are other ways and byways of influence behind these juxtapositions. For instance, whether or not the American officers in charge of the denazification of German musicians read what Mann wrote about his country, they rendered his abstractions into post-war policy. The officials of the American military administration of Germany had greater ambitions to change its culture of classical music than their English, French, or Russian counterparts.[25] For the American occupiers the notion that one could reform Germany's national character without confronting its musical legacy was absurd. Music had clearly contributed crucially to Germans' sense of superiority over other peoples, which had in turn caused so much suffering among its neighbours since Germany's foundation as a state. To re-educate Germans from obedient and xenophobic aggressors into tolerant and peaceful democrats required, therefore, that one somehow confront German music itself. As Edward Kilenyi, head of the American administration of musical life in Munich, noted, music had "furnished unlimited material for racist, mystic incantations" and "served as an emotional inspiration for the intense nationalism so typical of the German nation." Music, wrote the refugee musicologist Alfred Einstein in a *New York Times* editorial, "has become the intoxicating drug of nationalism."[26]

Still, Germany's intense relationship to its music was easier to diagnose than to cure. It was one thing to recognize the interpenetration of music and politics and quite another to figure out how to disentangle them, retaining the music but ditching the politics. The impact of these administrators on German musical life and attitudes thus tended towards the meagre and transitory.[27] Officials could shut down institutions, submit musicians to searching inquiries into their actions and motivations during the Nazi years, forbid a handful from performance, require a few more to go to special re-education programs, reopen institutions only under new direction, and fiddle with concert programs so that blacklisted composers such as Mendelssohn or allegedly neglected twentieth-century compositions or simply music not by Germans would be heard. But all this activity added up to considerably less than the sum of its parts, and people whom the Americans had proscribed had a way of tuning up their instruments again as soon as the Americans handed back control of orchestras and operas to the Germans. Within the American military government as a whole the musical officers had little clout at the higher levels of post-war administration. Meanwhile, the inconsistency of Allied occupation policy on the question of music undermined even their dogged efforts. As Elizabeth Janik has shown, the Russian occupiers of Berlin "successfully cast themselves as champions of German cultural tradition" and "oversaw a comprehensive reactivation of musical life in Berlin" even before their Allied counterparts arrived in July 1945 (hence, the loudspeaker Edgar Morin heard issuing forth Beethoven by the Brandenburg Gate was owned and operated by the Soviets).[28]

Little wonder, then, that scholars studying this record have tended to lament the lost opportunities or to adopt the elegiac tone appropriate to the depiction of doomed yet noble undertakings. The Americans, writes historian David Monod, "failed to prevent the reassertion of German confidence in their own cultural superiority or the cover-up of classical music's collaboration in the crimes of National Socialism." "Many of us who love music," he concludes, "remain troubled by this legacy."[29] Michael Kater has suggested that no real denazification took place, nor did musicians ever understand "what that was all about." The whole process rested on the "paradoxical assumption that denazified artists would aid in the construction of a freedom-loving, democratic society." The "serious-music tradition," he concludes, "was by and large the same as it had been, autonomously in the Weimar Republic and captured in the Third Reich."[30]

Yet returning to the theme of fracturing, discontinuity, and a German identity that even music could not make whole again, the very fact that the Allies, especially the Americans, attempted the denationalization of German musical life made changes in ways that may not be easily assessed but are nevertheless real. Their efforts to determine the degree of musical culpability in the catastrophe of the Third Reich did not in themselves fracture German identity or dissolve the wholeness of national life. But the Allies did actively witness the reality of a shattering, of a disruption beyond all measure; they forced a confrontation of sorts, the consequences of which cannot be reduced to their success or failure at labelling people musical collaborators and ejecting them from the concert hall. In the words playwright Michael Frayn has put in the mouth of a famously compromised German from another walk of life, Werner Heisenberg, "you can never know everything about" the nature of an object in the world "because we can't observe it without introducing some new element into the situation."[31] One can draw two conclusions by analogy, that yes, the enterprise was bound to fail by virtue of its muddled purposes (Kater's "paradoxical" may be too kind), but that no, it was not a complete failure because the very act of scrutinizing musical life, identifying its ideological dimension, and trying to measure its involvement in the regime changed it (but therein, as Frayn/Heisenberg has it, lies the uncertainty).

Take, for instance, the case of Wilhelm Furtwängler, one of the greatest conductors of the twentieth century and the subject of controversy during and after the Third Reich, at home and abroad, object of numerous biographical treatments, and the central figure in a film based on Ronald Harwood's celebrated play, *Taking Sides.* After the highest-profile denazification procedure in the cultural community, Furtwängler returned to conducting in May 1947, his reputation far from intact. On 29 July 1951 he conducted Beethoven's Ninth at the reopening of the Bayreuth Festival. That event bore all the hallmarks of an exercise in overcoming the past by somehow contriving to ignore it. Furtwängler stood in for Wagner himself, who had conducted the Ninth Symphony on the occasion of the laying of the cornerstone of his new festival hall in 1872 – not to mention for Richard Strauss, who had conducted the Ninth at the opening of the Bayreuth Festival of 1933. Now Furtwängler was carrying on, symbolically laying a new cornerstone, as commentators at the time inevitably observed. His soloists themselves were more or less compromised by their activities during the Nazis years – his soprano, Elizabeth Schwarzkopf, had actually belonged to the party, though she concealed this fact for years.[32] Thus, one might justifiably take the performance as proof of a cultural arrogance so complete that nothing, not even utter defeat and an unprecedented exposure of crimes in which all were complicit, could deflate it. From such a perspective the Bayreuth performance was shameless. Yet the very obviousness of the scene surely must give us pause. It took place in 1951, not twenty or thirty or fifty years later, when one might argue that people had forgotten the past. Furtwängler's hearing before the American denazification tribunal was hardly past at all, and it had been a public trial, receiving extensive press coverage. Thus, Furtwängler's biographer Sam Shirakawa refers to "an endless rapturous *frisson*" one feels in listening to the performance of the Ninth even now, the source of which he attributes to everyone in attendance, Furtwängler most of all, knowing what had happened and what was at stake. The Bayreuth Ninth of 1951 continues to be the best-selling of all Furtwängler recordings and not just in Germany. His case suggests the impossibility of the task American music officials set themselves, for words or no words, famous conductors or not, music does not easily yield up any clear-cut message. Perhaps, as Shirakawa believes, the performance was a "manifesto of consolation, renewal, and psychic healing," but at the very least, we can be quite sure that its very existence attested to the enormity of the disruption.[33]

Bayreuth and the Transformation of Musical Tradition

Because of the way that history exposed his qualities, both as artist and as public figure, in a particularly inescapable way, Furtwängler is a unique musical figure. Nevertheless, his story draws us ever back to the broader problem of cultural citizenship and the German musical tradition. Except for Furtwängler devotees, his appearance in Bayreuth in 1951 is overshadowed by the larger historical circumstance of Bayreuth reopening at all. Bayreuth does not embody the entire German musical tradition, though one can easily forget this in the midst of the rhetorical excess – pinnacle and essence of German culture, ultimate symbol of German extremism, simulacrum of the German nation, and so on – that often accompanies its description. The mere history of Wagner's reception as the most German of composers constitutes a scholarly literature of considerable, and expanding, girth. But because it was so publicly a centre of the nationalist agitation of the 1920s and of the national triumphalism of the 1930s, Bayreuth's reopening in 1951 suggested to the unsympathetic observer a degree of intransigent Teutonomania that was difficult to endure. Its financial recovery was made possible largely by an organization of ex-Nazis and conservative nationalists, led by a successful insurance salesman named Gerhard Rossbach, who had founded, amid his other right-wing adventuring in the Weimar Republic, a touring musical youth group, the Spielschar Ekkehard, known as singing ambassadors of anti-republican sentiments.[34] Worse and worse, Winifred Wagner remained very much on the scene in Bayreuth, unapologetic about her close friendship with Hitler and often impossible to ignore, despite having handed over control of the festival to her two sons, Wieland and Wolfgang.[35] Bayreuth seemed to enact cultural continuity of an undesirable sort, its survival powerful evidence that Germany did not so much start over as paper over and then carry on as before.

Yet to believe that post-war Bayreuth's main achievement is to make a great deal of noise that effectively drowns out debate about its past and Germany's past is to ignore abundant evidence of the opposite phenomenon – that, in fact, Bayreuth's, and the entire Wagner family's, main achievement has been to serve as a permanent provocation to debate, about Bayreuth and about Germany's past. There have been the audibly dissenting family members, from Friedelind to Gottfried to Nike, all of whom over the years have published widely read books in denunciatory mode.[36] There have been the speeches, the memoirs, the interviews both outrageous and thoughtful. And, most of all, there have been the performances themselves, year in and year out, *Ring* after *Ring*, *Meistersinger* after *Meistersinger*, not to mention all the rest, and each one a commentary on the past to such a degree that even deliberately traditional productions of the operas provoke debate about the impossibility of tradition.

But the hallmark of New Bayreuth, as it came to be called under Wieland Wagner's direction, was not tradition at all, in fact, but the boldest, most radical innovation. Each of Wieland's stark, striking productions proved a revelation, in Frederic Spotts's apt description, "as moving and powerful to some" as they were "incomprehensible and outrageous to others."[37] Determined as he was to uncover a universal human condition hidden beneath all the layers of history and myth, both in the operas and surrounding them, Wieland ran the risk – and was duly accused – of taking things to an extreme in a typically Germanic fashion. Wieland also spoke rarely, and then curtly, about his own closeness to Hitler, his own struggles with his past, and his motivation in constructing such a radically new Wagner for the world to experience. But presumably he thought the productions spoke for themselves, more sincerely than mere speeches of contrition could have done.

One has only to look to the East German response to Wieland's Bayreuth to get a sense of how much he represented to his contemporaries the rejection of the past, for better or, in this case, much for the worse. On achieving statehood in 1949 East Germany had continued to follow the lead of its Soviet mentor, in cultural as in all matters, and, as we have seen, the Soviet occupation authorities had positioned themselves from the outset as the rescuers, not the cleansers, of Germany's musical tradition. The Soviet example authorized East German leaders and citizens alike to cultivate a highly traditional version of musical life, without apology. "It falls to us, the musicians of the DDR, to demonstrate daily to our colleagues in West Germany how the great humanistic tradition of German musical culture has found its true home in our worker-and-farmer state," wrote editor Hansjürgen Schaefer in *Musik und Gesellschaft*, the mouthpiece of the state-run Association of German Composers and Musicologists. Here "the ideas of peace and freedom represented by the great masters of the past find their realization," he continued, "and will serve as an example to all men of good will in West Germany, strengthening them in their struggle against Adenauer's atomic war-mongering."[38] As for Wieland Wagner, an "open discussion" of a new production of *Die Meistersinger* in Leipzig provided the occasion to criticize his "radical efforts" in Bayreuth as "swinging the pendulum too far" in one direction. Wieland's "Catholicized and cosmopolitanized" *Meistersinger*, his "equally cosmopolitan and socially unconnected" *Ring*, and the "mystical confusion" of his *Parsifal* all betrayed the authentic radicalism of Richard Wagner himself, who had been, it seems, a social realist *avant la lettre*.[39]

Still, however one judges the Wagners morally, as prominent men and women in dark times, Bayreuth under Wieland and even after Wieland has been a veritable workshop in the uses of memory, the maintenance of continuity, and the deliberate fostering of disruption and change. Its material has been of the most unruly sort – powerfully emotional music the impact of which on any given person can certainly not be fully controlled or directed. Bayreuth is a monument to the renewal of national tradition through a continual process of self-criticism, in the mode of Richard von Weiszäcker's celebrated meditation in 1985 on memory and reconciliation. But Bayreuth also and inevitably carries other less hopeful connotations. There is no starting over with community.

Musical Memorials

Challenges to any unexamined musical consolation on the part of Germans are not confined to the lingering influence of Mann's troubled examinations of selfhood and nationhood, to the dubious successes – or definite failures – of denazification, or to the bold recasting of seemingly irretrievable traditions. In ways that many people have experienced, German composers and performers have been leaders in the use of music as a means to memorialize the suffering their own country brought about in the twentieth century.[40] In *A Survivor from Warsaw* Arnold Schoenberg created, in Theodor Adorno's premature assessment, the only successful work of art after Auschwitz.[41] Others wrote soundtracks to films documenting the horrors, or collaborated on musical tributes to lost Jewish culture, or performed at concerts of international reconciliation, or published and promoted the compositions of composers killed during the war and in the camps.[42] The possibilities have been infinite, and the sheer number of new compositions and memorializing performances has been vast. Nor can one say that much commonality exists among these musical acts of commemoration, beyond their necessarily ironic testimony to a fracturing of lives and communities that music seems, of all the arts, best able to evoke. For Schoenberg and for the Darmstadt serialist composers, the challenge to German musical tradition, with all its ideological baggage, had to take the form of a radical stylistic break.[43] In a world filled with evil without redemption or end, music that confronted such a past had to *sound* different; for instance, there could be no consoling tonal resolutions, no "passing dissonances," to use that expressive musico-analytic term for a disharmony on its way to a new harmonic convergence. For others, one senses something of that late nineteenth-century German militarists' mantra, the *Flucht nach vorne*, welcoming of a confrontation one might hope to win through sheer nerve. Wieland Wagner's defiant embrace of his grandfather's music had that quality to it, as does Hans Werner Henze's own Ninth Symphony. In the words of music critic Paul Griffiths, this work is a confrontation with the "Germany ... inscribed in the memories on which the symphony is based, the Germany in which Mr Henze grew up and in whose army he had to serve" and with his "Germanic" musical heritage of "Bach, Beethoven, Wagner, Mahler, and Schoenberg."[44] From Schoenberg to Henze and many more in between, only more music could sober up Germans after a century or more of musico-nationalist intoxication.

Demystifying of German Music

Finally, in the past decades the community of scholars, both inside and outside Germany, has provided much of the impetus towards loosening the bond that has existed and that still exists between Germans and music. Mann and Adorno, the inspired generalizers, hover behind much of the more empirical work that has appeared – on Wagner as a German problem; on modernism and authoritarianism; and on culture, civilization, and capitalism. The effect of their influence has often been, practically speaking, to mark off Germany's classical music as uniquely powerful, uniquely tragic, and in either case uniquely attuned to the German psyche in ways that neither they nor anyone else has ever been able satisfactorily to explain. These most German of intellectuals had their bureaucratic counterparts, the American denazification officers, who also left their mark on post-war scholarship. The officers' legacy has been a series of irresolvable academic debates about how to judge correctly the behaviour during the Third Reich of men such as Richard Strauss and Wilhelm Furtwängler. These debates have accompanied a tendency to regard the Third Reich in isolation from what came after it, to see it as, crudely put, the nazification of Germans, which must therefore be followed by their denazification through whatever means possible.

But neither the Germans nor the world at large need remain forever stuck in what Jeremy Eichler has called, in reference to Furtwängler, the "opposing cults of adoration and vilification."[45] Take the example of Richard Strauss, whose decisions to remain in Germany and to accept the leadership of the Reich Music Chamber in 1933 have baffled and dismayed many observers. Pamela Potter recently proposed, as part of a broader effort to understand German musical identity in the context of German history, that it is time "to look at him not for what he might or should have been but for what he unquestionably was: musician, composer, international celebrity, German, late romanticist, advocate for copyright protection, and senior citizen." We have "virtually exhausted archival material," she argues, and "indulged our fascination with the lives of the famous and with the Nazis"; now we must use these materials more constructively, "to gain insight" into the "complex fabric of popular reaction to Nazi dictatorship."[46]

What applies to Strauss, no matter how great his eminence, applies to all other Germans caught up in this musical community and conscious of their musical citizenship. The beginning of a new millennium may have made possible some longer perspective on music's long run in German history, a perspective that reasserts the continuity of German involvement in music but without the meta-rational aura. If music has remained a meaningful part of the way Germans identify themselves as a culture, then we need to regard this long-standing identification not as a great mystery like Mozart's or Beethoven's genius. Some aspects of Beethoven may remain marvellously inexplicable, but the attachment of Germans to him is not so, as several books have already shown.[47] Nor should we regard the conjunction of Germans and music as the product of inertia or a stubborn refusal to change or a deplorable sense of prideful superiority – all things that carry some suggestion of *ought*, as in the Germans ought to have found some other way to enjoy music or the Germans ought not to have loved their music so much. Elements of persistence in the relationship between Germans and music are matters that can be investigated historically and contextually. They are the product of action and deliberation, and they are as much an outcome of destruction and flux as is a new building project or a change in government. What we are seeing and hearing is persistence, not sameness; culture, not recalcitrance; and a constantly renewing sense of belonging, not inborn grace. Culture in this sense is a way to change as well as a way to stay together.

Let me close as I began, with Daniel Barenboim's reflections on music, society, change, exile, home, and the Germans' relation to "their music," which is also his and all of ours. "The great German musician," he observed, "will always have a visceral reaction to the Beethoven and Brahms that he or she grew up with, almost something atavistic from the stomach – which he or she will not have with *La Mer* by Debussy, even if the musician plays it marvellously." This is because the Germans "relate to it on the level of culture." Music, "because it doesn't have to do with explicit ideas" is an encounter with "fluidity," with "the idea that things change, evolve, and not necessarily for the best." Some great music, he believes, "has two faces: one towards its own time and one towards eternity." This gives it a timelessness that is really a quality of being "permanently contemporary." Music, from this perspective, "is everything and nothing at the same time" and, as such, beyond the reach of our words.[48]

Notes

Introduction

1 Quoted in the *Oxford Companion to Classical Music*, ed. Simon Hornblower and Anthony Spawforth (Oxford: Oxford University Press, 2014), 527.
2 Edgar Istel, "Goethe and Music," *The Musical Quarterly* 14, no. 2 (1928): 216.
3 Quoted in Toby Thacker, *Music after Hitler, 1945–1955* (Farnham, UK: Ashgate, 2007), 28.
4 Margalit Fox, "Kurt Masur Dies at 88: Conductor Transformed New York Philharmonic," *New York Times*, 9 July 2016. http://www.nytimes.com/glogin?URI=http%3A%2F%2Fwww.nytimes.com%2F2015%2F12%2F20%2Farts%2Fmusic%2Fkurt-masur-new-york-philharmonic-conductor-dies.html%3F_r%3D1.
5 Celia Applegate, "Introduction: Music among the Historians," *German History* 30, no. 3 (September 2012): 329.
6 Key contributions to this effort include Richard Leppert and Susan McClary, eds, *Music and Society: The Politics of Composition, Performance, and Reception* (Cambridge: Cambridge University Press, 1989); and Lydia Goehr, *The Imaginary Museum of Musical Works: An Essay in the Philosophy of Music* (Oxford: Oxford University Press, 2006).
7 A sign of the times was the launching in 2008 of Oxford University Press's book series, *The New Cultural History of Music*, edited by Jane Fulcher. In the first volume the interdisciplinary musicologist Vanessa Agnew showed how European discourses concerning music helped to articulate the meaning of human agency and cultural difference in the European and non-European worlds; *Enlightenment Orpheus: The Power of Music in Other Worlds* (New York: Oxford University Press, 2008).

8 Clifford Geertz, "Art as a Cultural System," in *Aesthetics*, ed. S. Feagin and P. Maynard (New York: Oxford University Press, 1997).

9 See Peter Jelavich on the position of cultural history, "caught in the No Man's Land between interpretation and causal explanation"; "Method? What Method? Confessions of a Failed Structuralist," *New German Critique* 95 (1995), 76.

10 John Toews, "Integrating Music into Intellectual History: Nineteenth-Century Art Music as a Discourse of Agency and Identity," *Modern Intellectual History* 5, no. 2 (2008): 309–10.

11 "What Is German Music? Reflections on the Role of Art in the Creation of the Nation," *German Studies Review* 15 (Winter 1992): 21–32; "How German Is It? Nationalism and the Idea of Serious Music in the Early Nineteenth Century," *19th Century Music* 21, no. 3 (Spring 1998): 274–96.

12 Albrecht Riethmüller, "'Is That Not Something for *Simplicissimus*?' The Belief in Musical Superiority," in Celia Applegate and Pamela Potter, eds, *Music and German National Identity* (Chicago: University of Chicago Press, 2002), 290.

13 See especially Celia Applegate and Pamela Potter, "Germans as the 'People of Music': Genealogy of an Identity," in Applegate and Potter, *Music and German National Identity*, 1–35.

14 Peter van der Merwe, *Roots of the Classical: The Popular Origins of Western Music* (Oxford: Oxford University Press, 2004), 151.

15 Peter Burke, *Popular Culture in Early Modern Europe*, 3rd ed. (Farnham, UK: Ashgate, 2009), 103.

16 "Laß endlich schweigen, o Republic, Militärmusik! Militärmusik!" quoted in Christian Lankes, *München als Garnison im 19. Jahrhundert*, 2 vols (Berlin: E.S. Mittler, 1993), 2: 497.

17 David Blackbourn, Review of Neil MacGregor's *Germany: Memories of a Nation*, *The Guardian*, 23 December 2014, accessed 9 July 2016. http://www.theguardian.com/books/2014/dec/23/germany-memories-nation-neil-macgregor-review

1. How German Is It?

1 This chapter is a lightly revised version of: "How German Is It? Nationalism and the Origins of Serious Music in Early Nineteenth Century Germany," in *19th Century Music* 21, no. 3 (Spring 1998): 274–96. © 1998 by the Regents of the University of California. Reprinted by permission of the University of California Press. Some passages have been deleted and a scattering of new bibliographic references included.

2 This project comes to the fore in Richard Taruskin, *Oxford History of Western Music,* esp. in Vol. 4, *The Nineteenth Century* (Oxford and New York: Oxford University Press 2005); for examples of how one can look at the German tradition differently see esp. 119–24, 187–250, 411–22, 703–30, 745.

3 Paul Henry Lang, *Music in Western Civilization* (New York: W.W. Norton, 1941), 487, 488, 490; Howard D. McKinney and W.R. Anderson, *Music in History: The Evolution of an Art* (New York: American Book Company, 1940); Donald N. Ferguson, *A History of Musical Thought,* 3rd ed. (Westport, CT: Greenwood Press, 1959); Donald Jay Grout, with Claude V. Palisca, *A History of Western Music,* 3rd ed. (New York: W.W. Norton, 1980).

4 Robert Pascall, *Romanticism, 1830–1890,* Vol. 9 of the *New Oxford History of Music,* ed. Gerald Abraham (New York: Oxford University Press, 1990), 540.

5 McKinney and Anderson, *Music in History,* 707.

6 Lang, *Music in Western Civilization,* 939.

7 Ferguson, *A History of Musical Thought,* 535.

8 See David Josephson, "The German Musical Exile and the Course of American Musicology," *Current Musicology* 79/80 (2005): 9–53.

9 Pascall, *Romanticism,* 536–42. For an excellent example of more recent work that interprets a set of German compositions in the nineteenth century as a kind of national exoticism, see Barbara Eichner, *History in Mighty Sounds: Musical Construction of German National Identity, 1848–1914* (Martlesham, UK: Boydell Press , 2012).

10 Ibid., 540.

11 Joseph Kerman, "How We Got into Analysis, and How to Get Out," *Critical Inquiry* 7 (1980), 314–15.

12 Hans Lenneberg, *Witnesses and Scholars: Studies in Musical Biography* (New York: Gordon and Breach, 1988), 85.

13 James Hepokoski, "The Dahlhaus Project and Its Extra-musicological Sources," *19th Century Music* 14 (1991): 225.

14 William Weber, *Music and the Middle Class: The Social Structure of Concert Life in London, Paris and Vienna* (London: Holmes & Meier, 1975), 75–6.

15 Sanna Pederson, "A.B. Marx, Berlin Concert Life, and German National Identity," *19th Century Music* 18 (1994): 87–107; Stephen Rumph, "A Kingdom Not of This World: The Political Context of E.T.A. Hoffmann's Beethoven Criticism," *19th Century Music* 19 (1995): 50–67.

16 A similar, equally de-legitimizing strategy is pursued by Martha Woodmansee, one of the literary authorities cited by Pederson. In *The Author, Art, and the Market: Rereading the History of Aesthetics* (New York: Columbia University Press, 1994), Woodmansee ingeniously interprets the motivation behind Schiller's bad-tempered conflicts with the popular writer

Ludwig Berger as a bid for a larger market share, or at least greater market security, on the part of the author of the *Letters on the Aesthetic Education of Man.* Nationalism serves the same function in Pederson's argument as the market does in Woodmansee's: as a means of revealing additional motivations behind seemingly disinterested statements of aesthetic intent.

17 Pederson, "A.B. Marx, Berlin Concert Life," 89; Rumph, "A Kingdom Not of This World," 58.

18 Pederson, "A.B. Marx, Berlin Concert Life," 89.

19 Rumph, "A Kingdom Not of This World," 65.

20 Ibid, 67; Pederson, "A.B. Marx, Berlin Concert Life," 89.

21 Pederson, "A.B. Marx, Berlin Concert Life," 89, 107.

22 Rumph, "A Kingdom Not of This World," 59.

23 It is also somewhat misleading to characterize it as a "project engineered primarily by aristocrats" (Rumph, "A Kingdom Not of This World," 52–3). While it is true that many reformers were aristocrats, the Prussian nobility, insofar as it represented a *Stand*-based opinion, bitterly opposed reform, the essence of which was the enhancement of the capacities of the bureaucratic state at considerable cost to the power and privileges of the old estates. For a summary of the reform period, see Thomas Nipperdey, *Deutsche Geschichte, 1800–1866: Bürgerwelt und starker Staat* (Munich: C.H. Beck, 1984), esp. 31–81. A more recent summation (since the publication of Rumph's article) of the diffuse and by no means universal patriotic fervour of the period can be found in Christopher Clark, *Iron Kingdom: The Rise and Downfall of Prussia* (Cambridge, MA: Harvard University Press, 2006), 312–44, 350–74. Stein alone has nationalist credentials of this sort and even these can be easily misconstrued if taken out of context.

24 Rumph, "A Kingdom not of this World," 58; James Sheehan, *German History, 1700–1866* (Oxford, 1989), 386. Rumph reproduces some of the central tenets of the subsequent nationalist myth of liberation, by which the *Volk* themselves were said to have achieved victory over Napoleon. There was a limited effort on the part of some German princes to mobilize national patriotism during the Napoleonic wars, but largely as a way to put pressure on those among the German princes who remained loyal to Napoleon.

25 See esp. Michael Jeismann, "Was bedeuten Stereotypen für nationale Identität und politisches Handeln," in *Nationale Mythen und Symbole in der zweiten Hälfte des 19. Jahrhunderts,* ed. Jürgen Link and Wulf Wülfing (Stuttgart: Klett-Cotta, 1991), 84–93; and Reinhart Koselleck, *Vergangene Zukunft: Zur Semantik geschichtlicher Zeiten* (Frankfurt, 1979).

26 Pederson, "A.B. Marx, Berlin Concert Life," 106–7.

27 Ibid. Marx does not use the phrase "the German people." He typically addressed himself to the "*gebildete Kreise,*" the educated public, a group that

played a key role in the emerging national movement but was nevertheless not the same thing as the German people.

28 The first and still compelling statement of this orientation to the world is Friedrich Meinecke, *Cosmopolitanism and the National State*, trans. Robert B. Kimber (1907; Princeton: Princeton University Press, 1970).

29 Pederson's interpretation of Hegel as the creator of a philosophy of history that glorified Prussia ("A.B. Marx, Berlin Concert Life," 90–1) is not an uncommon one, though Hegel scholar Schlomo Avineri goes to some lengths to revise it. The problem is that if one reads only secs 341ff. of the *Philosophy of Right*, then Hegel does indeed seem wholly Prussocentric. But if one begins with sec. 340, the abstraction of Hegel's vision from the particularity of Prussia c. 1830 becomes clear (or at least clearer). See Avineri, "Hegel and Nationalism," *Review of Politics* 24 (1962): 461–84.

30 That seems to be the source of Rumph's lament that Isaiah Berlin did not think of including Beethoven among his disillusioned Romantics ("A Kingdom Not of This World," 7).

31 Pierre Bourdieu and Loïc J.D. Wacquant, *An Invitation to Reflexive Sociology* (Chicago: University of Chicago Press, 1992), 12.

32 Carl Dahlhaus, *The Idea of Absolute Music*, trans. Roger Lustig (Chicago: University of Chicago Press, 1989).

33 Bernd Sponheuer, *Musik als Kunst und Nicht-Kunst: Untersuchungen zur Dichotomie von "hoher" und "niedrer" Musik im musikästhetischen Denken zwischen Kant und Hanslick* (Kassel: Bärenreiter Verlag, 1987). He also sees the national distinctions between German and Italian music as superficial labels for more general qualities; the debate was in that sense not about nationality or nationalism but about aesthetics (see esp. 22, 33). While not an entirely satisfactory explanation, Sponheuer at least leaves the discussion where it primarily belongs, in the social sphere of aesthetic and intellectual creation.

34 Andreas Mayer uses a similar methodology to address the problems of this era in "'Gluck'sches Gestöhn' und 'welsches Larifari': Anna Milder, Franz Schubert und der deutsch-italienische Opernkrieg," *Archiv für Musikwissenschaft* 52 (1995): 171–204.

35 Arno J. Mayer, *The Persistence of the Old Regime: Europe to the Great War* (New York, 1981); Tia DeNora, *Beethoven and the Construction of Genius: Musical Politics in Vienna, 1792–1803* (Berkeley and Los Angeles: University of California Press, 1995). Both authors' conclusions about the continuing importance of aristocratic patronage have been vigorously disputed.

36 Some 60 per cent of the German population changed rulers in the course of the period of French hegemony; see Sheehan, *German History*, 251.

37 Christoph-Hellmut Mahling argues that the quality of musicianship among court orchestral musicians was also in decline at the end of the eighteenth century; "The Origins and Social Status of the Court Orchestral Musician in the 18th and Early 19th Century in Germany," in *The Social Status of the Professional Musician from the Middle Ages to the 19th Century*, ed. Walter Salmen, trans. Herbert Kaufman and Barbara Reisner (Hillsdale, NY: Pendragon Press, 1983), 240.

38 On the complexities of local social distinctions, see the classic study by Mack Walker, *German Home Towns: Community, State, and General Estate, 1648–1871* (Ithaca, NY: Cornell University Press, 1971). An example of the struggle to maintain status that this multiplicity necessitated can be found in J.J. Quantz's account of his early wandering years, when he tried, at the time unsuccessfully, to hold onto the relatively respectable title of *Stadtpfeiffer*, reported in Charles Burney, *The Present State of Music in Germany, the Netherlands, and United Provinces*, Vol. 2, facsimile ed. (1775; London: Travis and Emery, 1969), 165–73.

39 Hans Engel, *Musik und Gesellschaft: Baustein zu einer Musiksoziologie* (Berlin: Hans Schneider Verlag, 1960); Arnfried Edler, "The Social Status of Organists in Lutheran Germany from the 16th through the 19th Century," in Salmen, *Social Status*, 89.

40 Heinrich W. Schwab, "The Social Status of the Town Musician," in Salmen, *Social Status*, 31–60; Dieter Krickeberg, "On the Social Status of the *Spielmann* ("Folk Musician") in 17th and 18th Century Germany, Particularly in the Northwest," in Salmen, *Social Status*, 95–122.

41 The literature on the origins of concerts is rich, in contrast to many other areas of music's social history. See esp. Hanns-Werner Heister, *Das Konzert: Theorie einer Kulturform* (Wilhelmshaven: Heinrichshofen's Verlag, 1983); the more general treatment in Walter Salmen, *Das Konzert: Eine Kulturgeschichte* (Munich, 1988); and a recent general contribution, Michael Thomas Roeder, *Das Konzert*, Handbuch der musikalischen Gattungen, Vol. 4 (Laaber: Laaber Verlag, 2000).

42 Mack Walker coined this term and developed its definition in *German Home Towns*, in which he argues for the uselessness of the category "bourgeois" or "middle class" in the German case. Such a category obscures essential and consequential differences between the "experiences and habit" of, for instance, a guildsman and a state bureaucrat (see 111–28).

43 Klaus Hortschansky, "The Musician as Music Dealer in the Second Half of the 18th Century," in Salmen, *Social Status*, 192. The definitive account of relations among composers, publishers, and the public is Alex Beer, *Musik zwischen Komponist, Verlag und Publikum: Die Rahmenbedingungen des*

Musikschaffens in Deutschland im ersten Drittel des 19. Jahrhundert (Tutzing: Hans Schneider Verlag, 2000).

44 Carl Maria von Weber, *Writings on Music,* ed. John Warrack, trans. Martin Cooper (Cambridge: Cambridge University Press, 1981), 318–19.

45 The study of notions of honour in regard to the musician's profession would be a fascinating undertaking. Concern about their honour seems to have undergone a shift over the course of the eighteenth century, defining its meaning and importance within much wider circles than those of German home town life: hence C.P.E. Bach's sharp "note to the public" in 1769 on the matter of a pirated edition of J.S. Bach's *Four-Part Chorales,* claiming that the "honor of the great deceased as well as my own honor as compiler has been most sharply offended"; repr. in *The Bach Reader,* ed. Hans T. David and Arthur Mendel (New York, 1966), 271. On music as a dishonourable trade, see chap. 3 of this volume, "Musical Itinerancy in a World of Nations," and more generally, Werner Danckert, *Unehrliche Leute: die Verfemten Berufe* (Bern and Munich: Francke Verlag, 1963).

46 Walker, *German Home Towns,* 130.

47 Ibid., 129. Charles McClelland, *State, Society, and University in Germany, 1700–1914* (Cambridge: Cambridge University Press, 1980), 3.

48 Hans H. Gerth, *Bürgerliche Intelligenz um 1800: Zur Soziologie des deutschen Frühliberalismus* (1935; Göttingen: Vandenhoeck & Ruprecht, 1976), 34. See also McClelland, *State, Society, and University,* 34–58.

49 McClelland, *State, Society, and University,* 97.

50 Hortschansky, "Musician as Music Dealer," 217. He attributes much of the scramble to engage in musical commerce as a response to this crisis.

51 Bourdieu and Wacquant, *Reflexive Sociology,* 11–17.

52 See McClelland, *State, Society, and University,* 61, 106, 110–11.

53 A distinction between court and state is important in this connection because, of course, many courts continued to support music in the form of ceremonial and chamber music as well as opera and theatre music.

54 Cited by Christoph-Hellmut Mahling, "The Origins and Social Status of the Court Orchestra Musician," in *The Social Status of the Professional Musician,* 238–9.

55 Note that one way to settle the issue is simply to be vague, as Dahlhaus is with the help of German abstraction: referring to the origins of Bach's significance for the Romantics, he writes of the "tying together [*Verknüpfung*] of the romantic metaphysic of absolute music with the patriotic idea of an epoch of German music"; Dahlhaus, "Zur Entstehung der romantischen Bach-Deutung," *Bach Jahrbuch* 64 (1978): 197.

56 Burney, *Present State of Music,* 2: 70, 340, 343.

57 The phrase is Hagen Schulze's in *The Course of German Nationalism: From Frederick the Great to Bismarck, 1763–1867*, trans. Sarah Hanbury-Tenison (Cambridge: Cambridge University Press, 1991), 46.

58 See esp. T.J. Reed, *The Classical Centre: Goethe and Weimar, 1775–1832* (Oxford: Clarendon Press, 1980), 17–19. For these sentiments, Reed makes particular use of Goethe's 1795 essay "Literarischer Sansculottismus."

59 William Weber argues that the process of what we might call the national inscription of music happened first in eighteenth-century England. See *The Rise of Musical Classics in Eighteenth-Century England: A Study in Canon, Ritual, and Ideology* (Oxford: Oxford University Press, 1992).

60 Meinecke, *Cosmopolitanism and the National State*, 10, 14, 15, 42.

61 David and Mendel, *Bach Reader*, 294; Forkel, *Über Johann Sebastian Bachs Leben, Kunst und Kunstwerke* (Leipzig, 1802), preface.

62 On the importance of philhellenism to the educated elite and it sense of national culture, see the classic study by E.M. Butler, *The Tyranny of Greece over Germany* (1935; Cambridge: Cambridge University Press, 2012); and the more recent study by Suzanne L. Marchand, *Down from Olympus: Archeology and Philhellenism in Germany, 1750–1970* (Princeton: Princeton University Press, 1996). A number of German musician-scholars in the first decades of the nineteenth century also undertook to investigate the place of music in the classical world and world view.

63 From "Literarischer Sanscullottism," 239ff, cited in Reed, *Classical Centre: Goethe*, 17–18.

64 Here, of course, his judgments on Beethoven have long been compared unfavourably with those of, say, E.T.A. Hoffmann, who had a lot more panache than Zelter as well. For a defence specifically of Zelter's views on Beethoven, see Cornelia Schröder, *Carl Friedrich Zelter und die Akademie* (Berlin: Deutsche Akademie der Künste Verlag, 1959), 50–1. She blames A.B. Marx for spreading the idea that Zelter, a "Berliner Philistine" according to Marx, had not understood Beethoven's genius. Marx's assessment was certainly influenced by his own Romantic determination to pose as the leading champion of Beethoven in north German musical circles.

65 For stimulating reflections on reception history and a demonstration of a new form of it, very similar to the approach this article takes, see Mayer, "'Gluck'sches Gestöhn' und 'welsches Larifari.'"

66 See Dalhaus, Introduction, in *Studien zur Musikgeschichte Berlins im frühen 19. Jahrhundert*, ed. Carl Dahlhaus (Regensburg: Bosse Verlag, 1980), 7.

67 Carl Freiherr von Ledebur, *Tonkünstler Lexicon Berlins von den ältesten Zeiten bis auf die Gegenwart* (Berlin: L. Rauh, 1861), 661–2.

68 Carl Friedrich Zelter, *Darstellungen seines Lebens*, ed. Johann-Wolfgang Schottländer (Weimar: Goethe-Gesellschaft, 1931), 3–5.

69 There is some disagreement in the historical record on this point. Zelter himself claimed in his letter of introduction to the king in 1804 (which included a brief account of his life and musical development) that his association with George ended because the man died; letter from 1 August 1804, repr. in Schröder, *Carl Friedrich Zelter*, 104–5.

70 As Zelter's life indicated, these worlds, static home town and mobile urban, existed side by side in central Europe up until the founding of the German Empire in 1871, by which time most traces of home town economic and political constitutions had disappeared. A city like Berlin, in other words, was both home town and modernizing city; this enabled ambitious but little-educated men from the *Bürgertum* of the guilds, like Zelter, to become "movers and doers" and thereby mix with people of higher education, wealth, and birth. Zelter had attended a gymnasium, the Joachimthalsche, for a few years, and good masons were among the most scientifically educated of the guilds. Still his acquaintance with literature and philosophy was meagre.

71 *Singakademie zu Berlin: Festschrift zum 175 jährigen Bestehen*, ed. Werner Bollert (Berlin: Rembrandt Verlag, 1966), 11; on its history see also Gottfried Eberle, *200 Jahre Sing-Akademie zu Berlin* (Berlin: Nicolai, 1991); Georg Schünemann, *Die Singakademie zu Berlin, 1791–1941* (Regensburg: Gustav Bosse Verlag, 1941).

72 It is worth noting that, though respectable, directing the Singakademie did not in fact put enough bread on the table, and with a family of eleven children to support, Zelter retained his living from masonry until sometime around 1820.

73 Goethe said as much to A.W. Schlegel: "If ever I have been curious to make the acquaintance of an individual, it is with this Herr Zelter. This union of two arts is so important, and I wish to know much about both and their mutual connection"; quoted in Schröder, *Carl Friedrich Zelter*, 46.

74 Quoted in Walter Victor, *Carl Friedrich Zelter und seine Freundschaft mit Goethe* (Berlin, 1970), 25.

75 For a rebuttal of such attitudes, see Lorraine Byrne Bodley, "A Musical Odyssey: Thirty-Five Years of Correspondence between Goethe and Zelter," in *Goethe and Zelter: Musical Dialogues*, trans. Lorraine Byrne Bodley (Farnham, UK: Ashgate, 2009), 1–28 ; see also my review of her translation and interpretation in *Music and Letters* 93, no.1 (2012): 123–6

76 Robert Spaethling, *Music and Mozart in the Life of Goethe* (Columbia, SC: Camden House, 1989), 21–3.

77 In the conclusion of the memorandum, Zelter apologized if his ideas seemed too "forward" (*dreist*); see Schröder, *Carl Friedrich Zelter*, 79.

78 Humboldt was the major force in Zelter's eventual achievement of Academy of Arts recognition; he read the sixth draft of the memorandum and wrote to the king that he was "fully in agreement" with all its suggestions. Humboldt himself was not much interested in music, although his brother Alexander, in contrast, was a regular participant in the Mendelssohn family's Sunday musical soirees. See Paul R. Sweet, *Wilhelm von Humboldt: A Biography* (Columbus: University of Ohio Press, 1980), esp. 2: 107, 393.

79 A "wohltätigen Einfluß auf die Sittlichkeit"; Zelter, "Erste Denkschrift, " in Schröder, *Carl Friedrich Zelter*, 78.

80 Zelter used the phrase in a letter to Goethe on 15 June 1830, cited in *Der Briefwechsel zwischen Goethe und Zelter*, ed. Max Hecker, 3 vols (Leipzig: Insel Verlag, 1913–18), 297.

81 See Schünemann, *Carl Friedrich Zelter: Der Mensch und sein Werk* (Berlin: Berliner Bibliophilen Abend, 1937).

82 "Diese Bildung besteht in einer Tätigkeit innerer oder Gemüthskräfte, wodurch der Mensch an sich selbst, vollkommner und also edler wird"; Zelter, "Zweite Denkschrift," December 1803, in Schröder, *Carl Friedrich Zelter*, 82.

83 Zelter, "Erste Denkschrift," in Schröder, *Carl Friedrich Zelter*, 75.

84 For instances see Schröder, *Carl Friedrich Zelter*, 129, 132, 125.

85 Sweet, *Wilhelm von Humboldt*, 2: 3–88.

86 Humboldt and Schiller, quoted in Meinecke, *Cosmopolitanism and the National State*, 45–6.

87 Zelter, "Vierte Denkschrift," in Schröder, *Carl Friedrich Zelter*, 111.

88 Letter to Ludwig Tieck, repr. in Martin Geck, *Die Wiederentdeckung der Matthäuspassion im 19. Jahrhundert: Die zeitgenössischen Dokumente und ihre ideengeschichtliche Deutung* (Regensburg: Bosse Verlag, 1967), 46.

2. Music in Place

1 This chapter is a slightly shorter version of "Music in Place: Perspectives on Art Culture in Nineteenth Century Germany," in *Localism, Landscape, and the Ambiguities of Place: German-Speaking Central Europe, 1860–1930*, ed. David Blackbourn and James Retallack (Toronto: University of Toronto Press, 2007), 39–59. Reprinted with the permission of the University of Toronto Press.

2 Among other state-of-the-field manifestos, see Lynn Hunt, ed., *The New Cultural History: Essays* (Berkeley: University of California Press, 1989); and

Victoria Bonnell and Lynn Hunt, eds, *Beyond the Cultural Turn: New Directions in the Study of Society and Culture* (Berkeley: University of California Press, 1999).

3 Matthew Arnold, *Culture and Anarchy* (Cambridge: Cambridge University Press, 1996), 6.

4 David Blackbourn, "A Sense of Place: New Directions in German History," The 1998 Annual Lecture of the German Historical Institute, London (London: GHI Publications, 1999), 5.

5 Robert Sack, *A Geographical Guide to the Real and the Good* (New York: Routledge, 2003), 4.

6 Walter Benjamin, "The Work of Art in the Age of Mechanical Reproduction," *Illuminations*, ed. Hannah Arendt, trans. Harry Zohn (New York: Schocken Books, 1969), 224.

7 R. Murray Schafer, "Music and the Soundscape," in *The Book of Music and Nature*, ed. David Rothenberg and Marta Ulvaeus (Middletown, CT: Wesleyan University Press, 2001), 58. The scholarly literature of sound studies is large and growing. For an overview of how sound studies has developed since this essay was first published in 2007, see Daniel Morat, "Zur Geschichte des Hörens: Ein Forschungsbericht," *Archiv für Sozialgeschichte* 51 (2011): 695–716, and Morat, ed., *Sounds of Modern History: Auditory Cultures in 19th and 20th-Century Europe* (New York: Berghahn Books, 2014).

8 John Connell and Chris Gibson, *Soundtracks: Popular Music, Identity, and Place* (London: Routledge, 2003), 1.

9 Two exceptional studies of how place might be integrated into the history of musical culture take Paris as their place: James Johnson, *Listening in Paris: A Cultural History* (Berkeley: University of California Press, 1995); and Anselm Gerhard, *The Urbanization of Opera: Music Theatre in Paris in the Nineteenth Century*, trans. Mary Whittall (Chicago: University of Chicago Press, 1998).

10 Terry Eagleton, *The Idea of Culture* (Oxford: Oxford University Press, 2000), 20.

11 A lively guide to the Bayreuth phenomenon is Frederic Spotts, *Bayreuth: A History of the Wagner Festival* (New Haven: Yale University Press, 1994).

12 See, for instance, "Art and Revolution" (1849), "The Artwork of the Future" (1849), "A Communication to my Friends" (1851), "Opera and Drama" (1852), and "A Glance at the German Operatic Stage of Today" (1873), all available in the William Ashton Ellis translations at the Wagner Library website, accessed 10 July 2016, http://users.belgacom.net/wagnerlibrary/prose/index.htm.

13 Cited in Matthew Wilson Smith, "Bayreuth, Disneyland, and the Return to Nature," in *Land/Scape/Theatre*, ed. Elinor Fuchs and Una Chauduri (Ann Arbor: University of Michigan Press, 2002), 254.

14 Quoted in Spotts, *Bayreuth*, 41.
15 Wilhelm Heinrich Riehl, *Kulturgeschichtliche Charakterköpfe*, 2nd ed. (Stuttgart: J.G. Cotta, 1892), 447, 453.
16 Ibid., 448–9, 453.
17 Richard Wagner, "Über deutsches Musikwesen," in *Gesammelte Schriften und Dichtungen* (Leipzig: E.W. Fritzsch, 1871), 1: 152; Riehl, *Charakterköpfe*, 480.
18 Wagner, "Über deutsches Musikwesen," 152–4.
19 Riehl, *Charakterköpfe*, 514, 480–4.
20 On the explosion in publishing for home performance in the decades of the 1860s and 1870s, see Andreas Ballstaedt and Tobias Widmaier, *Salonmusik: zur Geschichte und Funktion einer Bürgerlichen Musikpraxis*, Archiv für Musikwissenschaft, Band 28 (Wiesbaden: F. Steiner Verlag, 1989). See also Irmgard Keldany-Mohr, *'Unterhaltungsmusik' als soziokulturelles Phänomen des 19. Jahrhunderts: Untersuchung über den Einfluss der musikalischen Öffentlichkeit auf die Herausbildung eines neuen Musiktypes* (Regensburg: Bosse Verlag, 1977); Karl Gustav Fellerer, *Studien zur Musik des 19. Jahrhunderts: Musik und Musikleben im 19. Jahrhundert* (Regensburg: Bosse Verlag, 1984); and Thomas Christensen, "Public Music in Private Spaces: Piano-Vocal Scores and the Domestication of Opera," in *Music and the Cultures of Print*, ed. Kate van Orden (New York: Taylor & Francis, 2000), 67–94.
21 Wilhelm Jakob Jung, *Musikgeschichte der Stadt Ludwigshafen am Rhein vom Jahre 1850 bis 1918*, ed. Siegfried Fauck (Grünstadt/Pfalz: Emil Sommer Verlag, 1968), 84.
22 Carl Dahlhaus, *Nineteenth-Century Music*, trans. J. Bradford Robinson (Berkeley: University of California Press, 1989), 151.
23 See Monica Steegmann, ed., *Musik und Industrie: Beiträge zur Entwicklung der Werkschöre und Werksorchester* (Regensburg: Bosse Verlag, 1978).
24 The cultural import of the military bands is explored in chapter 10.
25 Sophie Hutchinson Drinker, *Brahms and His Women's Choruses* (Merion, PA: self-published, 1952).
26 Lucien Hölscher, "Die Religion des Bürgers: Bürgerliche Frömmigkeit und Protestantische Kirche im 19. Jahrhundert," *Historische Zeitschrift* 250 (1990): 595–630.
27 Johannes Brahms, *Johannes Brahms: Life and Letters*, edited by Styra Avins, translated by Josef Eisinger and Styra Avins (New York: Oxford University Press, 1997), 250, 258, 448.
28 Ibid., 258–9.
29 Dana Gooley, *The Virtuoso Liszt* (Cambridge: Cambridge University Press, 2004), 199.
30 Ibid.

31 See, for example, Jonathan Bellman, ed., *The Exotic in Western Music* (Boston: Northeastern University Press, 1998).

32 Richard Wagner, "On German Music" (1840), trans. William Ashton Ellis, available at *The Wagner Library*, http://users.belgacom.net/wagnerlibrary/prose/wagongm.htm, accessed 10 July 2016.

33 Returning to Hungary for the first time since childhood, he publicly accepted the sabre of honour from Magyar nationalists at his first concert, thus bringing down upon himself a storm of criticism in the French and German press, where he was accused of having repudiated his French and German loyalties in favour of narrow, backward-looking militarists. Gooley, *Virtuoso Liszt*, 157.

34 On the regional compass of most travel, see Siegfried Weichlein, *Nation und Region: Integrationsprozesse im Bismarckreich* (Düsseldorf: Droste Verlag, 2004).

35 "Busts of composers provide a great addition to the room of any musician or person who appreciates good music ... Mozart busts are one of the most popular items in the bust gallery ... If Mozart is not your style, perhaps a Beethoven bust would better suit." See http://www.statue.com/site/composer-busts.html, accessed 10 July 2016.

36 Richard Taruskin, *The Oxford History of Western Music*, Vol. 3: *The Nineteenth Century* (New York: Oxford University Press, 2004), 467–8.

37 Harold C. Schonberg, *The Great Pianists* (New York: Simon and Schuster, 1963), 253.

38 Quoted in Paul Henry Lang, *Music in Western Civilization*, with a new foreword by Leon Botstein (New York: W.W. Norton, 1997), 776.

3. Musical Itinerancy in a World of Nations

1 This chapter represents a lightly revised version of an essay first published as "Musical Itinerancy in a World of Nations: Germany, Its Music, and Its Musicians," in *Cultures in Motion* ed. Daniel T. Rodgers, Bhavani Raman, and Helmut Reimitz (Princeton: Princeton University Press, 2014), 60–86. Reprinted by permission of Princeton University Press.

2 Letter, Brahms to Clara Schumann, 18 November 1862, in *Johannes Brahms: Life and Letters*, ed. Styra Avins, trans. Styra Avins and Josef Eisinger (Oxford: Oxford University Press, 2001), 258; Jan Swafford, *Johannes Brahms: A Biography* (New York: Vintage, 1999), 496.

3 See, for instance, Jeffrey Richards, *Imperialism and Music: Britain 1876–1953* (Manchester: University of Manchester Press, 2001).

4 James Clifford, *Routes: Travel and Translation in the Late Twentieth Century* (Cambridge, MA: Harvard University Press, 1997), 17.

5 Ibid., 2–3.
6 William Weber, *The Great Transformation of Musical Taste: Concert Programming from Haydn to Brahms* (Cambridge: Cambridge University Press, 2008), 21.
7 On the musicological subject of "exoticism" in music, see Jonathan Bellman, *The Exotic in Western Music* (Boston: Northeastern University Press, 1998); and Ralph Locke, *Musical Exoticism: Images and Reflections* (Cambridge: Cambridge University Press, 2009).
8 The term and the mapping metaphor come from Fernand Braudel, *The Mediterranean and the Mediterranean World in the Era of Philip II*, trans. Siân Reynolds (Berkeley, CA: University of California Press, 1998), 835. On "mapping" literary culture see Franco Moretti, *Atlas of the European Novel, 1800–1900* (London: Verso, 1998) and *Graphs, Maps, Trees: Abstract Models for a Literary History* (London: Verso, 2005).
9 Akira Iriye, *Cultural Internationalism and World Order* (Baltimore: Johns Hopkins University Press, 1997), 2.
10 A distinction between hard and soft national boundaries informs this discussion; see Prasenjit Duara, *Rescuing History from the Nation: Questioning Narratives of Modern China* (Chicago: University of Chicago Press, 1997), 65.
11 Nate Schweber, "For Two Jazzmen, Work Meant Life on the Road," *New York Times*, 15 February 2009.
12 Heinrich W. Schwab, "The Social Status of the Town Musician," in Walter Salmen, ed., *The Social Status of the Professional Musician from the Middle Ages to the 19th Century*, trans. Herbert Kaufman and Barbara Reisner (New York: Pendragon Press, 1983), 33–59.
13 Johann Beer, "Teutsche Winternächte," in *Sämtliche Werke*, ed. Ferdinand van Ingen and Hans-Gert Roloff (Bern: Peter Lang, 2005), 7: 117–19.
14 To name but a few: see Werner Danckert, *Unehrliche Leute: die Verfemten Berufe* (Munich: A. Franke, 1963). Danckert, trained as a concert pianist and then as a musicologist, subjected his richly original mind to the dreary predictability of racial science in the 1930s, eventually joining the Nazi party and the cultural bureaucracy of Alfred Rosenberg. After the war he wrote many works of what we would now call ethnomusicology. See also Kathy Stuart, *Defiled Trades and Social Outcasts: Honor and Ritual Pollution in Early Modern Germany* (Cambridge and New York: Cambridge University Press, 1999), and Carsten Küther, *Menschen auf der Strasse* (Göttingen: Vandenhoeck & Ruprecht, 1993), and *Räuber und Gauner in Deutschland*, 2nd ed. (Göttingen: Vandenhoeck & Ruprecht, 1987).
15 The definitive study is Walter Salmen, *Der fahrende Musiker im europäischen Mittelalter* (Kassel: Bärenreiter, 1960).

16 The most famous example of this was, of course, the Bach family, of whom more than fifty members were professional musicians, for the most part in Thuringia.

17 Dieter Krickeberg, "The Folk Musician in the 17th and 18th Centuries," in Salmen, *Social Status*, 101.

18 Henry Raynor, *A Social History of Music, from the Middle Ages to Beethoven* (London: Barry & Jenkins, 1972), 68.

19 Martin Wolschke, *Von der Stadtpfeiferei zu Lehrlingskapelle und Sinfonieorchester* (Regensburg: Gustav Bosse Verlag, 1981), 33–6.

20 Ralf Gehler, "Dorf und Stadtmusikanten im ländlichen Raum Mecklenburgs, zwischen 1650 und 1700," in *Historical Studies on Folk and Traditional Music*, ed. Doris Stockman (Copenhagen: International Council for Traditional Music, 1997), 47–58.

21 Steven Rose, "The Musician-Novels of the German Baroque: New Light on Bach's World," *Understanding Bach* 3 (Bach Network UK), http://www.bachnetwork.co.uk/ub3/ROSE.pdf, 363–4, accessed 28 July 2016.

22 James Sheehan, *German History, 1770–1866* (Oxford: Oxford University Press, 1990), 153.

23 These novels were quite popular in their day but only rediscovered in the twentieth century, though not uncritically. Hans Menck said of Beer's Jan Rebhu that he expressed "only the unique and historically bounded experiences of the musician's condition in his time," not the nature of a true artist; *Der Musiker im Roman* (Heidelberg: C. Winter, 1931), 28. See also Richard Alewyn, *Johann Beer: Studien zum Roman des 17. Jahrhundert* (1932: Heidelberg: Universitätsverlag Winter, 2012), and George Schoolfield, *The Figure of the Musician in German Literature* (Chapel Hill: University of North Carolina Press, 1956). Stephen Rose, *The Musician in Literature in the Age of Bach* (Cambridge: Cambridge University Press, 2011) is now the starting point for exploring this literature.

24 James Hardin, *Johann Beer* (Boston: Twayne, 1983), 27. See also Gordon J. Burgess, "*Die Wahrheit mit lachendem Munde": Comedy and Humor in the Novels of Christian Weise* (Bern: Peter Lang, 1990).

25 Alan Menhennet, *Grimmelhausen the Storyteller: A Study of the "Simplician" Novels* (Columbia, SC: Camden House, 1997), 13.

26 On the limitations of *Simplicissimus* as a guide to the life of Grimmelshausen or the sufferings of the Germans, see Robert Ergang, *The Myth of the All-Destructive Fury of the Thirty Years' War* (Pocono Pines, PA: The Craftsman, 1956); see also Geoffrey Parker, ed., *The Thirty Years' War*, 2nd ed. (London: Routledge, 1997), 210–16.

27 Suspicion of music in western Christianity constitutes a very long strand of thought and practice that predates the Reformation, and despite Martin Luther's ringing endorsement of music as the greatest gift of God after salvation, some Pietist sects tried to do away with service music altogether.

28 His musical tracts included *Ursus Murmurat* (The Bear Growling), *Ursus Vulpinatur* (The Bear Scheming), *Bellum Musicum* (The Musical War), *Musicalische Discurse,* and *Schola Phonologica,* the latter a work of instruction in music theory and harmonization that remained unpublished in his lifetime. All are now available in modern printed editions; Vol. 12 of Johann Beer, *Sämtliche Werke* (Bern: Peter Lang, 2005). See also Michael Heinemann, "Stil und Polemik: Zur Musikanschauung von Johann Beer," *Beer 1655–1700, Hofmusiker, Satiriker, Anonymus: eine Karriere zwischen Bürgertum und Hof,* ed. Andreas Brandtner and Wolfgang Neuber (Vienna: Turia + Kant, 2000), 117–46.

29 The figures of the wandering musician and the wandering Jew share obvious affinities, though the latter carries none of the positive traits associated with the musicians. These intersecting cultural formations have received extensive scrutiny in the rich literature on Richard Wagner's music; see esp. Marc A. Weiner, *Richard Wagner and the Anti-Semitic Imagination* (Lincoln: University of Nebraska Press, 1997).

30 Beer placed Printz in a madhouse cell in his satirical novel *Narrenspital* (Fools' Asylum).

31 See Andreas Angler, "'Ich bin kein Spiel-mann: die Verteidigung des bürgerlichen Status und das künsterlishe Selbstbewusstsein der Hauptfiguren in den Musiker-romanen von Wolfgang Caspar Printz," *Daphnis: Zeitschrift für mittlere Deutsche Literatur* 30, no. 1 (2001): 333–54.

32 Joseph Kerman and Gary Tomlinson, *Listen,* 6th ed. (New York: Bedford St Martins, 2008), 100.

33 Erich Reimer, *Die Hofmusik in Deutschland, 1500–1800: Wandlungen einer Institution* (Wilhelmshaven: Florian Noetzel Verlag, 1991), 16–17.

34 On musical life especially, see Tanya Kevorkian, *Baroque Piety: Religion, Society, and Music in Leipzig, 1650–1750* (Aldershot, UK: Ashgate, 2007). For a comparison, see Gerald Lyman Soliday, *A Community in Conflict: Frankfurt Society in the Seventeenth and Early Eighteenth Centuries* (Hanover, NH: Brandeis University Press, 1974). In Frankfurt the struggles between the aristocracy and the burgher-citizens impeded the development of its cultural life until later in the century.

35 See Christoph Wolff, *Johann Sebastian Bach: The Learned Musician* (New York: W.W. Norton, 2001); for his immersion in the politics of the Dresden court

see Ulrich Siegele, "Bach and the Domestic Politics of Electoral Saxony," in *The Cambridge Companion to Bach*, ed. John Butt (Cambridge: Cambridge University Press, 1997), 17–34.

36 Mack Walker, *German Home Towns: Community, State, and General Estate* (Ithaca, NY: Cornell University Press, 1983), 130; Hardin, *Johann Beer*, 38.

37 Quotations from Wolff, *Learned Musician*, 179, 2, 237–38.

38 Walker, *German Home Towns*, 2–3.

39 Hans Leo Hassler (1564–1612) travelled to Venice at age twenty and brought back the new polychoral style of the early baroque.

40 Cited in Klaus Hortschansky, "The Musician as Music Dealer in the Second Half of the 18th Century," in Salmen, *Social Status*, 217.

41 J.F. Reichardt, "An junge Künstler," *Musikalisches Kunstmagazin* 1 (1782): 5.

42 Reimer, *Hofmusik*, 125–41.

43 This is one of the more famous of the genre and one of only two that have been translated into English, thanks to the work of James Hardin and the Camden House Press. See Kuhnau, *The Musical Charlatan*, trans. John R. Russell, intro. James Hardin (Columbia, SC: Camden House, 1997).

44 Ibid., 1–2.

45 Ibid., 4.

46 *Collegia musica* participated in the transnational movement of German musical institutions. The Moravian Brethren emigrants to North America established *collegia musica* in many of their communities, in Pennsylvania and North Carolina.

47 Kuhnau, *Charlatan*, 4.

48 Ibid., 4, 7–8, 20–1.

49 Mattheson has been the subject of a considerable amount of recent scholarship. For a brief overview of his life see especially Holger Böning: "Johann Mattheson – ein Streiter für die Musik und sein Wirken als Hamburger Publizist," in *Johann Mattheson als Vermittler und Initiator: Wissenstransfer und die Etablierung neuer Diskurse in der ersten Hälfte des 18. Jahrhunderts*, ed. Wolfgang Hirschmann and Bernhard Jahn (Hildesheim: Olms Verlag, 2010), 19–60. Böning is also the author of the most recent and extensive Mattheson biography: *Der Musiker und Komponist Johann Mattheson als Hamburger Publizist: Studie zu den Anfängen der Moralischen Wochenschriften und der deutschen Musikpublizistik* (Bremen: Edition Lumiere, 2011).

50 He even briefly (1713–14) published his own version of the English taste-making weeklies the *Tatler* and the *Spectator*.

51 Otto Dann, *Nation und Nationalismus in Deutschland, 1770–1990* (Munich: C.H. Beck, 1993), 39.

52 Johann Mattheson, *Das neu-eröffnete Orchestre* (Hamburg: Schiller, 1713), 200–31. http://reader.digitale-sammlungen.de/en/fs1/object/display/bsb10599040_00001.html, accessed 19 July 2016.

53 He gave the periodical a suitably verbose subtitle, laden down with claims to erudition (which given his polemics against musical pedants may be regarded as ironic) – "searching critiques and assessments of the many opinions, arguments, and objections," designed "to eradicate ... all vulgar error and to promote a freer growth in the pure science of harmony." It appeared between 1722 and 1726.

54 The title is essentially untranslatable – "complete" is no problem, but no single English term encompasses the functions of organizer, performer, and composer required of the eighteenth-century Capellmeister, which is why it is usually left in German. An English translation does exist: Ernest C. Harriss, *Johann Mattheson's* Der vollkommene Capellmeister*: A Revised Translation with Critical Commentary* (Ann Arbor, MI: UMI Research Press, 1981).

55 On the meaning of "patriot," see the discussion of "Bürger," an even more complicated term, in *Geschichtliche Grundbegriffe*, ed. Otto Brunner, Werner Conze, and Reinhart Koselleck, 8 vols. (Stuttgart: E. Klett, 1987–92), 1: 686.

56 This section essentially copied and then expanded upon on a contemporary French treatise of 1737 called *Discours sur l'harmonie d'un Anonyme*, now known to be the work of the dramatist Jean-Baptiste-Louis Gresset, who is remembered mainly for the comic story *Vert-Vert*, about a foul-talking parrot in a convent. Mattheson was also a great reader of travel literature; his claims about the Chinese, for instance, seem to have been derived from his reading of the Jesuit Martino Martini's seventeenth-century *History of the Great and Renowned Monarchy of China.* Johann Mattheson, *Der vollkommene Capellmeister*, Neusatz des Textes und der Noten, ed. Friederike Ramm (Kassel: Bärenreiter, 2012), 83, 89; pt I, chap. 5, paras 4, 31, 32.

57 Koselleck, "Volk, Nation, Nationalismus, Masse," in Brunner, Conze, and Koselleck, *Geschichtliche Grundbegriffe*, 7: 305–6.

58 "Der Italiener aber nimmt das Geld und geht davon"; Mattheson, *Neu-eröffnete Orchestre*, 215. http://reader.digitale-sammlungen.de/en/fs1/object/display/bsb10599040_00001.html, accessed 19 July 2016. Praetorius in the introduction to his Singspiel libretto, *Calypso, oder Sieg der Weissheit Ueber die Liebe*, quoted in Gloria Flaherty, *Opera in the Development of German Critical Thought* (Princeton: Princeton University Press, 1978), 69.

59 William Weber, *The Rise of Musical Classics in Eighteenth-Century England: A study in Canon, Ritual, and Ideology* (Oxford: Oxford University Press, 1992), 101.

60 By 1815 the United States had a Handel and Haydn Society in Boston, and many more such groups would follow. France developed its own version of institutionalized mass singing in the form of the Orphéon choral society, founded in Paris in the 1830s as a quasi-educational society for working-class men, but soon it became a mass male-voice choral movement with thousands of local branches.

61 Haydn's *Creation* was an even more transnational piece of music than Handel's oratorios. Its genesis lay in Haydn's trips to England in the 1790s and his exposure to the English Handel performances. An Englishman wrote the libretto for Haydn, and Baron Gottfried van Swieten, himself a key musical traveller, did the translation in Vienna in 1796. *The Creation / Die Schöpfung* may be the first piece of music published in a bilingual edition (1800).

62 Percy A. Scholes, *The Mirror of Music, 1844–1944: A Century of Musical Life in Britain as reflected in the pages of the* Musical Times (London: Novello, 1947), 2: 642.

63 Weber, *Rise of Musical Classics*, 127–41.

64 Hiller's star is beginning to rise among musicologists; see the recent translation of one of his key pedagogical texts: Johann Adam Hiller, *Treatise on Vocal Performance and Ornamentation*, ed. and trans. Suzanne J. Beicken (Cambridge: Cambridge University Press, 2001).

65 See Cecilia Porter, "The New Public and the Reordering of the Musical Establishment: the Lower Rhine Music Festivals, 1818–1867," *19th Century Music* 3 (1979–80): 211–24, and *The Rhine as Musical Metaphor: Cultural Identity in German Romantic Music* (Boston: Northeastern University Press, 1996), 169–77.

66 Brian Vick, *Defining Germany: The 1848 Frankfurt Parliamentarians and National Identity* (Cambridge, MA: Harvard University Press, 2002), 16, 22–3, 205–8.

67 Celia Applegate, *Bach in Berlin: Nation and Culture in Mendelssohn's Revival of the* St Matthew Passion (Ithaca, NY: Cornell University Press, 2005).

68 At the same time, Hans Georg Nägeli in Switzerland embarked on a similar process of musical improvement and historical revival, founding in 1805 the Zürich *Singinstitut*, publishing music for choral performance, and encouraging festival oratorio performances on the scale of the English ones.

69 Karen Ahlquist, "Men and Women of the Chorus: Music, Governance, and Social Models in Nineteenth-Century German-Speaking Europe," in *Chorus and Community*, ed. Karen Ahlquist (Urbana and Chicago: University of Illinois Press, 2006), 265–93.

70 Dieter Düding, "Nationale Oppositionsfeste der Turner, Sänger und Schützen im 19. Jahrhundert," in *Öffentliche Festkultur: Politische Feste in Deutschland von der Aufklärung bis zum Ersten Weltkrieg*, ed. Dieter Düding, Peter Friedemann, and Paul Münch (Reinbek bei Hamburg: Rowolt, 1988), 166–90.

71 Josef Eckhardt, "Arbeiterchöre und der 'Deutsche Arbeiter-Sängerbund'" in *Musik und Industrie: Beiträge zur Entwicklung der Werkchöre und Werksorchester*, ed. Monica Steegmann (Regensburg: Bosse Verlag, 1978), 45–106.

72 Jessica Gienow Hecht cites a representative of the Prussian cultural ministry in the early twentieth century, who claimed that the Germans had built their unity out of songs (and gymnastics); Gienow-Hecht, *Sound Diplomacy: Music and Emotions in German-American Relations, 1850–1920* (Chicago: University of Chicago Press, 2009), 34n102.

73 Quoted in Porter, *Rhine as Musical Metaphor*, 129.

74 William McNeill, *Keeping Together in Time: Dance and Drill in Human History* (Cambridge, MA: Harvard University Press, 2009), viii, 151–8. A different kind of demonstration of this phenomenon is Louise Erdrich's novel about German immigrants in a small town in South Dakota, *The Master Butchers Singing Club* (New York: Harper Collins, 2003).

75 Carl Friedrich Zelter, *Selbstdarstellung*, ed. Willi Reich (Zurich: Manesse Verlag, 1955), 71–2.

76 Erich Valentin, "Chor und Hausmusik," *Jahrbuch des deutschen Sängerbund* (1961): 80.

77 See Annette Friedrich, *Beiträge zur Geschichte des weltlichen Frauenchores im 19. Jahrhundert in Deutschland* (Regensburg: Bosse Verlag, 1961), 7–9.

78 See, for instance, the *Jahresbericht des Münchener akademischen Gesangvereines: XXVI. und XXVII. Vereins-Semester, November 1873 bis Oktober 1874* (Munich, 1874).

79 John Blacking, *How Musical Is Man* (Seattle, 1974), 107.

80 Carl Maria von Weber, "Fragments of a *Tonkünsters Leben*," in *Writings on Music*, ed. John Warrack, trans. Martin Cooper (Cambridge: Cambridge University Press, 1981), 318–19.

4. Music at the Fairs

1 This chapter is a lightly revised version of an essay first published as "Music at the Fairs: A Paradigm of Internationalism?" in *Crosscurrents: American and European Music in Interaction, 1900–2000 (Crosscurrents: Wechselwirkungen zwischen amerikanischer und europäischer Musik, 1900–2000)*, ed. Felix Meyer, Carol Oja, Wolfgang Rathert, and Anne Schreffler (Woodbridge, UK, 2013). Reprinted with permission of Boydell & Brewer Publishers.

2 "Music Supply Beats Demand," *San Francisco Examiner*, 24 April 1915, 7.

3 Wolfram Kaiser, "The 'Great Derby Race' Strategies of Cultural Representation at Nineteenth Century World Exhibitions," in *Culture and International History*, ed. Jessica Gienow-Hecht and Frank Schumacher (New York: Berghahn Books, 2003), 45–59.

4 Thomas Fleming, *Around the "Pan" with Uncle Hank* (New York: Nutshell, 1901), 24–6. https://archive.org/details/aroundpanwithunc00flemiala.

5 Annegret Fauser, *Musical Encounters at the 1889 Paris World's Fair* (Rochester, NY: University of Rochester Press, 2005).

6 Percy Allen Scholes, *The Mirror of Music, 1844–1944: A Century of Musical Life in Britain* (London: Novello, 1947), 35; see also Michael Musgrave, *The Musical Life of the Crystal Palace* (Cambridge: Cambridge University Press, 1995).

7 Fauser, *Musical Encounters*, 2.

8 For an overview of the fair see Mark Goldman, *High Hopes: The Rise and Decline of Buffalo, New York* (Albany: SUNY Press, 1983), 3–20. Web resources on the Pan-American exhibition are extensive. For an overview see http://www.buffaloah.com/h/panam/links.html, accessed 19 July 2016; for the most complete collection of musical images and contemporary articles see http://library.buffalo.edu/pan-am/exposition/music/, accessed 19 July 2016.

9 Craig R. Whitney, *All the Stops: The Glorious Pipe Organ and Its American Masters* (New York: Public Affairs, 2003), 22–4.

10 "Violent Storm Visits Buffalo in the Night," *Buffalo Evening News*, 6 July 1901. And, of course, after the assassination at the Temple of Music in September 1901 tourists flocked in even greater numbers to the site, protests were launched, in vain, against the planned demolition of the building, and so on.

11 Ben Macomber, *The Jewel City: Its Planning and Achievement; its Architecture, Sculpture, Symbolism, and Music; its Gardens, Palaces, and Exhibits* (San Francisco: John H. William, 1915), 150–7; and Frank Morton Todd, *The Story of the Exposition, being the official history of the international celebration held at San Francisco in 1915 to commemorate the discovery of the Pacific Ocean and the construction of the Panama Canal*, 5 vols (New York: G.P. Putnam's Sons, 1921), 2: 56–9

12 As he explained, "The public [will] not have any patience with efforts to educate it musically, and it [will] not derive any benefit from what it [does] not enjoy. The general music plan should have as its core a complete orchestra of about 80 players, around which [can] be built a scheme that would include something for everybody"; "Report of the Department of Music to the President of the Panama-Pacific International Exposition," Daniel E. Coshland San Francisco History Center, San Francisco Public Library.

13 Todd, *Story of the Exposition,* 2: 56.

14 Ibid., 2: 56–7.

15 Programs of the Boston Symphony Orchestra at the Panama-Pacific Exposition, Panama Pacific International Exposition Records, Bancroft Library, University of California, Berkeley, BANC MSS C-A 190 (hereafter PPIE Records), Carton 82, folder 6.

16 1 August 1915 was a day dedicated to the music of American composers, and in photographs of the event one can see them, looking slightly sheepish and seated in front of the Festival Hall. That it required a special day to celebrate American music testified, of course, to its marginal status.

17 Louis Moreau Gottschalk, *Notes of a Pianist* (Philadelphia: J.B Lippincott, 1881), 127.

18 Cited in Jessica Gienow-Hecht, *Sound Diplomacy: Music and Emotions in Transatlantic Relations, 1850–1920* (Chicago: University of Chicago Press, 2009), 164. See also Frank Trommler and Elliott Shore, eds, *German-American Encounters: Conflict and Cooperation between Two Cultures, 1800–2000* (New York: Berghahn Books, 2000).

19 Cited in Gienow-Hecht, *Sound Diplomacy,* 164–5.

20 On Beach see Arlene Block, *Amy Beach: Passionate Victorian* (Oxford: Oxford University Press, 1998), 197ff. After safely returning to the United States, Stewart signed a collective letter to President Woodrow Wilson, pleading the case for international understanding: "We the undersigned, returning from Germany, wish to combat the widespread opinion that Americans have been accorded ill treatment in Germany ... We have no desire to discuss the causes leading to the present European war. We wish only to state that from the beginning of the war we who have been in Germany during July, August, and a part of September have been accorded every courtesy and every care." "Open Letter to the President of the United States, from 787 Citizens of the United States from 36 States," undated, PPIE Records, Carton 135, folder 31.

21 Benjamin Wheeler to Theodor Lewald, 7 August 1912, PPIE Records, Carton 135, folder 28.

22 Ibid.

23 "Report of the Department of Music."

24 Rollin Smith, *Saint-Saëns and the Organ* (Stuyvesant, NY: Pendragon Press, 1992), 170.

25 Perhaps a better term than declassing might be democratization, but I am reluctant to use it because it hints at an absolute contradiction between democracy and hierarchy, which might be true in some purely philosophical sense but is less useful in trying to understand the mixing and messiness of cultural life, especially in the United States.

26 Tim Blanning, *The Triumph of Music: The Rise of Composers, Musicians, and Their Art* (Cambridge, MA: Harvard University Press, 2008).

27 Barbara Owen, "Technology and the Organ in the Nineteenth Century," in *The Organ as a Mirror of Its Time*, ed. Kerala Snyder (Oxford: Oxford University Press, 2002), 218–22.

28 For J.P. Sousa's views on the compatibility of cultural standards with consumer culture, see his autobiography: "If you look over the field of musicians, conductors and composers you cannot fail to be struck with the fact that those who are most famous, most popular with the people, and whose reputation has passed the frontiers of their respective countries are precisely those who have been … compelled to put forward the best that was in them by the beneficent law of the survival of the fittest, which has forced them to be ever upon the alert to conquer competition"; *Marching Along: Recollections of Men, Women, and Music* (Boston: Hale, Cushman & Flint, 1928), 189. Likewise, Victor Herbert expressed the view that "there is only one kind of music. There is good music … False notions regarding good music are fostered by three classes: poor interpreters who fail to bring out the beauty of good music; conductors who are pendants before they are musicians, and ragtime performers who discourage the belief that there is good music which everybody can comprehend"; quoted in Edward N. Waters, *Victor Herbert: A Life in Music* (New York: Macmillan, 1955), 345.

29 "Public of Today Wants Good Music: Greatest Melodies Have Simplest Tonal Form," *Los Angeles Times*, 19 May 1917.

30 Fairbanks to James Buchanan, 23 April 1915, reprinted in the *History of the Panama-Pacific International Exposition, comprising the History of the Panama Canal and a full account of the world's greatest exposition embracing the participation of the states and nations of the world and other events at San Francisco, 1915*, ed. and comp. James A. Buchanan (San Francisco: Pan-Pacific Press Association, 1917), 8.

31 Fritz Kreisler, *Four Weeks in the Trenches: The War Story of a Violinist* (Boston and New York: Houghton Mifflin, 1915).

32 Ibid., 86.

5. Mendelssohn on the Road

1 The Frankfurt legalities are described in R. Larry Todd, *Mendelssohn: A Life in Music* (Oxford: Oxford University Press, 2003), 347. This chapter is a revised and shortened version of an essay first published as "Mendelssohn on the Road: Music, Travel, and the Anglo-German Symbiosis" in *Oxford Handbook on the New Cultural History of Music*, ed. Jane Fulcher (New York:

Oxford University Press, 2011), 228–44. It is reprinted with the permission of Oxford University Press.

2 See chapter 3 in this volume, "Musical Itinerancy in a World of Nations" for more developed reflections on the "travelling culture" of music.

3 James Clifford, *Routes: Travel and Translation in the Late Twentieth Century* (Cambridge, MA: Harvard University Press, 1997), 2–3.

4 Akira Iriye, *Cultural Internationalism and World Order* (Baltimore: Johns Hopkins University Press, 1997).

5 Charlotte Moscheles, ed., *Recent Music and Musicians, as Described in the Diaries and Correspondence of Ignatz Moscheles,* trans. A.D. Coleridge (New York: Holt, 1873), 26–7.

6 Quoted in Emil F. Smidak, *Isaak-Ignaz Moscheles: The Life of the Composer and His Encounters with Beethoven, Liszt, Chopin, and Mendelssohn* (Aldershot, UK: Scolar, 1989), 68–9. The Rainer Family Singers are now credited with having made "Silent Night" popular throughout Europe, especially in England.

7 See Jonathan Bellman, *The Exotic in Western Music* (Boston: Northeastern University Press, 1998); and Ralph Locke, *Musical Exoticism: Images and Reflections* (New York: Cambridge University Press, 2009).

8 Letter, Mendelssohn to his family in Berlin, Llangollen, 25 August 1929, in *Felix Mendelssohn Bartholdy: Sämtliche Briefe,* ed. Juliette Appold and Regina Back (Kassel: Bärenreiter, 2008), 1: 380–1.

9 Todd, *Mendelssohn,* xx.

10 The classic account is Paul M. Kennedy, *The Rise of the Anglo-German Antagonism, 1860–1914* (Boston: Allen & Unwin, 1980).

11 Johann Mattheson, "Vom Unterschied der heutigen Italiänischen / Frantzösischen / Englischen und Teutschen Music," in *Das neu-eröffnete Orchestre* (Hamburg: Schiller 1713), 211, 219–20. http://reader.digitale-sammlungen.de/en/fs1/object/display/bsb10599040_00001.html, accessed 19 July 2016.

12 Panikos Panayi, *German Immigrants in Britain during the 19th Century, 1815–1914* (Oxford: Berg, 1995), 126–7.

13 Carl Dahlhaus, *Nineteenth Century Music,* trans. Bradford Robinson (Berkeley: University of California Press, 1991), 247.

14 Schumann, opening statement of the *Neue Zeitschrift für Musik,* 2 January 1835, 1.

15 G.W. Fink, "Mendelssohns Paulus," *Allgemeine musikalische Zeitung* 39 (March 1837): 209.

16 For the political and intellectual manifestations of this reformist view, see John Edward Toews, *Becoming Historical: Cultural Reformation and Public Memory in Early Nineteenth-century Berlin* (New York: Cambridge University Press, 2004).

17 Quoted in Todd, *Mendelssohn,* 337.

18 Simon McVeigh, "A Free Trade in Music: London during the Long 19th Century in a European Perspective," *Journal of Modern European History* 5, no. 1 (2007): 71.

19 Quoted in Emily Auerbach, "John Bull and His 'Land ohne Musik,'" *Victorian Literature and Culture* 21 (1993): 69.

20 Simon McVeigh, "The Society of British Musicians (1834–1865) and the Campaign for Native Talent," in *Music and British Culture, 1785–1914: Essays in Honour of Cyril Ehrlich,* ed. Christina Bashford and Leanne Langley (New York: Oxford University Press, 2000).

21 H. Davey, "Discoveries in English Musical History," *New Quarterly Musical Review* 3, no. 9 (May 1895): 35.

22 Karl Geiringer, *Haydn: A Creative Life in Music* (New York: W.W. Norton, 1946), 318. See also a surprisingly similar account in Richard Taruskin, *The Oxford History of Western Music,* 6 vols (New York and Oxford: Oxford University Press, 2005), 2: 555–9. In 1938 Geiringer had fled Vienna, where he was curator of the library and the archives of the Gesellschaft der Musikfreunde. Although a Roman Catholic himself, both his parents had been Jewish. His own desire to see Haydn and indeed all of the great Viennese composers whose papers he had curated and whose biographies he wrote speak for the German nation rather than the Germans who had forced him to flee seems palpable in these observations.

23 Quoted in Nicholas Temperley, *Haydn: The Creation* (New York: Cambridge University Press, 1991), 21.

24 Zelter, review of the published full score, *Allgemeine musikalische Zeitung* 4 (1801–2), excerpted and translated by Nicholas Temperley in the appendix to his *Haydn,* 92. Zelter clearly regarded this as an opportunity also to pontificate a bit in his self-appointed role as guardian of the Bach legacy: "Eager young composers may have noticed that all the fugal choruses are light, supple, and free and that in all this great work there is not a single strict fugue," wrote Zelter, but "let them be warned that such ease and freedom are possible only for someone who knows how to write a strict fugue with all its trappings."

25 Percy A. Scholes, *The Mirror of Music, 1844–1944: A Century of Musical Life in Britain as Reflected in the Pages of the* Musical Times (London: Novello, 1947), 2: 642. See also the complete program of the Boston Peace Jubilee by Patrick Sarsfield Gilmore, *History of the National peace jubilee and great musical festival: Held in the city of Boston, June, 1869, to commemorate the restoration of peace throughout the land* (Boston: Lee & Shepard, 1871), 432–42.

26 Todd, *Mendelssohn,* 548.

27 Weber, *Rise of Musical Classics,* 127–41.
28 K.A. Appiah, "Against National Culture," in *Text and Nation: Cross-disciplinary Essays on Cultural and National Identities,* ed. L. Garcia-Morena and P.C. Pfeiffer (Columbia, SC.: Camden House, 1996), 175–6.

6. A.B. Marx's Cosmopolitan Nationalism

1 This chapter is an expanded and lightly revised version of an article that appeared as "The Internationalism of Nationalism: Adolf Bernhard Marx and German Music in the Mid-nineteenth Century," *Journal of Modern European History,* Special Issue, "Demarcation and Exchange: 'National Music' in 19th Century Europe," ed. Sven Oliver Müller, 5, no. 1 (2007): 139–59. It is reprinted with permission of C.H. Beck Verlag, publishers of the *Journal of Modern European History.*
2 Richard Taruskin, Commentary, "Roundtable on European Nations, Musical Nationalisms, and the Writing of Music Histories," Annual Meeting of the American Musicological Society, Los Angeles, 2–4 November, 2006.
3 Richard Taruskin, "Nationalism," *Grove Music Online. Oxford Music Online* (Oxford University Press), http://www.oxfordmusiconline.com.proxy.library.vanderbilt.edu/subscriber/article/grove/music/50846, accessed 19 July 2016.
4 Benedict Anderson, *Imagined Communities: Reflections on the Origin and Spread of Nationalism,* 2nd rev. ed. (New York: Verso, 1991), 46.
5 Edith Wharton, *The Age of Innocence* (1920; New York: Penguin, 1996), 3–4.
6 An exemplary work is Dana Gooley, *Virtuoso Liszt* (Cambridge: Cambridge University Press, 2004), the first sentence of which reads "Virtuosity is about shifting borders."
7 One review, in *Music and Letters,* of Peter Rummenhöller's *Musiktheoretisches Denken im 19. Jahrhundert,* characterizes Marx as one of a group of nineteenth-century "reactionaries," whose "antiquated systems" are of "total irrelevance" to contemporary music theory and pedagogy – a more extreme view than most, to be sure, but not untypical; H.F.R., untitled review, *Music and Letters* 49, no. 2 (1968): 189–90. Recently, scholars have found more to admire in Marx. See, for instance, the work of Michael Spitzer, especially "Marx's *Lehre* and the Science of Education: Towards the Redemption of Marx's Pedagogy," *Music and Letters* 79, no. 4 (1998): 489–526; and "Convergences: Criticism, Analysis and Beethoven Reception," *Music Analysis* 16, no. 3 (1997): 369–91; and of Scott Burnham, ed. and trans., *Musical Form in the Age of Beethoven: Selected Writings on Theory and Method by*

A.B. Marx (Cambridge: Cambridge University Press, 1997), and *Beethoven Hero* (Princeton: Princeton University Press, 1995).

8 "die Stimme für die Seele Europa's zu verlieren und zu einer blossen Vaterländerei herabzusinken"; Friedrich Nietzsche, *Jenseits von Gut und Böse*, Project Gutenberg, http://www.gutenberg.org/ebooks/7204, accessed 19 July 2016.

9 Carl Dahlhaus, *Nineteenth-Century Music*, trans. J. Bradford Robinson (Berkeley: University of California Press, 1989), 37.

10 Carl Dahlhaus, "Nationalism and Music," in *Between Romanticism and Modernism*, trans. Mary Whittall (Berkeley: University of California Press, 1980), 80–1.

11 Prasenjit Duara, *Rescuing History from the Nation: Questioning Narratives of Modern China* (Chicago: University of Chicago Press, 1995), 65–6.

12 Brian Vick, *Defining Germany: The 1848 Frankfurt Parliamentarians and National Identity* (Cambridge, MA: Harvard University Press, 2002), 173, 188.

13 Marx later wrote, "How would it have been possible to realize my plans, ever more turning in an artistic and scholarly direction, in Stralsund or any other such provincial city, without university, without library, without opera!" Adolf Bernhard Marx, *Erinnerungen, aus meinem Leben*, 2 vols (Berlin: Otto Janke Verlag, 1865), 2: 19.

14 On cultural and political nationalism, see Vick, *Defining Germany*, 16–17.

15 On several of these issues, see Arno Forchert, "Adolf Bernhard Marx und seine Berliner allgemeine musikalische Zeitung," in *Studien zur Musikgeschichte Berlins im frühen 19. Jahrhundert*, ed. Carl Dahlhaus (Regensburg: Bosse Verlag, 1980), 381–404. On Marx's championing of Beethoven, his prime example of an underappreciated contemporary composer, see Robin Wallace, *Beethoven's Critics: Aesthetic Dilemmas and Resolutions during the Composer's Lifetime* (Cambridge: Cambridge University Press, 1986), 45–64; and Sanna Pederson, "A.B. Marx, Berlin Concert Life, and German National Identity," *19th Century Music* 18, no. 2 (Fall 1994): 87–104. English translations of Marx's Beethoven articles may be found in *The Critical Reception of Beethoven's Compositions*, ed. Wayne M. Senner, Robin Wallace, and William Meredith (Lincoln, NE: University of Nebraska Press, 1999), 59–77, 90–5, 111–12.

16 On the philosophical origins of this dichotomy see Bernd Sponheuer, *Musik als Kunst und Nicht-Kunst: Untersuchungen zur Dichotomie von 'hoher' und 'niederer' Musik im musikästhetischen Denken zwischen Kant und Hanslick* (Kassel: Bärenreiter Verlag, 1987). For a deeply researched, socio-economic explanation of it, see Axel Beer, *Musik Zwischen Komponist, Verlag und*

Publikum: Die Rahmenbedingungen des Musikschaffens in Deutschland im ersten Drittel des 19. Jahrhunderts (Tutzing: Hans Schneider Verlag, 2000).

17 Marx, *Erinnerungen*, 1: 82.

18 Ibid., 2: 56–9.

19 Jürgen Habermas, *The Structural Transformation of the Public Sphere*, trans. Thomas Burger with Frederick Lawrence (Cambridge, MA: MIT Press, 1981), 33.

20 James Brophy, "The Public Sphere," in *Germany, 1800–1870*, ed. Jonathan Sperber (Oxford: Oxford University Press, 2004), 185.

21 Marx, *Erinnerungen*, 2: 56; Marx, "Abschied des Redakteurs," *Berliner Allgemeine Musikalische Zeitung* (hereafter *BAMZ*) 7, no. 52 (24 December 1830): 414–16.

22 Vick, *Defining Germany*, 40.

23 See note 21, above.

24 See, for instance, Spitzer, "Marx's 'Lehre' and the Science of Education," 489–526.

25 A.B. Marx, *Die Musik des neunzehnten Jahrhunderts und ihre Pflege* (Leipzig: Breitkopf & Härtel, 1873), 12, 16.

26 A.B. Marx, *Anleitung zum Vortrag Beethovenscher Klavierwerke* (Berlin: Otto Janke Verlag, 1863), 3–4.

27 Wallace, *Beethoven's Critics*, 51–2.

28 Marx compared the Kantian era of the Leipzig *Allgemeine Musikalische Zeitung* and "new period" of his journal, which he described in a torrent of Hegelian concepts: "coming into being," "development and further development," "concatenation of emergence and consciousness," and so on. See his "Andeutung des Standpunktes der Zeitung," *BAMZ* 2, no. 52 (28 December 1825): 421.

29 Ibid.; Marx, *BAMZ* 2, no. 45 (9 November 1825): 358; *BAMZ* 2, no. 51 (21 December 1925): 407; *BAMZ* 5, no. 1 (2 January 1828): 1.

30 Marx, *BAMZ* 2, no. 52 (28 December 1825): 421; *BAMZ* 2, no. 35 (24 August 1825): 281.

31 Marx, *BAMZ* 3, no. 47 (22 November 1826): 384.

32 Marx, "Wer is zu der Theilnahme an der Zeitung berufen?" *BAMZ* 4, no. 1 (3 January 1827): 2–3.

33 Marx, *Musik des neunzehnten Jahrhunderts*, 38, 41.

34 Ibid., 41; Marx, "Wer ist zu der Theilnahme an der Zeitung berufen?" *BAMZ* 4, no. 1 (3 January 1827): 2–3

35 Ibid.

36 Vick, *Defining Germany*, 40.

37 Marx, *Musik des neunzehnten Jahrhunderts*, 23.

38 For a full account of the role of Marx in Mendelssohn's famous revival, see my *Bach in Berlin: Nation and Culture in Mendelssohn's Revival of the St Matthew Passion* (Ithaca, NY: Cornell University Press, 2005).
39 Marx, "Hoechst wichtige und glückliche Nachricht," *BAMZ* 5, no. 17 (23 April 1828): 131–2. See Applegate, *Bach in Berlin*, esp. 80–124.
40 Marx, *BAMZ* V, 13 (26 March 1828): 97; *BAMZ* 4, no. 52 (26 December 1827): 424.
41 Marx, *Erinnerungen*, 1: 86.
42 Marx, "Bekanntmachung," *BAMZ* 6, no. 9 (28 February 1829): 65.
43 Marx, "Zweiter Bericht über die Passionsmusik," *BAMZ* 6, no. 11 (14 March 1829): 80–1.
44 Marx, "Hoechst wichtige und glückliche Nachricht," *BAMZ* 5, no. 17 (23 April 1828): 131–2.
45 Marx, "Blick ins Ausland," *BAMZ* 6, no. 11 (14 March 1829): 86;"Vierter Bericht über die Passionsmusik," *BAMZ* 6, no. 13 (28 March 1829): 100.
46 B. [anon.], "Grosse Passion von Johann Sebastian Bach," *BAMZ* 6, no. 12 (21 March 1829): 93.
47 See for instance, Marx, *Erinnerungen*, 2: 1–17.
48 Vick, *Defining Germany*, 176.
49 Marx, *Erinnerungen*, 1: 82.
50 Wallace, *Beethoven's Critics*, 45, 50. See also Elisabeth Eleonore Bauer, *Wie Beethoven auf den Sockel Kam: Die Entstehung eines musikalischen Mythos* (Stuttgart: J.B. Metzler Verlag, 1992); Sanna Pederson, "A.B. Marx, Berlin Concert Life, and German National Identity," *19th Century Music* 18 (1994): 87–107.
51 Marx, *BAMZ* 2, no. 12 (14 March 1825): 95.
52 Pederson argues that Marx's advocacy of Beethoven's symphonies reflected a "strategy" to "delimit the symphony by positioning its 'other,' foreign opera, and by establishing this other's undesirable nature"; "A.B. Marx, Berlin Concert Life," 89; see also chapter 1, above.
53 Marx,"Ueber die Musik bei Schauspielaufführungen: ein Vorschlag zu Gunsten der Bühnen-Orchester," *BAMZ* 2, no. 42 (19 October 1825): 333.
54 Marx, *BAMZ* 3, no. 52 (27 December 1826): 421.
55 This excerpt, from an 1854 translation of one of Marx's pedagogical works, was also reprinted in Novello's *Musical Times* in 1855 (see discussion below, pp. 151–2). A.B. Marx, *General Musical Instruction: An Aid to Teachers and Learners in Every Branch of Musical Knowledge*, trans. George Macirone (1854; repr. Cambridge and New York: Cambridge University Press, 2012), 106.
56 Marx, *BAMZ* 3, no. 45 (8 November 1826): 357–9.
57 Marx, *Musik des neunzehnten Jahrhunderts*, 27.

58 Ibid., 6–7.
59 Marx, *Erinnerungen,* 2: 67. See also Andreas Mayer, "'Gluck'sches Gestöhn' und 'welsches Larifari': Anna Mildern, Franz Schubert und der deutsch-italienische Opernkrieg," *Archiv für Musikwissenschaft* 7, no. 3 (1995): 171–218.
60 Marx, *Musik des neunzehnten Jahrhunderts,* 27, 64–7.
61 Marx, *BAMZ* 2, no. 35 (24 August 1825): 283; Marx, *Musik des neunzehnten Jahrhunderts,* 9.
62 Marx, *BAMZ* 2, 3 (19 January 1825): 23 (translation my own). Cited also in Pederson, "A.B. Marx, Berlin Concert Life," 91.
63 Marx, *BAMZ* 1 12 (15 March 1824): 108.
64 Marx, *BAMZ* 2, 3 (19 January 1825): 23.
65 Marx, *BAMZ* 3, no. 45 (8 November 1826): 358.
66 Bernd Sponheuer, "Reconstructing Ideal Types," in *Music and German National Identity,* ed. Celia Applegate and Pamela Potter (Chicago: University of Chicago Press, 2002), 36–58.
67 Marx, *BAMZ* 2, no. 21 (25 May 1825): 168.
68 Marx, *Musik des neunzehnten Jahrhunderts,* 38.
69 See Bernarr Rainbow, *The Land without Music: Musical Education in England, 1800-1860, and Its Continental Antecedents* (London: Novello, 1967), esp. 57, 111–68.
70 A.B. Marx, *The Music of the Nineteenth Century and Its Culture,* trans. C. Natalia Macfarren (London: Robert Cocks, 1854), 11.
71 On Novello's career, see Victoria L. Cooper, *The House of Novello: Practice and Policy of a Victorian Music Publisher, 1829–1866* (Aldershot, UK: Ashgate, 2003).
72 Novello's prospectus for his new version of Mainzer's periodical is cited in Imogen Fellinger, et al., "Periodicals, II, 5: Europe," *Grove Music Online, Oxford Music Online,* http://www.oxfordmusiconline.com.proxy.library.vanderbilt.edu/subscriber/article/grove/music/21338pg2, accessed 19 July 2016.
73 Alfred Novello, *The Musical Times and Singing Class Circular* 6 (15 January 1855): 154.
74 A.B. Marx, "Objects of Musical Education and Their Time," *Musical Times* 7 (1 July 1855): 59–60; 7 (15 July 1855): 75–6; 7 (1 August 1855): 86.
75 Marx, *General Musical Instruction,* 114–15.
76 Marx, *Musik des neunzehnten Jahrhunderts,* Foreword.
77 Marx, *Erinnerungen,* 1: 162–3.
78 Marx, *Musik des neunzehnten Jahrhunderts,* 79.
79 See chapter 5, above, for an explanation of this term; K.A. Appiah, "Against National Culture," in *Text and Nation: Cross-disciplinary Essays on Cultural and*

National Identities, ed. L. Garcia-Morena and P.C. Pfeiffer (Columbia, SC.: Camden House, 1996), 175–6.

7. Schumann's German Nation

1 This chapter is a revised and expanded version of an essay that appeared as "Robert Schumann and the Culture of German Nationhood," in *Rethinking Schumann,* ed. Roe-Min Kok and Laura Tunbridge (Oxford, 2010), 3–14. It is reprinted with permission of Oxford University Press.

2 The complete passage concerning Schumann reads: "Mit seinem Geschmack, der im Grunde ein kleiner Geschmack war, (nämlich ein gefährlicher, unter Deutschen doppelt gefährlicher Hang zur stillen Lyrik und Trunkenboldigkeit des Gefühls) … dieser Schumann war bereits nur noch ein deutsches Ereigniss in der Musik, kein europäisches mehr, wie Beethoven es war, wie, in noch umfänglicherem Maasse, Mozart es gewesen ist – mit ihm drohte der deutschen Musik ihre grösste Gefahr, die Stimme für die Seele Europa's zu verlieren und zu einer blossen Vaterländerei herabzusinken"; Friedrich Nietzsche, *Jenseits von Gut und Böse,* paragraphs 244, 245: Project Gutenberg, http://www.gutenberg.org/ebooks/7204, accessed 20 July 2016. For the translation used here see Friedrich Nietzsche, *Beyond Good and Evil: Prelude to a Philosophy of the Future,* ed. and trans. R.J. Hollingdale (Harmondsworth, UK: Penguin, 1973), 158–9.

3 Ute Bär, ed., *Robert Schumann und die Französische Romantik: Bericht über das 5. Internationale Schumann-Symposium der Robert-Schumann-Gesellschaft am 9. und 10. July 1994 in Düsseldorf,* Schumann Forschungen, Vol. 6 (Mainz: Schott, 1997).

4 Richard Wagner, "Judaism in Music," in *Judaism in Music and Other Essays,* trans. William Ashton Ellis (Lincoln: University of Nebraska Press, 1995), 117.

5 Prasenjit Duara, *Rescuing History from the Nation: Questioning Narratives of Modern China* (Chicago: University of Chicago Press, 1995), 65–6.

6 K.A. Appiah, "Against National Culture," in *Text and Nation: Cross-Disciplinary Essays on Cultural and National Identities,* ed. Laura Garcia-Morena and Peter C. Pfeiffer (Columbia, SC: Camden House, 1996), 175–6.

7 Immanuel Kant, "Perpetual Peace," in *Kant: Political Writings,* Cambridge Texts in the History of Political Thought, ed. H.R. Reiss, trans. H.B. Nisbet (Cambridge: Cambridge University Press, 1991), 106.

8 This association was less intense after he gave up the editorship of the *Neue Zeitschrift für Musik,* but he still remained a musician committed to music's place in literary culture. This aspect of Schumann is essential to John Daverio's interpretation of his compositional output as a whole: he was

"perhaps the first in western musical history to view the art of composition as a kind of literary activity"; Daverio, *Schumann: Herald of a New Poetic Age* (Oxford: Oxford University Press, 1997), vii.

9 Leon Plantinga, *Schumann as Critic* (New Haven: Yale University Press, 1967), 48.

10 Quoted in Ronald Taylor, *Robert Schumann: His Life and Work* (New York: Universe, 1982), 267.

11 Brian Vick, *Defining Germany: The 1848 Frankfurt Parliamentarians and National Identity* (Cambridge, MA: Harvard University Press, 2002), 22.

12 Quoted in Taylor, *Schumann.* 267.

13 Plantinga, *Schumann as Critic,* 24.

14 Jürgen Habermas, *The Structural Transformation of the Public Sphere: An Inquiry into a Category of Bourgeois Society,* trans. Thomas Burger (Cambridge, MA: MIT Press, 1989), 9.

15 Quoted in Plantinga, *Schumann as Critic,* 14.

16 Robert Schumann, *On Music and Musicians,* repr. ed. (Berkeley: University of California Press, 1983), 194.

17 As quoted in Daverio, *Schumann,* 197.

18 The difficulty in assessing Schumann's attitudes towards Jews stems from the paucity of what he wrote about them and from the ambivalence the National Socialist cultural authorities showed towards him. On the one hand, Nazi authorities deemed him "hardly heroic," as Lily Hirsch has written in a revelatory article on the subject, too hostile to Wagner and too admiring of Mendelssohn and Brahms. On the other hand, various Nazi musicologists went to great efforts to make the case for him as sympathetic to the Nazi world view and secretly antagonistic to Mendelssohn. See Lily E. Hirsch, "Segregating Sound: Robert Schumann in the Third Reich," in *Rethinking Schumann,* ed. Roe-Min Kok and Laura Tunbridge (Oxford: Oxford University Press, 2011), 51–66.

19 Vick, *Defining Germany,* 40.

20 Ibid., 39.

21 Kant, "What Is Enlightenment?" in *Political Writings,* 54–60.

22 Vick, *Defining Germany,* 39.

23 Plantinga, *Schumann as Critic,* 23.

24 Schumann, *On Music and Musicians,* 130.

25 Quoted in Susanna Grossmann-Vendrey, *Felix Mendelssohn Bartholdy und die Musik der Vergangenheit* (Regensburg, 1969), 151; Schumann to Wilhelm Götte, 2 October 1828, in Robert Schumann, *Jugendbriefe,* 2nd ed. (Leipzig, 1886), 37–8.

26 Joseph [Giuseppe] Mazzini, *An Essay on the Duties of Man Addressed to Workingmen* (New York: Funk and Wagnalls, 1898), 59–60.

27 Schumann, *Music and Musicians,* 196.
28 Felix Mendelssohn to Karl Klingemann, 10 December 1831, in *Letters,* ed. G. Selden-Goth (London: Paul Elek, 1946), 184.
29 Schumann, *Music and Musicians,* 193.
30 Theodor Uhlig, "Zeitgemässe Betrachtungen," *Neue Zeitschrift für Musik* 33 (23 April 1850): 168.
31 Schumann to Liszt, 31 May 1849, in *Schumanns Briefe: Eine Auswahl,* ed. Karl Storck (Elberfeld: Greiner und Pfeiffer, 1905), 188–9.
32 Schumann to D.G. Otten, 2 April 1849, in *Robert Schumanns Briefe: Neue Folge,* ed. F. Gustav Jansen (Leipzig: Breitkopf & Härtel, 1886), 254–5.

8. The Musical Worlds of Brahms's Hamburg

1 This chapter is an expanded and revised version of an essay that first appeared as "Of Sailors' Bars and Women's Choirs: The Musical Worlds of Brahms' Hamburg" in *Patriotism, Cosmopolitanism, and National Culture: Public Culture in Hamburg, 1700–2000,* ed. Peter Uwe Hohendahl (New York and Amsterdam: Rodopi Press, 2003), 181–92. It is reprinted here with permission of the Rodopi Press.
2 Jan Swafford, "Did the Young Brahms Play Piano in Waterfront Bars?" *19th Century Music* 24 (Spring 2001): 268–75; Styra Avins, "The Young Brahms: Biographical Data Re-examined," *19th Century Music* 24 (Spring 2001): 276–89.
3 See Kurt Hofmann, *Johannes Brahms und Hamburg: Neue Erkenntnisse zu einem alten Thema* (Hamburg, 1986).
4 Richard Evans, *Death in Hamburg: Society and Politics in the Cholera Years, 1830–1910* (Oxford: Clarendon Press, 1987), 36–7.
5 Quoted in Gisela Jaacks, *Hamburg zu Lust und Nutz: Bürgerliches Musikverständnis zwischen Barock und Aufklärung, 1660–1760* (Hamburg: Verein für Hamburgische Geschichte, 1997), 25–6.
6 *Allgemeine musikalische Zeitung* 1 (17 October 1798): 46.
7 *Musikalische Correspondenz* (Speyer), 7 (1791), 13 (1792).
8 "Hamburg," *New Grove Dictionary of Music and Musicians,* ed. Stanley Sadie, 12 vols (London and New York: Oxford University Press, 1980), 8: 66–7.
9 Jan Swafford, *Johannes Brahms: A Biography* (New York: Vintage Books, 1997), 189–90, 194.
10 This is not to say that the eighteenth century did not have its own distinctive form of non-aristocratic musical life, but lively and widespread though "musical understanding" was among the middle classes, the institutions of a sustained musical culture – regular concerts, voluntary associations,

professional organizations, musical journalism, and so on – existed more sporadically or not at all. See Jaacks, *Hamburg zu Lust und Nutz.*

11 David Gramit, *Cultivating Music: The Aspirations, Interests, and Limits of German Musical Culture, 1770–1848* (Berkeley: University of California Press, 2002); Michael P. Steinberg, *Listening to Reason: Culture, Subjectivity, and Nineteenth-Century Music* (Princeton: Princeton University Press, 2006).

12 See Celia Applegate, *Bach in Berlin: Nation and Culture in Mendelssohn's Revival of the* St Matthew Passion (Ithaca, NY: Cornell University Press, 2010).

13 Josef Sittard, *Geschichte des Musik- und Concertwesens in Hamburg vom 14. Jahrhundert bis auf die Gegenwart* (Altona: A.C. Reher Verlag, 1890), 2, 93–4.

14 Bryan Wilson, *Religion in a Secular Society* (London: C.A. Watts, 1966), xiv; Lucien Hölscher, "Religion des Bürgers: Bürgerliche Frömmigkeit und Protestantische Kirche im 19. Jahrhundert," *Historische Zeitschrift* 250 (1990): 605.

15 Evans, *Death in Hamburg*, 102.

16 Sittard, *Geschichte*, 290–95.

17 Gottfried Eberle, *200 Jahre Singakademie zur Berlin* (Berlin: Nicolai, 1991), 23–31; Applegate, *Bach in Berlin*, 128–47.

18 *Allgemeine Musikalische Zeitung* (Leipzig) 29 (12 December 1827): 167.

19 Sittard, *Geschichte*, 298.

20 Ibid., 302–4. Before 1829 and Mendelssohn's revival of the *St Matthew Passion* Carl Heinrich Graun's 1755 setting of Karl Wilhelm Ramler's Passion libretto *Tod Jesu* was the most often performed Passion oratorio in German-speaking Protestant Europe. It remained in the choral society repertoire throughout the nineteenth century.

21 Lucien Hölscher, "Säkularisierungprozesse im deutschen Protestantismus des 19. Jahrhunderts," in *Bürger in der Gesellschaft der Neuzeit*, ed. Hans-Jürgen Puhle (Göttingen: Vandenhoeck & Ruprecht, 1991), 249–51.

22 Sophie Drinker, *Brahms and His Women's Choruses* (Merion, PA: Self-published, 1952), 9–75.

23 See, for example, Rebecca Grotjahn, ed., *Deutsche Frauen, Deutscher Sang: Musik in der deutschen Kulturnation* (Munich: Allitera, 2009); and Dietmar Klenke, *Der Singende "deutsche Mann": Gesangverein und deutsche Nationalbewusstsein von Napoleon bis Hitler* (Münster: Waxmann, 1998). Barbara Eichner has recently shown how the nineteenth-century "musical constructions of national identity" produced a vast array of operas, oratorios, and cantatas, many written for Germany's dense network of organized amateur singers; *History in Mighty Sounds: Musical Constructions of German National Identity, 1848–1914* (Woodbridge, UK: Boydell & Brewer, 2014). Most of these works took as their subject matter the ancient Germans

in conflict with Rome, for instance, Max Bruch's *Frithjof* or Heinrich Hofmann's *Armin*.

24 Leon Botstein, *The Compleat Brahms: A Guide to the Musical Works of Johannes Brahms* (New York: W.W. Norton, 1999), 306.

25 James Sheehan, *German History, 1770–1866* (Oxford: Oxford University Press, 1989), 145–6.

26 Sittard, *Geschichte*, 304–5.

27 Josef Sittard's history of concert life in Hamburg, compiled at the end of the nineteenth century, contains exhaustive lists of visiting virtuosi, as well as excerpts from local reviews of their performances; ibid., 233–48, 265–89.

28 Hector Berlioz, *Memoirs of Hector Berlioz*, ed. Ernest Newman (New York: Dover, 1966), 303–4.

29 Evans, *Death in Hamburg*, 4.

30 "*die schönste Ehre und grösste Freude die mir von Menschen kommen kann*"; Hofmann, *Johannes Brahms und Hamburg*, 45.

9. What Difference Does a Nation Make?

1 This chapter is an expanded and updated version of a paper presented to the "Workshop on Art and Society in the Long Nineteenth Century" at the German Historical Institute in Washington, DC, in December 2002. It incorporates extracts from chapters on "Culture and the Arts" in two of the volumes of the *Short Oxford History of Germany*: *Germany, 1800–1870*, ed. Jonathan Sperber (Oxford and New York: Oxford University Press, 2004), 115–36; and *Imperial Germany, 1871–1918*, ed. James Retallack (Oxford and New York: Oxford University Press, 2008), 106–27. These passages are reprinted here with permission of Oxford University Press.

2 Françoise Forster-Hahn, "Modernity and the Building of Nation," in *Imagining Modern German Culture 1889-1910*, ed. Françoise Forster-Hahn (Washington, DC: National Gallery of Art, 1996), 9.

3 Friedrich Nietzsche, "David Strauss, the Confessor and the Writer," in *Untimely Meditations*, trans. R.J. Hollingdale, Cambridge Texts in the History of Philosophy (Cambridge: Cambridge University Press, 1997), 5–6.

4 Friedrich Meinecke, *The Age of German Liberation, 1795–1815*, trans. Peter Paret and Helmuth Fischer (Berkeley: University of California Press, 1977), 19.

5 Isaiah Berlin, *The Roots of Romanticism* (Princeton: Princeton University Press, 1999): xi, 1, 22, 134.

6 "Fifth Letter," in Schiller, *On the Aesthetic Education of Man*, ed. and trans. E.M. Wilkinson and L.A. Willoughby (Oxford: Oxford University Press, 1967), 25.

7 T.J. Reed, *Schiller* (Oxford: Oxford University Press, 1991), 68–9.
8 Schiller, *Aesthetic Education*, cxxxiii.
9 Nicholas Boyle, *Goethe: the Poet and the Age* (Oxford: Oxford University Press, 2000), 2: 230, 233.
10 James Sheehan, *Museums in the German Art World* (Oxford: Oxford University Press, 2000), 46; Schiller, *Aesthetic Education*, cxxxiii.
11 Rochlitz, "Die Verschiedenheit der Urtheile über Werke der Tonkunst," *Allgemeine musikalische Zeitung* 1 (1799): 505; Nina D'Aubigny, *Briefe an Natalie über den Gesang* (Leipzig, 1803), 1–2; "The serious thing is the true joy," from Seneca the Younger, which was the motto of the original Leipzig concert society of the 1770s.
12 Meinecke, *German Liberation*, 21.
13 Jim Samson, "Music and Society," in *The Late Romantic Era, from the mid-19th Century to World War I*, ed. Samson (Englewood Cliffs, NJ: Prentice Hall, 1991), 4.
14 Sheehan, *Museums in the German Art World*, 83.
15 Lydia Goehr, *The Imaginary Museum of Musical Works* (Oxford: Oxford University Press, 1992), 205.
16 Natorp quoted in David Gramit, *Cultivating Music: The Aspirations, Interests, and Limits of German Musical Culture, 1770–1848* (Berkeley: University of California Press, 2002), 138–9.
17 Ulrich Tadday, *Die Anfänge des Musikfeuilletons: Der kommunikative Gebrauchswert musikalischer Bildung in Deutschland um 1800* (Stuttgart: J.B. Metzler, 1993), 13–14, 65–7, 155.
18 Leon Plantinga, *Schumann as Critic* (New Haven: Yale University Press, 1967), 16–22.
19 See Axel Beer, *Musik zwischen Komponist, Verlag und Publikum: Die Rahmenbedingungen des Musikschaffens in Deutschland im ersten Drittel des 19. Jahrhunderts* (Tutzing: Hans Schneider, 2000).
20 Gerhart Baumann, "Goethe: 'Über den Dilettantismus,'" *Euphorion* 46 (1952): 350.
21 Ibid., 351.
22 See Wilfried Gruhn, *Geschichte der Musikerziehung: Eine Kultur- und Sozialgeschichte vom Gesangunterricht der Aufklärungspädogogik zu ästhetisch-kultureller Bildung* (Hofheim: V.-G. Wolke Verlag, 1993), 93–4.
23 Nicolaus Petrat, *Hausmusik des Biedermeier im Blickpunkt der zeitgenössischen Fachpresse, 1815-1848* (Hamburg: Wagner Verlag, 1986), 24–5.
24 Robin Lenman, John Osborne, and Eda Sagarra, "Imperial Germany: Towards the Commercialization of Culture," in *German Cultural Studies*, ed. Rob Burns (Oxford: Oxford University Press, 1995), 13–14.

25 David Friedrich Strauss, *The Old Faith and the New: A Confession*, trans. Mathilde Blind (New York: Holt, 1873), 3.
26 Nietzsche, *Untimely Meditations*, 3–4.
27 Ibid., 3.
28 Ibid., 6–7, 10.
29 Gordon Craig, *Germany, 1866–1945* (Oxford: Oxford University Press, 1978), 215.
30 Wolfgang J. Mommsen, "Culture and Politics in the German Empire," in *Imperial Germany, 1867–1918: Politics, Culture, and Society in an Authoritarian State*, trans. Richard Deveson (New York: Bloomsbury, 1995), 119–40.
31 Ulrich Schleunes, "Die Kunst als Staatsaufgabe im 19. Jahrhundert," in *Kunstverwaltung, Bau- und Denkmal-Politik im Kaiserreich*, ed. Ekkehard Mai and Stephan Waetzoldt (Berlin: Gebr. Mann Verlag, 1981), 10, 13.
32 See, for instance, Klaus Nohlen, "Baupolitik im Reichsland Elsaß-Lothringen, 1870–1918: Stadterweitung und Kaiserpalast in Straßburg," Harold Hammer-Schenk, "'Wer die Schule hat, hat das Land!' Gründung und Ausbau der Universität Straßburg nach 1870," and Lothar Burchardt, "Hochschulpolitik und Polenfrage: Der Kampf um die Gründung einer Universität in Posen," all in Mai and Waetzoldt, *Kunstverwaltung, Bau- und Denkmal-Politik im Kaiserreich*, 103–64.
33 See Barbara Miller Lane's characterization of architectural historiography in *National Romanticism and Modern Architecture in Germany and the Scandinavian Countries* (Cambridge: Cambridge University Press, 2000), 13.
34 The essay was originally a lecture, delivered first in Munich in 1933 and subsequently on a lecture tour to Amsterdam, Paris, and Brussels. The furious reaction to it by nationalist musical notables and National Socialists was such that, while vacationing in Switzerland after the tour, Mann decided with great reluctance not to return to Germany. Thus began his sixteen-year exile. Mann, *Pro und Contra Wagner*, trans. Allan Blunden (Chicago: University of Chicago Press, 1986), 134. See also Alex Rehding, *Music and Monumentality: Commemoration and Wonderment in Nineteenth-Century Germany* (Oxford: Oxford University Press, 2009), 3–18.
35 Matthew Jeffries, "Imperial Germany: Cultural and Intellectual Trends," in *Nineteenth-Century Germany: Politics, Culture and Society, 1780–1918*, ed. John Breuilly (London: Bloomsbury Academic, 2001), 234–5.
36 Richard Wagner, "What is German?" in *Richard Wagner's Prose Works*, 8 vols, Vol. 4, *Art and Politics*, trans. William Ashton Ellis (New York: Broude Bros, 1966), 155.
37 Theodor Billroth on its larger reception history, quoted in Michael Musgrave, *Brahms: A German Requiem* (Cambridge: Cambridge University Press, 1996), 61 and passim.

38 S. Baring-Gould, *Germany: Present and Past* (New York: H. Holt, 1879), 328.
39 Abigail Green, *Fatherlands: State-Building and Nationhood in Nineteenth-Century Germany* (Cambridge: Cambridge University Press, 2001), esp. 97–147.
40 Ibid., 120–1.
41 Nicholas Vazsonyi, *Richard Wagner: Self-Promotion and the Making of a Brand* (Cambridge: Cambridge University Press, 2010),169–204.
42 George Bernard Shaw, *The Perfect Wagnerite* (Mineola, NY: Dover Books, 1967), 127.
43 Lenman, Osborne, and Sagarra, "Imperial Germany," 22–3.
44 Albrecht Riethmüller, "'Is That Not Something for *Simplicissimus?!*' The Belief in Musical Superiority," in *Music and German National Identity*, ed. Celia Applegate and Pamela Potter (Chicago: University of Chicago Press, 2002), 300.
45 Carl Dahlhaus, *Nineteenth-Century Music*, trans. J. Bradford Robinson (Berkeley: University of California Press, 1989), 8–15.
46 Leon Botstein, ed., *The Compleat Brahms: A Guide to the Musical Works of Johannes Brahms* (New York: W.W. Norton, 1999), 89, 151.
47 Wilhlem Jakob Jung, *Musikgeschichte der Stadt Ludwigshafen am Rhein vom Jahre 1850 bis 1918*, ed. Siegfried Fauck (Ludwigshafen am Rhein: Stadtarchiv, 1968), 84.
48 Christoph-Hellmuth Mahling, "Werkschöre und Werkskapellen im Saarländischen Industriegebiet," in *Musik und Industrie: Beiträge zur Entwicklung der Werkschöre und Werksorchester*, ed. Monica Steegman (Regensburg: Bosse Verlag, 1978), 107–12.
49 See Christopher Fifield, *Max Bruch: His Life and Works* (Woodbridge, UK: Boydell, 2005), 54; and Barbara Eichner, *History in Mighty Sounds: Musical Constructions of German National Identity, 1848–1914* (Woodbridge, UK: Boydell, 2014), 213–17, 241.
50 Quoted in Gerhard Baumann, "Goethe: Über den Dilettantismus," *Euphorion: Zeitschrift für Literaturgeschichte* 46 (1952), 350.
51 Jim Samson, "Music and Society," 15.
52 See, for instance, John Breuilly, "The National Idea in Modern German History," in *The State of Germany: The National Idea in the Making, Unmaking, and Remaking of a Modern Nation-State*, ed. John Breuilly (London: Longman, 1992).

10. Men with Trombones

1 *Times Literary Supplement* 5607 (17 September 2010). For a shorter discussion of German military music see Celia Applegate, "'Eine große Nachtmusik': Musik und Militär im Deutschland des 19. Jahrhunderts," in *Kommunikation*

im Musikleben: Harmonien und Dissonanzen im 20. Jahrhundert, ed. Sven Oliver Müller, Jürgen Osterhammel, and Martin Rempe, trans. Sven Oliver Müller (Göttingen: Vandenhoeck & Ruprecht, 2015).

2 For probing and suggestive studies of the entanglement of the music and the arts of war in early modern Europe see Jutta Nowosadtko, Matthias Rogg, and Sascha Möbius, eds, *"Mars und die Musen": Das Wechselspiel von Militär, Krieg und Kunst in der Frühen Neuzeit, Herrschaft und Soziale Systeme in der Frühen Neuzeit*, Vol. 5 (Berlin: LIT Verlag, 2008), 247–321.

3 Quoted in Susan Witt-Stahl, *"…But his soul goes marching on": Musik zur Ästhetisierung und Inszenierung des Krieges* (Karben: CODA Verlag, 1999), 12.

4 Jakob Vogel, *Nationen im Gleichschritt: Der Kult der 'Nation in Waffen' in Deutschland und Frankreich, 1871–1914* (Göttingen: Vandenhoeck & Ruprecht, 1997), 274.

5 C.A. Bayly, *The Birth of the Modern World, 1780–1914: Global Connections and Comparisons* (Oxford: Oxford University Press, 2004), 2.

6 An extensive historiography already exists concerning the role of the military as a whole in society, and it includes tantalizing but minimal references to military music. For Germany see Thomas Rohkrämer, *Der Militarismus der "kleinen Leute": Die Kriegervereine im Deutschen Kaiserreich* (Munich: Oldenbourg Verlag, 1990); Ute Frevert, *A Nation in Barracks: Modern Germany, Military Conscription and Civil Society*, trans. Andrew Boreham with Daniel Brückenhaus (Oxford: Oxford University Press, 2004); Frank Becker, *Bilder von Krieg und Nation: Die Einigungs-Kriege in der bürgerlichen Öffentlichkeit Deutschlands, 1864–1913* (Munich: Oldenbourg Verlag, 2001); Ralf Pröve, *Militär, Staat und Gesellschaft im 19. Jahrhundert* (Munich: Oldenbourg Wissenschaftsverlag, 2006). For European comparative perspectives see Christian Jansen, ed., *Der Bürger als Soldat: die Militarisierung europäischer Gesellschaften im langen 19. Jahrhundert, ein internationaler Vergleich* (Essen: Klartext Verlag, 2004); and Vogel, *Nationen im Gleichschritt.* Jann Pasler, *Composing the Citizen: Music as Public Utility in Third Republic France* (Berkeley: University of California Press, 2009) is probably the fullest effort we have to integrate military music into a broad musico-cultural history, but her discussions of military music are nevertheless limited and scattered.

7 Ludwig Degele, *Die Militärmusik: ihr Werden und Wesen, ihre kulturelle und nationale Bedeutung* (Wolfenbüttel: Verlag für musikalische Kultur und Wissenschaft, 1937), 158.

8 For general perspectives on the development of European, esp. German, military bands see Bernhard Höfele, *Die Deutsche Militärmusik: Ein Beitrag zu ihrer Geschichte* (Cologne: Luthe, 1999), 89–105; see also Höfele's and Wilhelm

Probst's entry on "Militärmusik" in *Die Musik in Geschichte und Gegenwart: Allgemeine Enzyklopädie der Musik*, Vol. 6 (Basel: J.B. Metzler, 1997); David Whitwell, *The Nineteenth Century Wind Band and Wind Ensemble in Western Europe* (Northridge, CA: Whitwell Books, 1984); Jeremy Montagu, et al., "Military Music," in *Grove Music Online*, http://www.oxfordmusiconline.com.proxy.library.vanderbilt.edu/subscriber/article/grove/music/44139?q=Military+Music&search=quick&pos=2&_start=1#S44139.2, accessed 24 July 2016.

9 H.G. Farmer, *The Rise and Development of Military Music* (London: Wm Reeves, 1912), 2; Peter Panoff, *Militärmusik in Geschichte und Gegenwart* (Berlin: K. Siegesmund, 1938), 1–3. One could cite many more examples; the notion of an ancient and natural association of music-making and war informs all popular histories of the genre.

10 Frank Heidlberger, "Betrachtungen zur Rolle der Militärmusik in der abendländischen Kunstmusik," in *Militärmusik und "zivile" Musik: Beziehungen und Einflüsse*, ed. Armin Griebel and Horst Steinmetz. Bericht über ein Symposion beim Tag der Musik am 14. Mai 1993 in Uffenheim (Uffenheim: Forschungsstelle für frankische Volksmusik, 1993), 9. For a musicological exploration of these military "topics" see Raymond Monelle, *The Musical Topic: Hunt, Military and Pastoral* (Bloomington: Indiana University Press, 2006). For a more embracing formulation of the relationship see Anselm Gerhard, "Der Krieg als Vater musikalischer Dinge: Fragen zur Militarisierung der Kunstmusik in den Jahrzehnten um 1800," in Nowosadtko, Rogg, and Möbius, *'Mars und die Musen'*, 291–301.

11 Michael Schramm, "Funktionsbestimmte Elemente der Militärmusik von der Frühen Neuzeit bis zum 19. Jahrhundert," in Nowosadtko, Rogg, and Möbius, *"Mars und die Musen,"* 247–60.

12 Hans von Bülow, "Zur preussischen Militärmusik," *Neue Zeitschrift für Musik* 49, no. 1 (1858): 5. Jacob Adam Kappey's entry on the "Wind-Band" in the 1910 edition of *Grove's Dictionary* considered him, along with Adolphe Sax, one of the two men who revolutionized military music in the nineteenth century; George Grove, *Grove's Dictionary of Music and Musicians*, 5 vols (New York: Macmillan, 1910), 5: 537.

13 This account of his early life originated from a biography of Wieprecht written in 1882 by August Kalkbrenner and partially based on Wieprecht's autobiography, which is no longer extant except in the form of lengthy quotations in Kalkbrenner. Most accounts of Wieprecht's life originate from this contemporary, quasi-hagiographic account by the music director of the 42nd Infantry Regiment of the Prussian Army; August Kalkbrenner, *Wilhelm Wieprecht, director der sämtlichen musikchöre des Gardecorps: Sein Leben und Wirken* (Berlin: E. Prager, 1882), 6–20.

14 Reinhard Koselleck coined the term *Sattelzeit* to characterize the period 1750–1850; see his *Practice of Conceptual History: Timing History, Spacing Concepts*, trans. Todd Samuel Presner (Stanford: Stanford University Press, 2002), 154–69; and David Blackbourn, "'The Horologe of Time': Periodization in History," *Publications of the Modern Language Association of America* 127, no. 2 (March 2012): 303. On the transformation of city musical establishments see Martin Wolschke, *Von der Stadtpfeiferei zu Lehrlingskapelle und Sinfonieorchester* (Regensburg: Bosse Verlag, 1981).

15 Wieprecht quoted in Kalkbrenner, *Wieprecht*, 15. On the importance of "musical knowledge" in the emergence of modern musical culture and of Rochlitz as journalist, see Celia Applegate, *Bach in Berlin: Nation and Culture in Mendelssohn's Revival of the St Matthew Passion* (Ithaca, NY, 2005), 60–98.

16 Wieprecht quoted in Kalkbrenner, *Wieprecht*, 18.

17 Ibid., 18–19.

18 See chapter 1.

19 Nor, as he later confided to a colleague, did Wieprecht himself want to join the military in the probably vain hope of improving its music-making from the inside out (Kalkbrenner, *Wieprecht*, 18).

20 The attractively percussive "Turkish music" with its drums, tambourines, cymbals, triangles, and bells was an especially popular musical "topic" or exotic gesture in the period of Viennese classicism. Its influence is familiar to classical-music lovers under the term "Janissary music" – it can be heard in the fourth (choral) movement of Beethoven's Ninth Symphony. The Janissaries formed the corps of the Ottoman military bands. They were also shock troops in the Ottoman Army. For a brief summary of the phenomenon, see Heidlberger, "Betrachtungen," in Griebel and Steinmetz, *Militärmusik und "zivile" Musik*, 14.

21 The best clarinetist would occasionally be designated the band's *Musikmeister*. See Johannes Reschke, *Studien zur Geschichte der brandenburgisch-preussischen Heeresmusik* (Inaug. diss., Berlin, 1936), 41. It was not unusual for serious composers to compose for these ensembles; Mozart, Beethoven, Mendelssohn and many others wrote occasional works for the small woodwind and brass ensembles; Hans Heinz Stuckenschmidt, "Militärmusik," *Querschnitt* 13, no. 4 (1933): 6.

22 For an eighteenth-century view on proper military concertizing see Johann Friedrich von Fleming, *Der vollkommene teutsche Soldat* (1726: repr. ed. Graz: Akademische Druck- u. Verl. Anstalt, 1967), 181, 376; see also Höfele, *Die deutsche Militärmusik*, 126–9.

23 Wilhelm Wieprecht, *Die Militair-musik und die militair-musikalische Organisation eines Kriegsheeres: hinterlassene Denkschrift von Wilhelm Wieprecht* (Berlin, 1885), 5.

24 For a useful layman's guide to valves see Adam Carse, *Musical Wind Instruments* (1939; repr ed. New York: Dover, 2002), 6.

25 *Allgemeine musikalische Zeitung* (Leipzig), 29 (December 1827): 890–1.

26 This achievement was a particular source of pride for him and an aspect of his unlikely authority as a civilian among soldiers; Kalkbrenner, *Wieprecht,* 22. See also Gasparo Spontini (former music director of the Prussian Court Opera) letter to Wieprecht, 5 June 1846, in ibid., 51.

27 In 1867, in response to the personal request of Napoleon III, Wieprecht wrote a memorandum on the requirements for "a well-organized military music" (eine gut organisirte Militairmusik), stressing centralization and standardization in musical practices and musical knowledge from Kapellmeister to tuba player; Wieprecht, *Militair-musik,* 5.

28 Rosemary Hughes, ed., *A Mozart Pilgrimage, Being the Travel Diaries of Vincent & Mary Novello in the year 1829,* trans. and comp. Nerina Medici di Marignano (London: Novello, 1955), 274–5.

29 See letters to Wieprecht from Giacomo Meyerbeer and Franz Liszt, among others, for testimonials about his skill in adapting their own compositions to military bands (Liszt, 18 July 1856; Meyerbeer, 9 April 1858); repr. in Kalkbrenner, *Wieprecht,* 52–5. Along the way he also acquired a uniform (designed, allegedly, by the king), then an invented commission to go with it, and then finally a more conventional position of command, viz. the soldier/musicians; Höfele, *Die Deutsche Militärmusik,* 129–35; for a description of the uniform, see Kalkbrenner, *Wieprecht,* 28.

30 Advanced training for military band leaders remained a perennial problem, and over the years many solutions were proposed. A formal proposal in 1878 from the Allgemeine Deutsche Musikerverband for a network of conservatories for military musicians, with a flagship institute in Berlin, went nowhere. In 1887 the army allowed a limited number of band leaders to undertake a three-year course of study at the Berlin Music Conservatory (Hochschule für Musik), but the program was plagued with problems and in the end probably had only a minor impact. See Josef Eckhardt, *Zivil- und Militärmusiker im Wilhelminischen Reich* (Regensburg: Bosse Verlag, 1978), 53–5; and Reschke, *Studien zur Geschichte der brandenburg-preussische Heeresmusik,* 55.

31 In 1845 the Viennese correspondent for Leipzig's *Die Grenzboten* reported that Wieprecht was studying Habsburg military bands because Prussian ones had not yet reached the "perfection" (*Vollkommenheit*) of Austrian military musicians; "Aus Wien," *Die Grenzboten* 4 (1845): 525.

32 Whitwell, *Nineteenth Century Wind Band,* 40; see also Panoff, *Militärmusik,* 155; Kalkbrenner, *Wieprecht,* 49–53.

33 In 1897 the Ministry of War formally required that all military bands follow the Wieprechtian system of size and instrumentation; most were already doing so. The question of numbers is vexing: bands included shifting numbers of supernumerary musicians off the books. An interwar study estimated that something more like 20,000 men were employed as military musicians during the Second Empire, two-thirds of them off the books (Richard Thielecke, "Die soziale Lage der Berufsmusiker in Deutschland," unpublished diss., University of Frankfurt, 1921; cited in Eckhardt, *Zivil- und Militärmusiker,* 48).

34 See ibid., 11–42.

35 Andreas Masel, "Wechselwirkungen zwischen Militärmusik und 'ziviler Musik': Ein Überblick am Beispiel Bayerns im 18. und 19. Jahrhunderts," in Griebel and Steinmetz, *Militärmusik und "zivile" Musik,* 23–5.

36 Eckhardt, *Zivil- und Militärmusiker,* 28.

37 Ibid., 61.

38 Erich Tremmel, "Die Bedeutung der Bürgermilitärmusik für die Entwicklung der Blaskapellen in Bayern," in Griebel and Steinmetz, *Militärmusik und "zivil" Musik,* 55–60.

39 Thomas Bruder, *Nürnberg als bayerische Garnison von 1806 bis 1914: Städtebauliche, wirtschaftliche und soziale Einflüsse* (Nuremberg: Stadtarchiv, 1992), 492–3. For a similar case see Ulrich Hettinger, *Passau als Garnisonstadt im 19. Jahrhundert* (Augsburg: Wissner, 1994), 270, 274.

40 Eckhardt, *Zivil- und Militärmusiker,* 58–60, 75–85.

41 Jim Samson, "Music and Society," in *The Late Romantic Era: from the Mid-19th Century to World War I,* ed. Jim Samson (Englewood Cliffs, NJ: Prentice Hall, 1991), 14–16.

42 "Such a fortunate coincidence might be described as luck," he continued, "but luck of that kind is an attribute of genius"; Siegfried Kracauer, *Orpheus in Paris: Jacques Offenbach and the Paris of his Time,* trans. Gwenda David and Eric Mosbacher (New York: Alfred A. Knopf, 1938), 62.

43 Clifford Geertz, "Art as a Cultural System," in *Aesthetics,* ed. S. Feagin and P. Maynard (Oxford: Oxford University Press, 1997), 112.

44 Hector Berlioz, *Memoirs of Hector Berlioz from 1803 to 1865,* trans. Rachel Holmes and Eleanor Holmes (New York: Dover, 1932), 325.

45 Ibid., 326. Wieprecht's *Franc-Juges* overture transcription has become a standard part of the brass band repertoire and is often used as a competition piece, mainly because of the dramatic qualities that the brass setting gives it – precisely what Berlioz himself first experienced in Berlin.

46 *Zapfenstreich* corresponds roughly to "taps," or "tattoo," in Anglo-American terms the signal for the end of the day, the return to barracks; the Russian

"taps" too was a simple trumpet fanfare. See Höfele, *Der Grosse Zapfenstreich von Wieprecht: Particell und Geschichte* (Norderstedt: Books on Demand GmbH, 2012), 48.

47 "*Zur lauten Bewunderung hingerissen,*" *Allgemeine Zeitung (Augsburg)* 24 (2 September 1838): 2010.

48 Kalkbrenner, *Wieprecht*, 42–8; Höfele, *Der Grosse Zapfenstreich*, 47–52.

49 It is also performed on important occasions, such as the fiftieth anniversary of *Bundeswehr*'s foundation. Bundeswehr portal: https://www.bundeswehr.de/portal/a/bwde/!ut/p/c4/NUzBCoJAFPyj97RL1i2RILp1qPSy7OprXdRdeT4Voo9vDZqBmYFhBiuM9HpxVosLXvf4xLJ2R7OCWRuCSZicdKzpJQSWZ9_02pIHExNNK7WsluCVVsZN6g308xYf22_c18GTbCrkxUW1rCUwjIGl35qZOTbgGiyTtMjTffJH-snO2f1aZbtDcclvOA7D6Qs9QRd7/, accessed 25 July 2016. Invariably, the ceremony goes forward in the face of protest and catcalls from citizens appalled by militarism. Several recent studies by Germans, who tend to be less inclined to give a free pass to this particular aspect of their heritage than are Anglo-American historians, regard it as an unacceptable holdover from a militaristic past. See especially Witt-Stahl, "*...But his soul goes marching on.*" For the ceremonial context see Hans Ehlert, ed., *Militärisches Zeremoniell in Deutschland*, Potsdamer Schriften zur Militärgeschichte, Vol. 6 (Potsdam: MGFA, 2008); for the politics of military tradition in West Germany see Donald Abenheim, *Reforging the Iron Cross: The Search for Tradition in the West German Armed Forces* (Princeton: Princeton University Press, 1988), esp. 11–46. For a sociological analysis see Ulrich Streuten, "Der große Zapfenstreich: Eine soziologische Analyse eines umstrittenen Rituals," Duisburger Beiträge zur soziologische Forschungen, No. 2/1999: http://www.ssoar.info/ssoar/bitstream/handle/document/11653/ssoar-1999-steuten-der_groe_zapfenstreich.pdf?sequence=1, accessed 25 July 2016.

50 See, for example, Wieprecht, *Militair-musik*, 8, 23, 31.

51 On the "nocturnalization" see Craig Koslovsky, *Evening's Empire: A History of the Night in Early Modern Europe* (Cambridge: Cambridge University Press, 2011), 1–18.

52 On the "invention" of a particular kind of anti-French animus see Ute Schneider, "Die Erfindung des Bösen: Der Welsche," in "*Gott mit uns*": *Nation, Religion und Gewalt im 19. und frühen 20. Jahrhundert*, ed. Gerd Krumeich and Harmut Lehmann (Göttingen: Vandenhoeck & Ruprecht, 2000), 35–52.

53 See Mona Ozouf, *Festivals and the French Revolution*, trans. Alan Sheridan (Cambridge, MA: Harvard University Press, 1988), which has little to say about music. See also Laura Mason, *Singing the French Revolution: Popular*

Culture and Politics, 1787–1799 (Ithaca, NY: Cornell University Press, 1996); Malcolm Boy, ed., *Music and the French Revolution* (Cambridge: Cambridge University Press, 1992); and Pasler, *Composing the Citizen*, 94–134.

54 Achim Hofer, *Studien zur Geschichte des Militärmarsches*, 2 vols (Tutzing: H. Schneider, 1988), 1: 113. See also Heidlberger, "Betrachtungen," in Griebel and Steinmetz, *Militärmusik und "zivile" Musik*, 9–22.

55 Quoted in Richard Taruskin, *The Oxford History of Western Music*, 6 vols (New York, Oxford University Press, 2005), 2: 86, 88.

56 Wieprecht almost certainly encountered Spontini's earlier operas during his Dresden period. On another kind of intersection of grand opera with society see Anselm Gerhard, *The Urbanization of Opera: Music Theater in Paris in the Nineteenth Century*, trans. Mary Whittall (Chicago: University of Chicago Press, 1998).

57 Kalkbrenner, *Wieprecht*, 65. The American musician Amy Fay provided a lengthy and amusing account of this event in her *Music-Study in Germany* (London: Macmillan, 1896), chap. 9: https://archive.org/details/musicstudyingerm00faya, accessed 25 July 2016.

58 The historical literature on these broad topics of nationalism and militarism is extensive. For Germany see Frevert, *Nation in Barracks*; Eckhard Trox, *Militärischer Konservatismus: Kriegervereine und 'Militärpartei' in Preussen zwischen 1815 und 1848/49* (Stuttgart: Steiner, 1990); Rohkrämer, *Der Militarismus der "kleinen Leute"*; Becker, *Bilder von Krieg und Nation*; and Benjaman Ziemann, "Sozialmilitarismus und militarische Sozialisation im deutschen Kaiserreich, 1870–1914," *Geschichte in Wissenschaft und Unterricht* 54 (2002): 148–64. For comparative perspectives on Europe and the United States see Manfred F. Boemeke, Roger Chickering, and Stig Förster, *Anticipating Total War: the German and American Experiences, 1871–1914* (Cambridge: Cambridge University Press, 1999); Jansen, *Der Bürger als Soldat*; and Dirk Bonker, *Militarism in a Global Age: Naval Ambitions in Germany and the United States before World War I* (Ithaca, NY: Cornell University Press, 2012).

59 Arjun Appardurai, "The Grounds of the Nation-State: Identity, Violence and Territory," in *Nationalism and Internationalism in the Post-Cold War Era*, ed. K. Goldmann, U. Hannerz, and C. Westin (London: Routledge, 2000), 141.

60 Christian Jansen, "Einleitung: Die Militarisierung der bürgerlichen Gesellschaft im 19. Jahrhundert," in Jansen, *Bürger als Soldat*, 10–13; Frevert, *Nation in Barracks*, 149–50; Michael Geyer, "The Past as Present: The German Officer Corps as Profession," in *The German Professions, 1800–1950*, ed. Geoffrey Cocks and Konrad Jarausch (Oxford: Oxford University Press, 1990), 183–212.

61 Vogel, *Nationen im Gleichschritt*, 11–12, 15–16, 18–19, 21, 82, 275.

62 Thomas Rohkrämer, "Der Gesinnungsmilitarismus der 'kleinen Leute' im Deutschen Kaiserreich," in *Der Krieg des Kleinen Mannes: Eine Militargeschichte von unten*, ed. Wolfram Wette (Munich: Piper, 1992), 95–109; and *Der Militarismus der 'kleinen Leute.'*

63 Becker, *Bilder von Krieg und Nation*, 7, 34–5, 160.

64 Matthew Jefferies, *Contesting the German Empire, 1871–1918* (London: Wiley-Blackwell, 2008), 27. Jefferies provides an account of the *Sonderweg* debate. A more recent assessment is Sven Oliver Müller and Cornelius Torp, eds, *Imperial Germany Revisited: Continuing Debates and New Perspectives* (New York: Berghahn, 2011).

65 Stuckenschmidt, "Militärmusik," 241.

66 Frevert, *Nation in Barracks*, 141.

67 Barbara Stambolis, "Schützenfeste: Militärfolklorismus, historischer Karneval, Imitation oder Persiflage höfischer und militärischer Vorbilder," in *Das politische Zeremoniell im Deutschen Kaiserreich, 1871–1918*, ed. Andreas Biefang, Michael Epkenhans, and Klaus Tenfelde (Düsseldorf: Droste Verlag, 2009), 354.

68 Derek Linton, *"Who Has the Youth, Has the Future": The Campaign to Save Young Workers in Imperial Germany* (Cambridge: Cambridge University Press, 1991), 68, 157.

69 *Die Preussische Armeemarschsammlung, 1815–1839*, 6 vols (Berlin: Schlesinger, 1839; repr. Vienna, 2007).

70 The definitive musicological account of the military march repertoire is Hofer, *Studien zur Geschichte des Militärmarsches*. The most important edition of the collection, available to the public (although expensive), was published in 1839 by the Schlesinger Press in Berlin.

71 Civilian leaders played a much more important role in French military band ceremonies; see Vogel, *Nationen im Gleichschritt*, 284–91.

72 In German-speaking Europe, musical journals had written occasional pieces on military music since 1807. Periodicals devoted entirely to military musical matters were rare. They included *Le Moniteur musical militaire* (Paris; founded 1865); *Lyra: Blätter für Militär- und Civil Musiker* (Relitz; founded 1869); the *Militär-Musiker-Almanach für das deutsche Reich*, an unofficial register of all military bands intended to "win new patrons and friends" for military music, published at irregular intervals between 1879 and 1914 (ed. Emil Prager; Berlin, 1897, 1); and the *Deutsche Militär-Musiker-Zeitung* (Berlin; founded 1879). The latter lasted until 1944. Among the few books written about military music before Wieprecht's own work and that of his faithful biographer Kalkbrenner was Jean-Georges Kastner, *Manuel*

Général de Musique Militaire (Paris: L'Institut de France, 1848). Kastner was an Alsatian of German heritage, an important promoter of Adolphe Sax and his new instruments, and a mentor to Wieprecht. He became well known in Germany only after Hermann Ludwig wrote a long and laudatory biography of him, highlighting his "German nature"; *Johann Georg Kastner, ein elsässischer Tondichter, Theoretiker, und Musikforscher: Sein Werden und Wirken*, 2 vols (Leipzig: Breitkopf & Härtel, 1886), 1: 3.

73 J.A. Kappey, *Military Music: A History of Wind Instrumental Bands* (London: Boosey, 1894), 1.

74 Quoted in Ludwig, *Johann Georg Kastner*, 2: 250. Comettant is a key figure in Jann Pasler's *Composing the Citizen*. He is cited with approval by his German contemporary Hermann Ludwig, also an advocate for military music's civic importance.

75 Wieprecht, *Die Militair-musik*, 5. Wieprecht's description of "a well-organized military music," however, never alludes to the enormous expansion of its role in civilian life, for which he was at least partially responsible.

76 Kastner, *Manuel Général de Musique Militaire*, 4; Friedrich Guthmann, "Forderung an die militärische Musik," *Allgemeine musikalische Zeitung* 9, no. 25 (1807): 391.

77 Whitwell, *Nineteenth Century Wind Band*, 67–9.

78 Jeffrey Richards, *Imperialism and Music: Britain, 1876–1953* (Manchester: Manchester University Press, 2001); John M. McKenzie, *Imperialism and Popular Culture* (Manchester: University of Manchester Press, 1987); Martin Clayton and Bennett Zon, eds, *Music and Orientalism in the British Empire, 1780s –1940s* (Aldershot, UK: Routledge, 2007).

79 Joseph Roth, *Radetzkymarsch: Roman* (1932: Munich, 1998); English translation, *The Radetzsky March*, trans. Joachim Neugroschel (Woodstock, NY: Overlook Press, 1995).

80 Rob Boonzajer Flaes, *Brass Unbound: Secret Children of the Colonial Brass Band* (Amsterdam: Koninklijk Instituut de Tropen, 2000), 10.

81 David G. Herbert, *Wind Bands and Cultural Identity in Japanese Schools* (Dordrecht: Springer, 2011), 20–6. Herbert also discusses the extremely limited extent to which western tonal music had been heard – and suppressed – in Japan through the work of missionaries, especially Jesuits in earlier centuries. See also Wolfgang Suppan, "Deutsche Militärmusiker in Japan in der frühen Meiji-Ära (seit 1868), in *Festschrift für Christoph-Hellmut Mahling zum 65. Geburtstag*, ed. Axel Beer, Kristina Pfarr, and Wolfgang Ruf, 2 vols (Tutzing: Schneider, 1997): 1379–401.

82 See note 22, above.

83 Pelin Kadercan treats the subject briefly in her work on later importations of European musical expertise, "The Unlikely Architects of Modern Turkish National Identity? The Case of German Refugees from the Third Reich (1933–1972)," PhD diss., University of Rochester, 2012.

84 See Timothy D. Taylor, *Beyond Exoticism: Western Music and the World* (Durham, NC: Duke University Press, 2007), 50.

85 On the general context of German-British contacts see David Blackbourn, "As 'dependent on each other as man and wife': Cultural Contacts and Transfers," in *Wilhelmine Germany and Edwardian Britain: Essays on Cultural Affinity*, ed. Dominik Geppert and Robert Gerwarth (Oxford: Oxford University Press, 2008), 15–37.

86 Pasler, *Composing the Citizen*, 290.

87 Wieprecht played a medley of opera themes from *Le prophète* by Giacomo Meyerbeer, a composer who embodied the alleged "Jewish rootless cosmopolitanism" so despised by the anti-Semites and Wagnerians but like Wagner a great favourite in transcriptions of his music for wind bands. See Wieprecht, *Militair-musik*, 28–37; and Ludwig, *Kastner*, 2: 247–51.

88 This event was advertised as a celebration of the end of the American Civil War and the Franco-Prussian War. See George Upton, *Musical Memories: My Recollections of Celebrities of the Half-Century, 1850–1900* (Chicago: A.C. McClurg, 1908), 200–10.

89 Julian Ralph, *Harper's Chicago and the World's Fair, the Chapters on the Exposition Being Collated from and Approved by the Department of Publicity and Promotion of the World's Columbian Exposition* (New York: Harper & Bros, 1893), 306.

90 As Stewart explained, "The public [will] not have any patience with efforts to educate it musically, and it [will] not derive any benefit from what it [does] not enjoy." "Report of the Department of Music to the President of the Panama-Pacific International Exposition," Daniel E. Coshland San Francisco History Center, San Francisco Public Library. See also chapter 4.

91 Upton, *Musical Memories*, 198.

92 Ibid., 202.

93 By the second half of the nineteenth century a long tradition already existed in western music – from Monteverdi's *Combattimento di Tancredi e Clorinda* in 1638 to Beethoven's *Wellingtons Sieg oder die Schlacht bei Vittoria* of 1813 to Carl Maria von Weber's cantata *Kampf und Sieg* of 1815 – of trying to reproduce the sounds of battle in music. The novelty of Gilmore's Peace Jubilee production is perhaps that he did so in the name of peace rather than, as was more common, as a celebration of victory.

94 Wieprecht, *Militair-musik*, 23, 25.

95 Quoted in Georg Kandler, "Deutsche Armeemärsche," in *Musik in Geschichte und Gegenwart*, ed. Friedrich Blume (Kassel: Bärenreiter Verlag, 1986), 9: 35–6.

96 Richard Wagner, "Über die Aufführung des 'Tannhäuser,'" in *Gesammelte Schriften und Dichtungen* (Leipzig: E.W. Fritzsch, 1872), 5: 186.

97 See especially the contributions by Monica Steegmann, Christoph-Hellmuth Mahling, and Wolfgang Korb in *Musik und Industrie: Beiträge zur Entwicklung der Werkschöre und Werksorchester*, ed. Monica Steegmann (Regensburg: Bosse Verlag, 1978). The volume includes a number of photographs, as eloquent in their own way as the text.

98 Nancy Reich, "Women as Musicians: A Question of Class," in *Musicology and Difference: Gender and Sexuality in Music Scholarship*, ed. Ruth Solie (Berkeley: University of California Press, 1993), 125–8.

99 An eloquent and canny defence of women's singing against such charges, couched in ladylike terms acceptable to her audience, was Nina D'Aubigny von Engelbrunner, *Briefe an Natalie über den Gesang als Beförderung der häuslichen Glückseligkeit und des geselligen Vernügens: Ein Handbuch für Freunde des Gesanges, die sich selbst, oder für Mütter und Erzeiherinnen, die ihre Zöglinge für diese Kunst bilden wollen* (Leipzig: Breitkopf & Hartel, 1803; rev. ed. 1824).

100 See, for instance, Gustave Kerker, "Opinions of Some New York Leaders on Women as Orchestral Players," *Musical Standard* (London), reprinted in *Women in Music: An Anthology of Source Readings from the Middle Ages to the Present*, ed. Carol Neuls-Bates (Boston: Northeastern University Press, 1996), 202–3.

101 On Berlioz see note 45. From time to time medical concerns were expressed, even concerning these men of "indefatigable lungs"; see, for instance, August Kalkbrenner, "Ist das Blasen auf musikalischen Instrumenten (ins. Bei der Marchmusik) gesundheitsgefährlich?" in Kalkbrenner, *Musikalische Studien und Skizzen* (Berlin: Parrhysius, 1903), 192–5.

102 Jacob Adam Kappey, the Prusso-Rhenish military bandsman who directed the British Royal Marines Band and wrote one of the earliest histories of military music, thought "an astonishing amount of nonsense" had been written and said about the superiority of natural trumpets (*Military Music*, 61). See also Hermann Eichhorn's long-definitive history of the trumpet, *Die Trompete in alter und neuer Zeit* (Leipzig: Breitkopf & Härtel, 1881), 81–3.

103 Weiprecht's phrase, obscure in its Germanic abstraction, was that he preserved the "*Urquell des Instrumentalwesens*"; letter, Wieprecht to Jean-Georges Kastner in 1867, quoted in Ludwig, *Johann Georg Kastner*, 2: 247–8.

104 Damen-Trompeter-Corps "Stefanie"; Janietz Elite Damen Blas Orchester; Herm. Brandt's Damen-Trompeter-Corps und Streich-Orchester: evidence for the existence of these groups is most abundant on blogs and eBay, where photographs of them abound. The most thorough and well-researched source is music historian Mike Brubaker's blog, TempoSenzaTempo: http://temposenzatempo.blogspot.ca/2011/10/postcards-of-german-ladies-orchestras.html, accessed 24 July 2016. See also the Internet Bandsman's Everything Within (IBEW) website for a treasure trove of "vintage" photographs from all over the globe: http://www.ibew.org.uk/vbbp-oz.htm, accessed 24 July 2016. The *Deutsche Militär-Musiker Zeitschrift* included many notices and advertisements but no mention of women's brass ensembles.

105 Frevert, *Nation in Barracks*, 150. For a study of militarism from the perspective of its critics in Imperial Germany see Nicholas Stargardt, *The German Idea of Militarism: Radical and Socialist Critics, 1866–1914* (Cambridge: Cambridge University Press, 1994).

106 Eckhardt, *Zivil- und Militärmusiker*, 14–15, 28–38; Martin Wolschke, *Von der Stadtpfeiferei zu Lehrlingskapelle und Sinfonieorcheste: Wandlungen im 19. Jahrhundert* (Regensburg: Bosse Verlag, 1981), 55–67.

107 Eckhardt, *Zivil- und Militärmusiker*, 71–100; *Militär-Musiker-Almanach* (Berlin: Parrysius, 1879), 436–37.

108 These were the Allgemeine Deutsche Musiker-Verband, founded in 1872, and the Zentralverband der Zivilmusiker Deutschlands, founded in 1902.

109 Eckhardt, *Zivil und Militärmusiker*, 100.

110 Hermann Eichhorn, *Militarismus und Musik* (Berlin: Schuster & Loeffler, 1909), 9.

111 Alexander Pfannenstiel, *Die Erhaltung der Militärkapellen – eine Kulturfrage* (Berlin: Parrysius, 1914), 4–14. Wieprecht's biographer August Kalkbrenner was another such defender of military music's principally musical importance; see his *Musikalische Studien und Skizzen*, 24.

112 Pfannenstiel, *Die Erhaltung der Militärkapellen*, 13.

113 On such contingencies, see Christopher Clark, *The Sleepwalkers: How Europe Went to War in 1914* (New York: Harper Books, 2013).

11. Women's Wagner

1 This chapter is a revised and expanded version of an essay, "Women's Wagner," to be published in a future special issue of *Act – Zeitschrift für Musik & Performance*, an online journal. The title of the special issue will be "Theater as Global Culture: Wagner's Legacy Today," edited by Anno

Mungen, Nicholas Vazsonyi, Julie Hubbert, Ivana Rentsch, and Arne Stollberg, http://www.act.uni-bayreuth.de/de/index.html. Passages from my essay appearing in that special issue are printed in this volume with permission of the journal and its editors.

2 Just within the past few years, several new biographies and studies of Wagnerian women have come out: Oliver Hilmes, *Cosima Wagner: The Lady of Bayreuth* (New Haven: Yale University Press, 2007); Jonathan Carr, *The Wagner Clan: The Saga of Germany's Most Illustrious and Infamous Family* (New York: Grove Press, 2009); Eva Rieger, *Friedelind Wagner*, trans. Chris Walton (Woodbridge, UK: Boydell Press, 2013), and *Richard Wagner's Women*, trans. Chris Walton (Woodbridge, UK: Boydell Press, 2011); Brigitte Hamann, *Winifred Wagner: A Life at the Heart of Hitler's Bayreuth*, trans. Alan Bance (New York: Harcourt, 2006); Nila Parley, *Vocal Victories: Wagner's Female Characters from Senta to Kundry*, trans. Gaye Kynoch (Chicago: University of Chicago Press, 2011).

3 "die bürgerliche Gesellschaft Europas und der Welt in ihren Bann zog und sich unterwarf"; "Ist es nicht das Wonnevolle, das Sinnlich-Sehrende, Sinnlich-Verzehrende, das Schwerberauschende, Hypnotisch-Strichende, das dick und üppig Abgesteppte, mit einem Worte das höchst Luxuriöse seiner Musik, was ihr die bürgerlichen Massen in die Arme trieb?" Thomas Mann, "Leiden und Grösse Richard Wagners," in Thomas Mann, *Gesammelte Werke, Band IX, Reden und Aufsätze* (Frankfurt: S. Fischer Verlag, 1960), 441. The English translation is that of Allan Blunden, *Thomas Mann: Pro and Contra Wagner* (Chicago: University of Chicago Press, 1985), 137.

4 Rebecca Grotjahn, "Playing at Refinement: A Musicological Approach to Music, Gender and Class around 1900," *German History* 30, no. 3 (2012): 395.

5 A former student, Dr James M. Shugert, created this web page. "The Virginia W. Strait Music Award," *HASD Educational Foundation*; http://www.hasdfoundation.com/virginia-w.-strait-music-award.html, accessed 26 July 2016.

6 Virginia Strait also owned a copy of Friedelind Wagner's effort to come to terms with her family's relationship to Hitler, written during the Second World War: *Heritage of Fire: The Story of Richard Wagner's Granddaughter* (New York, 1945).

7 Umberto Eco, "Towards a Semiotic Inquiry into the Television Message," in *Working Papers in Cultural Studies* (1972): 103. We have, of course, many accounts and analyses of Wagner's directing his works. The fullest is probably Heinrich Porges, *Rehearsing the "Ring": An Eye-Witness Account of the Stage Rehearsals of the First Bayreuth Festival*, trans. Robert L. Jacobs (Cambridge: Cambridge University Press, 2009), 1983. This piece appeared

first in the *Bayreuther Blätter* between 1881 and 1896 in a series of articles called "Die Bühnenproben zu den Bayreuther Festpielen des Jahres 1876."

8 Laurence Dreyfus, *Wagner and the Erotic Impulse* (Cambridge, MA: Harvard University Press, 2010); Eva Rieger, *"Leuchtende Liebe, Lachender Tod": Richard Wagners Bild der Frau im Spiegel seiner Musik* (Düsseldorf: Artemis & Winkler, 2009).

9 Laurie McManus, "The Rhetoric of Sexuality in the Age of Brahms and Wagner," PhD diss., University of North Carolina, 2011.

10 Dreyfus, *Erotic Impulse,* 1–39; see n6.

11 Amy Fay, *Music-Study in Germany, from the Correspondence of Amy Fay,* ed. Mrs Fay Pierce (New York: A.C. McClurg, 1886); https://archive.org/details/musicstudyingerm00faya, accessed 26 July 2016. The Dover reprint of the original 1880 edition touts it on the cover as the "classic memoir of the Romantic Era" (Mineola, NY: Dover, 2014).

12 Ibid., letters of 25 November 1870, 16 February 1871, 22 April 1871.

13 Ibid., letter of 27 July 1871.

14 Ibid., letter of 18 May 1871.

15 Ibid., letter of 26 February 1871.

16 "Solche Rohheit, solcher Mangel an jedem Anstand ist doch wohl noch nirgends zu finden gewesen, wie hier im neunzehnten Jahrhundert auf einer deutschen Bühne, vor einem Elite-Publicum von deutschen Männern und Frauen!"; Luise Büchner, "Weibliche Betrachtungen über den Ring des Nibelungen," in *Die Frau: Hinterlassene Aufsätze, Abhandlungen und Berichte zur Frauenfrage* (Halle: Hermann Gesenius, 1878), 362. Unless indicated otherwise, all translations my own.

17 "Auch ich bin in Arkadien geboren, d.h. auch ich habe einmal für Richard Wagner geschwärmt"; ibid., 356–7.

18 On the Arcadian tradition, see Erwin Panovsky, "*Et in Arcadia ego*: Poussin and the Elegiac Tradition," in *Meaning in the Visual Arts* (Garden City, NJ: Doubleday, 1955), 295–320.

19 "Welch' deutsches Herz hätte auch nicht höher schlagen"; "wahrhaft poetischen Stoffe der alten Sage und Geschichte"; "getragen durch eine Musik, die zwar neu und überraschend war sollen"; Büchner, "Weibliche Betrachtungen," 356.

20 On Wagner's skill in managing his own fame, see Nicholas Vaszonyi, *Richard Wagner: Self-Promotion and the Making of a Brand* (Cambridge: Cambridge University Press, 2012).

21 Quoted in Gerlinde Röder-Bolton, *George Eliot in Germany, 1854–55* (Aldershot, UK: Routledge, 2006), 67.

22 Quoted in the editors' introduction to George Eliot, "Recollections of Weimar," in *The Journals of George Eliot,* ed. Margaret Harris and Judith

Johnston, Cambridge Studies in Romanticism (Cambridge: Cambridge University Press, 2000), 217.

23 Eliot, "Recollections of Weimar," 233.

24 Anna Dzamba Sessa, *Richard Wagner and the English* (Teaneck, NJ: Fairleigh Dickinson University Press, 1979), 35–6.

25 "Dies sollte ein Deutscher Frauentag sein, und mehr als ein deutscher. Denn nicht nur die erste Frau Deutschlands ist es, die man zu feiern hat, es ist wahrscheinlich heute die erste Europas"; Thomas Mann, "Zum sechzigsten Geburtstag Ricarda Huch," in *Gesammelte Werke*, ed. Peter de Mendelssohn, 13 vols (Frankfurt: S. Fischer Verlag, 1960), 10: 429.

26 Ricarda Huch, *Du, mein Dämon, meine Schlange …: Briefe an Richard Huch, 1887–1897*, ed. Anne Gabrisch (Göttingen: Wallstein, 1998). For the history of the relationship, told novelistically, see also Anne Gabrisch, *In den Abgrund werf ich meine Seele: Die Liebesgeschichte von Ricarda and Richard Huch* (Zurich: Verlag Nagel & Kimche AG, 2000). The affair ended in part because the unstable psychological state of Ricarda's sister rendered a decision to abandon her unthinkable; nor does Richard seem to have been a very decisive man.

27 "Weißt Du, ich könnte 10 Jahr mit einem andern verheirathet gewesen sein, Du brachtest nur Deine Stimme einmal von ferne zu erheben, gleich läge ich zu Deinen Füssen als wärs ein Stück von Dir"; Ricarda to Richard, letter of 2 February 1892, in Huch, *Briefe*, 225.

28 "Auch ich war gestern in den Meistersingern (mag sie nicht, zu ausgeklügelt), auch mir ist ein Würgen in die Kehle gestiegen, wenn ich unsre Lage bedenke … Und dabei wächst eine wilde Sucht nach Ruhm täglich in mir an. Das ist das einzige, wovon ich noch Rettung für mich hoffe. Wenn ich Musik höre, z. b. gestern im Theater, steigen mir immer die Thränen auf und ich sehne mich nach Gedichten oder überhaupt nach Poesie wie nach einer Person, es ist so entsetzlich leer und wüst in mir. Und dann denke ich zuweilen, es kommt wohl vom Alter, und das macht mich dann vollends rasend. Ich hätte doch nicht gedacht, daß ich ein ganz bewegungsloses Leben so schlecht ertragen könnte. Ich bin unter lauter so schlichten, rechtlichen, legitimen Menschen und Verhältnissen und trabe für gewöhnlich so mit, und dann manchmal regt sich so eine Art Wildheit in mir, ich weiß nicht, so Gefühle wie etwa in Achill, als er in Mädchenkleidern steckte, oder wie ein alter Heidengott im Christenhimmel. Eben fällt mir ein, wenn ich nun ein wildes Pferd wäre, das man gefangen hätte, und das sich nun losgerissen hätte und in die Steppe hinaussprengte, wo man nirgends ein Ende sieht, und wie ich das denke, fange ich gleich an zu weinen. Es ist mir alles so schrecklich

verleidet, was soll nun daraus werden. Entweder ich gewöhne mich an dies öde Knechtsleben – na, dies ist zwar eigentlich alles Unsinn was ich da schreibe, es kommt ja doch wie es muß … Wärst Du doch plötzlich da … dann käme ein Augenblick, in dem ganze unerträgliche Wochen und Monate versänken, daß sie einen nachher nicht mehr belasteten." And later, "Mein Aufbäumungsparoxismus ist vorbei, und ich trotte wieder weiter. Die Matthäuspassion ist die schönste Musik, die ich noch gehört habe, nichts had jemals solchen Eindruck auf mich gemacht"; ibid., letter of 22 April 1892, 244–5.

29 Ibid.

30 Ibid., letters between 22 April and 6 May 1892, n19, 245–6.

31 Ibid., letters of 11 November 1892, and 23 February 1893, n19, 284, 311.

32 "Ich komme von Wagner immer mehr ab … Ein großer Genuß ist er schon, aber kein musikalischer"; ibid., letters of 18 February 1894, and 13 March 1894; "Ich halte garnichts mehr von Wagner," letter of 10 May 1894; "doch nur Conflikte geben kann," letter of 27 April 1897, n19, 396, 402, 420, 618.

33 Joachim Radkau, *Max Weber: A Biography*, trans. Patrick Camiller (Cambridge: Polity Press, 2009), 362.

34 Dreyfus, *Wagner*, 33n6.

35 Charlotte Teller, *The Cage* (New York, 1907), 94. The excerpt is from a longer account of the concert, a regular summer event for larger audiences and less well-to-do people than those who attended concerts in Orchestra Hall downtown; it took place in the old "Exposition Hall" from the World's Columbian Exposition of 1893 in Chicago. In the novel the concert on that evening was devoted entirely to orchestral excerpts from Wagner's operas, including "Siegmund's Love Song," "Tannhäuser's March," and "Evening Star."

36 Radkau, *Max Weber*, 162–3, 362.

37 Joseph Horowitz, *Wagner Nights: An American History* (Berkeley: University of California Press, 1994). 199–239.

38 Teller, *The Cage*, 96.

39 Peter Gay, *The Education of the Senses* (1984; New York: W.W. Norton, 1999), 458.

40 Chris Walton, *Richard Wagner's Zurich: The Muse of Place* (Rochester, NY: University of Rochester Press, 2007), 4. Walton's book is an important and often revelatory study of this crucially important period of Wagner's life.

41 Helen Horowitz, "'Nous Autres': Reading, Passion, and the Creation of M. Carey Thomas," *Journal of American History* 79, no. 1 (June 1992): 70.

42 Ibid.

43 Quoted in J. Horowitz, *Wagner Nights*, 228. Seidl and his intense but short Wagnerian reign in New York City (he died in 1898 at age forty-seven) is the subject of Horowitz's *Wagner Nights*.

44 Hermione Lee, *Virginia Woolf* (New York: Random House, 1999), 237–8.
45 Virginia Woolf, *The Years* (New York: Harcourt Brace, 1937), 184–5.
46 Anon. (later identified as Virginia Stephen), "Impressions at Bayreuth (from a Correspondent)," *Times* (London), 21 August 1909.
47 Ibid.
48 Paul Hindemith, *A Composer's World: Horizons and Limitations* (Cambridge, MA, 1952), 25.
49 Mann, "Leiden und Größe Richard Wagners," 367. Mann is referring to both Wagner and Henrik Ibsen in this passage.
50 Willa Cather, "A Wagner Matinee," *Everybody's Magazine*, 10 March 1904, 324–8. Willa Cather Archive, http://cather.unl.edu/ss011.html, accessed 26 July 2016.
51 Angela Diller, *The Story of Siegfried* (New York: Jonathan Cape & Harrison Smith, 1931), 30–1. Angela Diller was a prolific composer/arranger of music for beginning piano students. Many American children worked their way through the Diller-Quaile series of Solo Books and Duet Books for the piano. For an introduction to the work of Lynd Ward, see Art Spiegelman, "Introduction," in Lynd Ward, *Gods' Man; Madman's Drum; Wild Pilgrimage*, ed. Art Spiegelman (New York: Library of America, 2010).
52 George Eliot, *Middlemarch* (1871; Harmondsworth, UK: Penguin, 1965), 25–6.
53 Henry David Thoreau, *Walden and other Writings* (1854; New York: Modern Library, 1992), 8.
54 Mann, "Leiden und Größe Richard Wagners," 100.
55 J. Horowitz, *Wagner Nights*, 228.

12. *Hausmusik* in the Third Reich

1 Pamela Potter, *Most German of the Arts: Musicology and Society from the Weimar Republic to the End of Hitler's Reich* (New Haven: Yale University Press, 1998), 4–9, 37–45, 207–8; Michael Kater, *The Twisted Muse: Musicians and Their Music in the Third Reich* (New York, 1997), 130–4. This chapter is a lightly edited version of an essay first published in *Music and Nazism*, ed. Michael Kater and Albrecht Riethmüller (Laaber: Laaber Verlag, 2003), 136–49; reprinted by permission of the Laaber Verlag.
2 Richard Baum, "Der Arbeitskreis für Hausmusik," *Zeitschrift für Hausmusik* 2, no. 5–6 (1933): 75.
3 Walter Blankenberg, "Kasseler Musiktage 1933," *Collegium Musicum* 2, no. 4 (1933): 4.
4 Friedrich Blume, "Hausmusik," *Zeitschrift für Hausmusik* (formerly *Collegium Musicum*) 2, nos 5–6 (1933): 64. Hans Klein, in 1924, saw all musical

activities swinging purposelessly between a deracinated *Kunstmusik* and "that musical bastard," the operetta; see "Deutsche Musik," *Die Singgemeinde* 1, no. 1 (1924–5): 4.

5 See, for instance, Richard Baum, "Menschenwort und Offenbarung: Gedanken zur Deutschen Bach-Händel-Schütz-Feier 1935," *Zeitschrift für Hausmusik* 4, no. 1 (1935): 4; or Hans Joachim Moser, "Der Leierkasten und die musikalische Kultur," *Die Singgemeinde* 1, no. 1 (1924–5): 52–3.

6 Compare the concerns of the editors of the first edition of *Collegium Musicum* (1, no. 1 [1932]: 1–2), who worried that insufficient expertise would be available to support, educationally and technically, a renewed amateur instrumentalism, to those of the editors of *Die Singgemeinde* (1, no. 1 [1924–5]: 1–2), who were additionally concerned about a moral decay that made renewal of any kind difficult.

7 See, for instance, Potter's reference to an "amateur revolution" in the Weimar era; *Most German*, 4–9.

8 Andreas Schulz, "Der Künstler im Bürger: Dilettanten im 19. Jahrhundert," in *Bürgerkultur im 19. Jahrhundert: Bildung, Kunst, und Lebenswelt*, ed. Dieter Hein and Andreas Schulz (Munich: Beck Verlag, 1996), 34–52.

9 Bernd Sponheuer, *Musik als Kunst und Nicht-Kunst: Untersuchungen zur Dichotomie von 'hoher' und 'niederer' Musik im musikästhetischen Denken zwischen Kant und Hanslick* (Kassel: Bärenreiter Verlag, 1987).

10 The decade of the 1990s produced an enormous scholarly literature on the *Stadtbürgertum* or urban bourgeoisie, thanks to the multi-city project of Lothar Gall and his students. For overviews see Jonathan Sperber, "Bürger, Bürgertum, Bürgerlichkeit, Bürgerliche Gesellschaft: Studies of the German (Upper)Middle Class and its Sociocultural World," *Journal of Modern History* 69 (1997): 271–81; and my review of three of the volumes of the "Stadt und Bürgertum" series in *Journal of Modern History* 71 (1999): 492–6. None of these books supports a catastrophic view of nineteenth-century bourgeois development. Armed with impressive statistical tables and graphs, all confirm a picture of steady growth in influence and associational density and diversity over the course of the century. Research in this area has subsequently slowed down considerably.

11 For Leipzig see Pall Björnssen, "Making the New Man: Liberal Politics and Associational Life in Leipzig, 1845–1871," PhD diss., University of Rochester, 2000.

12 Thomas Nipperdey, "Verein als soziale Struktur in Deutschland im späten 18. und frühen 19. Jahrhundert," in *Geschichtswissenschaft und Vereinswesen im 19. Jahrhundert*, ed. Hermann Boockmann et al. (Göttingen: Vandenhoeck & Ruprecht, 1972), 1–44; Karl Gustav Fellerer, "Hausmusik," *Studien zur Musik des 19. Jahrhunderts* (Regensburg: Bosse Verlag, 1984), 267–92.

13 For a cultural history see Adrian Daub, *Four-Handed Monsters: Four-Hand Piano Playing and Nineteenth Century Culture,* trans. Erik Butler (Oxford: Oxford University Press, 2014), esp. 82–104.
14 Lucien Hölscher, "The Religious Divide: Piety in Nineteenth Century Germany," in *Protestants, Catholics, and Jews in Germany,* ed. Helmut Walser Smith (New York: Berg, 2001), 35; "Die Religion des Bürgers: Bürgerliche Frömmigkeit und Protestantische Kirche im 19. Jahrhundert," *Historische Zeitschrift* 250 (1990): 595–630.
15 Joe Perry writes, "Family music and singing were crucial for the construction" of the rituals of Christmas in the home; *Christmas in Germany: A Cultural History* (Chapel Hill: University of North Carolina Press, 2010), 10.
16 For Nazi-era appreciation of Riehl, see Josef Müller-Blattau, "Vorkämpfer für deutsche Musikkultur. Musikgeschichte und Musikpolitik bei Wilhelm Heinrich Riehl (1823–1897)," *Deutsche Musikkultur* 2 (1937): 19–27.
17 Riehl's most historical writings on music are contained in the three separately published volumes of his *Musikalische Charakterköpfe: Ein kunstgeschichtliches Skizzenbuch* (Stuttgart: Cotta, 1853, 1860, 1878). See also Dennis McCort, *Perspectives on Music in German Fiction: The Music Fiction of Wilhelm Heinrich Riehl* (Bern: Peter Lang, 1974).
18 Riehl, "Die göttliche Philister," in *Musikalische Charackterköpfe,* 3: 207–8.
19 Reinhart Koselleck, *Futures Past: On the Semantics of Historical Time,* trans. Keith Tribe (Cambridge, MA: MIT Press, 1985), 246–59.
20 Riehl's critique of Wagner began with a long essay called "Die Kriegsgeschichte der deutschen Oper; Vorstudien zu einem Charakterkopf der Zukunft," in *Musikalische Charakterköpfe,* 3: 243–408; it continued in later writings, culminating in a profile of Wagner, written in 1891, in which he denounced Wagner's "art dictatorship": "Richard Wagner," in *Kulturgesichtliche Charakterköpfe* (Stuttgart: Cotta, 1892), 453.
21 W.H. Riehl, *50 Lieder deutscher Dichter in Musik gesetzt* (Stuttgart: Cotta, 1856, 1859), and *Neue Lieder fürs Haus* (Leipzig: Breitkopf & Härtel, 1877); A. Reißmann, *Die Hausmusik in ihrer Organisation und kulturgeschichtlichen Bedeutung* (Berlin: R. Oppenheim, 1884).
22 Schulz, "Künstler im Bürger," 45–51.
23 Heino Eppinger, "Der Finkensteiner Bund und seine Zeitschrift," *Die Singegemeinde* 1, no. 1 (1924–5): 1.
24 Walter Blankenberg, "Zehn Jahre Bärenreiter-Verlag," *Zeitschrift für Hausmusik* 3, no. 2–3 (1934), 75.
25 Eppinger, "Der Finkensteiner Bund," 1–2.
26 Peter Gay, *Weimar Culture: The Outsider as Insider* (New York: W.W. Norton, 1968), esp. 102–18.

27 Ernst Sommer, "Politische Jugendbünde und Finkensteiner Singbewegung," *Die Singgemeinde* 9 (1932): 170.

28 Reprinted in Bruno Aulich and Ernst Heimeran, *The Well-Tempered String Quartet: A Book of Counsel and Entertainment for all Lovers of Music in the Home*, trans. D. Millar Craig (London: Novello, 1938): 41–5. The title of the German original was *Das Stillvergnügte Streichquartett* (Munich: Heimeran, 1936).

29 Eppinger, "Der Finkensteiner Bund," 2.

30 Potter, *Most German*, 41.

31 See Joseph Müller-Blattau, "Collegium Musicum," *Collegium Musicum: Blätter zur Pflege der Haus- und Kammermusik* 1 (1932): 4. Müller-Blattau became, of course, deeply involved in the Nazi cultural establishment; see Potter, *Most German*, 104, 107, 117, 135, 211.

32 See, for instance, Wilhelm Kamlah, "Die deutsche Musikbewegung," *Musik und Volk* 1 (1933): 9–14.

33 Fritz Jöde, "Hausmusik gestern und morgen," *Zeitshrift für Hausmusik* 3 (1934), 18–19; Herbert Just, "Tag der deutschen Hausmusik 1933," *Zeitschrift für Hausmusik* 3 (1934): 22–3.

34 Ian Kershaw, *Hitler, 1889-1936: Hubris* (New York: W.W. Norton, 1998), 527–31.

35 Detlev Peukert, *Inside Nazi Germany: Conformity, Opposition, and Racism in Everyday Life*, trans. Richard Deveson (New Haven: Yale University Press, 1987), 236–43; see also the chapter on National Socialism and provincial life in my book *A Nation of Provincials: The German Idea of Heimat* (Berkeley: University of California Press, 1990), 197–227. An enormous amount of scholarship on the question of the Volksgemeinschaft and everyday life in Nazi Germany has appeared since this essay was first published. One might begin with the work of Andrew Bergerson, *Ordinary Germans in Extraordinary Times: The Nazi Revolution in Hildesheim* (Bloomington: Indiana University Press, 2004); and Robert Gellately, *Backing Hitler: Consent and Coercion in Nazi Germany* (Oxford: Oxford University Press, 2002).

36 Saul Friedländer, *Reflections on Nazism: An Essay on Kitsch and Death*, trans. Thomas Weyr (1984; Bloomington: Indiana University Press, 2000); Peter Williams, "The Idea of *Bewegung* in the German Organ Reform Movement of the 1920s," in *Music and Performance during the Weimar Republic*, ed. Bryan Gilliam (Cambridge: Cambridge University Press, 1994), 149.

13. To Be or Not to Be Wagnerian in Leni Riefenstahl's Films

1 This chapter is a lightly edited version of an essay first published in Ingeborg Majer-O'Sickey, Neil Christian Pages, and Mary Rhiel, eds, *Riefenstahl Screened: An Anthology of New Criticism* (New York: Continuum

Press, 2008), 179–201. It is reprinted here with permission from the Continuum Press.

2 It is worth noting that Benjamin himself was not thinking about Wagner or the Gesamtkunstwerk when he wrote this. Walter Benjamin, "The Work of Art in the Age of Mechanical Reproduction," in *Illuminations: Essays and Reflections,* trans. Harry Zohn (New York, 1969), 241. For a recent reassessment of the meaning and history of the term Gesamtkunstwerk see David Imhoof, Margaret Menninger, and Anthony Steinhoff, eds, *The Total Work of Art: Foundations, Articulations, Inspirations* (New York: Berghahn, 2016).

3 Doris Bergen, *War and Genocide: A Concise History of the Holocaust* (New York: Rowman & Littlefield, 2003), 33.

4 Jonathan Petropoulos, for example, an otherwise astute analyst of Nazi aesthetics, misleadingly identifies the music of *Triumph of the Will* as that of Wagner's *Die Meistersinger von Nürnberg,* in his "Leni Riefenstahl, Coy Propagandist of the Nazi Era," *Wall Street Journal* (11 September 2003). In his *Artists Under Hitler: Collaboration and Survival in Nazi Germany* he writes that in *Triumph of the Will* she "added a rich, stirring soundtrack, drawing mostly on Wagner's music" (New Haven: Yale University Press, 2014), 244.

5 Scott D. Paulin explores the broader "metatheoretical" question of why Wagner's name is "inescapable" within "discourses on film and its music" in "Richard Wagner and the Fantasy of Cinematic Unity: The Idea of *Gesamtkunstwerk* in the History and Theory of Film Music," in *Music and Cinema,* ed. James Buhler, Caryl Flinn, and David Neumeyer (Hanover, NH: Wesleyan University Press, 2000), 58–84.

6 Linda Schulte-Sasse, *Entertaining the Third Reich: Illusions of Wholeness in Nazi Cinema* (Durham, NC: Duke University Press, 1996), xviii.

7 Lutz Koepnick, "Fascist Aesthetics Revisited," *Modernism/Modernity* 6, no. 1 (1999): 54. He fully develops and substantiates these arguments in *The Dark Mirror: German Cinema between Hitler and Hollywood* (Berkeley: University of California Press, 2002).

8 Ibid., 52.

9 Ibid., 54.

10 Brian Winston, "Triumph of the Dull," *Sight and Sound* 11 (2001): 60.

11 Leni Riefenstahl, *Leni Riefenstahl: A Memoir* (1987; New York: St Martin's Press, 1993), 11.

12 There is no evidence that Busoni ever published this work she attributed to him under that title, and thus one can only take Riefenstahl's word for it that she was dancing to an original, uncatalogued Busoni work, not the more widely known works titled "Valse Caprice," by Franz Liszt or Cecile

Chaminade or Gabriel Fauré, all available in published sheet music in the 1920s. That Busoni wrote such a work for her is not impossible; he did compose a number of short dance pieces, both for orchestra and for two- or four-handed piano performance.

13 See Mary Rhiel, "The Ups and Downs of Leni Riefenstahl: Rereading the Rhythms of the Memoirs," in *Riefenstahl Screened: An Anthology of New Criticism*, ed. Neil Christian Pages, Mary Rhiel, and Ingeborg Majer-O'Sickey (New York: Continuum Press, 2008), 202–17.

14 Riefenstahl, *A Memoir*, 46, 57, 61.

15 André Levinson, "The Modern Dance in Germany," *Theatre Arts Monthly* 13 (February 1929): 143–53. The rapidly changing shape of the musical repertoire for early twentieth-century dance has not been exhaustively studied. The best discussion of music and dance in the early twentieth century is that of Karl Toepfer, *Empire of Ecstasy: Nudity and Movement in German Body Culture, 1910–1935* (Berkeley: University of California Press, 1997), 321–33.

16 Toepfer, *Empire of Ecstasy*, 321.

17 Ibid., 322.

18 That said, Laban's Wagnerian moments seem confined to two points in his life. The first Wagnerian moment came during the First World War, which Laban experienced from the bohemian idyll of Monte Verità in Switzerland, where Parsifal's natural innocence and Tannhäuser's sandals seemed especially attractive to people searching for a new style of life. The second Wagnerian moment came, unsurprisingly, during the first years of the Third Reich, when he wrote, sincerely or opportunistically or both, about the supreme importance of Wagner as a dramatist – "I always say that the greatest German dramatist showed us dancers what to do." See Martin Green, *Mountain of Truth: the Counterculture Begins; Ascona, 1900–1920* (Hanover, NH: University Press of New England, 1986), 110, 123, 244–5; and Lillian Karina and Marion Kant, *Hitler's Dancers: German Modern Dance and the Third Reich*, trans. Jonathan Steinberg (New York: Berghahn, 2003), 11–21, 303–38.

19 The latter was not as uncommon a choice as it might seem. Ippolitov-Ivanov was well known at the beginning of the twentieth century as a kind of lesser Rimsky-Korsakov (his teacher). In the national-romantic-exoticist mode, he had immersed himself in the culture of the non-Russian peoples of Georgia and composed in 1894 a group of instrumental works called *Caucasian Sketches*. Riefenstahl choreographed a dance to the last and most popular of these, the "Procession of the Sardar," a work that, not unlike Ravel's now infamous *Bolero*, combined a moody yet forceful melody in an exoticized

minor mode with steadily intensifying rhythmic and dynamic elements. The whole package, with Riefenstahl presumably hurling herself about the stage with ever faster, more frantic movements, earned her, so she reported, tumultuous applause and calls for encores. She called her Ippolitov-Ivanov dance *Caucasian March*; Riefenstahl, *A Memoir*, 37.

20 She had appeared, to be sure, in a previous film, *Paths to Strength and Beauty* (1925), but anonymously, one dancer among many in one of Mary Wigman's ensemble pieces, "*Der Wanderung*."

21 Riefenstahl, *A Memoir*, 56; on this period in her life see also Steven Bach, *Leni: The Life and Work of Leni Riefenstahl* (New York: Knopf, 2007), 33–46.

22 Riefenstahl, *A Memoir*, 34.

23 Klaus Kreimeier, *The Ufa-Story: A History of Germany's Greatest Film Company, 1918–1945*, trans. Robert and Rita Kimber (New York: Hill & Wang, 1996), 122ff.

24 Herbert Windt, "*Tiefland*: the Opera and the Film," unpublished essay dated 17 December 1953 and reprinted as an appendix to David B. Hinton, *The Films of Leni Riefenstahl*, 3rd ed. (Lanham, MD: Scarecrow Press, 2000), 124.

25 The scholarly literature on film music is substantial and growing fast. Among the most significant are Claudia Gorbmann, *Unheard Melodies: Narrative Film Music* (Bloomington, IN: Indiana University Press, 1987); Nicholas Cook, *Analysing Musical Multimedia* (Oxford: Oxford University Press, 1998); James Buhler, Caryl Flinn, and David Neumeyer, eds, *Music and Cinema* (Hanover, NH: Wesleyan University Press, 2000); Caryl Flinn, *The New German Cinema: Music, History, and the Matter of Style* (Berkeley: University of California Press, 2004); Nora Alter and Lutz Koepnick, *Sound Matters: Essays on the Acoustics of Modern German Culture* (New York: Berghahn, 2004); Miguel Mera and David Burnand, eds, *European Film Music* (Aldershot, UK: Routledge, 2006); Konrad Vogelsang, *Filmmusik im Dritten Reich: Die Dokumentation* (Hamburg: Facta, 1990); Ute Rügner, *Filmmusik in Deutschland zwischen 1924 und 1934* (Hildesheim: G. Olms, 1988).

26 See, for instance, Giuseppe Becce and Hans Erdmann, *Allgemeines Handbuch der Film-Musik*, 2 vols (Berlin: Schlesinger, 1927).

27 Interestingly, Paulin's otherwise illuminating article on the Wagner Gesamtkunstwerk myth does not mention Becce. See note 5, above.

28 Max Steiner, the Viennese-born émigré film composer, took parallelism to comic extremes, as when the club-footed Leslie Howard, in the 1935 film of Maugham's *Of Human Bondage*, limped around to the accompaniment of a Steiner-eloquent musical motif, not unlike that of Wagner's Mime. See, among the more amusing accounts of the phenomenon, Joseph

Lanza, *Elevator Music: A Surreal History of Muzak, Easy-Listening, and other Moodsong*, rev. and expanded ed. (Ann Arbor: University of Michigan Press, 2004), 59–60.

29 Theodor Adorno and Hanns Eisler, *Composing for the Films* (1947; New York: Continuum, 2007), 47.

30 Cook, *Analysing Musical Multimedia*, 65.

31 Pierre Bourdieu, *Distinction: A Social Critique of the Judgment of Taste*, trans. R. Nice (Cambridge: Cambridge University Press, 1984); Brian Currid, *A National Acoustics: Music and Mass Publicity in Weimar and Nazi Germany* (Minneapolis: University of Minnesota Press, 2006), 120–3.

32 Kathryn Kalinak, *Settling the Score: Music and the Classical Hollywood Film* (Madison, WI: University of Wisconsin Press, 1993), 7.

33 The best account of Windt's life and work is that of Reimar Volker, *"Von oben sehr erwünscht": Die Filmmusik Herbert Windts im NS-Propagandafilm* (Trier: WVT Wissenschaftler Verlag, 2003).

34 Martin Thrun, *Neue Musik im deutschen Musikleben bis 1933*, 2 vols (Bonn: Orpheus Verlag, 1995), 2: 498.

35 He did credit Schoenberg with opening up new compositional paths for him; see Volker, *"Von oben sehr erwünscht,"* 5–7.

36 "Ich werde nie zu den Neuerern gehören, die um jeden Preis 'modern' sein wollen; anderseits bin ich nicht Reaktionär genug, die Erweiterungen durch die Moderne zu unterschätzen und mich ihrer nicht da zu bedienen, wo ich sie für angebracht und berechtigt halte"; Herbert Windt, "Warum Andromache?" *Blätter der Staatsoper* 12, no. 8 (March 1932): 5–6; cited in full in Volker, *"Von oben sehr erwünscht,"* 7.

37 Henning Eichberg et al., *Massenspiele. NS-Thingspiel, Arbeiterweihespiel und olympisches Zeremoniell* (Stuttgart: Frommann-Holzboog, 1977); Manfred Frank, "Vom 'Bühnenweihespiel' zum 'Thingspiel'. Zur Wirkungsgeschichte der 'Neuen Mythologie' bei Nietzsche, Wagner und Johst," *Poetik und Hermeneutik* 14 (1989): 610–38; William Niven, "The Birth of Nazi Drama? Thing Plays," in *Theatre under the Nazis*, ed. John London (Manchester: Manchester University Press, 2000), 54–95; Johannes M. Reichl, *Das Thingspiel. Über den Versuch eines nationalsozialistischen Lehrstück-Theaters (Euringer-Heynicke-Möller), mit einem Anhang über Bert Brecht* (Frankfurt: Dr Misslbeck, 1988); Rainer Stommer, "'Da oben versinkt einem der Alltag ...' Thingstätten im Dritten Reich als Demonstration der Volksgemeinschaftsideologie," in *Die Reihen fast geschlossen. Beiträge zur Geschichte des Alltags unterm Nationalsozialismus*, ed. Detlev Peukert, et al. (Wuppertal: Hammer, 1981), 149–73; Rainer Stommer, *Die inszenierte Volksgemeinschaft: Die "Thing-Bewegung" im Dritten Reich* (Marburg: Jonas Verlag, 1985).

38 Volker, *"Von oben sehr erwünscht,"* 7–8.

39 "Sieben Fragen an zwölf Komponisten," *Film-Kurier* (31 December 1938); and "Musikalische Pionierleistung im Olympia-Film: Herbert Windt: Das Wort 'untermalen' müßte verboten werden," *Film-Kurier* (11 April 1938). See also "Warum Musik im Film?" *Jahrbuch der Deutschen Musik, 1943* (Leipzig: Breitkopf & Härtel, 1943): 182–5. For a fuller discussion of Windt and the debates about the status of film music in the Third Reich see Volker, *"Von oben sehr erwünscht,"* 12–22.

40 To place this tyranny of the visual, or "ocularcentrism," in a long historical perspective see Martin Jay, *Downcast Eyes: the Denigration of Vision in Twentieth-Century French Thought* (Berkeley: University of California Press, 1994); and David Levin, *Modernity and the Hegemony of Vision* (Berkeley: University of California Press, 1993). On the dominance of ocularcentrism over sound in particular see Alter and Koepnick, *Sound Matters.*

41 Martin Loiperdinger, *Rituale der Mobilmachung: Der Parteitagsfilm Triumph des Willens von Leni Riefenstahl* (Opladen: Leske + Budrich, 1987).

42 Michel Delahaye, "Leni and the Wolf: Interview with Leni Riefenstahl," *Cahiers du Cinéma in English* 5 (1966): 49–55.

43 For a rich array of scholars who have fallen into the Wagner trap see Volker, *"Von oben sehr erwünscht,"* 75–7.

44 Ibid., 58–9, 66–7.

45 Ibid., 68.

46 This radio address of Goebbels is quoted in virtually every text, German and English, on music in the Third Reich. For a particularly strong treatment of the issue see Reinhold Brinkmann, "Wagners Aktualität für den Nationalsozialismus: Fragmente einer Bestandaufnahme," in *Richard Wagner im Dritten Reich,* ed. Saul Friedländer and Jörn Rüsen, (Munich: Verlag C.H. Beck, 2000), 106–41; Goebbels quotation on 126.

47 At the same time Volker's careful analysis of Windt's compositional procedures, in particular his motivic work, casts considerable doubt on Riefenstahl's own account of how she herself seized the baton and did the conducting, because she became frustrated by Windt's seeming inability to conduct his eighty-man orchestra in synchronization with the images (Riefenstahl, *A Memoir,* 165). In order to match particular motif with particular image, as the score succeeds in doing, Windt had to master very precise timing in the compositional process itself, not simply in the performance. Riefenstahl's self-dramatizing account seems built on the assumption that music is music, one just plays it at different tempi – an assumption consistent with her simplistic approach to musical expression altogether.

48 Volker, *"Von oben sehr erwünscht,"* 79.
49 Paulin, "Richard Wagner and the Ideal of Cinematic Unity."
50 See, for instance, Frederic Spotts, *Bayreuth: A History* (New Haven: Yale University Press, 1996), 195.
51 Volker, *"Von oben sehr erwünscht,"* 15, 20.
52 Koepnick, "Fascist Aesthetics," 54.
53 Bergen, *War and Genocide*, 23.
54 Roger Hillman, *Unsettling Scores: German Film, Music, and Ideology* (Bloomington: Indiana University Press, 2005), 27.
55 Borgmann was an accomplished film music composer, whose most famous (notorious) product was the score for the 1933 film *Hitlerjunge Quex*.
56 For a complete account of the melody, lyrics, and anything else one might need to know about the Horst-Wessel-Lied see George Broderick, "Das Horst-Wessel-Lied: A Reappraisal," *International Folklore Review* 10 (1995): 100–27.
57 See Georg Kandler, *Deutsche Armeemärsche; ein Beitrag zur Geschichte des Instrumentariums, des Repertoires, der Funktion, des Personals und des Widerhalls der deutschen Militärmusik* (Bad Godesberg: Hohwacht Verlag, 1962); and Joachim Toeche-Mittler, *Armeemärsche* (Neckargemünd: Spemann, 1971).
58 See chapter 10 in this volume.
59 An important starting point is a short pamphlet by Georg Kandler (1902–73), which he first wrote as a memorandum to the war ministry: *Die kulturelle Bedeutung der deutschen Militärmusik* (Berlin: Kandler, 1932).
60 Beyond expanding the musical forces in existing bands and re-establishing ones that had been allowed to dissolve, the new regime also created a number of new musical corps for new military units, including the Luftwaffe, the SS, and the Leibstandarte Adolf Hitler.
61 Bernhard Höfele, *Die Deutsche Militärmusik: Ein Beitrag zu ihrer Geschichte* (Cologne: Luthe, 1999), 137–68.
62 As Windt put it, "und zwar nach innen, nicht nach aussen," or, expansively translated, "and indeed not superficially but in the inner apprehension [of the viewer/listener]"; Herbert Windt, "Warum Musik im Film?" 182. The lyrics to "*Ich hatt' einen Kameraden*" would have come easily to the mind of any German hearing the tune. They are "Ich hatt' einen Kameraden, / Einen bessern findst du nit. / Die Trommel schlug zum Streite, / Er ging an meiner Seite|: Im gleichen Schritt und Tritt.:| // Eine Kugel kam geflogen: / Gilt's mir oder gilt es dir? / Ihn hat es weggerissen, / Er liegt mir vor den Füßen |: Als wär's ein Stück von mir: |," and so on. The German communists and anti-fascists of the Thälmann Brigade in Spain also adopted this tune, writing new words but in a similar spirit of simple soldierly comradeship and sacrifice.

63 Michael Mackenzie, "From Athens to Berlin: The 1936 Olympics and Leni Riefenstahl's *Olympia*," *Critical Inquiry* 29 (Winter 2003): 304–5; Vogelsang, *Filmmusik im Dritten Reich*, 12.

64 Transcript of Riefenstahl's appeal to the Filmbewertungsstelle included, as Appendix D, in Cooper C. Graham, *Leni Riefenstahl and Olympia* (Metuchen, NY: Scarecrow Press, 1986), 288.

65 Transcript in Graham, *Riefenstahl*, 288.

66 Windt, in 1938 pressbook, quoted in ibid., 177.

14. Saving Music

1 Daniel Barenboim and Edward W. Said, *Parallels and Paradoxes: Explorations in Music and Society*, ed. Ara Guzelimian (New York: Vintage, 2002), 21. This chapter is a lightly revised and expanded version of an article first published as "Saving Music: Enduring Experience of Culture" in *History and Memory* 17, no. 1–2 (Spring-Winter 2005): 217–37; it is reprinted with permission from Indiana University Press.

2 The latter quote came from Franz Brendel's 1852 treatise on the history of music. See Bernd Sponheuer, "Reconstructing Ideal Types of the 'German' in Music," in *Music and German National Identity*, ed. Celia Applegate and Pamela Potter (Chicago: University of Chicago Press, 2002), 55.

3 Richard Wagner, "What Is German?" in *Art and Politics*, Vol. 4 of *Richard Wagner's Prose Works*, trans. William Ashton Ellis (Lincoln: University of Nebraska Press, 1995), 150, 167, 169.

4 Dilthey, quoted in Erich Reimer, "National Consciousness and Music Historiography in Germany, 1800–1850," *History of European Ideas* 16 (1993): 721.

5 Quoted in Pamela Potter, *Most German of the Arts: Musicology and Society from the Weimar Republic to the End of the Third Reich* (New Haven: Yale University Press, 1998), 4.

6 Both remarks of Schoenberg, in 1919 and in 1921, are quoted in Reimer, "National Consciousness," 721.

7 Quoted in Marc Weiner, *Undertones of Insurrection: Music, Politics, and the Social Sphere in Modern German Narrative* (Lincoln: University of Nebraska Press, 1993), 39.

8 Wilfried Gruhn, *Geschichte der Musikerziehung* (Darmstadt: Wissenschaft Buchgesellschaft, 1993), 213–52.

9 Potter, *Most German of the Arts*, 6–9; see also chapter 12 in this book.

10 Potter, *Most German of the Arts*; Alan E. Steinweis, *Art, Ideology, and Economics in Nazi Germany: the Reich Chambers of Music, Theater, and the*

Visual Arts (Chapel Hill: University of North Carolina Press, 1993). For a brief summation of this period, see Pamela Potter and Celia Applegate, "Germans as the 'People of Music': Genealogy of an Identity," in Applegate and Potter, *Music and German National Identity*, 24–8.

11 Herbert Just, "Tag der deutschen Hausmusik 1933," *Zeitschrift für Hausmusik* 3 (1934): 22–3; Fritz Jöde, "*Hausmusik* gestern und morgen," *Zeitschrift für Hausmusik* 3 (1934): 18–19.

12 Doris Bergen, "Hosanna or 'Hilf, O Herr Uns': National Identity, the German Christian Movement, and the 'Dejudaization' of Sacred Music in the Third Reich," in Applegate and Potter, *Music and German National Identity*, 140–54.

13 Gottfried Eberle, *200 Jahre Sing-Akademie zu Berlin: 'Ein Kunstverein für die heilige Musik'* (Berlin: Nicolai, 1991), 196–7.

14 Estaban Buch, *Beethoven's Ninth: A Political History*, trans. Richard Miller (Chicago: University of Chicago Press, 2003), 220.

15 For discussion of how the consciousness of disruption entered into German collective life, see Konrad Jarausch and Michael Geyer, *Shattered Past: Reconstructing German Histories* (Princeton: Princeton University Press, 2003), esp. 317–40.

16 Richard Jakoby, "Introduction: A Land of Music," in *Musical Life in Germany: Structure, Development, Figures*, ed. Richard Jakoby, trans. Eileen Martin (Bonn: Music Information Council, 1997), 6–8.

17 "Ohne Musik wäre das Leben ein Irrtum"; Friedrich Nietzsche, *Götzen-Dämmerung*, in *Werke in Drei Bänden* (Munich: Carl Hanser, 1955), 947.

18 It is no coincidence that Wolf Lepenies's flawed exploration of culture and politics, *The Seduction of Culture*, begins with a musical anecdote and uses Mann as the touchstone for all the arguments the book seeks to advance; *The Seduction of Culture in German History* (Princeton: Princeton University Press, 2006). See my review of the book in the *American Historical Review* 112, no. 3 (June 2007): 802–4.

19 Thomas Mann, "Germany and the Germans," *Addresses Delivered at the Library of Congress, 1942–49* (Washington, DC: Library of Congress, 1963), 47–8.

20 Hans Vaget, "National and Universal: Thomas Mann and the Paradox of 'German' Music," in Applegate and Potter, *Music and German National Identity*, 156; Mann, "Germany and the Germans," 64.

21 Vaget, "National and Universal," 158, 164.

22 Mann, "Germany and the Germans," 63–4.

23 See Joy Calico, *Arnold Schoenberg's* A Survivor From Warsaw *in Postwar Europe* (Berkeley: University of California Press, 2014), esp. 20–40.

24 Roman Polanski tried a variation on this theme in his film adaptation of Wladyslaw Szpilman's Holocaust memoir, *The Pianist*. In Polanski's version a

rather menacing German officer listens while a starving, freezing Szpilman struggles through a Chopin ballade (in the book he recounts playing the Nocturne in C sharp minor, but that work evidently lacked the virtuosic display Polanski found appropriate to his mise-en-scène). The performance being more than adequate, the German is moved to allow this Jew to live. See Wladyslaw Szpilman, *The Pianist*, trans. Anthea Bell (New York, 1999), 177–87.

25 Elizabeth Janik, *Recomposing German Music: Politics and Musical Tradition in Cold War Berlin* (Leiden: Brill, 2005); David Monod, *Settling Scores: Music Control in the American Zone, 1945–1952* (Chapel Hill: University of North Carolina Press, 2005); Toby Thacker, *Music after Hitler, 1945–1955* (Farnham, UK: Ashgate, 2007); David Tompkins, *Composing the Party Line: Music and Politics in Early Cold War Poland and East Germany* (Purdue, IN: Purdue University Press, 2013).

26 Kilenyi and Einstein quoted by Monod, *Settling Scores*, 98.

27 Pamela Potter has written a provocative analysis of how denazification had an unexpected victory in shaping not so much post-war Germany as post-war *historians* of Germany, leading them to write the history of the arts in Germany as if "Nazi aesthetics" was a coherent set of artistic values that existed in consistent opposition to modernism. See Potter, *Art of Suppression: Confronting the Nazi Past in Histories of the Visual and Performing Arts* (Berkeley: University of California Press, 2016).

28 Janik, "'The Golden Hunger Years': Music and Superpower Rivalry in Occupied Berlin," *German History* 22, no. 1 (January 2004): 81.

29 Monod, *Settling Scores*, 263.

30 Michael Kater, *Composers of the Nazi Era: Eight Portraits* (Oxford: Oxford University Press, 2000), 272–6.

31 Michael Frayn, *Copenhagen* (London: Methuen, 1998), 67.

32 Schwarzkopf earns a high place of dishonour in Michael Kater's account of the Nazi years, *The Twisted Muse: Musicians and Their Music in the Third Reich* (Oxford: Oxford University Press, 1997), 61–4.

33 Sam H. Shirakawa, *The Devil's Music Master: The Controversial Life and Career of Wilhelm Furtwängler* (Oxford: Oxford University Press, 1992), 484–5.

34 Bruce Campbell, "Kein schöner Land: The Spielschar Ekkehard and the Struggle to Define German National Identity in the Weimar Republic," in Applegate and Potter, *Music and German National Identity*, 128–39.

35 See Brigitte Hamann, *Winifred Wagner: A Life at the Heart of Hitler's Bayreuth*, trans. Alan Bance (New York: Harcourt, 2006).

36 The two most prominent books are Nike Wagner, *The Wagners: The Dramas of a Musical Family* (Princeton: Princeton University Press, 2001); and

Gottfried Wagner, *Twilight of the Wagners: The Unveiling of a Family's Legacy* (New York: Picador, 1999). A much earlier contribution was Friedelind Wagner, *Heritage of Fire: The Story of Richard Wagner's Granddaughter* (New York: Harper and Bros, 1945).

37 Frederic Spotts, *Bayreuth: A History of the Wagner Festival* (New Haven: Yale University Press, 1994), 238.

38 Hansjürgen Schaefer, "Zum neuen Jahre," *Musik und Gesellschaft* 11 (January 1961): 1.

39 Werner Wolf, "Die Musiktheater und die Leipziger 'Meistersinger,'" *Musik und Gesellschaft* 11 (January 1961): 34.

40 See Julia Goodwin, ""Breaking Down Barriers: Music and the Culture of Reconciliation in West Berlin, 1961–1989," PhD diss., University of Rochester, 2007; Amy Wlodarski, "'An Idea Can Never Perish': Memory, the Musical Idea, and Schoenberg's *Survivor from Warsaw*," *Journal of Musicology* 24, no. 4 (2007): 581–608; Wlodarski, "Sounds of Memory: German Musical Responses to the Holocaust, 1945–1967," PhD diss., Eastman School of Music, University of Rochester, 2007.

41 Amy Wlodarski, "Memory as Method: Mnemonic Structures in Schoenberg's *A Survivor from Warsaw*," in *form follows function – zwischen Musik, Form, und Funktion* (Hamburg, 2005); Calico, *Arnold Schoenberg's* A Survivor from Warsaw.

42 To cite only one item of a steady stream of press coverage of these phenomena: Allan Kozinn, "Hearing Music Silenced by the Nazis," *New York Times*, 26 March 2003.

43 Gesa Kordes, "Darmstadt, Post-War Experimentation, and the West German Search for a New Musical Identity," in Applegate and Potter, *Music and German National Identity*, 205–17.

44 Paul Griffiths, "Facing Challenges of Greatness and Mortality," *New York Times*, 18 February 2001.

45 Jeremy Eichler, "The Man Who Kept the Music Playing (for Hitler), *New York Times*, 31 August 2003.

46 Pamela Potter, "Strauss and the National Socialists: the Debate and its Relevance," in *Richard Strauss: New Perspectives on the Composer and his Work*, ed. Bryan Gilliam (Durham, NC: Duke University Press, 1992), 108–9, 111.

47 Buch, *Beethoven's Ninth*; David Dennis, *Beethoven and German Politics* (New Haven: Yale University Press, 1996).

48 These quotations are drawn, I hope not arbitrarily though certainly out of various contexts, from Barenboim's conversations with Edward Said, as well as from his essay, "Germans, Jews, and Music." All are published in *Parallels and Paradoxes*; see esp. 4–5, 11–12, 52, 146–7, 159–61, 174.

Index

GERMAN AND EUROPEAN STUDIES

General Editor: Jennifer J. Jenkins

1 Emanuel Adler, Beverly Crawford, Federica Bicchi, and Rafaella Del Sarto, *The Convergence of Civilizations: Constructing a Mediterranean Region*
2 James Retallack, *The German Right, 1860–1920: Political Limits of the Authoritarian Imagination*
3 Silvija Jestrovic, *Theatre of Estrangement: Theory, Practice, Ideology*
4 Susan Gross Solomon, ed., *Doing Medicine Together: Germany and Russia between the Wars*
5 Laurence McFalls, ed., *Max Weber's 'Objectivity' Revisited*
6 Robin Ostow, ed., *(Re)Visualizing National History: Museums and National Identities in Europe in the New Millennium*
7 David Blackbourn and James Retallack, eds., *Localism, Landscape, and the Ambiguities of Place: German-Speaking Central Europe, 1860–1930*
8 John Zilcosky, ed., *Writing Travel: The Poetics and Politics of the Modern Journey*
9 Angelica Fenner, *Race under Reconstruction in German Cinema: Robert Stemmle's Toxi*
10 Martina Kessel and Patrick Merziger, eds., *The Politics of Humour in the Twentieth Century: Inclusion, Exclusion, and Communities of Laughter*
11 Jeffrey K. Wilson, *The German Forest: Nature, Identity, and the Contestation of a National Symbol, 1871–1914*
12 David G. John, *Bennewitz, Goethe,* Faust: *German and Intercultural Stagings*
13 Jennifer Ruth Hosek, *Sun, Sex, and Socialism: Cuba in the German Imaginary*
14 Steven M. Schroeder, *To Forget It All and Begin Again: Reconciliation in Occupied Germany, 1944–1954*
15 Kenneth S. Calhoon, *Affecting Grace: Theatre, Subject, and the Shakespearean Paradox in German Literature from Lessing to Kleist*
16 Martina Kolb, *Nietzsche, Freud, Benn, and the Azure Spell of Liguria*
17 Hoi-eun Kim, *Doctors of Empire: Medical and Cultural Encounters between Imperial Germany and Meiji Japan*
18 J. Laurence Hare, *Excavating Nations: Archeology, Museums, and the German-Danish Borderlands*

19 Jacques Kornberg, *Pope Pius XII's Dilemma: Facing Atrocities and Genocide in the Second World War*

20 Patrick O'Neill, *Transforming Kafka: Translation Effects*

21 John K. Noyes, *Herder: Aesthetics against Imperialism*

22 James Retallack, *Germany's Second Reich: Portraits and Pathways*

23 Laurie Marhoefer, *Sex and the Weimar Republic: German Homosexual Emancipation and the Rise of the Nazis*

24 Bettina Brandt and Daniel Purdy, eds. *China and the German Enlightenment*

25 Michael Hau. *Performance Anxiety: Sport and Work in Germany from the Empire to Nazism*

26 Celia Applegate, *The Necessity of Music: Variations on a German Theme*

www.ingramcontent.com/pod-product-compliance
Lightning Source LLC
LaVergne TN
LVHW090800070826
844660LV00022B/1045

* 9 7 8 1 4 8 7 5 2 0 4 8 9 *